Argument and Audience

Presenting Debates in Public Settings

Argument and Audience

Presenting Debates in Public Settings

by

Ken Broda-Bahm

Daniela Kempf

William Driscoll

International Debate Education Association

New York • Amsterdam • Brussels

Published in 2004 by
The International Debate Education Association
400 West 59th Street
New York, NY 10019

Library of Congress Cataloging-in-Publication Data

Broda-Bahm, Kenneth T., 1963–
     Argument and audience : presenting debates in public settings / By Ken
Broda-Bahm and Daniela Kempf.
          p. cm.
     Includes bibliographical references and index.
     ISBN 0-9720541-3-8 (pbk.)
     1. Debates and debating. I. Kempf, Daniela, 1969- II. Title.
     PN4181.B76 2004
     808.5'3--dc22

                                        2004007628

Printed in the United States of America.

Contents

Preface

In September, 2002, as the people of the United States began to consider the possibility of a war on Iraq, students at Marist College in Poughkeepsie, New York, gathered to hear a public debate between two advocates—one, a U.S. Army colonel who favored an attack, and the other, a professor of social studies who opposed military action. The event proved to be lively, with frequent interruptions for applause, as well as boos and cheers. Because they were participants in a live event, the audience members became involved in a dramatic way. "Marist College debate coach Maxwell Schnurer, who organized the event, said watching arguments over the issue on television makes 'people feel as though they're not invited to the table.' But 'public debates are conversational lightning,' he said. 'They affect us.'"[1]

We wholeheartedly agree with Dr. Schnurer—public debates do affect us. More than that, they are an integral part of any society that is truly open. An open society, as defined by the philosopher Karl Popper, is a society based on the recognition that nobody has a monopoly on the truth, that different people have different views and interests, and that there is a need for institutions to protect the rights of all people to allow them to live together in peace. Public debates offer a unique opportunity for the articulation of different views and interests in a forum that is characterized by reasonable argument and personal respect.

Debate has changed our lives, as it has changed many other lives. For Ken, debate helped transform a rather shy boy from a military family into a young man who found as a teacher, coach, author, and advocate that he could influence with the power of words, and later into a (yes, somewhat older) man who found, again and in a new career, that a fascination with words, ideas, and audiences continues to serve as a profound calling. For Daniela, a native of formerly socialist Croatia, debate finally channeled all the previously unsatisfied yearnings for free speech and open public debate, nonexistent in her country and so many others when she was growing up, and made her eager to share this epiphany with others. We can both say with confidence that debate helped to make us and many of our students into more tolerant people and conscientious citizens of the world. We have had the privilege of seeing firsthand the difference that public debates can make in countries that face past and present threats to the ideal of respectful civil discourse—countries like the United States and many transitioning countries in East and Central Europe and around the world.

We owe the idea for this book and its realization to the Southeast Europe Youth Leadership Institute and its staff and students, who all contributed to the project with their insights and who served as our permanent inspiration and focus group. We are thankful to all of our students and colleagues at Towson University and Marymount Manhattan College for shaping us into the teachers that we are and for allowing us to test-run this material. We are indebted to the International Debate Education Association for promoting debate in the United States and all over the world and for giving this book a publishing home. We would like to recognize and extend our thanks also to Gordon Mitchell, Max Schnurer, Alfred Snider, the Baltimore Urban Debate League and many others who play a role every day in helping to reawaken public debate in America and elsewhere. Finally, we are grateful to all of our debate coaches, mentors, colleagues, family and friends who contributed to this book by making us who we are.

Ken Broda-Bahm
Daniela Kempf
William Driscoll
March 2004

---

1. Nik Bonapartis, "Professor, Colonel Debate Iraq War," *Poughkeepsie Journal*, September 26, 2002.

Part One

Public Debate in Context

Chapter One

A Rationale for Public Debates

The student council and the university community as a whole were divided on the issue. The student bookstore at a mid-sized university in the Western United States had for years sold the adult magazine *Penthouse* in the student bookstore. A recent issue, however, featured a series of photographs showing models in various states of undress with fake bruises and blood, some even playing "dead." The publication of this issue of the magazine, and the fact that it was sold in the university's student-owned and student-controlled cooperative bookstore, brought about a furious response from several groups on campus. Women's groups and others argued that the images linked sex with violence and as a result promoted the ideas of rape, battery, and hatred toward women. They argued that this issue and future issues of the magazine should be withdrawn from the student bookstore. Others, however, argued that however much some may dislike the images, a commitment to free expression (and specifically, the first amendment to the U.S. Constitution protecting free speech) required that this magazine not be censored. They believed that the magazine should remain for sale in the student bookstore. The dispute came to a head when one member of the student council, Yvonne, introduced a motion to remove the magazine from the bookstore, and another member of the student council, Eric, emphatically opposed it.

As various individuals and groups on campus began taking sides, it was soon clear that the situation was ripe for an important public debate. The debate team for this university (whose membership at the time included one of your authors) decided to step into this dispute, not to take one side or the other, but to promote an intelligent exchange of views. After quickly picking a time and a place for the debate, members of the team approached

Eric and Yvonne, the two members of the student council who had taken opposing views on this conflict. Offering to provide each side with an assistant to help them prepare, the debate team encouraged Eric and Yvonne to debate each other in a public forum. The debate would provide an open and fair hearing of the arguments on all sides and would serve as a useful way to receive student input. As such, the team argued, the debate would help the student council make the best decision.

Agreeing to the debate, Yvonne and Eric began preparing their arguments. Their respective assistants from the debate team acted to ensure that each side came up with the best arguments and that the arguments were organized and supported by research. Arguing for the continued sale of the magazine, Eric found evidence questioning the argument that violent images cause violent behavior. In addition, he developed an extended argument that defended the principle of free expression, and pointed out that because the university was government-supported, a decision to remove the publication would amount to government suppression of speech, which is against the U.S. Constitution. Yvonne anticipated this argument, of course, and her response focused on drawing a distinction: there is a difference between the government banning a publication and an individual merchant (the student-owned bookstore in this case) deciding not to sell a particular publication; the Constitution doesn't require all merchants to sell all publications. In fact, Yvonne planned to argue that if we accept the principle of free expression, then we must accept that the merchant has a right to choose what to sell and what not to sell. In addition, Yvonne found evidence from a variety of sources that argued that exposure to sexually violent images tends to increase a person's tolerance of violence against women.

When the day came for the debate, the university union, the largest space on campus, was filled beyond capacity. Advertisements for the debate had been targeted to a number of groups including feminist and civil libertarian organizations. Students and professors of psychology, law, gender studies and media studies also had a clear interest in the themes of the debate. Individuals stood at the back and in the aisles when all the chairs were taken and listened as Yvonne and Eric each presented their sides of the argument. They defined, developed, and disputed the idea of free expression; they explored the issue of how one can measure the effect of media images; and they discussed the findings and the flaws of specific psychological studies on the effects of violent pornography. Eric and Yvonne not only made speeches, but questioned each other directly, while several microphones placed in the audience allowed those attending to have a voice as well. The debate didn't result in a "winner" per se, and may or may not have had an effect in the student council's ultimate decision to keep selling the magazine, but the best indication of the debate's success was this: once the debate had formally concluded, easily one-third of the audience stayed and discussed the issue—with each other, with the members of the debate team who had helped prepare, and with Yvonne and Eric. The debate represented an ideal example of the role that public debates can play in helping people develop their ideas, share their views, and ultimately reach intelligent and responsible decisions.

Public debates may of course happen in a variety of settings. An advocacy group might sponsor a debate on the death penalty; a local town council might host a debate on whether their town should pursue economic development. Candidates for a public office might debate about the best plan for improving national health care. What links all of these events together are a few common elements.

Definition of Public Debate

While the terms "public" and "debate" are familiar enough, a definition of the phrase as we use it in this text is important. We see public debates as more or less formal events in which advocates on opposing sides of a controversial issue make use of argument and the power of speech to express their own points of view and react to opposing points of view for the benefit of a large and non-specialized audience. While the chapters to follow will identify a number of specific dimensions and considerations regarding format, content, support, and attention to audience and situation, several common elements can be identified in everything that we consider a public debate:

- *Controversy*: An issue, a question, or a problem; something that is unsettled and that ought to be settled
- *Opposition*: There are two or more parties who have opposing views of the issue, question or problem
- *Argumentation*: The parties have committed to the use of arguments and will support their claims with reasoning and evidence

- *Engagement:* The parties have committed to focus not only on their own views but also on the views of their adversaries

- *Audience:* The argumentation is presented to a particular or general audience, adapted to their level of comprehension, and aims to gain their understanding or agreement.

While these parameters are broad enough to include a large number of diverse events, we would like to be clear in identifying a few events that we purposely do not include. Panel discussions can be considered events in which a number of speakers address a common topic. Without opposition—without participants' willingness to identify and commit to distinct and incompatible positions on a topic—we cannot term these events "debates." Most debating that occurs at formal competitive tournaments can certainly be considered debate but not "public debate," because it generally takes place in front of a specialized judge rather than an audience, and in many to most cases it takes place in relative privacy, with few parties other than the judge in attendance. Similarly, debates in tournament settings that are designed to mimic the experience of debating in front of a public audience are also not considered public debates. While there is an unquestioned educational value to simulations, such as those promoted by America's National Educational Debate Association (NEDA), in which the judge is expected to view and evaluate the debate as a common audience member would, these events are best seen as preparation for public debates, but not public debates as such. In addition to requiring a genuine audience, the public debate also requires a commitment to argumentation. The airwaves are presently filled with talk shows featuring controversy and opposition, but because participants frequently oppose each other by shouting, insulting or even throwing chairs, rather than by offering reasons, these events generally shouldn't be considered public debates either. Finally, an element of engagement with the arguments of the other side is important as well. While high profile exchanges between candidates for national office, such as the U.S. presidency, are commonly called "debates," critics have argued that because candidates often simply answer questions posed by a journalist/moderator and don't directly address each other's arguments, these events are more accurately called "joint press conferences" rather than public debates. Our view is that such events are debates only to the extent that they feature direct engagement in argumentation and direct clash between points of view offered by the adversaries.

A public debate, then, occurs in any setting in which advocates on two or more opposed sides of a controversy engage each other through arguments before an audience. The remainder of this chapter will develop a rationale for public debates. We intend this rationale to serve not only as a justification for the subject matter of this book, but more importantly as a resource for individuals who need to persuade others of the value of public debates. Of course, if you yourself were not already a believer in the value of public debating, you probably would not be reading this book. However, at some point you may find yourself in the position of having to justify the value of a public debate to a student council (as in the example above), a city government, a potential opponent or expert guest, or an organization that may supply funds to sponsor public debates. In all of these cases, you will need arguments on the benefits of public debates. In the following sections, we offer arguments to support three general claims: public debates build skills, contribute to the public sphere, and help an organization meet its goals.

Public Debates Build Skills

Perhaps the most common justification for debating in all of its forms is the argument that it builds a specific set of very important skills. For the debater, the advisor, the attentive audience member or the moderator/judge, public debates promote skills in both communication and critical thinking.

Communication Skills

In front of an audience of dozens, hundreds, or more; possibly under the glare of television lights; facing an opponent and a situation that are only partially predictable, the public debate has all of the makings for a public speaking experience of the greatest intensity. The pressure of knowing that many eyes and ears will be attending to you and the spontaneity of having to respond to a line of reasoning as it develops both ensure that a public debate is a situation demanding all of your resources as a speaker. The more experience in such a setting that a speaker has, the greater the chance that the speaker will gain the sensitivity and the virtuosity to excel.

The presence of the audience and the likelihood that the public debate has emerged out of a concern for a real issue both raise the stakes for the advocate. Public debates demand the development of basic skills such as employing variety and emphasis in voice; developing eye contact with as much of the audience as possible; controlling and employing facial expression, gesture and movement; creating and communicating clear organization and comprehensible logical connections; and selecting concise, appropriate, memorable, and vivid language. Public debates also emphasize extemporaneous presentation; this is a demanding style in which the speaker is neither presenting memorized or pre-written material nor speaking from the top of her head, but is instead actively fitting prepared knowledge and ideas to the needs of the moment. The audience is obviously and palpably present and for that reason, they demand adaptation: a speaker's goals must be based upon what the audience is likely to understand and appreciate. In addition, the fact that public debates involve a flow of development from argument presentation to argument conclusion emphasizes the need to think of an overall strategy and not simply a message. Because each speaker in a public debate is confronted by a present and engaged opponent, debaters must anticipate the arguments of others and react accordingly. Finally, the presence of an audience promotes a realization of the importance of good communication habits. Two university debate coaches with long histories of promoting on-campus public debates have observed that "when confronted with an audience that participates in the debate through its questions and comments, students recognize that their ideas must be structured clearly, that their language must be understandable, and that their delivery must be dynamic and their speaking rate comprehensible." [1]

With all of these considerations, the public debate requires a great deal of grace under pressure. Despite the high stakes, though, some participants may find the setting of a public debate easier and more pleasant than other comparable speech settings. Rather than being based on an assigned or casually selected topic, public debates often emerge from timely issues of great salience and importance to speakers, and it is easier to speak about something that is personally important to you. In addition, the competitive elements of debate, and the fact that there is implicitly or explicitly a winner, makes it more like a game, and it is more pleasant to engage in a game than to complete an assignment. Finally, the fact that they are focusing on opponents and a goal makes it possible for nervous speakers to diminish their self-awareness a bit by directing their energies toward their adversaries and not toward themselves.

For the audience members, the public debate also provides a setting in which to develop the communication skills of listening, evaluating, and in some settings, participating as a speaker as well. Today of course, many citizens receive their information from the electronic media—small "sound bites" of information from either the radio or the television. It is more challenging to attend to a speech in its entirety, and this experience engages the audience more fully by inviting them to appreciate the speaker's overall structure and strategy. It is more challenging still to follow a line of argument through several speeches as it is disputed back and forth. In this way, public debates encourage activity and engagement on the part of the audience by rewarding sustained attention.

Public debates are a unique setting for developing not only competence, but superior performance in all dimensions of oral communication. In an essay focusing on America's Bicentennial Youth Debates, held in 1976, two researchers found that "students with debate experience were significantly better at employing the three communication skills (analysis, delivery, and organization) than students without that experience."[2]

Critical Thinking Skills

California was one of the first states in the U.S.A. to include "critical thinking" among the required elements of study, defining the concept as comprising "an understanding of the relationship of language to logic, which would lead to the ability to analyze, criticize, and advocate ideas, to reason inductively and deductively, and to reach factual or judgmental conclusions based on sound inferences drawn from unambiguous statements of knowledge or belief." [3] Basically, critical thinking includes the ability to understand the support for claims and to test that support. These skills are involved when advocates fully explore the arguments for their side of the question, and anticipate the arguments of the other side of the question; when debaters research and analyze the reasoning and the evidence that is used to support the claims in the debate—whether to refute or to defend—they are using critical thinking skills. American President John F. Kennedy once said, "A good debater must not only study material in support of his own case, but he must also, of course, thoroughly analyze the expected arguments of his opponent."[4] This requires public debaters to be critics not only of the claims of their adversaries, but of their own claims as well. To think like your opponents, it is necessary to see your own weaknesses as well.

Critical thinking is seen as one of the most salient benefits of debate generally. After reviewing the empirical research on the question, there is "presumptive proof," as one researcher concluded, for believing that debate provides precisely the critical thinking benefits described above.[5] An additional group of authors concluded, "Many researchers over the past four decades have come to the same general conclusions. Critical thinking ability is significantly improved by courses in argumentation and debate and by debate experience."[6] One of the most recent works on the subject was a "meta-analysis" of nineteen previous studies on the relationship between experience in debate and similar activities and critical thinking, and that review concluded "this summary of existing research reaffirms what many ex-debaters and others in forensics, public speaking, mock trial, or argumentation would support: participation improves the thinking of those involved."[7]

While some of this research has focused on debate as it occurs in a classroom or a tournament context, some confidence in the inference that public debates promote comparable critical thinking benefits can be gained from the fact that the basic elements that constitute critical thinking (analyzing, advocating, evaluating) are as prominent in public debates as they are in any other format. The practitioner of tournament debating may well benefit from the relative frequency of the debates (for some college debaters as many as ten debates on a given weekend). But the public debater might benefit from the proportionately greater attention that is being paid to one setting, one case, and one opponent. The focus on the public debate as a single unique event, rather than just one in a string of debates, encourages the debater to plan more thoroughly and to reason more deeply on the comparatively limited possibilities for argument in this one setting. At least when it is done well, the public debate—by adding additional elements such as moderator and audience—has the potential to promote a deeper experience in critical thinking.

An additional critical thinking benefit to the public debate must also be added: the benefit to the audience. Attentive audience members at a public debate will not only hear and appreciate the speakers, but they will also follow and evaluate a line of argumentation. This means critically understanding claims, searching for their logical support and implication, and weighing the relative strength of competing claims. In this way, the active audience member of a public debate will be participating in a critical thinking process that parallels the thinking of the advocates themselves.

Public Debates Contribute to the Public Sphere

The benefits of debate have convinced many secondary schools and universities throughout the world to include debate programs within their activities and curricula. Modern debate, however, focuses much of its energies on preparing for debating tournaments, relatively large gatherings at which students from a number of different schools and programs will compete largely out of the public's eye. The corollary is that the benefits of modern debate are gained largely by participants, not by the public. We see that public debates can significantly broaden the benefits of debate by contributing to the public sphere.

Interscholastic debate did not always avoid the public eye. Before there were tournaments, the way in which one college or university would debate another was fairly direct: one school's team would travel to the other school and they would debate in front of an audience. Often teams would string together several such events and go on a debating "tour." As the debate tour gave way to the debate tournament, teams were able to debate many more schools in much less time at a fraction of the cost. Much was gained, but one thing was lost: the audience. In time, debate tournaments established their own context in their own setting—one in which debates moved from the auditorium to the common classroom. The new audience—the often solitary judge—quickly became a specialist in possession of a very specific way of viewing, structuring, and talking about the debate. Debate developed into a powerful tool for developing skills in analysis, research and criticism. The rhetorical role of presenting ideas in a clear and lively fashion to an untutored audience in large part vanished from many debate communities.

The idea of public debate on school campuses is not dead—that much can be seen in international debates, parliamentary debating societies, and the occasional intramural debate tournament. And yet it is clear that the vast majority of the energy of most of the national and international debate organizations is focused on preparing for and planning tournaments. Given the demands of competition, it is also quite likely that a clear majority of program directors' and coaches' time is also directed away from the campus and away from potential audiences. As one commentator noted about American universities, "campus debates or intramural debate contests have become nonexistent on most college campuses."[8]

The loss of the audience has not gone unnoticed or unmourned, however. In America at least, the increased distance between debates and the audience has led to persistent calls for a recovered audience in academic debate. Some voices have called for a reorientation in theory. These arguments have ranged from the belief that the initial presumption for one side or the other should be based on the natural-state opinions of the audience (i.e., their opinions before being influenced by a debate),[9] to the argument that the importance of an issue should be determined by the audience's own "issue agenda,"[10] to the concept that reasoning that best comports with a public's rationality should be preferred,[11] and finally to the belief that debate should be viewed as a narrative in which audiences freely evaluate arguments "in terms of their own cultural beliefs, values, and experiences."[12] Other voices have called for a reorientation in debate structure and organization. While the Cross Examination Debate Association's original goal of "striking a balance among analysis, delivery, and evidence"[13] reveals the purpose of fostering a form of debate that is closer to audience standards, more explicit attempts in this direction can be found in more recent organizations. The National Educational Debate Association, for example, has dedicated itself to promoting "the stylistic and analytical skills that would be rewarded in typical public forums (i.e., courts, Congress, the classroom, civic gatherings, etc.)."[14] The organization is dedicated to an explicitly audience-oriented view of appropriateness: "Ideally, a debate is an exchange that, when witnessed by a member of the general public, would be viewed as comprehensible and enlightening."[15]

It is important to note, however, that the "recovered audience" sought by these perspectives and prescriptions is a theoretical construct, rather than a reality. That is, the purpose of these initiatives is to alter tournament-style debating so that it conforms to the normative standards of a presumed audience. What these prescriptions do not contain is a means for recovering an actual audience. Their audience is simulated. While simulating the experience of an audience within the confines of tournament debating is a beneficial, possibly indispensable element in preparing speakers for audience debates, such simulations do not re-create the public function of a debate in front of a general audience. To put it another way, a presumed audience gains no benefits from the debate, and the real public remains untouched.

In fact, tournament debating can limit the benefits gained by the debaters themselves in their capacity as citizens. That is, there is a danger when the educational task of preparing debaters focuses exclusively on tournament preparation. As Gordon Mitchell of the University of Pittsburgh noted, such a focus can serve to distance debaters from the very topics and ideas that they discuss:

> Academic debaters nourished on an exclusive diet of competitive contest round experience often come to see politics like a picturesque landscape whirring by through the window of a speeding train. They study this political landscape in great detail, rarely (if ever) entertaining the idea of stopping the train and exiting to alter the course of unfolding events. The resulting spectator mentality deflects attention away from roads that could carry their arguments to wider spheres of public argumentation.[16]

Debate's movement from an audience-centered forum to a tournament-centered laboratory and its resulting avoidance of the public sphere ought to be viewed in a larger context as well. Numerous social critics have noted fundamental changes in the character of public dialogue over the past few decades. A reliance on one-way channels of information, for example, risks transforming citizens from active partners in the production of knowledge and opinions to mere consumers of information. Membership in a mass audience can have the effect of making people feel like witnesses to the dramas of democratic life, and not participants. In addition, there is the risk that a "public sphere" of deliberative decision-making is being replaced on the one hand by the technical decisions of experts and on the other hand by the purely personal experiences and opinions of individuals. Electronic sources have potential for facilitating group dialogue, but even they often find themselves channeling the public's views in an atomized fashion: as public opinion data or as personal narratives. A proliferation of sources of information—Internet sites, cable television channels, and desktop-published magazines and newspapers—has contributed to a segmentation of audiences, meaning that even as modern communication reaches more and more people, those who are reached are more targeted, more specialized, and less "public." Northwestern University professor Thomas Goodnight, for example, has lamented that "issues of significant public consequence, what should present live possibilities for argumentation and public choice, disappear into the government technocracy or private hands."[17]

The consequences of this decline in the public sphere are crucial to any society that prides itself on an active citizenry. Converted to information consumers, citizens become atomized, and begin to lack the psychological capacity that permits them to feel a responsibility for, and an ownership in, the affairs of their society and their government. "The results of the deterioration of public debate," two Harvard professors wrote, "include a loss of public faith in democratic institutions, a distrust of government, and reduced public participation."[18]

Public debates have the potential to play their own part in restoring the public sphere by encouraging the general population to experience an actual and sustained engagement with issues. By promoting a dialogue between parties on opposing sides, and between experts and non-experts, public debates facilitate a deeper level of interaction than that which is normally afforded by vehicles of mass communication. While an audience member may choose to be passive at a public debate, as much as they are passive as a television watcher, the dynamics of the public debate provide several incentives for a greater level of involvement. The first is participation. Audience members attending a live public debate have a direct opportunity to be heard. By their comments, their applause, and their very presence at the debate, they send a message. The second reason is evaluation. Even when public debates are televised or otherwise presented to a mass audience, the back-and-forth of the exchange encourages audience members to investigate and re-examine their own views. The third reason is improved information. Public debates provide a better chance to develop arguments fully as well as a better chance to expose shallowness and deceit. In calling for regular televised debates on issues of American national policy, Phillip and Jody Heyman of Harvard recently wrote, "A thirty-second advertising spot can be false or empty without embarrassment. In contrast, a thirty-minute televised debate among proponents of both sides of an issue is far more likely to embarrass emptiness and to expose falsity."[19]

For students as well, public debates offer opportunities to learn in a new way—a way that is intimately connected to the intellectual life of a community. As Gordon Mitchell of the University of Pittsburgh noted,

> By creating forums where salient and pressing contemporary issues can be debated and discussed in a robust, wide-open fashion, students can lend vibrancy to the public sphere. Public debates represent sites of social learning where the spirit of civic engagement can flourish, ideas can be shared, and the momentum of social movements can be stoked.[20]

By promoting a greater number of on-campus debates, university and secondary school programs could serve the functions of teaching advocacy and educating audiences without sacrificing the argumentation laboratory that tournament debating has become. As a complement to (not a substitute for) current debate activities, programs should expand the practice of on-campus debating. Public debates can be incorporated in argumentation and public speaking classes, integrated into student government and elections, connected to on-campus political clubs, or linked to international traveling teams. One additional way to promote audience debates would be to reprise the invitation-style debate of America's previous century: a team from one school can travel to another school for the purpose of debating in front of an audience. The travel need not be an additional expense. All over the world, thousands of schools already travel on a regular basis—as often as every weekend for some—to debate tournaments in other parts of their countries. Adding a public debate on the Thursday or Friday evening before the beginning of a weekend tournament is an easy and inexpensive way to promote public debates in conjunction with the tournament schedule. Such an addition can also provide a tournament with a "public face" that will allow administrators and members of the general public to develop a positive image of the debate program and the debate activity.

By contributing to interactive public dialogue, public debates can help society at a fundamental level. President John F. Kennedy wrote, "The give and take of debating, the testing of ideas, is essential to democracy. I wish we had a good deal more debating in our institutions than we do now."[21]

Public Debates Help Organizations Meet Their Goals

We have looked at the benefits of public debates at an individual level (building skills) as well as at a societal level (promoting the public sphere). A final category of benefit relates to the organizations that support debates. Whether they are competitive debating clubs, activist organizations, government agencies, educational institutions, or political clubs, any group that seeks to carry a message to the public can benefit from public debates. While potential benefits may be as numerous and specific as the goals of these groups, public debates can be seen as yielding the following general outcomes for organizations:

- *Promoting visibility* by allowing the group receive attention for its message
- *Providing information* by educating audience in a dynamic way
- *Attracting new membership, audiences, and partners*
- *Leveling the playing field* by allowing smaller, less recognized or less powerful groups to compete on an equal footing
- *Motivating existing membership* by providing an exhilarating and even addictive experience

Promoting Visibility.   No matter what other goals an organization has, one basic need is to be seen and recognized. To attract sponsors, clients, audience's, and partners; to get its message out; to form an identity and to be appreciated for what it does, an organization needs first to be noticed. Public debates offer a unique means to attract a form of attention that would be difficult to obtain through comparable events. Hosting a speaker, giving an award, and issuing a press release are all potential ways to communicate, but particularly for media outlets that focus on conflict and controversy, a debate is inherently more worthy of attention. For the same reason that an announcement of a new policy is not as newsworthy as a dispute over a new policy, a debate naturally fits into media priorities and audience interests. "Debate is an activity thick with motivation and laden with drama, meaning, and purpose,"[22] Professor Mitchell wrote, and as a result it provides a unique way to capture interest and attention.

Providing Information.   Conveying information in some form or other is a common objective for all kinds of organizations. While newsletters, narratives, panels, and individual speakers all serve to convey information, the dynamic of a debate has unique benefits. Its embedded conflict promises a more interesting exchange: people who might cringe at listening to a lecture might welcome listening to a debate—even if it conveys essentially the same information. In addition, a debate is unique in not only informing on a particular point of view, but also capturing the diversity of opinions contained in an issue. Even though U.S. presidential debates involve less direct interaction than other forms of public debate, one study found that people who watched those debates were more likely to understand the common issues and to recognize each candidate's stance on an issue accurately.[23]

Attracting New Membership, Audiences, and Partners.   With rare exceptions, school debating clubs and programs are always attempting to find new members. Those of us who coach university programs, for example, can identify with the experience of having long-term, successful, and (we think) visible programs, while still encountering students who say, "I didn't know this college had a debate team." Hosting frequent and well-publicized public debates is one way to spread awareness to potential members. Without fail, after every public debate there are a few individuals who will drift toward the stage to chat with the debaters or the coaches about the possibility of joining the team. Organizations other than debating teams benefit from this attention as well. By bringing together representatives of different organizations and by targeting still more organizations in your advertising, your public debate can serve as a 'networking' opportunity which allows you to identify new audiences and potential partners.

Leveling the Playing Field.   One important element of debate is its formal equality. In most formats at least, speakers receive equal time in which to state their views, with no restrictions on what they say. In many formats, speakers receive a direct opportunity to question the other side. Public debates limit opportunities to introduce unfair elements into the public dialogue. They limit opportunities to monopolize attention by "filibustering" (or refusing to yield to another speaker), by interrupting, or by speaking louder or longer than an opponent. The power of money—so essential for political campaigns that must buy advertising time and send promotional letters—counts for little in a public debate; it is impossible to defeat a debate opponent by spending more money than he does. This element of the public debate not only keeps the exchange civil, it also has the potential to allow smaller, less recognized or less powerful groups to compete on an equal footing with larger, more familiar, or more powerful groups. In the U.S. for example, there is a recent movement to bring debate to urban, inner-city, secondary schools.[24] By targeting schools with high populations of racial minorities and needs that go beyond the available resources, this movement seeks to use debate as a method of empowerment. Public debates within a program such as this provide an ideal opportunity to hear the voices of marginalized groups: groups that we are used to hearing about, but not always used to hearing from.

The civil rights activist, Malcolm X, who learned public debating while an inmate at the Norfolk Prison Colony, later used debate as his preferred method of engagement. Robert Branham, who explored this aspect of Malcolm X's development, explained that this preference came from debate's unique ability to expand the "mainstream" of political discourse:

> Debate was Malcolm X's primary mode of public address. Its use represented a deliberate rhetorical choice regarding how his ideas might best be advanced. The debate format accorded equal standing to his then-radical ideas and enacted the politics of confrontation that he espoused as essential for African-American dignity.[25]

Motivating Existing Membership.   A final benefit to public debates can be found in the experience of the debate itself, in its exhilarating and even addictive quality. Hosting public debates is an excellent means to provide members of your organization with an experience that is likely for many to be intrinsically satisfying. For many, in fact, this benefit may make the preceding pages of this chapter quite unnecessary. Generations of students have embraced debating, not because it is educational (though it is) and not because it improves the life of the *polis* (though it does), but because it is fun. The game-elements, the need for quick thinking, the unpredictability of the situation, the possibility of winning the capitulation of an adversary or the assent of an audience, can all make the debate experience seem like an end in and of itself. This element of debating was probably never described better than by Malcolm X himself:

> I will tell you that right there, in the prison, debating, speaking to a crowd, was as exhilarating to me as the discovery of knowledge through reading had been. Standing up there, the faces looking up at me, the things in my head coming out of my mouth, while my brain searched for the next best thing to follow what I was saying, and if I

could sway them to my side by handling it right, then I had won the debate—once my feet got wet, I was gone on debating.[26]

Notes

1. C. DeLancey, and H. Ryan, "Intercollegiate, Audience Style Debating: *Quo Vadis*," *Argumentation and Advocacy* 27 no. 2 (1990): 50.

2. W. D. Semlak, and D. Shields. "The Effect of Debate Training on Students' Participation in the Bicentennial Youth Debates," *Journal of the American Forensic Association* 13 (1977): 194.

3. G. Dumke, "Chancellor's Executive Order 338. (Long Beach: California State University, Chancellor's Office, 1980).

4. C. Streit, ed., *Freedom and Union* (1960): 7.

5. K. R. Colbert, "Enhancing Critical Thinking Ability Through Academic Debate," *Contemporary Argumentation and Debate* 16 (1995): 52–72.

6. C. Keefe, T. Harte, and L. Norton, *Introduction to Debate*, (New York: Macmillan, 1992): 33–34

7. M. Allen, S. Berkowitz, S. Hunt, and A. Louden, "A Meta-analysis of the Impact of Forensics and Communication Education on Critical Thinking," *Communication Education* 48 no. 1 (1999): 28.

8. M. J. Woolsey, "A Historical Look at the Advantages of Intramural Debate Tournaments," (Paper presented at the annual meeting of the Speech Communication Association. San Diego, CA).

9. J. M. Sproule, "The Psychological Burden of Proof: On the Evolutionary Development of Richard Whately's Theory of Presumption," *Communication Monographs* 43 (1976): 115–129.

10. J. Bartanen, and D. Frank, "The Issues-Agenda Model," *The Forensic of Pi Kappa Delta* 69 (1983): 1–9. J. Bartanen, and D. Frank, "The Issues-Agenda Model," in *Advanced Debate*, ed. D. A. Thomas and J. Hart, 408–416 (Lincolnwood, IL: National Textbook, 1987).

11. R. O. Weiss, "The Audience Standard," *CEDA Yearbook* 6 (1985): 43–49.

12. T. A. Hollihan, P. Riley, and K. Baaske, "The Art of Storytelling: An Argument for a Narrative Perspective in Academic Debate," in *Argument and Social Practice: Proceedings of the Fourth SCA/AFA Conference on Argumentation*, ed. J. R. Cox, M. O. Sillars, and G. B. Walker, 807–824 (Annandale, VA: Speech Communication Association, 1985).

13. Constitution of the Cross Examination Debate Association, art. 2, sec. 1, http://ceadebate.org/.

14. Statement of Objectives of the National Debate Education Association, sec. 1, http://www.neda.us/doc.php?article_id=40.

15. Ibid.

16. G. R. Mitchell, "Pedagogical Possibilities for Argumentative Agency in Academic Debate," *Argumentation and Advocacy* 35 (1998): 46.

17. G. T. Goodnight, "The Personal, Technical, and Public Spheres of Argument: A Speculative Inquiry into the Art of Public Deliberation," *Journal of the American Forensic Association* 18 (1982): 225.

18. P. Heyman, and J. Heyman, "The Fate of Public Debate in the United States," *Harvard Journal on Legislation* 33 no. 2 (1996): 519.

19. Ibid., 523.

20. Mitchell, "Pedagogical Possibilities for Argumentative Agency," 48–49.

21. Streit, *Freedom and Union*, 7.

22. Mitchell, "Pedagogical Possibilities for Argumentative Agency," 51.

23. W. J. Benoit, D. J. Webber, and J. Berman. "Effects of Presidential Debate Watching and Ideology on Attitudes and Knowledge," *Argumentation and Advocacy: The Journal of the American Forensic Association* 34 no. 4 (1998): 163–172.

24. M. W. Wade, "The Case for Urban Debate Leagues," *Contemporary Argumentation and Debate* 19 (1998): 60–65.

25. Robert J. Branham, "I Was Gone on Debating: Malcolm X's Prison Debates and Public Confrontations," *Argumentation and Advocacy* 31 no. 3 (1995): 135.

26. Malcolm X, with Alex Haley, *The Autobiography of Malcolm X* (New York: Grove Press, 1965): 184.

Chapter Two

The History of Public Debates

Who were the first debaters? Where did debate originate? When? And where does the word "debate" come from, anyway? Many great books have been written about the history of rhetoric in general and the history of debate in particular, especially political debate. Here, we are presenting only a sliver of that wealth of knowledge and information, in order to provide the historical context for public debates.

Debate and the Beginnings of Democracy

Debate (from the Old French word *debat-re*, meaning "to fight" and the Latin word *batluere*, meaning "to beat") has probably always existed in one form or another, ever since human beings first developed the capacity to speak and to reason. The beginnings of public debate—understood as debates with broader social impact—are usually linked by historians with the beginnings of democracy. Even though the word "debate" may be of more recent provenance (dating from the Middle Ages), the activity of debate can be traced as far back as the fifth century B.C.

Syracuse

Debate is first mentioned in the realm of public life in Syracuse, a Greek colony founded on the island of Sicily. In 467 B.C., Syracusans and their allies drove the tyrant Thrasybulus from the throne, and instituted a democracy. The new government was quickly faced with a refugee problem: Syracusans who had been exiled by Thrasybulus started to return home—and they wanted to reclaim the land that had been taken from them by the tyrant. These refugees had to present their claims for restitution in court. Since

there was no written record about their usurped land, and no documenta-
tion that they ever owned it, they had to persuade the court by oral argumentation. The outcome of each case was decided by the audience in the
court, composed mainly of regular citizens, sometimes numbering in the
hundreds. Those refugees whose speeches were more persuasive would end
up getting more land. Skill at speaking produced financial rewards.

When plaintiffs realized that they needed to speak well in order to
succeed, a business opportunity emerged. Lessons in rhetorical skill and
persuasion were soon being offered to the plaintiffs to help them become
more effective in court, and the first teachers of speech and debate emerged.
"Rhetoric" was the term used back then, without the somewhat negative
connotation it carries today—although (as we will explain below) there
were notable opponents of rhetoric, among them the philosopher Socrates.
(The word "rhetoric" comes from the Greek *rhetorike tekhne*, meaning "the
craft of speaking.")

Athenian Democracy and Pericles

As we mentioned before, the birth of debate is closely connected with the
beginnings of democracy. The first known form of democracy (from the
Greek *demos*, meaning "people" and *kratia*, meaning "rule") in Western
civilization is named Periclean democracy, after the Athenian statesman
Pericles. From 461 to 430 B.C., Pericles was a leader of Athens, the largest city-state in Greece, and was known for making significant social and
political reforms that contributed to the advancement of democracy. Since
city-states in ancient Greece were relatively small, there was no need for
representative government. All adult male citizens could debate on a wide
variety of issues and vote directly in the popular assembly, the *ecclesia*,
which was convened almost every week. Women and slaves could not vote
(neither could they speak in the assembly), and only men born in Athens
could be its citizens. In effect, even though this was a direct democracy (as
opposed to a representative democracy of most modern nations, including
the United States) that allowed citizens to decide without intermediaries on
all state matters, only a minority of the population in fact had the opportunity and the right to speak and debate in the popular assembly. Still, the
ecclesia became an important political and public forum, where debate and
argument flourished.[1]

The Athenian courts also provided ample opportunities for debating and argumentation. There were no professional attorneys, and litigants were expected to argue their own cases in front of large juries, sometimes consisting of more than five hundred citizens. Socrates was tried in such a court in 399 B.C., where he spoke in his own defense before he was executed for impiety and "corrupting the youth of Athens." The outcome was decided by majority vote,[2] so debating and public speaking skills became crucial tools for success (though they did not help Socrates much).

Sophists and Protagoras vs. Plato and Socrates

The first paid teachers of rhetoric who started their careers in the courts of Syracuse expanded their clientele with an increasing demand for their services, and traveled to other city-states to teach young men the virtues and skills of good citizenry, including the art of dialectic, argument and debate. These first teachers and philosophers in Athens were called Sophists (from the Greek *sophos*, meaning "clever, or wise"). With the rise of Athenian democracy and systematic higher education, the Sophists' influence grew and they became powerful forces in ancient Greek political and social life.

One of the first and best known Sophists was Protagoras (480-411 B.C.), a philosopher and teacher famous for his relativistic view that "Man is the measure of all things; of the things that are, that they are; of the things that are not, that they are not."[3] The individual he claimed, is the only valid measuring instrument, the only criterion of reality. There is not one Truth, but many. Although in Protagoras' view there is no ultimate truth or falsehood in the traditional sense, there is a pragmatic standard of better or worse: "Some appearances are better that others, though none is truer."[4] (Plato, *Theaetetus*) The appearance of the moment is subordinated to a higher standard, the end or purpose of human nature and society. Since societies and individuals' needs differ, there is no all-embracing, universal "good for man."

Because of this, Protagoras strongly believed that every issue has at least two sides, and since each individual sees things differently, the more reason there is for deeper examination. The truth on one side needs to be tested by the truth of the other side, and no ultimate or absolute appeal can be made to settle such questions once and for all. The truth (or rather, the best solution) emerges from the clash of arguments. The good proposal is the one that survives debate, and the advocates of both sides have the burden of proving their sides the stronger. Feeble representation is a neglect of responsibility.

Protagoras put this philosophy into practice by teaching his students to engage in *dissoi logoi* or "double" speeches, taking turns in speaking *pro et contra*, for and against, on every issue. He believed that by teaching his students, young citizens, how to argue effectively on a wide variety of issues by examining and debating all the possible sides of those issues, they would be able to put the best ideas forward and let everyone in the public forum make a more informed decision about which proposals to adopt for the good of the state.

Socrates (470–399 B.C.), the famous philosopher and teacher, fiercely protested this notion, especially in Plato's dialogue *Theaetetus*, where he examined the meaning of knowledge and truth. (There are no extant texts by Socrates himself; his ideas are known primarily from the dialogues of Plato, in which he appears as a character—although Plato often uses Socrates as a mouthpiece for his own views.) Plato (428–348 B.C.) considered Protagoras and other Sophists to be nothing more than an ancient version of modern-day spin doctors. In his view, they taught their students to manipulate others, by selling them their opinions (*doxa*), rather than true knowledge (*episteme*). Plato did not believe in the "man measure" idea, because, for him, there is only one truth, one reality. His scorn for the Sophists survives to this day in the form of the word "sophistry," which means false reasoning or argumentation, especially when used to deceive.

The fortunes of rhetoric took another turn at the hands of Plato's successor Aristotle (384–322 B.C.), whose treatise *Rhetoric* is probably the most influential work in the history of the field. Aristotle's theories have been consulted from the time of Rome down to the present day—and you will find that we make repeated use of his concepts throughout this book. (We will also pay due regard to Aristotle's theory of logic, since he is commonly regarded as the inventor of formal logic.)

Rome

The Roman democracy differed from that of ancient Greece, though debate still had a central role in the decision-making process. Designated representatives, rather than all citizens, discussed matters of the state in the

Roman Senate. The tradition of public debate and public oratory survived in the open-air Forum, however; there, the elevated platform (the *rostrum*) provided a venue for speeches and debates that ranged from eulogies to disputes about matters of national policy.[5]

The Roman courts were much more specialized than those of ancient Greece: the outcome was decided by a trained judge rather than a jury, and the cases were argued by skilled advocates. This resulted in the development of more sophisticated argumentative strategies and greater technical skill in debating.

Since it is hard to separate the development of debate from the history of rhetoric, which was a central discipline in Greek and Roman education, it is worth mentioning two of the foremost Roman orators and rhetoricians, Cicero and Quintilian. Cicero (106–43 B.C.) was a famous lawyer, statesman and orator, who produced among other works the *De inventione* (On Making Your Case) and the *De oratore* (On Being a Public Speaker). A century later, Quintilian (35–99 A.D.) wrote the *Institutio oratoria*, which is considered to be the first manual in public speaking. Quintilian strongly believed that the virtues of good citizenship can be taught, and that skill in rhetoric is essential for acquiring these virtues.

Other Cultures—India and East Asia

Ancient Greece and Rome, although predominant in the development of debate in the Western world, were not the only societies where debate had an important role. Other cultures have used debate as a form of inquiry as well, although sometimes in different contexts. Unlike in the West, where debate has flourished in politics and law, debate in the East has been part of religion and education.

India

Debating in India has its origins in religious ceremonies, and later served as an important medium for theological disputes. At first a minor diversion during religious sacrifices, debates became popular entertainment and were part of public assemblies. Indian kings even sponsored debating contests and offered prizes for the winners. To better prepare for such contests, debaters developed systematic instruction in logic, reasoning, and debate strategy, in which they paid special attention to matters of evidence (e.g., experience, examples, analogies and authoritative testimony). One of the first debate manuals was written in India describing the methods of debating and defending debate as being "necessary to protect the truth."[6]

East Asia

In China, debate had an important role in religious training and theological inquiry as well. The practice of "pure talk," as this form of debate was called, was conducted in circles of educated people, often taking the form of very long competitive debates including the audience. One person (the "host") would defend the thesis for debate and another (the "guest") would refute it. The audience would sometimes participate as well. Though structured as a game, the goal of these "pure talks" was to discover the truth about an issue that concerned everyone involved.

Feudal Japan also prized debates as an important part of scholarly life. There, debates focused primarily on literary and historical texts and were conducted informally among students. It was not until the 19th century that debate took a more organized form when religious and political debating societies were established in Japan.[7]

Medieval Universities

Based on the traditions of Aristotle and Cicero, debate and rhetoric had a central role in the curriculum of medieval universities. Debating blossomed in the 12th century all over Europe, and served to improve the understanding of texts and material being taught in the classroom; debates also developed oratorical and logical skills. Students became accustomed to attending public debates between their masters; they also were expected to present and defend their own theses in formal "disputations." Usually, the issues being debated were theological or philosophical. Typically, the debater used dialectic to "reconcile" differing positions in theological texts (e.g., passages in the work of one church authority that seemed to contradict another church authority), and then defended his reasoning against formal attacks.

As debate expanded beyond its narrow scholarly origins, it acquired new audiences in cities and courts, who saw debate as an entertaining forum for dialectical inquiry and intellectual dispute. Debate participants often brought their friends, so debating became a social event. However, debate issues and the sides that the participants argued remained largely abstract and artificial. As a result, these debates had little significance or political impact (not surprising, given the strict hierarchical rule that dominated medieval society). Debates were merely a form of entertainment.

As the Middle Ages gave way to the Renaissance, and the Renaissance gave way to the Enlightenment and the Age of Reason, debate firmly held its ascendancy in the academic world. From the 17th through the 19th centuries, the methods of Cicero and Quintilian—not to mention Latin disputations— were standard procedures in British and American universities. Debates were characterized by predetermined roles, rules and time limits. The audiences were largely academic and were integral parts of these debates: professors would usually take turns giving floor speeches, in the order of their rank. Opponents had to develop clear clash or controversy (Latin: *status controversiae*) and they were subjected to rigorous rules of argumentation. The debaters did not defend their real opinions, nor did they necessarily disagree with their opponents in real life. This exercise was still confined within the walls of the universities, just as in the Middle Ages; nevertheless, it had a profound influence on the development of political debate.

Political Debate

As in ancient Greece and Rome, debate is most consequential in the political realm. Outside of universities, religious institutions and the courts, debate finds its special social and political function in the development of European parliamentarism.

English Parliament

The English Parliament is thought to be the first governmental body to revive the political application of debate. Established in the 13th century during the reign of Edward III, the House of Commons became an increasingly important debate forum. Because of potential political ramifications, these debates were not made public until the 18th century; even then, the debaters were given fictitious names when parliamentary reports were published. Nonetheless, these debates were carefully recorded and reported;

their dissemination in the press helped to educate the public about issues of national importance.

The introduction of a public element in parliamentary procedures significantly influenced further development of democracy, as demands for the freedom of expression—that is, the freedom to speak without fear of punishment or prosecution—grew among members of Parliament. The lack of any immediate outside influences or threat of consequences turned out to be crucial for the return of political debate to its philosophical origins, in which all participants have an equal opportunity to examine issues freely, and to take sides and argue as they see fit.

American Congress

The colonial government in America was rooted in the practices of the British Parliament; as a result, public debate was part of the political process long before the American Revolution. As the movement toward independence took shape, debate took on significant importance, as politicians and public figures debated the propriety of severing ties with England— most notably in the Second Continental Congress, which produced the Declaration of Independence after intense debate. Similarly intense debates shaped the creation of the American Constitution in 1787. Even though the sessions of the Constitutional Convention took place behind closed doors (and were not disclosed to the public until fifty years later, when James Madison's notes were published), the arguments made by the participants were widely disseminated in the public press. (A recent collection of primary source material published by the Library of America, *The Debate on the Constitution*, runs to more than 2,000 pages in two volumes.)

After the ratification of the Constitution, the American Congress became the primary forum for the discussion of all national issues like states' rights, slavery and secession. Although sessions of the Senate were closed, debates in the House of Representatives were widely reported. Rules of procedure were highly important: in his 1801 book, *A Manual of Parliamentary Practice*, Thomas Jefferson, later to be elected president, prescribed strict rules of order in debates. Jefferson believed that "free argument and debate" are "natural weapons" in the service of truth, since "errors [cease] to be dangerous when it is permitted freely to contradict them."[8]

As in the past, debate was seen to have personal benefits for the debater. Debate training was thought to produce sound habits of mind, and skill in debate was taken as a sign of breeding, talent and personal worth. But political thinkers believed that debate bestowed its greatest benefits on the public and the body politic. Debate was seen as a way to produce carefully considered decisions; it was also seen as a way to enlighten the public about controversial issues. Woodrow Wilson, the president of Princeton University who went on to serve as American president from 1912 to 1920, thought that debate discouraged demagoguery; he advocated the creation of debating societies similar to those at European universities, primarily Oxford.[9]

Electoral Debates

In time, debate became so important that it entered the electoral process as well, and candidates running for office started conducting campaign debates with their opponents.

The most famous electoral debates (though not the first) were those between Abraham Lincoln and Stephen Douglas in 1858 as they campaigned for the office of U.S. senator from Illinois. The most controversial issue of those times was slavery. The critical question, as America expanded westward, was whether slavery should be permitted in the new territories. Many Northerners wanted to abolish slavery throughout the entire United States, not just in the North; minimally, they wanted slavery contained to the Southern states where it already existed. The Southern states saw the abolition movement as a threat to their autonomy, and they realized that if slave territory did not expand as the country expanded, they would gradually lose power. The issue divided the nation and threatened the existence of the Union. Lincoln and Douglas had seven debates, and each lasted several hours (the attention span of American audiences seemed to have been much longer back then!). Even though Stephen Douglas won the Senate seat, the debates propelled Lincoln into the national political arena and helped him become president in 1860.[10]

These and other electoral debates had a tremendous effect on educating the electorate, involving them in the issues of the time. Debates were well attended—thousands came to hear Lincoln and Douglas debate—and considered to be major events. They were significant as public business, producing meaningful discussion of nationally important issues, but they were also entertainment, and the participants were treated as celebrities.

Lincoln and Douglas, it should be remembered, were campaigning for a Senate seat, not the presidency. Even in the early 20th century, publicly campaigning for the presidency was regarded as "ungentlemanly" ; in any case, the size of the country and the comparative slowness of travel (note that in 1920 trains took over three days to go from New York to California) made reaching a significant portion of the population almost impossible. Following the precedent of successful candidates before him (among them Presidents Garfield, Harrison and McKinley), Warren G. Harding was elected president in 1920 after running a "front porch" campaign: he stayed at home in Ohio and spoke to his supporters (and the press) from the front porch of his house. Without significant campaigning by the candidates, there were no presidential debates—as a substitute, there were some debates conducted by surrogates. But the advent of radio, which carried the candidates' voices anywhere in the country, changed the nature of campaigning. In time, the candidates started debating themselves, and those debates have ever since been highly publicized.[11]

Debate in the Broadcasting Era

As radio stations spread across the United States in the 1920s, debate was carried from the U.S. Congress and town meetings into the national arena. Party representatives, reporters and members of political associations debated in shows like the "American Forum of the Air," or NBC's "America's Town Meeting of the Air," which started in 1935. These shows usually included time limits for the debaters and for audience questions. Sometimes a prize was awarded to the listener who asked the best question.

Presidential Debates in the United States

Presidential candidates did not debate each other directly on the air until 1948, when Republican candidates Harold Stassen, ex-governor of Minnesota, and New York Governor Thomas Dewey clashed in the primary election campaign in front of an audience estimated at between 40 and 80 million. The main issue they debated was: Should the Communist Party be outlawed? This was the first and last presidential broadcast debate limited to a single issue.[12]

Broadcast television was already established when Stassen and Dewey debated in 1948, but it was not until 1960 that a presidential debate was televised. That year, Richard M. Nixon, the vice president of the United States, debated four times against John F. Kennedy, U.S. senator from Massachusetts, before a national audience of over 66 million. In all of their debates, Kennedy fared much better; to many viewers he looked earnest and resolute, and answered questions with skill and humor, while Nixon looked tired and shifty-eyed.[13] The importance of physical image, though always present as a factor in debates, was greatly augmented by television. (Indeed, some scholars have noted that many voters who heard the debates on the radio—and did not see the physical contrast between the candidates—concluded that Nixon had "won" the debates.)

There were no presidential debates again until 1976—at least partly because the Republican candidate in 1968 and 1972 was Richard Nixon, who was not a man to make the same mistake twice. Since 1976, however, debates (in one form or another) have been a fixture on the political landscape. Because of the nature of radio and television, and the fact that the audience can tune in and out as they please or change channels, the expectations and style of debating have changed. Debates have become entertaining as well as educational. The debates themselves have become shorter and the list of issues discussed has become longer, with the result that superficiality has crept into a lot of the broadcast debates. In addition, presidential debates have become an amalgam of traditional debate and a press conference; in one format, a panel of questioners addresses a number of questions on many different issues to both candidates, who answer briefly and not always to the point. Kathleen Jamieson and David Birdsell think that while presidential debates in the United States offer an insight into a presidential candidate's personality, communicative style and vision of reality, they often fail to truly educate the public about the whole complexity of issues; often, the debates focus on irrelevant questions that provide better sound bites for the media.[14]

Parliamentary Debates

Congressional and Parliamentary debates remain vital in the decision-making process in every democratic country—but they always receive less coverage from the media than election debates. Only excerpts can be seen or heard on major TV and radio stations, and when debates are broadcast in their entirety (by public service cable stations such as C-SPAN), they are watched by only a handful of viewers. In the era of infotainment, nobody has the time, the patience or the attention span to follow long debates about issues that are sometimes unexciting (even if important). Long gone are the times when Lincoln and Douglas commanded the attention of their audiences for hours in a row.

With the fall of the Berlin Wall, debate found its place in the parliaments, media and schools of formerly communist countries as well. From Lithuania to Albania, debate is slowly but surely seeping into the pores of those societies. Debating associations and organizations are flourishing, as the youth of the post-communist nations take an active role in contributing to faster democratic and economic progress in their countries. The International Debate Education Association brings together youth from more than twenty formerly communist countries all over the world and helps them get integrated into the well-established democratic debating community; debate prepares them to serve in their own parliaments or to become active citizens in building open societies where once stood barbed wire and cement walls.

Conclusion

Debate has a rich history that spans over twenty-five centuries. It started as a precursor to and a manifestation of democracy in ancient Greece, and now precipitates the re-emergence of democracy all over the world. Even after all the major transformations debate has gone through, and the many forms it takes, the words of Pericles, spoken in his funeral oration for Athenians killed in battle, still ring true:

> We Athenians decide public questions for ourselves, or at least endeavor to arrive at a sound understanding of them, in the belief that it is not debate that is a hindrance to action, but rather not to be instructed by debate before the time comes for action. (Thucydides)), *Peloponnesian War* II, 34–36.

Notes

1. A. H. M. Jones, *Athenian Democracy* (Baltimore: Johns Hopkins University Press, 1986).

2. Robert J. Branham, *Debate and Critical Analysis: The Harmony of Conflict* (Mahwah, NJ: Lawrence Erlbaum, 1991): 6.

3 Plato, *Theaetetus*, translated and edited by John McDowell (Oxford: Oxford University Press, 1973): 152a.

4. Plato, *Protagoras*, translated and edited by C. C. W. Taylor (Oxford Clarendon Press, 1976).

5. Branham, 6.

6. Anthony Kennedy Warder, *A Course in Indian Philosophy* (Delhi, India: Motilal Banarsidass, 1970): 414–416.

7. Branham, 10.

8. Thomas Jefferson, *The Virginia Act for Establishing Religious Freedom-Draft* (1779), http://religiousfreedom.lib.virginia.edu/sacred/vaact_draft_1779.html

9. Woodrow Wilson, *Congressional Government* (repr. Gloucester, MA: Peter Smith, 1973): 143.

10. Kathleen Hall Jamieson, and David S. Birdsell, *Presidential Debates: The Challenge of Creating an Informed Electorate* (Oxford: Oxford University Press, 1978).

11. Ibid.

12. Ibid., 90–103.

13. Ibid., 140, 183.

14. Ibid., 163–193.

References

Barrett, H. *The Sophists*. Novato, CA: Chandler and Sharp, 1987.

Bizzell, P., and B. Herzberg, eds. *The Rhetorical Tradition*. Boston: Bedford Books, 1990.

Coby, P. *Socrates and the Sophistic Enlightenment*. Lewisburg, PA: Bucknell University Press, 1987.

De Bono, E. *Parallel Thinking—From Socratic Thinking to De Bono Thinking*. London: Penguin Books, 1994.

De Romilly, J. *The Great Sophists in Periclean Athens*. Oxford: Clarendon Press, 1992.

Dick, R. C. *Argumentation and Rational Debating*. Boston: WCB McGraw-Hill, 1978.

Diels, H., and R. K. Sprague, eds. *The Older Sophists*. Columbia: University of South Carolina Press, 1990.

Farrar, C. *The Origins of Democratic Thinking*. Cambridge: Cambridge University Press, 1988.

Finley, M. I. *Democracy Ancient and Modern*. New Brunswick, NJ: Rutgers University Press, 1973.

Guthrie, W. K. C. *The Sophists*. Cambridge: Cambridge University Press, 1971.

Habicht, W. *Der Literatur-Brockhaus*. Mannheim, Germany: Brockhaus, 1988.

Hall Jamieson, K., and D. S. Birdsell. *Presidential Debates: The Challenge of Creating an Informed Electorate*. New York: Oxford University Press, 1988.

Hanson, J. *NTC's Dictionary of Debate*. Lincolnwood, IL: National Textbook, 1996.

Harrison, R. *Democracy*. London: Routledge, 1993.

Herrick, J. A. *The History and Theory of Rhetoric*. Boston: Pearson Allyn and Bacon, 1996.

Kemp, R. *Lincoln-Douglas Debating*. Clayton, MO: Alan Company, 1984.

Kennedy, G. *The Art of Persuasion in Greece*. Princeton, NJ: Princeton University Press, 1963.

———. *The Art of Rhetoric in the Roman World 300 B.C.–A.D. 300*. Princeton, NJ: Princeton University Press, 1972.

Kerferd, G. B. *The Sophistic Movement*. Cambridge: Cambridge University Press, 1982.

Plato. *Plato's Republic*. Translated and edited by I. A. Richards. Cambridge: Cambridge University Press, 1966.

Plato. *Plato's Sophist*. Translated and edited by William Cobb. Totowa, NJ: Rowman and Littlefield, 1990.

Plato. *Protagoras*. Translated and edited by C. C. W. Taylor. Oxford: Clarendon Press, 1976.

Popper, K. R. "Plato as Enemy of the Open Society." In *Plato: Totalitarian or Democrat?* edited by Thomas L. Thorson. Englewood Cliffs, NJ: Prentice Hall, 1963.

Rankin, H. D. *Sophists, Socratics and Cynics*. London: Croom Helm, 1983.

Russell, B. *The History of Western Philosophy*. New York: Touchstone, 1995.

Schiappa, E. *Protagoras and Logos*. Columbia: University of South Carolina Press, 1991.

Silk, P., and R. Walters. *How Parliament Works*. London: Longman, 1995.

Thomas, D. A., ed. *Advanced Debate: Readings in Theory, Practice and Teaching*. Lincolnwood, IL: National Textbook, 1989.

Thorson, T. L., ed. *Plato: Totalitarian or Democrat?* Englewood Cliffs, NJ: Prentice Hall, 1963.

Thucydides. *The History of the Peloponnesian War.* Translated and edited by Richard Livingstone. Oxford: Oxford University Press, 1959.

Ueding, G. *Historisches Woerterbuch der Rhetorik.* Tuebingen, Germany: Max Niemeyer, 1992.

Vratovic, V. *Povijest Svjetske Knjizevnosti u Ssam Knjiga, 2. dio.* Zagreb, Yugoslavia: Liber–Mladost, 1977.

Wales, K. *A Dictionary of Stylistics.* Reading, MA: Addison-Wesley, 1989.

Wiese, J. *Lincoln-Douglas Debate: Values in Conflict.* Topeka, KS: Clark Publishing, 1993.

Chapter Three

An Ethical Perspective for Public Debates

Keep off the grass. Don't smoke. Form a line. Wait until your number is called. Keep your seat belt fastened. No talking. Wash your hands. No dogs allowed. Pay attention. Turn your cell phones off. Stand behind the line. Be on time. Say "thank you." Fill out the form completely. Place all bags on the conveyor belt. Follow me. Sign here. Read all the instructions. Place your tray table in the upright and fully locked position . . . Be good!

As a member of society, you may feel that your life is totally structured by rules—by lists of what you must do and what you must not do. Perhaps that is your attitude toward the subject of "ethics" as well. After reading the chapter heading, you might approach this discussion warily, thinking that it too will just amount to more commands to *be good*. If that is your fear, rest assured. While we would never play down the importance of being good, our perspective in this chapter is that anything that deserves the name "ethics" can never be reduced to a simple list of what to do or what not to do. Instead, ethics is a perspective, a worldview even. While we will mention several things that should be done, and several things that should be avoided, we believe that such guidelines must stem from a common foundation, and can't simply be a list of disconnected commands, like the list above. The ethics of public debating in particular, because they relate to communication, have much more to do with relationships than with rules.

What does that mean? Let's start by considering the following true story. The year 2001 Tournament and Youth Forum, conducted by the International Debate Education Association (IDEA) and held in Saint Petersburg, Russia, ended with a final debate before an audience of more than two hundred students and teachers from twenty-six different countries. The two teams of debaters, who themselves represented several different nations, focused on the issue of cultural rights, with the affirmative side advocating a United Nations role in increasing educational opportunities for Europe's Roma population. The negative side was responsible for opposing this policy, and while other options certainly existed, they chose to argue that there was no need for such a policy. Appealing to broad racial stereotypes, these debaters argued that Roma children have no interest in learning anything and simply can't be taught. At a factual level, there are good reasons to doubt this conclusion.[1] Even in the audience there were living refutations to this claim since two Roma observers attended the program outside of their normal school year in order to gain education. Believing that the claims were not only wrong but insulting as well, both of these Roma participants left the room in protest, returning only when the debate ended and then only for the opportunity to address the audience and to defend, as forcefully as possible, the idea that the Roma should not be stereotyped as a people who don't seek out or benefit from education. Others spoke as well, the problem was laid bare and in the end both teams apologized for the way they had handled the issue.

One could hopefully say that these remarks from the final debate served to instigate an important discussion and may have raised the consciousness of those who witnessed it or heard of it. Still, there are better ways to promote understanding, and the story of this debate gone awry serves as an important reminder to all involved: participants and audience members alike need to view public debates from an ethical perspective, understanding that debates are better or worse, effective or worthless, noble or disgraceful based upon the degree to which the participants emphasize several elements of a good relationship: honesty, respect, and dialogue.

As broad as these elements are, a concern for ethics can't be contained or isolated in just one chapter. For that reason, you will see that we return to ethical considerations at a number of points in further chapters. This chapter, however, has the purpose of developing a point of departure for these applications. For the remainder of this discussion, we intend to develop this relational view of ethics by first exploring the connection between ethics and public debating, then identifying several elements of an ethical perspective, and finally discussing practical ways to promote and negotiate ethical guidelines in public debates.

Ethics and Public Debating

"Ethics" is a term that reflects the human concern for issues of what is right and wrong, fair and unfair, just and unjust in our conduct and our communication. The term stems from the Greek word *ethos* which the early Greek teachers of rhetoric saw as an aspect of character. Aristotle, who described the art of rhetoric as "the faculty of observing in any given case the available means of persuasion,"[2] noted that "character may almost be called the most effective means of persuasion."[3] The reason that your character may rival the importance of your arguments is found in the simple fact that because they lack the ability to verify every statement independently, audiences must trust, and trust is not given out indiscriminately. "We believe good men more fully and more readily than others," as Aristotle says, and "this is true generally whatever the question is, and absolutely true where exact certainty is impossible and opinions are divided."[4]

The relevance of this aspect of character to public debating is clear: when presenting your ideas to your audience, you are also presenting yourself. As you decide how to use researched information, how to characterize events and people, how to address your opponent and your audience, all of these choices will reflect something of your own character. Your knowledge, your trustworthiness, even your likeability are all a part of your message, and it is impossible to fully separate an audience's reaction to an idea from an audience's reaction to the source of that idea. To paraphrase Quintilian, the Roman teacher of communication, the effective public persuader is not just a good speaker, but also "a good person, speaking well."

Public debating, because it involves practical communication, reasoning, and adaptation, always involves choice. All issues involving choice are potentially moral issues. Because a public debate is aimed at a general audience, unethical debaters might be tempted to engage in demagoguery by appealing to popular emotion and prejudice rather than making arguments. The fact that most public debates are specific and solitary events also means that opponents and audience members will rarely have a chance to use the "next time" in order to point out an erroneous quotation or criticize a suspect strategy. The importance of ethics is fueled by the fact that public debates take place in a context in which it is impossible to check on the validity of each bit of information and unwise to call attention to each act that is arguably unethical. Few audiences enjoy watching debaters bicker over who is more moral, and that is why the ethics of any public debate should be established and understood before the debate even starts. Good public debates can be found where event organizers, advocates, and audiences are committed to a positive view of responsible communication. Rather than being a bitter struggle for your view to prevail by any means necessary, a public debate should ennoble you, your opponent, the audience, and the issue.

An Ethical Perspective for Public Debating

Philosophers have long contended with the issue of the origin of ethics. Precisely how do we arrive at a view of what is good and what is bad? Some may turn to religion to answer that question. Others may say that an act's value depends upon its consequences. Still others would say that you can't evaluate any human action without considering its intent. Some would say that morality is found in one's community and would depend on the group and the age in which someone lives. Finally, some would go further and say that ethics always depends on the situation, and that few actions are always wrong or always right.

While each of these outlooks may contribute to one's personal worldview on ethics, we would like to develop a perspective on public debate ethics that is rooted in the value of dialogue. From a public perspective, the goal of a debate in front of a large audience is to provide a fair and rational hearing of all sides of a controversy. While advocates' goals may be to win, and organizers' goals may be to attract attention to an issue, the goal of the debate, seen from the broadest possible perspective, is to introduce dialogue. For that reason, our perspective on ethics should be dialogic as well. One illustration of this perspective of ethical rhetoric as dialogue is provided by the father of dialogue himself. Plato's dialogue entitled *Phaedrus* uses a familiar metaphor in order to differentiate the self-interested arguer from the arguer with a more dialogic intent.[5] The attitudes of arguers to their audience can be compared to the attitude of lovers toward those they love. To Plato, the "evil lover" stalks the target of his affections as a hunter stalks his prey—the beloved becomes an objective and hence is reduced to an object, a goal to be won. The parallel to the evil lover is the argumentative "Lothario" who sees the audience as nothing more than a fitting target for seduction. The evil lover in this case is the debater who is driven by the desire for victory and sees other elements of the debate—reason, persuasion, understanding, communication—as means to that end only. Rhetorical misdirection and outright deception may be justifiable in the mind of this "lover" if they increase his chance of attaining his goal and capturing his audience.

One alternative to the evil lover is the "non-lover." While the non-lover lacks the insidious wiles of the evil lover, the non-lover also lacks passion. As the name would suggest, the non-lover is not invested—she cares little if she is successful or not. As a debater, the non-lover is one who may seek to inform the audience, but lacks an interest in genuinely moving the audience. A non-lover may not distort or deceive, but she also imperils dialogue by failing to attempt persuasion and motivated argument; the non-lover bypasses an opportunity for engagement.

Since we are talking about Plato, an ideal has to be involved, and the ideal in this case is the "noble lover." By pursuing her intended only in ways that suit their mutual interests and goals, the noble lover embodies the value of dialogue. Its parallel in the setting of a public debate lies in an advocate whose main motivation is to conduct an argument within a dialogic setting. Of course, noble lovers have viewpoints, and they are committed to defending those viewpoints with the best arguments available. But they have also committed to the idea of a debate—they have committed to a process that privileges the exchange of views and rewards the best of each side. In addition, they've committed to a view of the audience as a group in possession of independence, rationality and free choice. The noble lover definitely tries to persuade, but only by appealing to the audience's best judgment.

The view expressed in this chapter is that the ethics of a public debate are in large part determined by whether or not participants have taken the dialogic perspective of a noble lover toward their audience. A dialogic perspective on ethics can be captured in the following formula: strategies, attitudes and behaviors that promote reasoned and respectful dialogue are presumptively ethical, and those that do not are suspect.

In writing on the ethics of argument, professor Stanley Rives argued that the debater has three main responsibilities: "(1) the responsibility to research the proposition thoroughly to know truth, (2) the responsibility to dedicate his effort to the common good, and (3) the responsibility to be rational."[6] To these responsibilities, professors Karyn and Donald Rybacki added a fourth: "the responsibility to observe the rules of free speech in a democratic society."[7] We believe that a dialogic perspective includes these four responsibilities—which must, however, be expanded in two important ways. The first element, the responsibility to research, should be seen more broadly as a responsibility to prepare fully. Beyond gathering needed evidence, advocates have a responsibility to the audience and to the issues to take preparation seriously. The last element, the responsibility to preserve free speech, should be broadened as well. Advocates and audiences should observe free speech because doing so respects individual views and individual autonomy. So it is really respect—for people and for their ideas and experiences—which is the final responsibility of the public debater. As a result of these modifications, we can identify four cornerstone responsibilities of the public debater:

- *A commitment to full preparation*
- *A dedication to the common good*
- *A respect for rational argument*
- *A respect for ideas and people*

Let's consider each of these responsibilities in greater detail and look at some of the resulting guidelines.

A Commitment to Full Preparation

By spending time at a public debate, an audience is doing more than simply spending; they are actually investing. The time and the effort that it takes to follow a public debate attentively are given in the hope that there is some sort of return or benefit for the listener. The audience's reasonable expectation of benefit creates an obligation on the part of the debaters to do their best to provide the audience with useful information presented in a way that interests and engages. A debater who wastes an hour in front of a large audience is wasting more than an hour. Indeed, he is wasting an hour for *each* member of the audience, and the resulting span of wasted time could be measured in days if not weeks or months. Without full preparation, opportunities for productive dialogue are limited. Thus is born the need for public debaters to commit to full preparation, and this obligation includes a number of elements.

Plan in Advance of the Debate. As much as experienced debaters are tempted to "wing it" or assume that inspiration will arrive in the heat of the moment, a public debate demands thorough preparation. This includes previewing the necessary arrangements, selecting and developing arguments, planning speeches and all of the other steps mentioned below. In chapter five, we discuss various advance steps to take in preparing for the debate.

Practice. There is no substitute for demonstrating your preparation by conducting a dry run of the debate. Ideally, you should practice in conditions that are as close as possible to those you can expect during the debate. In chapter nine, we discuss ways of practicing for the debate.

Know Your Subject. Audiences attend public debates in the hope of hearing, if not experts, then at least individuals with an informed perspective on the subject. Complete preparation for any public debate requires that advocates seek out answers to a number of different questions: What is the factual foundation of the controversy? Who are the major parties? What has happened up to now? When debaters take short cuts by relying on what they already know, or think they know, then they are limiting the potential for clash, risking insult to the audience and imperiling the possibilities for genuinely informed dialogue; solid knowledge is essential for a successful debate. (Even so, we will note that a debate is not a quiz show: no one is expected to know every fact, and no one wins a debate *simply* by knowing more facts. "I don't know" is often a perfectly appropriate answer during questioning.)

Make Reference to External Research Material When Necessary. A primary element of the need to prepare is the need to inform yourself on the topic. By researching the subject matter, you are avoiding error and presenting a more comprehensive argument in favor of your side. You will notice in the section above that we developed the responsibilities of the arguer by consulting Professor Stanley Rives and Professors Karyn and Donald Rybacki. By beginning with the thoughts of these authors and adding our own, we are participating in a conversation with other scholars—and that, after all, is what research is. Turning to external authorities doesn't limit your originality; rather, it permits you to participate along with others in an ongoing discussion of the topic. In chapter eleven we discuss more fully the need to provide evidentiary support and the best methods for developing it.

Avoid Representing the Thoughts of Others as Your Own.   If, in writing this chapter, we had read the professors mentioned above, and then just presented the four elements of responsibility without reference to their work, we would have committed plagiarism. Plagiarism (originating from *plagiarius*, the Latin word for "kidnapper") is the act of representing the ideas or words of another as your own. It can be global (stealing an entire speech) or partial (stealing a particularly good sentence, or an example). The solution to plagiarism is simply to give credit when you are using the words or ideas of another. Information that is in the public domain (e.g., the fact that Quintilian was Roman) doesn't need to be cited, but when taking material that is unique due to its judgment, reasoning, phrasing, or structure, you need to be careful to cite the original source of the information.

Identify Your Sources.   Instead of saying, "I remember reading somewhere that . . ." or "Scientists say . . ." advocates should let listeners and opponents know where their information comes from. Information from a source that is unidentified or vague is difficult to evaluate and may simply be discarded. Remember also that oral speeches do not have footnotes: the fact that a reference for your claim exists isn't likely to be impressive to an audience unless they are given some detail about that source. While you don't have to give every detail about your source (page numbers and specific dates, for example, are often omitted) it is a good rule of thumb to provide the audience with as much detail as they need at that moment to understand and evaluate the source of information.

Ensure That Your References Are Not Exaggerated or Distorted.   Because you are a debater, it is natural that you will want to make the best possible case for your side. When you refer to an author to support one of your arguments, make sure that you are giving the argument as much force as the author would give it, *but no more*. If an author said, "some would say that globalism is beneficial, but they haven't studied the issues," it would be grossly inaccurate and unethical to quote the author as saying "globalism is beneficial." If an author said that free trade was "a way" to promote international understanding, it would be grossly distorting and unethical to paraphrase the author as saying that free trade was "the only way" to promote international understanding. When you represent an author's views, the critical question of fairness is this: Would that author agree to the way in which you have used his or her words, including your selection, emphasis, and implication?

Ensure That You Are Using Fully Accurate and Legitimate References.   It should go without saying, of course, but fabricating support by inventing an expert who doesn't exist or creating a quotation that was never published represent the absolute lowest points of advocacy. Even if you believe that something like this was probably said by someone, it is never acceptable to lie about evidence. Because it is impractical to verify independently every reference used in a public debate, the survival of intelligent advocacy in this context depends on trust. To violate that trust is to inflict the gravest wound to the dialogue.

A Dedication to the Common Good

Inherent in the act of choosing debate over other potential means of persuasion is a willingness to place the common good over one's own interests. The purely self-interested persuader would probably prefer an uninterrupted monologue to a debate in which an opponent receives equal billing and equal time. By choosing debate, you commit to a process that showcases both sides—a process that may or may not help your "side" conceived narrowly, but a process that will serve the common good by promoting complete understanding and fair judgment. An ethical perspective on public debate includes a commitment to these ends.

It is impossible to say categorically which motives are appropriately oriented to the common good and which motives are purely personal; nevertheless, we offer six items of advice regarding motivation.

Examine Your Goals.   It may sound obvious, but our first suggestion is simply to ask yourself why you are participating in a public debate. Are you interested in the thrill of competition? The pride you feel in your ability to defeat an opponent? The glory and admiration you expect to receive from the audience? There is nothing ignoble in any of these motivations, but one goal that should be present, and the goal that should take precedence if it conflicts with any of the previously mentioned goals, is the objective of helping an audience understand a complex issue and make a reasonable decision. A debater wouldn't ask an audience to vote for her side because

"I want to win . . ." Similarly, an ethical arguer should not expect to sway an audience with appeals that are primarily self-serving.

Ensure That You Would Be Comfortable Having the Audience Know Your Real Motivation.   While there is no mathematical test for separating an unethical motivation from an ethical one, one easy way to test your motives is to ask yourself if you would be comfortable being fully frank in sharing your goals with your audience. For example, imagine your discomfort in saying to an audience, "I am hoping that this next example is going to cause you to have so much sympathy that you don't notice the fact that I'm using some pretty questionable statistics." That discomfort is a good sign that any such strategy would be suspect.

Address the Debate to the Audience's Level of Understanding.   Many forms of competitive debate are evaluated by technical experts only. If these judges are accustomed to faster speech and technical language, then it seems appropriate to give that to them. In public debates, on the other hand, you usually address a general audience, and while audience members have a responsibility to try to understand, ultimately the question of whether the debate is enlightening or incomprehensible is in the debaters' hands. Addressing the audience using terms that they don't understand or in a style of speech that they find incomprehensible makes as much sense as debating in French for an audience that understands only Russian.

Share Information.   Those focusing on the debate as a battle might be disturbed at the prospect of sharing information with the "enemy." Viewed from the perspective of the debate's larger goals, however, sharing information (specifically, main arguments and sources of information) can only improve the quality of debate. For those still focused on individual performance, remember that you can only look good if your opponent presents a reasonable challenge—sharing information will help that happen. In chapter nine we consider more fully the question of what information should be shared in what situations.

Choose Depth Over Breadth.   While you may put maximum pressure on your opponent by including every good argument that you can think of, that strategy is also likely to overwhelm the audience and result in insufficient development and explanation. A few fully developed arguments are always going to be more conducive to dialogue than a profusion of more shallow arguments.

Privilege Content Over Competition.   The exhilaration of debating—showing your skills, besting your opponent—can be an important motivator. An emphasis on the common good, however, requires you to remember that audiences are rarely interested in personal rivalries and instead want to see debate as a contest in ideas; they don't go to a debate because they want to see a horse race. Before and after the debate, any public comments you make should emphasize the value of the exchange of ideas, rather than predictions or proclamations of victory. During the debate, your attention should focus on showing that your arguments have the most merit, not on showing that you are the best debater.

A Respect for Rational Argument

Public debates are more than an opportunity to showcase your speaking skills or state your point of view. They are opportunities for argument and for the reasoned exchange of views. This interest in dialogue requires an emphasis on reasons.

Make Your Reasoning Explicit.   As we will develop in chapter 10, a central factor of argument in any context is that it always addresses the question "why?" In a public debate this question may be silent or it may be quite vocal, but debaters have a responsibility to provide an answer in each argument that they make. Statements like "my support for this is . . .", "here is why . . ." and "the reason for this is . . ." should run throughout the debate. In order to prevent the debate from becoming a simple exchange of position-statements, debaters should identify their reasoning and not rely on what they assume to be true or obvious.

Avoid Basing Arguments Solely Upon Your Audience's Prior Beliefs.   As we will emphasize in chapter 10, reasoning in any public context must *account for and include* audience beliefs, but this is not a license simply to parrot audience views without offering reasons. Speaking to an audience of hunters, for example, you could probably rely on their belief that people should have the right to own guns, but there are three practical reasons to provide justification for this premise anyway: it will reinforce the audience's beliefs, inoculate them against your opponent's efforts to change their minds, and demonstrate that you are holding up your end of the debate. The less practical but probably more important reason not to rest too comfortably on audience opinion is to promote the dialectical function of the debate: reasoning that isn't made explicit and resides instead only in the minds of the audience is hard to attack or defend, and less likely to lead to understanding or resolution.

Attack the Argument Not the Person. "My opponent is still very young and inexperienced . . . scarcely knows English . . . can't grasp the complexities of my argument . . . looks funny . . . dresses badly." All of these statements fail to promote rational dialogue by substituting an attack on the person for an attack on the argument. While there are a few circumstances in which the character and honesty of the advocate is a relevant issue (for example, in a debate between political candidates one *may* argue that character predicts future policy choices), in many cases the character assault merely covers for an inability to address the arguments. In most public contexts, debates are best conceived as contests between ideas, which happen to be represented by people, not contests between people.

Avoid Appeals to Fallacious Reasoning. Reasoning solely based on audience beliefs may be termed *argumentum ad populum* just as attacking the person rather than the argument may be termed *argumentum ad hominem*. Like other fallacies, these strategies subvert reason by offering an appearance of proof. Other "tricks" of reasoning include bandwagon appeals ("everyone thinks it is so . . ."), reasoning from too few or atypical examples ("I know in my town it is true that . . ."), slippery slope ("if we require licenses for guns, what is to stop us from requiring licenses for everything?"), and many others. These fallacies short-circuit the reasoning that should be central to the dialogic function of the debate. In chapters 10 and 11, we review some strategies for identifying, avoiding, and attacking these arguments.

Clarify Arguments and Refutations at the First Opportunity. The public debate on the sale of violent pornography which was discussed at the beginning of chapter 1 illustrates the need for this standard. In the very last moments of this debate, Eric, the student council member supporting the continued sale of *Penthouse* magazine in the university's bookstore, introduced the argument that exposure to pornography *reduces* violence, backing it up with a particular study. Since this was the last speech of the debate, the other side had no opportunity to respond. This tactic, called "sand-bagging" in competitive debate circles, impairs the dialogic function of the debate by robbing one side, and the audience as well, of the opportunity to give a fair hearing to both sides. Luckily in the pornography debate this dirty trick didn't pay off. A member of the audience happened to have information on this study. In the audience comment section, he not only presented evidence criticizing the study's findings, but he also took Eric to task for waiting to present the argument only when his opponent couldn't respond. When debaters hide arguments or delay arguments, rational dialogue suffers, and for that reason advocates have an obligation to clarify their own arguments and respond to opponent's arguments at their first opportunity to do so. The saying that "silence is consent" implies that if you fail to answer one of your opponent's arguments, then you have agreed to that argument (which doesn't necessarily mean that the debate is over—it just means that you grant them that one point). To answer the argument only later, after you've had time to think or to realize the implications, is unfair because it denies your opponents their best opportunity to defend their argument against your attack.

Evaluate Arguments Based on the Reasons Offered.   As an audience member or judge of a public debate, you may be tempted to base your assessment of the debate on the credibility or speaking skills of the debater, or the extent to which the debater's views mirror your own. While these considerations can't be dismissed, you should be committed—whether as a spectator, participant, or judge—to the debate's dialogic function of allowing a comparison of reasoning. In chapter 18 we outline a method of debate evaluation that moves through the process of identifying issues, comparing the reasoning of both sides, selecting the better argument in each case, and finally putting it together into a judgment for one side or the other. Evaluating a debate in this way takes some practice and patience, but it shows greater respect for rational dialogue than evaluations based on surface characteristics, such as the likeability or wit of a particular speaker.

A Respect for Ideas and People

An essential element of a debate is that it is a human encounter, one that respects reason over force, arguments over assertions, and persuasion over demagoguery. One assumption of this text is that if you did not respect your opponent, your audience, and the process of a reasoned exchange of views, then you would probably not choose to engage in a public debate. In its Statement of Ethical Principles, the American Cross Examination Debate Association notes the need to promote respect, both for people and for the process of debate.

> Furthermore, students should remember that debate is an oral, inter-active process. It is the debater's duty to aspire to the objective of effective oral expression of ideas. Behaviors which belittle, degrade, demean, or otherwise dehumanize others are not in the best interest of the activity because they interfere with the goals of education and personal growth. The ethical CEDA debater recognizes the rights of others and communicates with respect for opponents, colleagues, crit-ics and audience members. Communication which engenders ill-will and disrespect for forensics ultimately reduces the utility of forensics for all who participate in it and should, therefore, be avoided.[8]

Aside from a simple recognition of respect for all parties and the process itself, there are several important elements that we see.

Avoid Name-Calling, Personal Categorization, and Harassment. While most of us are smart enough to avoid making gratuitous insults to our hosts, our audience or our opponents, many public debates still provide opportunities for insensitivity and incidents such as the one described at the beginning of this chapter. The negative team in that debate, by wrapping their arguments in gross generalizations and ethnic stereotypes of Roma people, failed to show respect to specific audience members, for the reasoning process, and for simple human diversity. Even if there had been no Roma in the audience, arguments along these lines would have been offensive—perhaps especially so. That is, it would have been even worse if no Roma had been there to defend themselves.

In these and other situations, there is a tension between a desire to promote an open forum free from restrictions on speech and the desire to maintain a civil dialogue. The Cross Examination Debate Association, the American organization that promotes policy debate, addresses this balance in its sexual harassment policy in words that are worth quoting and adopting:

> It is the nature of the academic debate community to provide a forum for the robust expression, criticism and discussion (and for the tolerance) of the widest range of opinions. It does not provide a license for bigotry in the form of demeaning, discriminatory speech actions and it does not tolerate sexual [or, we would add, racial,

ethnic, religious, national, linguistic, or sexual-preference] harassment.... In the debate community, the presentation of a reasoned or evidenced claim about a societal group that offends members of that group is to be distinguished from a gratuitous denigrating claim about, or addressed to, an individual or group such as those enumerated above. The former is bona fide academic behavior while the latter may demean, degrade or victimize in a discriminatory manner and, if so, undermines the above principles.[9]

Applying these principles in practice requires no small amount of consideration and sensitivity. As a rule, however, public debaters should avoid the use of names or attributes that are considered derogatory, seriously question any argument that is based on generalizations about broad human categories (national, ethnic, linguistic, religious, or gender), and remember that every person, even those whose views we do not share, is entitled to basic human respect.

Appeal to the Best in Your Audience.   In his first inaugural address in 1861, President Abraham Lincoln urged his listeners at the time, and generations since, to unite on common ideals, appealing to what he termed "the better angels of our nature." In a context of public debate, we focus on these "better angels" when we appeal to an audience's compassion, intelligence and honesty. We dishonor dialogue, however, when we appeal to vanity, specious nationalism, pure self-interest, or prejudice of any kind. The rhetorical theorist Edwin Black[10] noted that the ethics of communication can be assessed not only by the persona or character that a speaker conveys but also by a "second persona" that is a speaker's view of his audience. This second persona is a rhetorical reflection—an image of the audience as seen by the speaker. For example, let's say that in a debate before students, a student debater argues that a change to their school's honor code is a good idea because it will allow students to cheat more effectively without getting caught. In this case, he would be communicating a specific image of the audience—namely that he sees them as people who would applaud the opportunity to cheat. He communicates not only his own persona (someone who advocates cheating) but also a second persona (an audience that appreciates cheating). Most obviously, he would be offering a grave insult to the students, but even if such an appeal were effective in a given context it would remain unethical because it appeals to an unethical motivation. Such appeals can corrupt not only the speaker but the audience as well. As

Black said, "In all rhetorical language we can find enticements not simply to believe something but to *be* something. We are solicited by the discourse to fulfill its blandishments with our very selves."[11] For this reason, the public debater ought to be evaluated not only for what she presents of herself, but also for what she presents of her view of the audience. An ethical advocate strives to focus her appeals on an audience's "better angels."

Preserve the Value of Free Expression.   All debates will at least attempt to restrict discourse to a more or less specific topic (see chapter 6, "Crafting A Proposition"), but there is a world of difference between topic restriction and viewpoint restriction. Consistent with the values of debate in the public sphere, organizers and participants should avoid any *a priori* effort to exclude a particular viewpoint. While adhering to the principles articulated above, advocates should consider themselves free to pick the best available argument and should not restrict themselves to whatever the audience considers most palatable. In an address in 1994, Colin Powell, later to become U.S. secretary of state, noted that "freedom of speech means permitting the widest range of views to be presented, however controversial those views may be. The [U.S. Constitution's] First Amendment right of free speech is intended to protect the controversial and even the outrageous word and not just comforting platitudes too mundane to need protection."[12] In promoting free expression in public contexts, a distinction deserves to be drawn between the freedom from censorship (a freedom that must be protected) and freedom from criticism (a freedom that ought never be protected). Sometimes in public dialogues, those who advocate unpopular viewpoints, and are criticized for it, will answer their opponents: "I have the right to my own views!" Certainly so, but as long as their opponents are saying, "You can express your view, but you are wrong," and not, "You can't express your view," then they are not censoring. On the contrary, we avoid censorship precisely in order to allow criticism.

Avoid Excessive Partisanship.   Those serving as advocates in a public debate are obviously supposed to be for one side and against another. Audience members as well are likely to lean more toward one side of the debate than toward the other. In the spirit of showing respect to people as well as ideas, however, audiences should avoid any displays that demonstrate contempt or disregard. Good-natured rooting for your side, of course, can add needed energy to a debate, but refusing to applaud for one side, booing a speaker or heckling in a mean-spirited fashion (see chapter 17, "Moderating the Debate") all constitute public displays of bad manners. Our assumption here is that if you were not interested in hearing and respecting both sides, you probably would not have come to a public debate.

Promoting Ethical Public Debates

We have attempted in this chapter to provide a relatively complete perspective on the ethical issues likely to arise in most public debates. Still, it is probable that there are other issues relating to specific topics, circumstances or participants that will suggest a need for additional application and development of the principles contained here. Most organizations that promote speech and debate competition have developed ethical guidelines that may be relevant to public debates.[13] While sections dealing with tournament procedures, eligibility and rules of competition are not likely to apply to public debates, those that relate more generally to the responsibilities of ethical advocacy can provide a useful additional resource. One advantage that organizations have in promoting ethical debating is continuity of contact. Within a community, regular meetings at tournaments and workshops can help groups of arguers develop ethical norms that are understood and observed. In addition, the governing boards, executive councils and general assemblies of these organizations have the ability to create binding and enforceable codes of conduct in a democratic way. Because they are usually staging one-time-only events, the organizers of public debates face greater challenges in promoting ethical behavior. In competitive contexts, the debater who uses inaccurate evidence in one tournament may well be caught at the next tournament. For public debates, however, there is likely to be no "next time." Expert judges who are trained to notice and penalize faulty logic and rhetorical tricks may not be present at a public debate. Rather than justifying a lighter standard of ethics for public debates, these considerations make it all that much more important for public debaters to commit themselves in advance to ethical advocacy.

When we are dealing with sponsoring organizations and opponents that we know, we can ideally rely on an unspoken understanding. In other contexts it may be advisable to make our ethical commitments explicit. One way to adapt the need for clear ethical commitments to the one-time nature of the public debate is to use a signed ethical compact. The purpose of an ethical compact is to set forth the advocates' mutual views on appropriate debating behavior in the form of an agreement that could exist on its own or could be incorporated into a larger agreement to debate that includes other elements such as format, topic, schedule and physical arrangements. While an ethical compact in itself is not likely to be enforceable on advocates who may after all still behave unethically even after agreeing not to, the existence of such a compact has several advantages nonetheless. First, it is explicit and thus reduces the possibilities for misunderstanding. Second, the positive act of affixing one's signature can serve as a strong rhetorical inducement to follow those commitments. Finally, the existence of the signed agreement can substantially increase the chance that an advocate who violated one of the principles can be effectively criticized for doing so after the fact. The possibility of being criticized for ethical violations is a powerful deterrent—especially so in high profile debates that involve the possibility of coverage by the mass media. In settings that are likely to be highly contentious, the compact could even be made public or be distributed to the audience prior to the debate. While it isn't always necessary, a signed agreement can promote clear understanding and deter unethical behavior, something that is in the interests of both sides.

We offer the following as one example of an ethical compact. Because such agreements, and ethics more generally, can be seen as the product of dialogue, your own compact may differ.

Ethical Compact for a Public Debate

We, the undersigned, having agreed to a debate on [your topic] on [a given day and time] and having committed ourselves to the belief that a free, fair, and full exchange of rational arguments contributes to a public dialogue that is more important than either of our personal goals, do agree and promise to uphold the following principles of ethical practice during our debate.

1. We see the debate as a forum for rational disagreement, not simply a vehicle for personal expression and competition.

2. We agree to make arguments and to support them explicitly with our knowledge, evidence or logical analysis.

3. We agree to state every argument in the clearest possible manner at the earliest opportunity and to the best of our ability, and not to hide, disguise, or delay arguments for the purpose of trapping our opponent.

4. We agree to address our arguments, in both matter and manner, to the audience's level of understanding, not allowing technicalities, jargon or rate of speech to interfere with audience comprehension.

5. When relying on factual knowledge, we agree to identify the source of our information whenever possible and to avoid knowingly misrepresenting a fact or inflating the certainty of our knowledge. At the same time we realize that the debate is not a quiz show and we will not expect our opponent to know every fact or detail.

6. When using evidence, we agree to identify and qualify our sources, and to quote and paraphrase in ways that are accurate and in keeping with the original author's manifest intent.

7. We agree that we will to the best of our ability avoid the use of unrepresentative examples, personal attacks, appeals to popular opinions and other logical fallacies.

8. We agree, within the limits of time, to respond to each important argument of our opponent at our first opportunity to do so, realizing that an argument not refuted is an argument granted. We will refrain from introducing new arguments into the debate at a time that would deprive our opponents of the opportunity to respond.

9. Whether we believe that the audience agrees with us at the start of the debate or not, we agree to use the debate to advance audience knowledge and understanding and to challenge and deepen their opinions, and not to simply tell them what we think they already believe.

10. We agree to treat each other with respect and to avoid name-calling and to focus on the arguments at hand and not on the irrelevant personal qualities or the debating skills of our opponents.

11. We agree, through our own behavior and our arguments in the debate, to treat all people and groups with respect and to avoid appeals to broad and unsubstantiated stereotypes regarding race, ethnicity, nationality, age, sex, sexual orientation or language.

12. We agree, within the constraints of relevance created by the topic, to respect free expression and understand that freedom of expression is not the same thing as freedom from criticism—all views are open to both expression and refutation.

13. We agree to encourage our supporters in the audience to show respect to both sides in the debate and to avoid any disruptive partisan displays.

14. We agree to exchange basic information no later than one week prior to the debate by sharing simple argument outlines and sources of information.

15. We agree that in comments to mass media organizations following the debate neither we nor our representatives or agents will emphasize the contest nature of the event as if it were a sports competition. Rather than declaring a winner or concentrating on debating feats or foibles, public comments will focus on the ideas presented.

x. _____   x. _____
    Signature   Signature

Notes

1. For example, experts from the Greater Toronto School Board tested Romani children who had emigrated from the Czech Republic and found that despite having been consigned to special schools for the educationally challenged, Roma immigrants were of completely normal intelligence and were able to be integrated successfully into Canada's public school system, as reported by the Roma Community Advocacy Center, Online: http://www.romani.org/toronto/FS7edu.html.

2. Aristotle, *Rhetoric,* translated and edited by W. Rhys Roberts (New York: Modern Library, 1954): Book 1, Chapter 2.

3. Ibid., 1356a.

4. Ibid.

5. A more modern application of this metaphor for rhetoric can be found in Wayne Brockriede's essay "Arguers as Lovers." Brockriede differentiates the "arguer as lover," who seeks mutual interest, from the "arguer as rapist," who substitutes

rhetorically violent power for compassion and altruism. *Philosophy and Rhetoric* 5 (1974): 1–11.

6. S. G. Rives, "Ethical Argumentation," *Journal of the American Forensic Association* 1 (1964): 84.

7. K. C. Rybacki, and D. J. Rybacki, *Advocacy and Opposition: An Introduction to Argumentation*, 4th ed. (Boston: Allyn & Bacon, 2000): 11.

8. Statement of Ethical Principles of the Cross Examination Debate Association, sec. 1. B.

9. Statement on Sexual Harassment of the Cross Examination Debate Association, quoted in P. Stepp, and B. Gardner, "How Well Are We Doing: Has the Sexual Harassment Policy in CEDA Debate Worked?" *Contemporary Argumentation and Debate* 22 (2001): 22–40.

10. E. Black, "The Second Persona," *Quarterly Journal of Speech* 56 (1970): 109–119.

11. Ibid., 119.

12. C. Powell, Commencement address at Howard University, in *Great Speeches for Criticism and Analysis*, 3rd ed., edited by L. Rohler and R. Cook (Greenwood, IN: Alistair Press, 1998): 319.

13. A good example is the American Forensic Association Code of Standards, http://www.americanforensics.org/afacode.html.

Chapter Four

Moving from Tournament Debating to Public Debating

A typical introduction to the world of public debating might go like this.

Ivana is an experienced debater. She learned the basics of debate at workshops and from coaches, competitors and more experienced teammates. She has spent the last couple of years honing her skills by going to frequent debate tournaments on the weekends. According to her coach and those who debate her, Ivana is pretty good. She prepares thoroughly, she is confident during rounds of debate, and she has a strategic knack for knowing which issues are going to be most persuasive to her judge. For all these reasons, when it comes time to pick debaters for one of the club's occasional public debates, Ivana's coach thinks that she would be ideal. Ivana manages to take a little bit of time away from her tournament preparation to prepare for the upcoming public debate, but for the most part she relies on her considerable tournament experience. "Debating in front of a big audience is going to be a little different," she says, "but I've been debating for years and I'm used to the pressure of several rounds a day against ruthless opponents, with experienced judges, and tons of preparation." So she concludes, "a nice and friendly public debate should be no sweat." When the event actually takes place, however, Ivana is taken by surprise. She knows that she needs to explain things a bit more than usual, but the words don't come easily and she finds herself stammering a bit and saying 'um" much more than usual. She finds herself using jargon or "debate words" that the audience doesn't understand. She thinks that her arguments are good, but half the time the audience doesn't seem to be paying attention. She uses excellent evidence, but learns after the debate that it didn't make much of an impression on the crowd. She thinks that she is speaking much more slowly and carefully than usual, only to be surprised when an audience member asks after the debate, "Why do you speak so fast?" She was proud of the fact that she was able to reveal very clearly a logical weakness in her opponent's argument, but was then stung by the revelation that some in the audience thought that she was being "rude" when she did this. In the end Ivana thought that the public debate was interesting, but she thought that in the future, she would prefer to stay in the world of the debate tournament where, she thought, the situation and the standards were more predictable. "I'll take the tournament," Ivana says, "there the judges know what they are doing, and I can just relax and debate without worrying about the audience misunderstanding every little thing."

While Ivana interprets her experience as an indication of the superiority of the debate tournament over the public debate, we believe that it simply reflects a failure to appreciate the uniqueness of the public debate situation. A public debate is much more than a conventional tournament debate with an added audience. In fact, we would reverse that equation and say that a tournament debate is best conceived as a practice arena for debates in broader and more public settings. And the conditions in this practice arena don't exactly match the conditions in the larger world. Tournament debate tends to happen within a community: a group of people that is formed and identified by their frequent interaction. Because they meet frequently at workshops, tournaments, and even social events, members of a competitive debate community develop a common perspective and worldview. They develop a common shorthand for explaining complex ideas, and common standards for what counts as a "good argument" and a "bad argument." Audiences for public debates don't get this opportunity. Instead of walking into the debate with a developed and specific worldview on what "debate" means, the audience walks in armed only with a general understanding of what counts as "a reason" and what counts as "good debate." What Ivana in our example interprets as a "misunderstanding" is simply a *different* understanding. And considering the fact that the most important arguments in life are likely to be in the larger world, not in the debate tournament, it is arguably a more important understanding.

This chapter is designed for individuals whose primary debate experience stems from a tournament environment. The first question from those who learned to debate by competing at events devoted just to debate and those who teach and prepare debaters for those events may be this: "How do public debates differ from the debates that I already know?" We feel that given the ubiquity of the tournament format as a vehicle for teaching debate, it is critical to provide a focused answer to that question in one chapter early in our text. An exploration of the differences between tournament debating and public debating is critical because for many who set out to present a public debate, their experience in tournament debating will shape the way that they go about preparing and staging the public event—and will also affect the way that they speak and argue. But even though tournaments offer unparalleled opportunities for the focused development of skills in proof, refutation, organization, strategy and expression, the debate tournament is not a perfect analog for general public argument. Adaptations must be made.

We will discuss matters such as argumentation, proof and delivery at some length later in this text; they are topics sufficiently important to warrant their own chapters. In this chapter, we will touch on these topics more briefly in the context of our theme—the differences between tournament debate and public debate. It is here that we mean to provide focused advice for those making the transition from debates in the educational microcosm of the tournament world to debates in the world at large. In other words, it is here that we will draw the principal comparisons between the two types of debate; we do not intend to make sustained comparisons throughout the rest of this book. Such sustained comparisons, we feel, would detract from our primary task—to describe the skills and procedures necessary to produce successful public debates—and would be of little help to readers without tournament experience. So, experienced debate competitors, this chapter is for you: if you mean to read just one chapter before engaging in a public debate, this is the one to read.

If, on the other hand, you are not a tournament-experienced debater, then this chapter may not carry the same relevance for you. Perhaps your own route to public debate hasn't been through the conventional debate tournament setting, but has instead been through political organizations, public advocacy groups, or a simple interest in your subject matter. If that is the case, then the present chapter's focus on differences between tournament debating and public debating might hold an academic interest for you, but you are likely to learn the most important lessons for preparing and presenting a public debate in subsequent chapters. (You will note, however, that we are not disinterested enough to suggest that you skip it!)

We will begin our comparison with a brief overview of tournament styles of debate. Next we will explain what we believe to be the dominant difference between tournament debating and public debating. Finally, we will explore more specifically a number of practical distinctions between the two settings.

Tournament Styles of Debate

Before delving into the differences between tournament styles and public styles of debating, it is helpful to provide a brief overview of the former— since even those readers who are experienced debaters may not be familiar with all of the various styles. The following section is meant simply to provide an explanation of our basis of comparison, not as an introduction to tournament styles of debating. While several published sources provide very complete overviews of these styles of debate,[1] the present section will provide a concise point of reference for some of the comparisons that we draw later in the chapter.

One element that is common to all tournament styles of debate is the tournament itself. A debate tournament shares the same basic elements of tournaments for other activities, games, or sports: a number of different competitors representing different teams or schools gathered at a common location for one or more days, multiple rounds of competition, a system for determining winners and making final awards. In the case of the debate tournament, generally it goes like this: a specific school decides to host a tournament, and invites a number of other schools (hence the term "invitational"). The schools that decide to attend bring a number of debaters or debating teams, a number of judges, and pay a set fee. On the day of the event, the tournament organizers match competitors against each other and assign judges, often employing relatively complex systems (sometimes computerized) for ensuring that debaters avoid competitors and judges from their own school or region, and are matched against competitors with a similar win-loss record; sometimes, judges are assigned who are mutually preferred by both sides in the debate based upon a form filled out prior to the tournament. Debates occur after a general posting is distributed that shows the room, the opponent, and the judge for each match. These scheduled debates, also called "rounds" of debate, generally occur between four and eight times during the initial phase of the tournament.

In each round, two debaters, or two teams of debaters, and one or more judges meet in an assigned room, with one side assigned to support a given proposition and the other side assigned to oppose it. Sometimes a few individuals other than the judge attend the debate, but just as often the judge is the only audience. The debate focuses on a common topic: a statement, also called a "proposition" or a "resolution," that one side opposes and the other side supports. After both sides complete a set sequence of speeches, the judge reaches a decision, either announcing it orally, recording it on paper, or both. Over the course of these initial debate rounds the debaters are required to support the proposition in some rounds, and to oppose the proposition in other rounds, with tournaments usually attempting to balance a team's rounds so that it debates an equal number of rounds in support of and in opposition to the proposition. Once these preliminary rounds are over, the teams with the best records continue to compete in "elimination rounds"; after each of these rounds, the losing team in eliminated from the tournament, while the winning team continues to compete. Some tournaments go directly from preliminary rounds to a final round; the winner of that round is declared the winner of the whole tournament, while the losing side is awarded second place. More commonly, tournaments include multiple elimination rounds before arriving at the finals: octa-finals (eight matches) are followed by quarter-finals (four matches), and then semi-finals (two matches). (Very large tournaments have been known to include sixteen matches in triple-octa-finals.)

The common elements of tournament debate, then, include the following:

- Multiple "rounds" of competition
- Assigned opponents, sides, and judges
- Recorded winners for each match
- A system of recognition for those who win the most

Individual styles of tournament debating, however, have their own unique attributes. The following brief sections should provide you with a working vocabulary on the styles that we'll mention in the rest of the chapter.

Parliamentary Debate

Parliamentary debate. Existing in a few different forms, parliamentary debate is a format that is loosely based on debate as it occurs in the British Parliament. The American style involves two teams of two individuals each: the "Government" (including a "Prime Minister" and a "Member of Government") and the "Opposition" (including a "Leader of Opposition" and "Member of Opposition"). By contrast, the style employed in Great Britain and many other countries and employed at the World Parliamentary Debate Championships (called the "British" or "Worlds" style) employs four such teams, two governments and two oppositions. Featuring propositions that are sometimes literal ("this house would expand stem cell research") and sometimes metaphoric ("this house would take a walk on the wild side"), parliamentary debate encourages debate that is creative in its interpretation of topics, well informed in its reliance on current events and common value conflicts, and witty in its attitude. (The topics for each round are usually announced only a few minutes before the debating actually begins—so quick-wittedness is a primary virtue in parliamentary competition.) Moving through a sequence of six or more speeches, the format also includes opportunities for questioning the opposition by interrupting their speeches ("points of information") or comments from the audience ("heckling"). The format generally requires a reliance on common knowledge only, barring the introduction of specifically researched facts or quotations. Finally, the format encourages a "public" standard of delivery that is conversational, civil, and ideally, appropriately humorous as well.

Policy Debate

A predominantly American format (with some notable offshoots in Japan and Eastern and Central Europe), policy debate is a very rigorous format in which two teams, each composed of two speakers, address a common topic that is generally debated for the entire year. Topics are very carefully phrased with an eye toward allowing the side supporting the resolution (the "affirmative") a wide degree of latitude in selecting a specific plan and the side opposing the resolution (the "negative") a number of different argument options. A recent U.S. topic, for example, was phrased "Resolved: That the United States federal government should adopt a policy of constructive engagement, including the removal of all or nearly all economic sanctions, with the government(s) of one or more of the following nation-states: Cuba, Iran, Iraq, Syria, North Korea." The resolution permits affirmative teams to select their own policies to advocate (their "plan") but requires negative teams to be ready to debate all predictable plans. Consequently, a very large amount of research is necessary. Generally beginning preparation on a topic over the summer, policy debaters usually amass a considerable number of written arguments (often filling four or five suitcase-sized tubs) prior to the first tournament. Norms that have built up over time around this form of debate, particularly in the United States, have encouraged a rapid rate of speech that allows teams to present a high number or arguments and to select, like chess players, which arguments to continue and which to sacrifice. While speeches are never interrupted, opportunities for questioning from the other side ("cross-examination") occur after the first four speeches. The format rewards thorough research, a great deal of advance preparation of arguments, and incredibly quick thinking during the debate.

Lincoln-Douglas Debate

This format receives its name from a series of public debates between Abraham Lincoln and Stephen Douglas for the Illinois seat of the U.S. Senate in 1858. Focusing largely on the question of slavery, the debates continue to convey the ideal of one person's ability to influence public attitudes and events. Today, Lincoln-Douglas debate is the only major format to feature, instead of teams, one speaker against another speaker. Existing chiefly in American high schools and universities, the format usually involves a total of five speeches: three for the affirmative (as in policy debate, the side that supports the resolution) and two for the negative (the side that opposes the resolution). Resolutions generally focus on public policy ("capital punishment is justified") or general value questions ("liberty is more important than life"). Lincoln-Douglas debaters will debate a topic, generally, for several months rather than an entire year, but they will gather published evidence and create prepared arguments in advance of the debate, like the policy debaters described above, but not on the same scale. Lincoln-

Douglas is promoted as a format that emphasizes advanced preparation, a basic understanding of philosophical and value conflicts, a moderate use of evidence, and a conversational approach toward delivery.

Karl Popper Debate

A relative newcomer to the debate world, the Karl Popper format is named after a Viennese philosopher who opposed the idea of absolute truth, embraced the notion of multiple perspectives, and developed the ideal of an "open society," based on a respect for different points of view, protection of minority rights, and a defense of free media. The Karl Popper format features two teams with three speakers per team. Each speaker presents one speech, and opportunities for questions ("cross-examination") occur after each side's first two speeches. The format usually focuses on resolutions of general value (e.g., "A nation's sovereignty ought to be valued over international order") but has recently included policy resolutions as well (e.g., "The United Nations should expand the protection of cultural rights"). Resolutions are sometimes kept for several tournaments, but more often they are used for only one tournament or even for only part of a tournament. The style encourages advance preparation, but also encourages creativity and the reliance on common knowledge and reasoning. The heavy reliance on quoted materials that is characteristic of American policy debate is not a feature of Karl Popper debate, but research is encouraged, and competitors frequently receive packets of published articles related to the resolution prior to the tournament. At present, the Karl Popper format is unique to areas of the world in which the Open Society Institute has fostered the development of debate programs: Eastern and Central Europe, the former Soviet Union, and Haiti.

All of these formats have their strengths: each emphasizes important aspects of inquiry and advocacy and each promotes the central value of debate: reasoned disagreement. However, each of the formats discussed is inescapably a *tournament* format—it is a way of debating in an educational setting in which we are *learning how to debate,* and *competing in debate.* Designed for these goals, and not the goals of educating, informing, or involving the general public, these formats reach the general public only infrequently and incidentally. Without a doubt, one's ability to debate in front of a general audience is enhanced by experience in these formats, but important differences nonetheless exist. In the next section, we explore several of the ways in which public debates differ from debates within the tournament formats described above.

A Paradigm Difference: Public Debates Are Centered on a General Audience

In communication, a paradigm—that is, a model or a pattern—is seen as a way of viewing an issue; a paradigm is an outlook or a perspective that touches upon everything. At a basic level, the difference between debating at a tournament and debating for a larger audience is reflected, not just in the existence of several specific considerations that you should have, but also in a basic outlook that should affect your entire approach to the debate. That basic difference, a "paradigm difference" in our view, is that rather than being centered upon competition or upon a judge, public debates ought to be centered on the audience.

In the most widely used American textbook on public speaking, Stephen Lucas writes that "good public speakers are *audience-centered*. They know the primary purpose of speechmaking is not to lord it over the audience or to blow off steam. Rather, it is to gain a *desired response* from listeners." [2] In the context of a public debate, that desired response is to sway the audience toward your view in the debate, or more broadly, to educate them on both sides of the dispute and to help them make a decision. To Lucas, audience centeredness means "keeping the audience foremost in mind at every step of speech preparation and presentation." [3] Every adaptation made in a public debate should be made toward that end: adaptations should be made in every case to help the audience to understand and appreciate the debate. As an outgrowth of this general attitude toward audience centeredness, we see several specific contrasts between public debate and tournament debate. To debaters and organizers who are moving from tournament debating to public debate, we make the following recommendations:

- Use a format and a topic suited to the audience's interests and involvement
- Debate for clarity, not for "correctness"
- Make it a priority to gain and maintain attention

- Display a heightened level of civility
- Adopt a more copious style
- Ground claims based upon a public standard of proof
- Speak conversationally

We will explore each of these contrasts in the sections below, noting the most important distinctions and adaptations that the competitive debater needs to make before making the transition to the public sphere. Later chapters will also explore the basic subjects of attention, proof, style, and delivery in much greater detail.

Use a Topic and a Format Suited to the Audience's Interests and Involvement

As we will explain at greater length in chapter 4, the topic for a public debate must be chosen only after carefully considering the needs of the public. Organizers must ask themselves what the public cares about or should care about; the answer drives the process of topic selection, as well as the crafting of debate propositions. It will be immediately clear to experienced debaters that tournament debate topics are chosen with different considerations in mind. Although tournament topics are often suggested or inspired by issues of public concern, the reaction of the public is not an integral part of the calculus that determines what topics will be. And, we might add, there is no compelling reason why this reaction *should* be weighed heavily: if the public is not watching the debates, then the requirements of the public do not need to be accommodated.

The corollary is that many tournament debate topics simply do not translate effectively into the very different setting of a public debate. This is not to say that these tournament topics are unimportant or unworthy of consideration; rather, they do not translate because they were designed to perform a different function, and to satisfy a different set of needs. Take, for example, the topics used in policy debates. They are chosen based on a number of very specific standards: roughly equal argument options for both sides, easy access to research materials, sufficient scope to permit a wide number of affirmative approaches, sufficient precision and focus to prevent affirmative teams from offering clearly irrelevant proposals. These standards are geared toward crafting a proposition that promotes detailed policy analysis and fair debates over an extended period of time. These interests are far less relevant when we are dealing with a public debate that is a one-time-only event. In addition, the precision and careful attention to language with which policy topics are framed can result in a fairly long and confusing topic. Consider the topic, "Resolved: That the United States federal government should increase regulations requiring industries to decrease substantially the domestic production and/or emission of environmental pollutants." This topic doesn't do the job of quickly and memorably conveying the subject of the debate and the phrasing (an "increase" that requires a "decrease" in one thing "and/or" another), while legally precise, would predictably cause confusion.

Much the same can be said of the topics used in other formats of tournament debate. Parliamentary debate topics, while generally having the advantage of greater simplicity, are not necessarily more suited to public debates. By working to facilitate the creative agency of the government side, parliamentary topics may end up providing little help to a potential audience trying to interpret the topic. "This house would go the distance" may indeed result in a lively debate on a virtual infinity of potential subjects, but if interested audience members can't predict the content from the topic, then they may not be there to witness the debate.

What, then, is the function served by a public debate topic? Rather than serving the function of guiding the argument choices of dozens, hundreds, or thousands of participants (by tightly controlling those choices in the case of policy debate and to a lesser extent Lincoln-Douglas and Karl Popper debate, or by forcing creative interpretation as in the case of many parliamentary topics), the public debate topic functions to attract and focus attention. The fundamental difference is that rather than promoting a specific educational experience, as tournament topics are designed to do, public debate topics ought to be designed to attract potential audience members and tell them what they are likely to hear. Control over argument content is most likely to be accomplished by agreement prior to the debate, not by the topic per se. Questions of salience (what topics are particularly "hot" right now?), interest (what issues affect my audience the most?), and comprehension (what questions are focused enough to be adequately addressed in one debate?) ought to guide public debate topic selection. More comprehensive advice on framing propositions is provided in chapter 6.

The bottom line is that debaters with tournament experience would do well to approach public debate topics with a fresh vision. It is tempting, we know, for experienced debaters to fall back on the tried and the true; if a topic has worked well in the tournament world, it is only natural to think of bringing it to the public in a different setting. But tournament debaters must remember that public debate is a brave new world—and old world ways may spell disappointment, rather than success.

Tournament debaters may also be tempted to transport the formats they know into the setting of public debate. As we will explain at length in chapter 7 ("Developing a Format"), tournament formats can provide very useful models for public debate formats—but we would caution experienced debaters to think before they leap. Once again, the needs of the public are of paramount concern in public debate, and organizers and debaters must consider them when creating, adapting, or importing a tournament format. Upon consideration, tournament veterans may conclude that a familiar and time-honored format will not work well in the public event they are planning.

Again, let's take a look at policy debate, and see how its format fits the needs of the public. Within the policy debate format, debates can last two hours or longer. That may be fine for the tournament judge, who is taking comprehensive notes and prides herself on attention to detail, but it is likely to be too taxing for the attention span of the average audience. In addition, connections between the formats and the duties of specific speakers may function well and seem quite logical to those schooled in the format, but may seem very odd to an audience. For example, in both parliamentary and policy styles, two speakers from the same side speak consecutively, without hearing from the other side, at a certain point in the debate. In both cases, this aspect of format is rationalized based on the practice of each speaker having a different duty or role to play. For the general audience member who is likely to be paying more attention to ideas than to speaker duties, it is likely to simply look repetitive: e.g., "We just heard from their side, so why is another speaker from the same side hitting us with it again?" There are other aspects of format that do serve the interests of the tournament environment, and potentially could be explained to the audience, but are likely to be more trouble than they are worth. For example, when the timekeeper in a parliamentary debate round raps his knuckles on the table to signify that points of information are now allowed, most audience members are likely to wonder, "Why is that man pounding on the table?" And then there are tournament behaviors that would strike the uninitiated as bizarre—e.g., the parliamentary habit of placing one hand on top of one's head to request a point of order.

An additional reason to consider modifying a tournament format for a public debate is to promote audience involvement. While parliamentary debate, in some settings, incorporates audience involvement, policy debate, Lincoln-Douglas debate, and Karl Popper debate all have no defined role for the audience other than "listener." This fails to take advantage of an opportunity: audiences attend public debates because they are interested, and interested people are likely to have something to say. Being audience centered in this case means being audience inclusive. A format that incorporates audience participation is likely to be much more interesting and much more conducive to the goals of public dialogue.

To sum up: we recognize that there are advantages to importing tournament topics and formats without alteration. For one thing, importing familiar procedures saves time and effort in preparing a public debate; what is more, it seems eminently sensible to use something that works—why reinvent the wheel? But we believe that the potential disadvantages of importing topics and formats are greater, simply because they may not suit the audience for whom the debate is staged. And the audience is the *raison d'être* of public debate.

Debate for Clarity, not for "Correctness"

All human communities, including communities of arguers, develop over time very specific patterns of what is appropriate and what is inappropriate. House builders rely on conventional forms and processes, bankers rely on time-honored modes and practices, and arguers rely on commonly held notions of correct forms of argument. Systems can always be challenged, of course, and communities do evolve. But within an argument community, such as a group of tournament debaters, the force of convention is very strong. Learning how to debate means learning how those who are more experienced than you are already debating. Attitudes about the appropriateness of this type of argument, or how to structure that type of argument, are passed on at workshops and reinforced at tournament awards assemblies.

As the arguments and practices of successful debaters are held up as models, other debaters learn to emulate. According to one argument theorist the community works to "determine certain allowed moves when arguing, and outlaw others."[4] The result over time is that the community develops a very specific, and quite unique, *modus operandi* that may be quite different from the practice of arguing outside that community.

It is also an aspect of communities that these conventional forms come to be seen as not just conventional, but also proper and correct: "The way we do this is not just our way, it is the right way, the best way, perhaps the only way." Debating communities strive to be self-critical but that doesn't prevent them from at times confusing the conventional with the correct.

In Lincoln-Douglas debating, for example, advocates addressing a value proposition like "The right to privacy is the most important individual right" are expected to identify a "criterion" that is conceived as a goal that society aspires to, and that the affirmative side upholds. A goal such as "individual self-actualization," for example, would then be supported by a "value premise" such as the claim that "individuals must be free from government interference in order to self-actualize." Other specific concepts and norms follow, and taken together they are seen by most participants as the correct way to do Lincoln-Douglas debate. If a participant can't answer the question, "What is your criterion?" or can't separate her "value premise" from the rest of her case, then she is presumed to be deficient in debating skill—she is someone who has not yet "learned how to debate."

Participants in Karl Popper debate have adopted many of the elements of American Lincoln-Douglas, but true to what we would expect of a community, they have modified them to suit their own experience. The "criterion," for example, also exists in Karl Popper debate, but it means something a little different. In Karl Popper debate, a "criterion" isn't necessarily a goal, but is instead a standard or a test (e.g., rights that serve as foundations for other rights are most important). If the affirmative "meets" its criterion (e.g., proves through its "contentions" that privacy is the common foundation for all civil rights) then it will have won the debate. An affirmative team that supplies arguments for the resolution but neglects to offer a "criterion" or clarify its "contentions," is seen as not debating properly, since it has failed to provide the judge with a clear and simple test for deciding who won.

We could, of course, offer many examples of this type of format-specific knowledge. Our purpose, though, is not to define tournament debate conventions fully, nor to disparage those conventions, but to remind you that audiences for public debates do not share those conventions—simply because they are members of "the public," not members of a debate community. As a result, there is no *intrinsic* advantage to following a set format in presenting your arguments. Now, we would like to be careful with that last statement: when we say there is no *intrinsic* advantage, we mean that following a set practice doesn't convey a benefit in and of itself. In a tournament setting, presenting an argument in the accustomed way has the benefit of fulfilling expectations and serving as a kind of verbal "shorthand" that allows us to avoid long explanations of the type of argument we are making, or the reason we are making it. In a public debate setting, however, relying on the accustomed mode doesn't necessarily convey an advantage.

This is not meant to suggest that conventional forms of argument learned in tournament settings have no value. On the contrary, they may help promote more intelligent debate, but only if they are presented in ways that clarify rather than confuse. The conception of argument in policy debate provides a good example. Traditionally, arguments in favor of a policy change are seen as having to answer four questions: Is there a significant problem? Is that problem caused by the current policy arrangements? Will the proposed change in policy solve or diminish that problem? Will the advantages of change outweigh any problems caused by change? These so-called stock issues of policy debate provide a rational and very useful template for clear argument in a number of contexts: personal arguments, essays, letters to a newspaper editor, and public policy speeches. So it would certainly be effective for a public debater to begin by saying, "First, let's look at the problems that exist now . . . ," before moving on to say, "Second, the reason these problems persist can be found in our current inadequate policies . . ." She could follow that with "Third, the solution we are offering you today would significantly reduce these problems . . ." and conclude with "Fourth, this solution could cause some short-term difficulty, but in the end it would bring much more good than bad . . ." This pattern of argument would present a clear and comprehensive analysis to the audience. However, in this case it would be the concepts themselves and not the formalism that would be meaningful to the audience—they would not be fitting what they heard into a predetermined (and expected) model, in the way that a policy debater in the audience might. But even if he approved of the pattern, that policy debater in the audience might be disappointed by the absence of the shorthand terms to which he was accustomed: "ill, blame, cure, and cost" (or, alternatively, "significance, inherency, solvency, and comparative advantage") are used to mean "the problem, the reasons for the problem, the solution to the problem, and the advantages of the solution." And yet if the speaker used these terms, they would mean nothing to the people in the audience who were not familiar with the conventions of policy debate; uninitiated listeners would simply be puzzled by statements like "and here is our inherency..." or "where is your solvency?" In this case employing the conceptual tool, with an eye toward remembering why the tool was considered useful in the first place would be a good idea, but a reflexive and automatic adoption of the terminology would be a bad idea. In chapters 13, 14, and 15, we consider a number of ways in which several concepts from tournament debating can be employed in ways that clarify rather than confuse.

Make it a Priority to Gain and Maintain Attention

Within a tournament setting, those who watch the debate are generally constrained to do so by their role. While they certainly aren't a captive audience, they are there because they are either judging the debate or, much less frequently, because they are watching the debate for a specific purpose (for example, competitors with a round off might attend in order to learn what another team is doing). Observers have an incentive for continued attention, judges for example knowing that they must provide a critique and rationale for decision at the end of the debate.

In contrast, an audience for a public debate may not have such a strong incentive. While they come to a debate to learn, to watch the clash of opinions, or to show support for their favored side in the debate, they are likely to feel less pressure to pay attention to every word. Also, it must be admitted, that thanks to politicians there is the perception (earned or unearned) that debates can be boring. Generations that have grown up on the feast of graphical images offered by television and movies, or have been schooled using methods that rely heavily on exercises, activities, and experiences, may find the idea of sitting and watching two static speakers for an hour or more to be a trial of unspeakable boredom, something to be endured, not savored.

But even when an audience doesn't relish the idea of a public debate, expectation is not destiny. A public debate, done well, will interest and involve the audience, leaving them informed and entertained as well. There are several elements necessary to making sure that your public debate captures the audience's attention.

First, Think of Attention as a Continuous Obligation, not a Right.   Speakers who have gone through all of the trouble of preparing for a public debate might be tempted to think that, "after all of that, the audience at least owes me its attention." That, however, isn't the case. Attention is a precious commodity and audiences don't give it for free; they don't give it just because you deserve it, but give it when they get something in return. What you have to give in return is something that meets an audience's interest. Thus, you should see your speech as continually carrying the burden, not just of responding to the other side, but of winning and re-winning the audience's interest by identifying elements of your argument that matter to them.

Second, Identify Audience Interests in your Appeals.   When you justify an argument in a tournament setting, it is often enough to provide anything that would be seen as a good reason to your judge, or to an imagined "universal audience." In the context of a public debate, appeals should directly involve your real audience. It is inevitable that to at least some extent an audience is going to view any controversy through the lens of their own experiences and priorities. A group of university students viewing a debate on proposed increases in law enforcement powers would think of how the proposal could increase security on campus, or how it could lead to harassment or racial profiling of the school's substantial minority population. A successful public debater wouldn't necessarily limit her appeal to those issues, but would be likely to give those arguments special emphasis because of their connection to the audience. While your debate will not always involve subjects that have a measurable impact upon your audience, you should think of creative ways to answer the question, *why should I care?* Many audiences, for example, might assume that unless they live in India or Pakistan, then they have no real reason to concern themselves over the struggle in the province of Kashmir. Such audiences would need reminders that educate them and encourage their attention: "India is one of our most important allies," or "Instability in Pakistan threatens to spread terrorism all over the globe, even to our country," or "Any conflict between two nuclear-armed states must concern the entire world."

Third, Keep Your Content Vivid.   Listening is a difficult task, and in settings in which audiences are not necessarily taking notes and not necessarily motivated to follow every point, debaters need to do more than simply lay our their arguments. Excellent public debaters help their audience experience their ideas, and not merely understand them. An idea is "vivid" if it in some way appeals to the senses. Asking an audience to imagine a scene, experience a moment, or follow a story all yield greater attention and involvement from the audience. A policy debater focusing on argument precision might content herself with the statistic that, in the current economy, more than a thousand people are losing their jobs every day. A public debater, on the other hand, might ask the audience to call to mind the largest church in their city, to imagine it filled to capacity, and then to imagine all of those people receiving a letter of dismissal from the only job they have: "That is how many people are losing their jobs every day in this economy."

Fourth, Don't Exclude Introductions, Conclusions, and Other Structuring Elements.   Because debate is a timed event, incentives toward efficiency exist in every format. Teams that are able to present more arguments, or more detailed arguments, don't necessarily win, but they enjoy the advantage of greater opportunities to score a win. This incentive to advance more arguments can sometimes cause debaters to cut corners: "introductions may be nice, but they don't win debates," "instead of offering a transition, I could simply say 'next...'" In a public setting, however, these structuring devices are not mere formalities, but are crucial tools for gaining the audience's attention, letting them know what to expect, and letting them know when the debater is moving from one idea to the next. Let's say that you offer your listeners these simple signposts: a preview at the beginning ("there are three main reasons for this, first..., second... and third... Now, let's explore each of these a bit more"), a summary at the end ("So, we've now seen that one reason is..., another is... and a final one is...."), and transitions in between ("now that you understand this first reason, I think that you'll find the second one even more compelling..."). With this kind of reinforcement, your audience doesn't just remember that you made some arguments, but actually remembers the arguments that you made.

chapter 13 in particular, but also chapters 14 and 15, will provide you with a number of ways to keep your content clear.

Fifth, Employ Humor Where Appropriate.   In some debate formats, parliamentary most notably, the ability to inject a bit of wit and humor is prized. As a way of "scoring" against an opponent and relieving the tedium of multiple rounds of competition, levity can bring some needed life to a tournament debate. Public audiences as well are likely to appreciate humor as long as it is tasteful (remember that it is a large and general audience, not a small group of your friends) and reasonably related to your subject area (not just a random joke used to start a speech), and as long as it doesn't occur at the expense of either your opponent or your argument's content. (For a more extended discussion of humor, see chapter 11, "Making Your Arguments Compelling.")

Display a Heightened Level of Civility

If you are used to debating in tournaments, then you are probably used to running into the same opponents on a fairly regular basis. This frequency of contact can build up some good-natured rivalries between specific opponents or teams. That rivalry (as long as it truly is good-natured) is not a bad thing at all. It adds a bit of fun to what could otherwise be a spiritless academic exchange, and judges are likely to appreciate the added energy as well.

Rivalries may be more difficult to decode for the public debate audience, however. A group that is unfamiliar with the norms of tournament debate may have difficulty differentiating between an attitude of "spirited play" and an attitude of battle. It is a common occurrence, for example, for audiences to express surprise at the end of the debate when they find out that advocates actually know and like each other. "Why were you so mean to each other during the debate?" the untutored audience member may ask, when the debater just feels that he was getting into the spirit of competition. If members of your audience have little experience witnessing public debate or other rational exchanges, then their main model for "debate" may be interpersonal conflict: they expect a verbal disagreement to look like two people fighting, and any apparent verbal or nonverbal indications of conflict can be seen as a confirmation of that expectation.

For this reason, it is a good idea for public debaters to make an extra effort to make sure that they appear civil to each other during the debate.

Civility is a general attitude, not inconsistent with friendly competition. It is difficult to define a complete code of civility for public debaters, but the following suggestions are a good start for making sure that your audience doesn't mistake rivalry for disrespect:

Refer Respectfully to Your Opponent.   Instead of calling your opponents "them," "the other side," or worse, use their names and, if appropriate, a title (Mr., Doctor, Professor). The phrase "my worthy opponent," however, risks sounding like a cliché (and has probably been said often enough with a sneer that it no longer carries its original meaning).

Make Positive Reference to the Other Side's Argument.   Of course, you will still assert superiority of your own argument, but you should treat your opponent's argument respectfully and positively: e.g., "they have a good point, but . . ." or "probably the best point that Sabina made was that . . ." Particularly when you have the upper hand in an argument, grace may require that you publicly give their arguments a bit more credit than you would give them privately.

Be Attentive and Respectful Even When You Aren't Speaking.   One of the great mistakes of debaters is to believe that when they are not speaking then they are somehow "offstage." That certainly isn't true of public debates—you are likely to be literally on stage and visible during all times during the debate and you should always assume that the audience is paying attention to you. By shaking your head "no," making a puzzled face, or frowning during an opponent's speech, you are only likely to decrease the audience's opinion of you. Instead, make it clear that even though you may be concerning yourself with your own notes for your upcoming speech, you are also paying full and polite attention to whomever is speaking. (One famous gaffe in a presidential debate occurred when President George H. W. Bush looked at his watch when his opponent was speaking; the audience interpreted it as a gesture meant to indicate boredom.)

Avoid Personal Attacks.   As chapter 3 explained, a debate is a contest between ideas, not people. Attacks on a person's intelligence, good will, or debating ability are mean-spirited and have no place in a civil debate.

Adopt a More Copious Style

The time-pressure of the debate tournament often leads to a preference for making your arguments in the fewest words possible. Repetition is wasteful when the clock is running on your speech time. For that reason, a statement like "the action that Alex and Terry ask you to consider may sound good, but unfortunately it poses an unacceptable risk to our economic stability, especially right now when the economy is already weak" is ideally replaced by a statement like "your plan destroys the economy." Those who are learning to debate in a tournament context may start out with the more expansive, more conversational expression, but gradually learn to practice the concision or "word economy" that allows them to communicate the same thought, or at least something close to the same thought, with fewer words and in less time. In the tournament setting, this word economy makes sense: the shorter expression not only spends less of your valuable speech time, it is also easier for the judge to write down.

This approach makes perfect sense in a setting in which participants and observers are keeping careful notes and paying a very high level of attention. In public settings, likely to be attended by more relaxed listeners, however, the approach is likely to be a burden. By maintaining a preference for short, staccato, telegraphic claims, debaters risk overwhelming their audience and saying much but really communicating little.

For this reason it is important for tournament-experienced debaters to remind themselves to relax their preference for word economy and to allow themselves a more expansive, more copious style. (From the Latin word *copia,* meaning abundance, copious means "abounding in thought or profuse in words.") To achieve a copious style, you must give your thoughts a fuller and more comprehensive expression. While, of course, no one wants to hear a speaker repeat, and repeat, and repeat a point that is already well-understood, Cicero's advice was that if one errs, it is better to err on the side of over- rather than under-explanation. Using the metaphor of language as a fine meal (itself an example of copiousness), Cicero wrote that "I shall provide such an abundance that there may be something left from the banquet, rather than let you go unsatisfied."[5] Of course, Cicero could have simply written "provide lots of explanation" but that wouldn't have made as much of an impression.

In order to break or at least weaken the habit of word economy, tournament-trained debaters should remember to include built-in emphasis by stating their claim a couple of different ways: "their proposal will pose unacceptable risk to our economic health. The prosperity that we enjoy may not be secure if we follow their advice." Freed from the burden of providing the most concise expression, public debaters may also free themselves to use devices that we normally associate with creative writing or poetry even (metaphor, alliteration, parallelism, for example) and to seize the opportunity for a simple, memorable statement. Strategies for making your language vivid, without overdoing it, are covered in chapter 11.

Ground Claims Based on a Public Standard of Proof

Tournament debaters, as discussed above, frequently inhabit communities characterized by frequent contact. Because debate is a game involving proof and disproof, some of the most powerful norms that emerge in debate communities have to do with what constitutes proof and what constitutes disproof. These norms differ from community to community. In Karl Popper debate, for example, a participant could refer to an example that he remembered from some past reading, and it would be considered proof. In policy debate, however, that example, unless it were accompanied by a direct quotation, would simply be considered a self-serving anecdote, not verifiable evidence. In parliamentary debate, it would be considered "specialized knowledge" which also is not proof because it is irrelevant to the *reasoning* contest that is debate. All of this, of course, would be a mystery to a general audience because they are not schooled in the specific norms of what constitutes proof according to each debate community.

Although those within debate communities may like to believe that their notions of acceptable or conventional proofs are simply hard reflections of reality, they are of course subjective preferences that are in some ways better and in some ways worse than the preferences of other communities and the preferences of publics at large. Public debaters trying to offer proof to their own audience need to start, not by just importing the standards of the debate community, but by analyzing their audience (a subject covered in the next chapter) and communicating arguments that are understandable and meaningful. Whether the norms for proof in your tournament debate community amount to primarily providing quotations, primarily referencing examples, or primarily dealing with common knowledge and logic, these norms encompass an *aspect* of proof but fail to embody the broad spectrum of proof as it is likely to be perceived by an audience.

Of all debate communities, the one with the norms of proof that are most rigorous, but also the most challenging to public audiences, is policy debate. Modern policy debate clearly prefers proof by authority, and quotations form the heart of the preliminary speeches, with debaters simply making a short statement, then reading a quotation, then making another short statement, then reading another quotation, throughout the debate. The quotations are usually just preceded by the last name of the author and year of publication ("Anderson in '01") and are usually not explained or reinforced by the debater's own words since the goal is to build the most complete and most comprehensively supported case possible in the time available. While this approach creates a challenging contest for the trained participants and judges, common audience members are likely to see it as a mystery: quotations from unidentified sources that are not themselves explained in clear conventional language are not likely to be seen as proof. For this reason, policy debaters making the transition to the public sphere are likely to be much better served using a few well-explained and well-qualified quotations. The quotations themselves should be seen as *a way* to support the speaker's own arguments, and not the arguments themselves. The speaker's own words should provide the main arguments and should not be seen as mere transitions between quotations. Sources should be fully identified and qualified. Rather than saying, "Anderson in '01" a public debater should say "Dr. Denise Anderson of the Centers for Disease Control in Atlanta looked at the situation this year, and she concluded that . . ." The quotations themselves should be relatively short—long enough to provide a reason as well as a conclusion, but not so long that they substitute for the speaker's own reasoning. It is probably a good rule of thumb that in order for a speech to be seen as a speaker's own work, quoted material should be no more than about a quarter of the overall speech content.

Of course expectations of proof will vary by audience. More educated and informed audiences are likely to want more, and casual entertainment-oriented audiences are likely to want less. Chapter 10 will develop a more comprehensive outlook toward adopting a more public style of reasoning for audience debates. In general, the public debater should strive to use facts their audience understands, authorities they respect, and opinions they trust.

Speak Conversationally

It occurs with regularity, often serving as its own somewhat humorous initiation to public debate: the tournament-experienced debater prepares for a public debate and receives perhaps the most common words of advice for that setting: "slow down!" When the debate occurs the debater perceives himself to be moving at a snail's pace. Crucial arguments are sacrificed because of the slow speed that he feels he is forced into. Yet at the end, and despite his perception that his words have been flowing out at a glacial speed, the debater hears the audience's first reaction: "you spoke so *fast!*" An experienced debater's conception of "slow" is often simply much faster than an audience's conception of "average."

This is of course most obviously true for policy debaters, since their format often emphasizes speed, but it occurs often enough with debaters schooled in other formats. With experience, your brain learns to generate thoughts and sentences with greater and greater ease and speed, and the mouth follows. The audience is simply not used to hearing someone who has been trained to generate and express thoughts in quick succession, particularly if they are speaking in a way that maximizes argument generation and minimizes explanation.

This problem may stem from more than just speed. If a debater merely slows the pace of words, but maintains a very concise, and word-economical style of expression, then the flow of arguments is likely to *seem* fast to the average listener simply because it is dense and more difficult to process than average conversation. Another element that adds to the perception of speed is the continuity of the pace. If a debater slows down, but never pauses, then again the speech may seem fast simply because the natural conversational breaks never occur. For this reason, the best advice on this score for the public debater is not just "slow down," but "speak in a conversational manner—as if you were explaining something to your mother or your father. Move at a moderate pace, but also pause, emphasize, and restate."

Your speech is more likely to be conversational (and comprehensible) if you present it extemporaneously—meaning that is prepared in advance, but delivered spontaneously. Tournament debating can emphasize the extremes of preparation, either so much that each word is considered critical and the entire speech is written down, or so little that momentary wit and inspiration are considered key and not even a speaker's main ideas are prepared ahead of time. Extemporaneous presentation is a happy medium between these two extremes. It means preparing in advance, but not going so far as to write the speech out exactly or memorize it. By familiarizing yourself with your ideas, but not necessarily your exact phrasing, you are increasing the chance that you'll be seen as thinking as you speak—not making things up off the top of your head, but not reading or reciting something from memory either. Elements of extemporaneous style are covered more completely in chapter 15, "Delivering Your Arguments Effectively."

Conclusion

Debate tournaments offer an irreplaceable opportunity to learn the skills of careful listening, information gathering, logical planning, advocacy, questioning, and refutation. Many of these skills are exactly the ones needed for the effective public debate advocate. The average tournament-trained debater, though, needs to commit to an audience-centered perspective before committing to a public debate. This picture can perhaps best be completed by returning to the example used to begin this chapter.

> A little while later, Ivana decided to try another public debate. Having learned from her experience the first time, this time she started by putting herself in the shoes of her audience: "Why are they interested in this debate? What do they already know about debate? What do they already know about the topic?" After some thought, Ivana began developing arguments that appealed directly to the audience's best interests. Rather than trying to fit in as many arguments as possible, she picked just a few, and used the extra time for some strategies for making those arguments as clear and interesting as possible. She even added a metaphor that would help the audience comprehend one of her more complicated points. After choosing to begin with a very involving story, Ivana provided her audience with a clear thematic development of her point of view—not structured in quite the same way as her tournament debate cases, but logical and easy to follow nonetheless. She didn't lighten up on her opponent one bit,

but she was always careful to refer to him respectfully and by name, and always to pay attention, and to be gracious even when attacking his reasoning. Finally, she slowed down and spoke conversationally. She didn't just decrease her pace, but she also added pauses and emphasis so that her words didn't sound mechanical but carried the cadence and rhythm of normal conversation. At the end of it all, Ivana thought "I'll definitely keep debating at tournaments—I love that too much to give it up. But I'll also not pass up an opportunity for a public debate. There is something about having that audience there that makes it quite a different game."

Notes

1. Introductory texts are available for a number of tournament debate formats: parliamentary debate (T. Goodnow Knapp, and L. A. Galizio, *Elements of Parliamentary Debate: A Guide to Public Argument*); policy debate (M. Fryar, D. A. Thomas, *Basic Debate*); Lincoln-Douglas debate (R. Kemp, *Lincoln-Douglas Debating*); and Karl Popper (W. Driscoll, *Discovering the World Through Debate: A Practical Guide to Educational Debate for Debaters, Coaches and Judges*).

2. S. E. Lucas, *The Art of Public Speaking*, 7th ed. (New York: McGraw Hill, 2001): 98.

3. Ibid., 98.

4. R. Maier, "Argumentation: A Multiplicity of Regulated Rational Interactions," in *Norms in Argumentation: Proceedings of the Conference on Norms, 1988* (Dordrecht, Holland: Foris, 1989): 132.

5. Cicero, "Topics," in *Cicero*, vol. 2, translated by H. M. Hubbell (Cambridge, MA: Harvard University Press, 1969).

Part Two

Preparing for a Public Debate

Chapter Five

Preliminary Steps

A tower of nine storeys begins with a heap of earth.
A journey of a thousand lis starts from where one stands.

—*Lao-Tzu,* Tao-Te Ching[1]

Introduction

We began this book with an account of a public debate held on a university campus. The debate, you will recall, focused on whether the campus bookstore should be allowed to sell *Penthouse* magazine. The debate was successful because the topic, the audience, and the debaters' objectives combined to form a harmonious whole. The topic was inspired directly by a recent event, the publication of an issue in which female models appeared bruised and beaten. The controversy was localized—that is, the debate questioned whether the magazine should be sold on the campus (not whether the magazine should be printed or distributed nationally). As a result, the student audience had a stake in the outcome of the debate; as campus citizens, they had a reason to care about what was sold in the campus bookstore. Finally, the mandate of the debaters was clear: each debater aimed to persuade the audience to adopt a clear position, either for or against the sale of the magazine. In short, the debate had a coherent internal logic; given the time, the place and the audience, the topic of the debate made perfect sense.

This chapter is devoted to a discussion of the preliminary steps that must be taken by anyone who undertakes the organization of a public debate. We have resurrected our original model because we think it provides a very useful ideal. The *Penthouse* debate worked precisely because the organizers carefully considered the audience, the situation, and their own objectives for having a debate. Such consideration, we believe, is essential if a debate is to be successful. The debate will fail if the organizers look at only one or two of these factors.

Our point may be clearer if we offer some examples of failed debates. Let's say that the organizers focus all of their attention on coming up with a good topic for the debate, and they decide that the debate should focus on the relationship of the United States and the new International Criminal Court (ICC). The issue is important, and genuinely controversial—if only because the United States supported the creation of the court for many years, but then refused to ratify the treaty authorizing the court when it was finally completed. One team of debaters is ready to defend current U.S. policy, while the other is eager to persuade listeners that the United States should reverse course and ratify the treaty. It is a fine topic for debate, then—but it will not lead to a successful debate if the debaters are members of a college debate team who are staging a demonstration debate at a junior high school assembly. The problem is that the average 12-year-old is unlikely to have any knowledge of the treaty, or of the court, and will have only a vague notion of what is meant by "jurisdiction" and "statutory criminal law." The proposed debate might work well for a college audience—although even then it might need the spur of current events to focus the issues and make them immediately vital. (An audience might be more interested in the question if they realized that the ICC as currently constituted could not prosecute Saddam Hussein.) Certainly, the debate would find a suitable audience in a school of foreign affairs, or at a conference of nongovernmental organizations.

A debate would also fail if organizers focused exclusively on the audience, without thinking enough about the situation or their own objectives. Say that the audience is the student body of a high school, and the debate organizers presume that their listeners are interested in rock and roll. After pondering various rock and roll controversies (e.g., whether Eric Clapton is a greater guitarist than Jimi Hendrix), they decide to create a debate inspired by an opinion piece someone has seen in a music magazine: "Rock and roll should acknowledge its debt to rhythm and blues and other forms of African-American folk music." The problem here is that while this issue may interest musicologists or sociologists, it is unlikely to stir the blood of the average teenager looking for new tracks to load on an MP3 player. It's also not clear how the organizers want to affect the audience: Is the debate supposed to change the behavior of the listeners? Is it supposed to change their attitudes? Is it meant simply to inform them? A debate about the morality of downloading music from the Internet might work very well indeed—but this topic, however sober and well-intentioned it may be, leads to a dead end.

To put it another way, debate organizers must *analyze*—they must analyze their own motives, the audience, the situation, the medium and their opponents. In the pages that follow, we will discuss each of these tasks separately, but we cannot emphasize too strongly that all of these issues are intertwined. Organizers may begin by asking, "Who is our audience?" but in almost the same breath, they must ask, "What do they care about and what should they care about?" and "How do we want to affect them?"

Analyzing Motives

The first question anyone organizing a public a debate should ask is "Why? Why are we having this public debate? What are we trying to get out of this? What do we hope to achieve?"

That brings us to the main difference between public and competitive debates. In a purely competitive debate the primary purpose is winning. The debaters are not concerned with changing the personal opinion of the judge who is listening to them—after all, the judge's vote is not supposed to be a register of her own personal opinion on the issue; it is supposed to be an assessment of the quality of the debate. The debaters are concerned, rather, with presenting a case that is stronger than the case of their opponents; they may even choose to write a case that is boring, but easily defensible. They don't particularly care if the judge finds them interesting; winning is all that matters.

In a public debate, by contrast, the debater's primary focus is on the audience and their response. Of course, the debaters want to do their best and "win" if a winner is to be chosen, but the primary purpose of a public debate is to affect the audience in some way.

The speaker's impact on the audience has been a serious consideration of rhetoricians since classical times. In his treatise *De Oratore*, the famous Roman statesman and orator Cicero (106–43 B.C.) discusses the speaker's goals when addressing an audience. A speech, he says, can have three main purposes: to teach or inform (*docere*); to move or persuade (*movere*); or to entertain (*delectare*).[2] Speakers can, of course, pursue more than one goal at the same time—it is certainly possible, for example, to teach in an entertaining way.

The purposes outlined by Cicero are still useful in creating an analytical framework for today's public debate. In the following discussion, we will subdivide Cicero's categories, and add few of our own. We see that a public debate can have six distinct goals. The organizers of a public debate must decide which of these goals they intend to pursue.

1. To Inform

Sometimes the goal of a debate is simply to give the audience the information they need to assess an issue for themselves. This goal is reflected in the motto of the Fox News Network: "We report, you decide." (Many critics, of course, claim that this is untrue, given the conservative bent of Fox's news coverage.) When they adopt this goal, debaters present both sides of a controversy, and each side argues its position forcefully; the primary purpose of the debate, however, is just to convey information, perhaps as a preparatory step for some persuasive efforts at a later date.

2. To Bring Attention to an Issue

Sometimes the primary aim of a debate is to get the issue on the table. If the debaters and organizers conclude that the target audience does not care enough about a certain issue, or is unaware of it and its importance, their motive would be to raise awareness about the issue. Even though the ultimate goal may be persuasion, in a case where the audience is not even aware that a problem exists, debaters may want to start with that limited goal in mind first. For example, if a school is having its budget cut by the government, the general public might not even know about the issue. Having a debate about whether cuts are justified might at least raise awareness and get people to read about it with more interest; it might even get people involved in resolving the issue. Similarly, a debate on whether the United States should ratify a treaty on the ban on land mines may be aimed at raising awareness about the issue with the general public. The debate may spur their interest and prompt them to get involved by making donations to organizations concerned with land mines and helping land mine victims, or by writing letters to their senators and to newspaper editors, or by contributing in some other way. Sometimes just raising awareness can do wonders for a cause.

3. To Persuade

Aristotle defined rhetoric as "the faculty of observing in any given case the available means of persuasion."[3] In other words, the primary task of rhetoric is to persuade the listener. This is all the more true in debate, specifically; debate has been seen, ever since the time of Protagoras (cf. chapter 2, on the history of public debates), as a fight of ideas, where debaters try to convince the audience to adopt their proposition, and not the one of their opponent. More often than not, persuasion will be the primary goal of a public debate.

Persuasion is paramount when debaters choose an issue on which most people have been following "conventional wisdom." For example, if most people are in favor of a war but are in favor without even analyzing the issue, then having a debate on whether the war is a good idea may force listeners to reconsider their positions. If the conventional wisdom says that the war makes sense, then the population is likely to hear the pro-war side of the debate every day. Putting the repressed antiwar message on an equal footing might itself be successful in persuading people to take the opposite view.

Other persuasive debates may start with a common core of agreement— and persuasive efforts can be focused on plans and policies. Both sides in a debate, for example, may agree that homosexual couples have legal rights comparable to the rights of heterosexual couples, but the debaters differ about the form those rights should take. One side may argue that the state should recognize marriage between homosexuals; the other side may argue that civil unions—similar but distinct—should be recognized. In any case, the goal of the debaters would be to persuade the audience about the merits of each policy.

4. To Move

When Cicero cited *movere* as one of the three main duties of the public speaker, he meant the term broadly; the speech should not only move the listeners emotionally, but it should also influence their will. That is, it should move them into action. Public speaking is an art that is, just like any other art, capable of moving and inspiring people. The debate can aim to provide spiritual uplift, or foster passion for a cause. Getting people to take some action is impossible without moving them, usually with emotional appeals, as a lot of highly influential leaders know very well. Pure logical reasoning does not move masses of people to wage war or overturn a government. Whether the ultimate goal of debaters is to rally their audience around a certain cause or political candidate, or to sign a petition, or to join a protest, the first thing they need to do is to move that audience (see discussion of audience analysis later in this chapter).

5. To Entertain

At one extreme, there are debates that have little purpose other than to entertain. Comedy debates are quite common, especially in British Commonwealth countries, where one university tradition is to hold "Pub Debates." The designation "pub" recognizes that the debate is "public"—but it also acknowledges the debate's location: pub debates are held in a pub! (They are, accordingly, raucous affairs.)

At another level, however, all debates must entertain. A debater is not going to capture much of an audience unless, on some level, the audience is having fun. So even when addressing the most serious topics, debaters should consider this goal. It is impossible to inform or persuade an audience about an important issue unless the audience is entertained enough to stay and listen to the debate.

6. To Display Skills

Sometimes the goal of the debate may be to teach about the activity itself. If you are recruiting new members for your debating society or debate team, or if you are coaching novice debaters, or if you are using debate as a teaching tool in the classroom, the debate is an end in itself, not just a means to achieve some of the goals mentioned above.

In sum, the debate organizers and the debaters themselves must carefully consider their goals and objectives before they do anything else; all of the other steps in a public debate should stem from the primary goals of the debate. At the same time, it is important to recognize that goals cannot be set without a due consideration of the other factors that must be analyzed. As we will discuss in the pages that follow, the audience—a "given" element in many public debates—will shape the possible objectives.

Analyzing the Situation

Everything takes place in a context. The debate is not an isolated event, but a response to a broader sociopolitical world and its context. Russian linguist and philosopher Michael Bahtin said that every utterance, every sentence (either spoken or written) is always geared toward an anticipated answer and is, indirectly or directly, an answer to something itself; it is in a dialogue with previously uttered and anticipated utterances; it interacts with the social context.[4] The audience will always listen to the debate within this broader context.

It is critical for debate organizers to understand the historical, cultural, social and political context of the audience, the setting and the topic. Timing affects the way that a topic is understood; debates about terrorism were very different before September 11, 2001. Similarly, the issue of tax cuts would be debated quite differently during an economic boom than during an economic slump. Organizers must ask themselves: What are the primary societal concerns of the moment? How familiar is the proposed topic to the potential audience? Is it something that they will immediately be interested in? Or is it something that will require some salesmanship? More important, how does the average listener feel about the topic? Is it something unlikely to inspire strong views because the public does not know much about the issue? (For example, most listeners outside of Africa would not be passionate about whether the European Union should support the new government in the Ivory Coast.) Is the topic something that would strike most people as so implausible that it would be a waste of time to listen to it (e.g., "Should the United States adopt a communist system of ownership?")? Or is the topic a "hot button" like abortion or religion? The analysis of the situation will determine many aspects of the debate.

First, the debate organizers have to consider whether a proposed topic is worth debating. They must ask themselves whether anyone would be interested in a debate about the conflict that has been formulated in the resolution. It may be true that most people care about the environment, but they might not care whether a riverside park should be managed by the state government or by the federal government. A topic might also fail if it seems that everyone would agree too readily with one side (for example, "Children should not be beaten for no reason."). Some topics might simply bore the listeners, no matter how much the issue is dressed up ("Should the Angolan government charge a 3% or 5% tariff on imported zucchini?")? Here, it is worth remembering the words of Lloyd Bitzer, who said that debate should spring from an exigency, which he defined as "an imperfection marked by urgency; it is a defect, an obstacle, something waiting to be done, a thing which is other than it should be."[5] Debaters need to analyze the situation in order to identify topics that call for urgent resolutions.

Second, debaters and organizers should carefully consider whom to invite. As discussed later in this chapter, the audience dictates how a debater should present the topic. But the topic also dictates which audience should be recruited.

Finally, organizers and debaters should think about how to market the debate. A hot button issue of the day needs no fancy marketing—for example, "Should we go to war?" But in other instances the audience might think that (1) the issue is resolved anyway, so there is no reason to care about the debate or (2) no matter how the issue is resolved, it will have no effect on them. When promoting the debate, organizers must make it a primary concern to answer the likely misgivings of the target audience. (For further discussion, see chapter 8, "Attracting Attention.")

Analyzing the Audience

A public debate preparation should be based on thorough audience analysis. Every public utterance is always a joint creation of meaning between the speaker and the audience, even if the audience is silent. In a public debate, there is always a mental give-and-take; the audience members listen to the debaters critically and participate in the debate actively, either by making speeches and asking questions from the floor, or by arguing with the speakers silently in their seats. The outcome of the debate will ultimately depend on its effect on the audience.

The audience is the most important "ingredient" of any public debate. Without the public, it would not be public. Some debates have more and some less audience participation, but whatever the format, knowing something about your audience, being able to anticipate how they would react, and adapting to their needs, attitudes and interests, is the key to success.[6]

Debaters can seek information about their audience through many different channels, depending on what is available to them. The most reliable is direct observation—if possible, it is best to get to know the audience from previous similar (or even different) settings, and to learn about their attitudes and interests firsthand. If direct prior observation is not an option, the systematic collection of data through opinion surveys and question-naires can be a good starting point. Sometimes it is even possible to conduct selected interviews, focus groups or opinion polls. (In today's world, most election campaigns depend on polling results for determining their direc-tion and crafting their messages.) A good resource for this type of informa-tion could also be the contact person of an organization or a group that is expected to attend the debate. If all else fails, reasonable assumptions based on intelligent inference and empathy can help. The important thing is to keep the central role of the audience in mind in every step of the debate preparation process.

Demographic Characteristics

Sometimes knowing even basic demographic information about the audi-ence can be a useful aid in predicting their orientation. (Not every type of information will be relevant in every single instance, however.)

Age/Generation.   Will most of the audience be younger or older? What generation do they belong to? A debate on social security will likely be more interesting for the Baby Boom generation than for a group of teenagers. By the same token, Generation Y (twenty something-year-olds) will probably find the issue of student loans from the government more riveting than would an audience of retirees.

Sex/Gender.   Biologically speaking, gender differences are rarely relevant for debates. What matters, however, is our socialized roles—how we think about masculinity and femininity in our society. These roles, of course, have a great deal to do with culture, and they differ from one society to another, from one community to another, even from person to person within one family. Although it is important to avoid stereotypes and hasty generaliza-tions, it is also wise not to disregard these differences; they should be consid-ered when choosing a topic and adapting it to the anticipated audience. The controversial issue of abortion, for example, affects women differently than men, aside from their political orientation and religious beliefs.

Race/Ethnicity.   Race and ethnicity can be very pertinent factors in the response of an audience, depending on the issue. Racial and ethnic groups sometimes have their own specific interests and needs, and debaters need to be aware of them in order to respond to them adequately. In the U.S., one is especially likely to encounter a racially and ethnically diverse audience. In order to avoid offending and alienating the audience, it is important to be culturally sensitive, while avoiding stereotypes, and to adapt the topic to the interests of a heterogeneous group.

Other demographic characteristics can also be important factors in audience analysis—e.g., socioeconomic background, occupation, religion, political orientation, education, etc. Knowing as much of this information in advance as possible can serve as a good predictor of how the audience will be affected by the debate.

Anticipating Audience Expectations, Needs and Interests

Why is this audience here? What do they expect to get out of this debate? What will they leave with? These questions should be asked before the debate is even planned. Aside from being crucial information for promotion purposes (this is discussed in a later chapter), knowing your audience's expectations, needs and interests is crucial to choosing the topic and constructing the case.

It is also important to find out how much the audience already knows about the topic. Debaters should beware of overestimating or underestimating their audience's knowledge. The best results will most likely be achieved if the information is kept just beyond their level of understanding. Remember the rule of the carrot and the mule: if you keep the carrot too close to the mule's muzzle, the mule will not move because there is no reason to; if you keep the carrot too far, the mule will not bother to move because it is out of reach.

What the audience thinks and knows about the debaters (what they have heard, read, assumed) will also affect the efficacy of their arguments. This is because the speaker's credibility is inevitably linked to his or her message. Aristotle discussed the importance of the speaker's character (*ethos*) at length in his book on rhetoric:

> Persuasion is achieved by the speaker's personal character when the speech is so spoken as to make us think him credible. We believe good men more fully and more readily than others: this is true generally whatever the question is, and absolutely true where exact certainty is impossible and opinions are divided . . . the speaker's character may almost be called the most effective means of persuasion he possesses.[7]

It is important to anticipate and understand the audience's assumptions in order to address them in the debate.

Determining Audience Attitudes Toward the Topic

Since debate is by and large about persuasion, anticipating the audience's attitudes about the issue on the table is essential. First, the attitude of the audience—favorable, neutral or unfavorable—will to a great degree determine the choice of arguments, reasoning, evidence, language, style, etc. Second, it is impossible to measure the outcome of the debate—that is, how it affected the audience—without knowing where they stood on the issue before they heard a debate on it. Many television polls commit this mistake because they poll the audience only after the event. These results say nothing about the debate's effectiveness because there is no basis for comparison—we do not know what the audience's attitudes were before the debate, so we do not know how or if they have changed. Of course, it is hardly possible to change listeners' minds completely with one debate, but a slight and instantaneous shift in the level of their conviction may happen. Sometimes a simple audience "before and after" questionnaire would do the trick, like the one below that shows a continuum from strong agreement (1) to strong disagreement (7). If conducted and collected right before the debate, and then again after the debate, certain shifts to the left (toward "agree") or the right (toward "disagree") may be noticed.

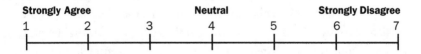

Favorable Audience

It seems unnecessary to try to persuade an already favorable audience, one that already agrees with us completely on an issue. However, believing that something is true and doing something about it are not the same. The debater's goals in speaking to a favorable audience could be to solidify and strengthen their attitudes, or to move them from theoretical approval to positive action.

Moving the audience usually requires an increased use of emotional arguments and appeals to what the audience cares about: their basic needs and core values. (Such arguments are what Aristotle termed *pathos*.) Debaters could ask the audience for personal involvement by showing them how their lives will be affected, or how their actions will create a difference. The goal could be to get the audience to make a public commitment (oral or written) by signing a petition or by raising their hands. It is also a good idea to provide the audience with several specific and easy alternatives for action. Another goal of debating in front of a favorable audience could be to make them carry on the message, to give them ammunition to persuade others—arguments, evidence, and responses to counterarguments. By listening to the debate, they will learn how to do it themselves.

Since the goal is to give the audience a sense of active participation, arguments are often presented in a compact form, where something is left out: either a major/minor premise, or a conclusion. This kind of reasoning uses enthymemes, or shortened syllogisms, which were recommended even by Aristotle in situations where speakers seek to create meaning jointly with the audience, thus making the audience feel much more involved in the process. (For a fuller discussion of enthymemes, see chapter 10, "Reasoning with Your Audience.")

Neutral Audience

The audience can be neutral for several reasons: a) they could simply be uninterested, b) they could be uninformed about the issue altogether, or c) they could know a lot about the issue, but remain undecided about the particular controversy under discussion. If the audience is neutral because they are uninterested, debaters should stress attention-getting factors; they should provide concrete illustrations of how the issue affects the audience, and sprinkle their remarks with humor and human interest. If the audience is uninformed, it is a good idea to emphasize clarifying and illuminating material such as explanations, definitions, examples, and restatements. Debaters should use a lot of visual aids, keep their language simple, and be exceptionally well organized. If people in the audience are undecided on the issue, debaters need to make a greater effort at establishing their credibility (Aristotle's *ethos*) by presenting new arguments that blend logical and emotional appeals; they should also make sure to recognize opposing arguments, and if they can, refute them. It is also important to offer new arguments rather than recycle those that have been heard already a hundred times; using more logical appeals is usually better for this type of audience.

Unfavorable Audience

Since an unfavorable audience is predisposed to reject the debaters and their message, the debaters should try to set limited, realistic goals for the debate. Even making the audience reexamine their convictions can sometimes be considered a big success. It is important to stress common ground with the audience—that is, common values, goals, and needs. Common ground establishes a basis for communication, which is the first step in addressing an unfavorable audience. Furthermore, debaters should base their cases on sound logic and extensive evidence; emotional appeals are likely to be rejected as "manipulation." Every step of reasoning should be explained; nothing should be taken for granted. The extensive use of factual and statistical evidence is needed, and debaters should always cite their sources. The refutation of counterarguments is crucial here. Special attention ought to be paid to establishing and projecting a credible image, an image of a calm, reasonable, fair, well-informed and congenial person. One common mistake is to be overly conciliatory; debaters should be firm, although they must avoid patronizing and being arrogant or sarcastic.

Analyzing the Medium

Marshall McLuhan, whose book *Understanding Media* was one of the seminal texts of the 1960s, wrote that "the medium is the message." In other words, the medium through which a message is sent is an essential part of the message itself. More than that, the medium shapes the message. Politicians, for example, typically craft their remarks to fit the medium of television news. They know that if they give a 30-minute speech, the news broadcast will not include the entire speech, or even a 5-minute excerpt from it. Instead, the speech will get 30 seconds, enough for a "sound bite"— a brief statement used by the networks to summarize what the speaker has said. As a result, politicians and their speechwriters work hard to come up with one pithy, entertaining, well-phrased statement to include in the speech. They often spend more time on this than on everything else in the speech. The bottom line is that they change what they say in order to suit the medium of television. (If, on the other hand, the politician was being interviewed for a magazine article, the importance of sound bites would recede; the politician might still want to provide a string of pithy quotes, but he would presume that his remarks would be quoted more extensively than on a TV broadcast.)

In the same way, debate organizers must analyze the medium through which their debate will be conveyed. Will the debate take place in an auditorium before a live audience? Will it be broadcast from a radio or television studio? Or will it take place before a live audience and also be covered by the broadcast media? We have emphasized above that debate organizers must analyze their audience, their situation and their goals. Here, we note that this analysis must be complemented by an analysis of the medium. A debate that would be ideal in front of a live audience might not work well at all if heard only on the radio.

At a minimum, the medium will affect the way that debate practitioners perform and interact with the audience. In a live debate, it is important to keep in mind the size of the audience and the setting. For example, is everyone seated around a table, or at least at the same level, or are the debaters up on a stage behind formal tables and podiums? Is the sound enhanced with microphones? Are there artificial lights that may "blind" the debaters and prevent them from seeing the audience (in which case they cannot "read" and adapt to the audience's nonverbal feedback)? A small group seated around tables calls for a less formal debating style. Grand hand gestures and a booming tone might strike the audience as pompous and artificial. Debaters should strive to be more conversational, as if taking part in an ordinary, private dialogue. At the opposite extreme, if the debaters have microphones and are positioned on stage in front of a large audience, a more exaggerated style may be appropriate—bigger gesture and more dramatic variations in pitch and tone are needed to "hold" the audience in such a setting.

If the debate is on radio, hand gestures obviously won't make much of a difference, and visual charts and diagrams must be left at home. More emphasis has to be put on voice and vocal interpretation. A lower voice register is generally perceived as more pleasant, especially on radio; there is an even greater need than usual for vocal inflections, a slower pace, clear enunciation, carefully placed emphasis, etc. (For a broader discussion, see the section vocal delivery in chapter 15, "Delivering Your Arguments Effectively.")

Television simulates a "live" situation, but viewers tend to expect a more polished, professional performance. Also, despite the fact that thousands (millions if you're lucky!) may be watching, it is in a strange way a very "personal" medium. Debates appear on a small screen in someone's living room, where the viewer may be watching in her pajamas, all by herself. This is why playing to a TV camera in the same way that you would play to a large live audience does not work: your presence on the screen will be out of scale with the intimacy of the surroundings. The TV audience will see a standard "live" performance as exaggerated; they will think that the debaters are lecturing to a wide group somewhere out of their range of vision, instead of having a nice casual one-on-one with them, the all-important viewers.

Combinations of different media are difficult to adapt to, because debaters have to appeal to different audiences for different media. For a lesson in this, it may be useful to attend a studio recording of a television talk show. This is a wildly different experience from watching the show on TV. In fact, the placement of cameras and stagehands sometimes makes it impossible for the "live" audience to see what is really going on. For the most part, the TV producers do not even care. The audience in the studio comprises a few hundred people, and they are not even watching the commercials. The TV audience may be hundreds of thousand or millions. The producers want to make sure the live audience laughs and claps when appropriate (pretty easy in our celebrity-obsessed culture), but this is where their interest in the live audience stops. For debaters, the experience would likely be different. In a debate, the live audience would be just as important or even more important than the broadcast audience—so debaters must find a way to play to them and the TV audience at the same time.

Conclusion

Without considering preliminary steps in debate preparation, like analyzing the motives, the situation, the audience, and the medium, even the most painstakingly researched and enthusiastically presented debate can be a failure. What exactly are we trying to achieve in this day and age, with this particular audience? And what do they have to gain from this? How are we going to convey this message most effectively? These questions should be on the minds of every public debater and debate organizer, from the minute they decide to have the debate until the very end of the process. Where you end is indeed determined by where you begin.

Notes

1. Quoted in Susan Radcliffe, ed., *The Oxford Dictionary of Thematic Quotations* (Oxford: Oxford University Press, 2000): 14.

2. Henry Hiz, "Cicero," in *The Encyclopedia of Philosophy*, ed. by P. Edwards (New York: Macmillan and the Free Press, 1967): 113–114.

3. Aristotle, *Rhetoric*, in *The Rhetoric and the Poetics of Aristotle*, translated by W. Rhys Roberts (New York: Modern Library. 1984): 24

4. V. Biti, *Pojmovnok Suvremene Knjizevne Teorije* (Zagreb, Yugoslavia: Matica Hrvatska, 1969); K. A. Wales, *A Dictionary of Stylistics* (London: Longman, 1969).

5. Lloyd F. Bitzer, "The Rhetorical Situation," *Philosophy and Rhetoric* 1 (1968): 1–14.

6. A brief note on the issue of adaptation and manipulation: Socrates scorned the Sophists for teaching their students to "manipulate" the audience. He accused them of persuading the public by appealing to them (and not the Truth); yet in another one of Plato's dialogues, he proposes that "wisdom-lovers" should appeal to people of "other types of souls" (Socrates called the general public "lower types") by getting to know them and understand their "loves" (preferences, tastes, motives), thus adapting their arguments (or choosing different types of arguments). According to Plato, Socrates thought that wisdom-lovers (philosopher-kings) should promise others the fulfillment of their loves (needs, wishes) to render their persuasion more effective (discussed in Plato's dialogues Gorgias and Phaedrus; J. A. Herrick, *The History and Theory of Rhetoric*). So the line between adaptation and manipulation has always been somewhat blurred, even for Socrates. One way to define the difference could be that adaptation serves to facilitate better communication, while manipulation advances only the speaker's interests to the detriment of the audience.

7. Aristotle, 25.

Chapter Six

Crafting a Proposition

Engineers have plans, scientists have hypotheses, writers have thesis statements, and debaters have propositions. A proposition is the subject you debate, expressed as a statement that one side supports and the other side opposes. Defined more formally as "a claim that expresses a judgment that decision-makers are asked to accept or reject"[1] propositions (also called resolutions) differ from "topics" by defining more precisely the judgment that is sought. While "gun control" is a topic, the statement "this nation should expand restrictions on gun ownership" is a proposition. Propositions come in several different forms. In tournament debates, propositions are often but not necessarily preceded by parliamentary or legislative language (e.g., "Resolved that ...", "Be it resolved that ...", "This house would..." or "This house believes..."); whatever its formulation, the proposition is a clear statement that forms the heart of the debate. For example:

> Be it resolved that hate speech ought to be censored for the good of society.
>
> This house would not sacrifice civil rights for security.
>
> Resolved that globalism threatens the natural environment.
>
> Religion and government don't mix.

One of the starting points for any public debate is crafting a proposition that clearly captures and communicates the basis for your intended debate. We say "crafting a proposition" rather than "picking a proposition" for an important reason. While it is common—certainly in tournament debate circles—to talk about "picking a proposition" for debates and speeches, that phrase suggests that there is a great stock of propositions out there and event organizers simply have to look over the list and select one. While it is possible to choose a proposition this way, and we do include a large list of potential propositions at the end of this chapter, we feel that good propositions are *made* rather than *found*. That is, taking into account the audience, the advocates, the situation, and the desired content for the debate, your best proposition will be *crafted* to meet those needs and won't simply be selected.

While you might think at first that it is natural to start with the proposition and then work your way to the arguments that each side is likely to make, in the case of a public debate the reverse method is probably more effective. Start by thinking about the kind of argument you would like to have. Considering those most likely to attend, what sort of exchange would they be most interested in seeing? Considering those who are likely to be advocates, what sort of themes would they be likely to sound, and what arguments would they see themselves making? Working from this expected outcome, a clear proposition can be fashioned that neatly communicates the themes addressed and clarifies the distinction between the two sides.

For example, a committee in charge of drafting a debate proposition for a summer youth conference in Slovenia approached the matter as follows. Considering that participants would come from more than thirty countries and that any potential sponsor would have to be interested in global issues in order to become involved, the planners envisioned practice debates and larger audience debates in which debaters grappled with the role of international institutions in building a global civilization. In the wake of severe terrorist attacks in the United States and subsequent military action, the planners also thought it fitting to include the question of whether justice through law could ever be successfully and consistently applied at a global level. Envisioning that one side's emphasis on human rights and justice would contrast with the other side's emphasis on principles of sovereignty and respect for other cultures, the committee saw a proposition begin to take shape. After reviewing recent literature on these general themes, the planners found that one of the most important conflicts centered on the recent criminal tribunals formed to address crimes against humanity in Rwanda and former Yugoslavia, as well as plans to ratify a convention bringing into being an International Criminal Court in the Hague. Believing that participants as well as audiences would benefit from a discussion of both general principles as well as practical applications, the planners decided that the question of an international criminal court served as a useful focus, with the arguments for human rights and internationalism on one side and the arguments for sovereignty and cultural distinctiveness on the other. Capturing and communicating this division, the planners settled on, "Resolved: That the nations of the world should support the creation of an international criminal court." In short, the process of crafting a resolution began with considering what the audience would care about and continued by focusing on broad themes and conflicts. In other words, the committee did not begin by putting a specific topic first and saying, "Let's do something about the criminal court"; rather, they settled on the topic of the court because it crystallized the conflict between human rights and national sovereignty.

This chapter will provide practical advice on developing a clear and useful proposition for your public debate. After discussing a few ways of selecting a subject for your debate, we will identify the functions of the proposition in a public debate, consider several elements of any good proposition, and then discuss some of the specific requirements of more particular types and modes of propositions, before finally concluding with a list of sample propositions.

Selecting a Subject for Your Public Debate

Many who have reached the planning stages for a public debate already have a topic in mind. Indeed, it is likely to be a concern for that topic area that motivated the decision to have a debate in the first place—that is what happened in the story with which we opened this text: a conflict on campus about the sale of *Penthouse* magazine led directly to a public debate that centered on issues of censorship, free expression, and the damaging effects of pornography. In many instances, though, the goal of having a debate may precede the identification of a specific subject for the debate. For those, the question "so what do we debate about?" is an important one. Before crafting a specific proposition, they will want to select a general topic area.

There are, of course, an infinity of possible topic choices and we will not even try to make a full listing. Depending on your own interests and those of your likely audience, the "right" topic is the topic that allows you to address issues that are important and worthwhile in a debate that is relevant, informative and entertaining to your audience. Selecting such a topic is the result of your own reflection and brainstorming. We can't suggest a surefire formula for that, but we can suggest that you begin by asking yourself a number of questions:

- Have there been any recent events that are dominating public discourse right now?
- These days when acquaintances meet, and finish talking about the weather, what do they talk about?
- What are my country's political leaders currently arguing over?
- Are there any new or proposed laws that have been the subject of controversy or criticism?
- What topics are being covered on the opinion pages of my local newspaper?
- That last time I got into a discussion about political or social issues, what was that discussion about?
- Are there any subjects that the debaters already know a great deal about?
- Are there any subjects that the debaters have an interest in learning more about?

If brainstorming along these lines fails to yield a topic, then another alternative is to visit the library and simply browse the current periodicals. An hour spent with recent publications should reveal a wealth of timely controversies. In addition, consulting the list of debate propositions at the end of this chapter might spark some ideas. One thing seems true: as long as ours is a world of many peoples, many cultures, and many priorities, there will be many subjects to debate.

Functions of the Proposition in a Public Debate

Texts on argumentation and debate often begin their description of the debater's role with a call for an analysis of the proposition, suggesting that debaters define terms, identify issues, and predict likely arguments. In calling for analysis following proposition selection, this advice assumes that the proposition has been delivered to the debaters by some outside agency; that it is has come down to them from those who have selected it. The debaters need to figure out what it means (or decide what it means.) While this may be the case for some public debates (for example, those that come at the end of a tournament and use the tournament's assigned proposition), more often a proposition will be selected with a specific public debate in mind and planners and the advocates themselves will be involved in crafting the proposition for their debate. Thus, in the case of a public debate, analysis by the debaters frequently precedes rather than follows proposition selection; the final proposition is not a matter of mystery that requires research, analysis and interpretation. Granted, our earlier example, recounting the creation of a proposition about the International Criminal Court, showed a proposition being crafted by a committee, rather than by the debaters themselves—but that example is still apposite here. Advocates who are planning for their own public debate could follow the same essential process described in the example; that is, they could begin with a consideration of the audience and the situation, move to a development of theme and preferred arguments, and finally craft a proposition that captured the conflict between those arguments.

In the setting of competitive educational debates, the function of the proposition is chiefly to "divide ground" by separating the argumentative responsibilities of one side from those of the other side, to limit the scope of the dispute, and to focus the judge's decision at the end of the debate. While these functions exist in some form in public debates as well, there are important differences.

Dividing the ground and limiting the scope of the debate, for example, are not necessarily the main purposes of a public debate proposition. Remember that a public debate is generally the product of specific planning (not a product of a randomly generated and assigned match-up); there are often other and better means for clarifying the content of the dispute. Joint planning and discussion (addressed in chapter 9) are often more effective since a negotiated agreement will do more to determine and clarify the goals and responsibilities of the two sides than the single sentence of the proposition. In tournament settings, the proposition itself is often a matter of contention—not surprising, given that it must be analyzed and interpreted, and each side can arrive at different conclusions about what the proposition "means" or what it is meant to include. (In competitive contexts, the proposition is often appealed to directly in order to rein in opponents who are seen as straying beyond the bounds of relevance—so-called topicality arguments.) Public debate audiences though, would be likely to see arguments about the proposition as bickering and the result of poor planning. In general, the public debate proposition is a communication device rather than an instrument of control. As a communication device, the proposition should be clear, should convey the scope of the dispute and should communicate the separation of the two adversaries' arguments in the public debate context. Broadly, we see the functions of the proposition in a public debate as follows:

- *To attract interest.* The debaters, the occasion, and the topic are the three main factors that generate interest in a public debate. For audiences seeking to attend in order to add to and focus their own understanding of important political and societal issues, it is likely that the topic is the most compelling element. In the wake of a terrorist attack on one's country, for example, the proposition "terrorists deserve justice delivered by soldiers, not by courts of law" is likely to be one that arouses passions on both sides of the issue.

- *To communicate the debate's central theme.* The proposition should identify the subject matter in a clear and simple phrase. "Resolved: That our government should provide for the general welfare" gives no clue to the real content of the debate, while "Resolved: That our government should guarantee a living wage for all working adults" is much clearer.

- *To communicate the debate's central division.* Finally, the proposition should provide potential audience members with an expectation of what sort of advocacy to expect from each side. "This house would reject the current intellectual property laws" may lead to good debate, but may also lead audiences to wonder whether the proposing side seeks stronger laws or no laws at all. "This house would strengthen claims to intellectual property" would be much more clear in letting the audience know what to expect from each side.

Because its main function is to communicate, the public debate proposition may differ in form from those commonly used in tournament settings. In 1942, American policy debaters addressed the following resolution: "Resolved: That the United States should take the initiative in establishing a permanent federal union with power to tax and regulate commerce, to settle international disputes and to enforce such settlements, to maintain a police force, and to provide for the admission of other nations which accept the principles of the union." It requires a fair bit of study before one realizes that the proposition is calling for a world government. While that level of specificity is often justified in tournament contexts, in a public debate it would communicate far better to say, "The United States should support the creation of a world government." The details (taxation, police power, international disputes) could be clarified by the advocates in advance and wouldn't need to be suggested in the proposition.

Just as policy debate propositions may be inappropriate for public debate because they convey too much, some tournament propositions—especially parliamentary debate propositions—may fail by conveying too little. In parliamentary debate, propositions are termed "straight" when they dictate a specific subject area, or "abstract" when they leave the content up to the imaginations of the debaters themselves. Authors Trischa Goodnow Knapp and Lawrence Galizio provide an example showing how the proposition "this house believes that someday my Prince will come" could be interpreted as calling for the election of a particular candidate for public office.[2] A highly entertaining and informative debate could ensue, of course, but the audience would not be likely to guess at that based on the topic. Abstract topics are often based on simple aphoristic phrases (like "you can't always get what you want," or "a stitch in time saves nine") and are not generally suited to a public debate's need to communicate content to a potential audience through the selected proposition. It's also worth reiterating, at this point, that the process of crafting a proposition begins with a consideration of the needs of the public—and it is hard to imagine that organizers would really envision an audience eager to hear why "This house would get down and dirty" (unless, of course, the debate was designed to satisfy nothing more particular than some broad desire for entertainment).

As we noted in our fourth chapter, many tournament propositions will not work in public debates, simply because they were designed to serve different functions. Tournament propositions are often designed so that they can be used many times, or even for an entire debating season. They identify a broad class of potential actions rather than a specific policy. For example, a proposition like "Resolved: That the United Nations should expand the protection of cultural rights" allows a variety of different approaches, with many possible plans of action being offered by the debaters addressing it. In this case, the proposition does not act simply as a statement to be proven true or false; rather, it acts as a parameter around potential cases, sort of a box from which debaters may choose their cases—and that is a good thing, given that the goal is to promote diverse argumentation over a long run. A public debate, however, has distinctly different goals, born of its nature as one-time event. There is really no need for a proposition whose breadth exceeds the specific case that is being put forward. To make the above proposition useful for a public debate, it must be more limited and focused. If debaters facing the proposition as originally formulated planned to argue that there should be better educational opportunities for Roma youth, then the communicative function of the public debate would be better served by dropping the broad formulation of the proposition, and recasting it as follows: "Resolved: That the United Nations should expand educational opportunities for Roma youth."

Rather than existing primarily to circumscribe or test the creativity of the advocates, the public debate proposition exists primarily to communicate the content of the event to a potential audience. For this reason, propositions are preferred that generate interest and highlight the central theme and division of the debate.

General Elements for Effective Propositions

A public debate proposition should embody elements of good communication which are essential in this context. Given the importance of language and the centrality of the proposition, crafting its specific language should take a bit of time and more than a little care. The following elements should be contained in any public debate propositions.

- *An identified controversy.* Although one of the purposes of debate may be to inform the audience (see chapter 5), the mere transmission of information does not constitute a debate. For a debate to occur, there needs to be controversy. There must be a question that reasonable people would answer differently. "What nations comprise NATO?" can be answered in only one way, with the appropriate information; "Should NATO membership be expanded?" will produce more than one answer. The existence of such a question forms the root of the proposition.

- *One central idea.* In order to provide a clear focus and an understandable sense of the responsibilities of each side, the proposition should center on one subject. Multiple subjects make it hard for debaters to take clear positions. Given the proposition that "Gambling and prostitution are immoral," debaters would essentially have to take on two cases: one against gambling and one against prostitution. Despite any perceived connection between two subjects, to combine both in the same proposition is to promote confusion. What would happen, for example, if the proposition's supporters won their case against prostitution, but lost it against gambling?

- *A single, simple declarative sentence.* Since the entire point of a proposition is to distill a controversy into a clear and comprehensible statement, the proposition should always be a single sentence. In order to communicate meaning to your potential audience quickly, it should be a simple sentence as well. A simple subject-verb-object pattern that avoids unnecessary modifiers and clauses will often produce a proposition that communicates the essential content in the fewest possible words. For example, the proposition might be, "The United States (subject) should sign (verb) the UN Convention on Genocide (object)," or "The European Union (subject) should support (verb) gay rights (object)." Phrasing a proposition as a question might be intuitive (especially since propositions are sometimes called "questions") but is not advisable because there may be too many possible answers, offering in no clear conflict of stances. "Is euthanasia ethical?" might be answered by neither a "yes" nor a "no" but with an "it depends." It is better to make the proponent's stance more certain by converting the question into a statement: "Euthanasia is unethical."

- *Clear burden of proof on the proposing side.* The proposition should be phrased so as to place the greater burden of proof on the proposing side. The burden of proof, a concept covered in greater detail in chapter 10, is the burden borne by the side that logically and psychologically has the first and greatest need to offer proof. Because those accused of crimes are usually presumed innocent, at least formally, the prosecution has the burden of proof. Similarly, in a public debate on the acceptability of world government, the side proposing that government would be seen as carrying a heavier burden by most audiences. That is, because of the current primacy of national governments, we would expect to hear why we should have a world government before needing to entertain reasons why we should not. Thus the proposition would make more sense if it supported world government, because that is the side that bears the heavier burden. It may be helpful to think of the burden of proof in terms of the conflict between change and the status quo. There is a presumption in favor of the existing situation, or status quo (the accused is innocent and "free"); the party that bears the burden of proof must argue to change the status quo (the accused should be judged guilty, and subject to imprisonment). In the same way, we do not currently have a world government; the side with the burden of proof must show why that situation should change.

- *Phrasing that includes a desired outcome, not just a disposition.* The proposition should let the audience know exactly what the side supporting the proposition is seeking. The proposition that states "Resolved: That the United States should change its policy toward Cuba" offers the disposition or attitude of the proposing side, but it does not say exactly what the proposing side wants to happen—it indicates that the proposing side is in favor of a change in policy, but it does not say precisely how the policy should be changed. If, however, we alter the proposition to read "Resolved: That the United States should remove economic sanctions on Cuba," then we have a clear sense of what outcome is desired by the proponents.

- *Phrasing that includes a conclusion only, not reasons.* The reasoning behind a conclusion is of course essential in a debate, but in order to promote clarity and add flexibility, the reasons are best left to the debaters and ought not be included in the proposition. The proposition, "This house believes that the death penalty is unacceptable because it devalues human life" would be better addressed as simply, "This house believes that the death penalty is unacceptable."

- *Two or More Identifiable and Reasonable Sides to the Issue.* Productive debate occurs when two (or more) opposing perspectives exist and both (or all) are capable of being supported by reasonable arguments. A statement like "The United States government should respect the rights of women" would be quite easy to support, but it is hard to imagine what argument, short of a call for outright male chauvinism perhaps, could be used to oppose it. Particularly if you are a party with an interest in one side of the proposition, before proposing it you should ask yourself, "would I be able to find reasonable arguments on the other side?" If not, chances are it is not a well-balanced proposition.

- *Neutral terminology.* While it is difficult to conceive of language as ever being truly and completely neutral, in crafting a proposition, you should strive to avoid terms that appear to slant the evaluation one way or another. "This house would oppose the heartless and vicious exploitation of animals by science" is better replaced by "This house would oppose the use of animals by science." Those opposing that proposition could conceivably justify "use" but would probably be hard-pressed to justify "vicious exploitation."

- [a]   *Avoidance of ambiguity.* Those crafting public debate propositions should make every attempt to select clear and concrete words, and to avoid formulations that leave unanswered questions. The proposition "the personal is political" in the right context may communicate quite a bit, but in other contexts would leave audiences scratching their heads about what is meant by "identity" or "personal" in this case. In addition, a formulation such as "Resolved: That nuclear weapons should be declared illegal" raises a question: "by whom should they be declared illegal?" The answer to that question would make a big difference in the ensuing debate. If this debate has been well prepared, of course, there would be no ambiguity in the minds of the debaters—in other words, they would not have left such a large question up in the air and would have agreed who would be making the declarations of illegality. There would be no reason, then, to create ambiguity for the public by leaving this mutual understanding out of the resolution. Finally, we note that the active voice ("The European Union should declare nuclear weapons illegal") is generally stronger and more direct than the passive voice ("Nuclear weapons should be declared illegal by the European Union.").

Types of Propositions

Beyond focusing on the common elements of any effective proposition, advocates may also be advised to consider the type of topic they are selecting. Various forms of debate as practiced in tournament settings focus on particular resolution types. For those settings, an analysis of topic-style is critical. Those involved in the planning or execution of public debates are less likely to require a topic of a specific type, but a consideration of the various styles of topic composition may yet be heuristic: it may lead you to consider alternative ways to package the content and theme of your debate. Debate propositions can be roughly grouped into three general types:

* *Propositions of policy* relate to actions by governments or by organizations:

    The nations of the world should implement the Kyoto Protocol limiting the effects of fossil fuels on the global environment.

* *Propositions of value* relate to evaluative stances taken by individuals or societies:

    The world's current dependence on fossil fuels is environmentally irresponsible.

- *Propositions of fact* relate to the truth of some condition or relationship:

  The world's dependence on fossil fuels is causing global warming.

These three types can be seen more simply as statements of *action* (it should be done, it should not be done), statements of *worth* (it is good, it is bad), and statements of *existence* or *classification* (it is, it is not). The distinctions between these three general types are not always perfectly clear. Propositions of value like "The death penalty is immoral" are often difficult to differentiate in practice from propositions of policy like "The death penalty should be abolished." The dashed-line in the model below signifies that it is difficult at times to distinguish where one category ends and another begins. For example, it is hard to say where the analysis of values ends and the advocacy of policies begins. Still the three general types do represent real differences in level of analysis and highlight the important relationship between dependence and responsibility. As we will explain at greater length below, the following diagram indicates that dependence decreases as responsibility increases—and each of the three types of proposition can be situated on the spectrum of change in those values.

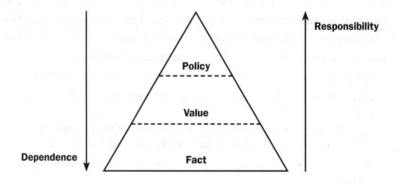

First, we must consider the relationship of the three types in terms of dependence. As the diagram indicates, policy claims are the most dependent of the three, because policy claims depend upon value claims, which in turn depend upon factual claims. The claim that "the nations of the world should implement the Kyoto Protocol limiting the effects of fossil fuels on the global environment" (a proposition of policy) is likely to rest on a number of value claims, including potentially the claim that "the world's current dependence on fossil fuels is environmentally irresponsible" (a proposition of value), which in turn would require that we had reached a number of factual conclusions, possibly including the conclusion that "the world's dependence on fossil fuels is causing global warming" (a proposition of fact). For this reason, there is an interdependence among these various proposition types: policy claims are supported by value claims, which are supported by factual claims. We seek a guaranteed livable wage (policy) because the free market is unfair (value) because large numbers of working citizens are unable to meet basic needs (fact). The base (factual claims) in this model is broader than the tip (policy claims) because for any given policy proposition there are likely to be several value claims supporting it, and for each value claim, there are likely to be several factual claims. For example, the policy claim that the "United Nations should expand protection of cultural rights" is likely not only to rest on the value claim that "cultural rights deserve protection" but also the value claim that "cultural rights are effectively protected by law" and even the value claim that "the United Nations is a legitimate organization." Similarly, the value claim that "cultural rights deserve protection" will depend on several factual claims: "language rights are threatened," "religious rights are threatened," "religion and language are critical to culture," etc.

Next, we must consider the relationship of the three types in terms of responsibility—and here, we are talking about the responsibility of the advocates who are making claims of these types. To start with the top level, policy claims: as we have just noted, policy claims depend upon the value claims and the factual claims that support them. In other words, the claim made at the policy level cannot be established, or proven true, unless the claims underneath it are also established or proven true. To use a simplified example: you cannot establish the claim that the world should endorse the Kyoto Protocol to reduce global warming unless it's factually true that the use of fossil fuels causes such warming. In other words, advocates are responsible not only for claims at the level of their proposition, but also for all levels below it. Advocates of a value proposition will be responsible for supporting the factual claims that undergird it as well, and advocates for a policy proposition must support both the underlying value claims as well as the underlying factual claims. If responsibility is taken to mean an advocate's logical need to account for related issues, then responsibility is highest for policy propositions and lowest for factual propositions. To illustrate, the proposition "immigration weakens U.S. economic performance" is at base a factual proposition, insofar as economic "weakening" can be measured in relatively objective terms such as the nation's gross national product and standard of living. In order to meet her responsibilities, the supporter of this proposition could be logically expected to show that such weakening occurs (the fact), but she would not be expected to show that immigrants are harmful to the nation on balance (the value) or that immigration should be restricted (the policy). A proponent could say, "Personally, I believe that the multicultural benefits of immigration outweigh any economic harms, but that is not the subject we are debating today. I am just charged to show that their economic effect is negative." Along the same vein, the proponent of a value proposition like "immigration is undesirable" would be expected to demonstrate actual harms (the facts) but could not be called upon to defend a particular action in opposition to immigration (the policy). Granted, anyone who criticizes the effects of immigration might be presumed to be calling for a limit on immigration, but other possibilities exist: improved immigration policy, a regulation of the types of immigrants admitted or the types of work made available, etc. The advocate of that proposition could reasonably say, "My role in this debate is to demonstrate the harms of immigration. Presuming that it is found to be harmful, then the next step would be to think about what we ought to do about it, but that would be another debate." Needless to say, the advocate of a policy proposition could not escape responsibility in that way. Thus, one important step in matching the proposition to your goals is to determine the extent of argumentative responsibility that advocates seek and select the proposition accordingly.

Another element in proposition selection relates to differences within each of these three general categories. There is another dimension to the proposition formed by the fact that different types of statements can be made within each of the three proposition types. Referring to this dimension as the proposition "attitude," we note that each of the proposition types can simply address the nature of something (descriptive), call for something new (imperative) or pose a contrast between two real or potential elements (comparative). These three possible attitudes combined with the three proposition types create the possibility for nine proposition styles.

Table 1: Proposition Types and Attitudes

		Proposition Attitude		
		Descriptive	**Imperative**	**Comparative**
Proposition Type	Policy	Addresses the nature of governmental/ organizational action.	Calls for governmental/ organizational action.	Contrasts two or more conflicting governmental/ organizational actions.
		Israel's stance toward terrorists is to shoot first and ask questions later.	*The United Nations should expand its protection of cultural rights.*	*The government is superior to the marketplace in guaranteeing quality health care.*
	Value	Addresses the nature of a societal/ personal stance.	Calls for a societal/ personal stance.	Contrasts two or more conflicting societal/personal stances.
		Society overvalues material success.	*We should embrace the principles of deep ecology.*	*When in conflict, liberty is more important than security.*
	Fact	Addresses the truth of some condition or relationship.	Calls for a finding of the truth of some condition or relationship.	Contrasts the likely truth or two or more conditions or relationships.
		Violence on television causes violence in society.	*The U.S. Supreme Court has legal justification to find that the death penalty discriminates against blacks.*	*The "conspiracy theory" is a more plausible explanation of the assassination of President John F. Kennedy than a "lone gunman" theory.*

The Importance of Proposition Type to the Public Debater

All of this, of course, must have some relevance to the public debate advocate or planner. Naturally, most general public debate audiences are likely to be unaware of these distinctions. Debaters in front of an audience are thus likely to get nowhere by claiming that "since this proposition is value descriptive, rather than value imperative, your arguments don't really apply." A taxonomy such as this is not useful as a tool to use in debates, and doing so would simply introduce terminology and distinctions that would be too expensive in the time their explanations would consume. That doesn't, however, mean that the distinctions are unimportant. We see the following benefits that can come from considering proposition styles in your public debate.

- *Proposition styles should be used to generate ideas.* The heuristic function of the proposition styles is that you might use the table above to consider different ways of addressing the same basic idea. For example, working with a topic like "freedom of expression" you might find that the subject is most interesting and most debatable when it is addressed as a comparative: e.g., "When the two conflict, the right to free expression is more important than the right to privacy."

- *Proposition styles should be fit to the type of arguments that advocates anticipate making.* Your sense of the debate should begin with an image of the types of clashes you expect would be most important to your debaters and most interesting to your audience. If you would like to focus on the subject of international human rights and justice and debaters plan to focus on the effectiveness or ineffectiveness of international treaties and institutions, then a policy imperative or comparative proposition is most appropriate.

- *Proposition styles should be fit to audience decision-making at the end of the debate.* If you expect your audience to vote or in some way indicate their stance at the end of the debate, then the proposition should be designed to facilitate that. For example, propositions that seek the most clear and direct response from the audience may be imperatives, e.g., "community service is an obligation for all citizens." For some audiences, actions may be easier to conceptualize than judgments, and the use of imperative propositions may be most advisable for planners seeking a clear audience decision at the end of the debate.

- *The construction of arguments, or "cases," should proceed from the proposition style.* The content and structure of arguments for or against a proposition will depend, to some degree, on the proposition style. Propositions that simply offer a judgment (like value descriptive propositions for example) will call for the articulation of some sort of standard of judgment followed by an argument that this standard is met. Propositions that call for some sort of change (like policy imperative propositions) on the other hand will encourage advocates to first indict the present policies and then move on to show the superiority of the changed policy.

Conclusion

Propositions in public debates play several unique communicative roles that are not found in other debate settings. Public debate propositions do not simply serve to limit the discussion and define the sides of the debate; they also play an important role in gaining attention and communicating the purpose of the debate. Topic analysis precedes the creation of the proposition in order to ensure that the proposition selected captures the controversy that advocates would like to embrace. Public debate propositions should not be designed to fit the requirements of any preexisting mold or model; their development is best guided by a complete analysis of the particular situation in which the debate will take place, with a proposition designed for that situation. Nonetheless, an analysis of several different proposition types may be useful in helping planners to consider multiple ways of approaching their intended subject of dispute.

Sample Propositions

Without knowing your particular situation, it is impossible for us to suggest appropriate propositions for your particular public debate. But we do think you may find it useful to look at propositions that have worked in other situations—you may find that they help you to generate ideas. Ideally, the phrasing of your proposition should stem from your own analysis of your audience, your debaters, and your situation. The following is certainly not an exhaustive list, but many of the most frequently debated social and political themes are represented. Some of these propositions make use of legislative or parliamentary language ("Resolved that . . ." or "this house believes . . .") and some do not—we would not say that one style is necessarily better than the other. In some cases, audiences may find phrases like "this house" to be odd and unnecessary; in our experience, however, some audiences find this phraseology fun, and it can add something to their experience. You should analyze your audience to decide whether to use this language in your debate.

Education

Resolved: That school vouchers would improve the quality of education.

This house would post the Ten Commandments in public school classrooms.

Competition is superior to cooperation in achieving excellence.

Resolved: That public education after high school ought to be a privilege and not a right.

A liberal arts curriculum is preferable to an employment-readiness curriculum in secondary schools.

Censorship of student publications by secondary school administrators is justified.

This house would reject the educational value of competition.

States should provide education only in their official language.

Environment

The development of natural resources ought to be valued above the protection of the environment.

Protecting the environment ought to be a higher governmental priority than encouraging economic growth.

Resolved: That globalism threatens the natural environment.

The nations of the world should implement the Kyoto Protocol to limit the effects of fossil fuels on the global environment.

The world's current dependence on fossil fuels is environmentally irresponsible.

The world's dependence on fossil fuels is causing global warming.

We should embrace the principles of deep ecology.

International Issues

Resolved: That U.S. troops should leave Korea.

Resolved: That the United States should not be the world's police force.

Resolved: That the United States should lift sanctions on Cuba.

National interest should be valued over moral principle in the conduct of foreign affairs.

A government owes no duty to protect the welfare and rights of citizens of other nations.

The United States ought to value global concerns above its own concerns.

A nation's sovereignty ought to be valued over international order.

The possession of nuclear weapons is immoral.

Nations should retaliate against terrorists.

The United States was justified in using the atomic bomb against Japan.

The People's Republic of China violates human rights.

The United Nations should expand the protection of cultural rights.

Resolved: That the nations of the world should support the creation of an international criminal court.

Terrorists deserve justice delivered by soldiers, not by courts of law.

The United States should support the creation of a world government.

Resolved: That NATO should expand its membership.

The United States should sign the UN Convention on Genocide.

The European Union should increase environmental regulations.

General National Issues

Resolved: That all citizens ought to perform a period of national service.

Resolved: That citizens ought to have the right to bear arms.

Risking human life to gain greater scientific knowledge is unethical.

Genetic engineering is immoral.

The death penalty deters crime.

Gay-parented families are harmful to children.

Resolved: That others conspired with Lee Harvey Oswald to kill President John F. Kennedy.

Resolved: That our government should guarantee a living wage for all working adults.

This house would strengthen claims to intellectual property.

Resolved: That the death penalty is never justified.

This house would oppose the use of animals by science.

Society overvalues material success.

Violence on television causes violence in society.

Resolved: That community service is an obligation for all citizens.

Political Process

Resolved: That civil disobedience in a democracy is justified.

Resolved: That society's obligation to the poor ought to be valued above individual economic freedom.

Capitalism provides for a better society than socialism.

The United States should abolish the electoral college.

Every citizen has a duty to participate in elections.

Religion and governments don't mix.

The government is superior to the marketplace in guaranteeing quality health care.

Majority/Minority & Race

Resolved: That English should be the official language of the United States.

Resolved: That white privilege should be addressed through the legal system.

This house would give reparations for slavery.

Resolved: That when in conflict, society's goal of eliminating discrimination ought to transcend an individual's right to participate in exclusive, voluntary associations.

Resolved: That a common culture is of greater value than a pluralistic culture.

Resolved: That individuals with disabilities ought to be afforded the same opportunities as able-bodied athletes.

Resolved: That the use of affirmative action to remedy the effects of discrimination is justified.

Rights

Resolved: That human rights ought not to be sacrificed for national security interests.

Resolved: That the restriction of civil liberties for the sake of combating terrorism is justified.

Mandatory drug testing of public officials is justified.

Resolved: That the protection of society's health interests is ensured through broad-based mandatory drug testing.

Testing for AIDS ought to be more important than personal privacy rights.

Resolved: That the public's right to know outweighs a candidate's right to privacy.

The public's right to know ought to be valued above national security interests.

Resolved: That an individual's freedom of expression is of greater value than social harmony.

Resolved: That hate speech ought to be censored for the good of society.

Community censorship of pornography is justified.

Governments have a responsibility to regulate the content of information available to their citizens through the internet.

Resolved: That laws which protect citizens from themselves are unjustified.

Capital punishment is justified.

The criminal justice system ought to place a higher value on rehabilitation than on retribution.

Terminally ill patients have the right to die.

Resolved: That physician assistance in the suicide of gravely ill patients ought to be legalized.

The school's right to search students and lockers is more important than a student's right to privacy.

The Boy Scouts should have the right to exclude gays.

Marijuana should be legalized.

Society should legally sanction homosexual marriages.

Resolved: That schools should teach acceptance of homosexuality.

This house would not sacrifice civil rights for security.

When in conflict, liberty is more important than security.

Notes

1. R. D. Rieke, and M. O. Sillars, *Argumentation and Critical Decision Making*, 4th ed. (New York: Longman, 1997): 46.

2. T. G. Knapp, and L. A. Galizio, *Elements of Parliamentary Debate: A Guide to Public Argument* (New York: Longman, 1999): 12.

Chapter Seven

Developing a Format

Perot: Let's take the next one. They say that we are spending more money against NAFTA than they are spending for it. That is not even close to truth. It is a matter of record how much Mexico has spent. It is a matter of record how much "USA NAFTA" has spent. You take our tiny little 'ole . . .

Gore: Why isn't it a matter of record how much you all spent? Can that be a matter of public record? Can you release those numbers?

Perot: I would really appreciate being able to speak.

Moderator: All right, go ahead. Well, it was a question he had raised . . .

Gore: It is a fair question, isn't it? I raised it earlier.

Perot: Excuse me. I would . . . .[to the moderator] It was my understanding that we'd have a format where you would ask the questions . . .

Moderator: Okay, but . . .

Perot: . . . and I would be able to . . . I am not able to finish. . . .

Moderator: . . . but if he makes a statement . . . I'm just trying to balance the . . .

Perot: Look, excuse me . . .

Moderator: . . . so that he answers yours and you answer his. Okay, go ahead.

Perot: I would just like to finish a sentence . . .

Moderator: Okay.

Perot: . . . just once before the program is over.

If the goal of public debate were simply to promote a spirited discussion, then it could be accomplished simply by putting opponents in the same room with an audience, a camera or a microphone and letting them go at each other. The resulting debate might be vigorous—but the debaters would probably spend just as much time arguing over whose turn it was to speak as they would arguing about substance. The purpose of a format for debate is to ensure that both sides get a fair opportunity to be heard. Usually taking the form of a sequence of timed opportunities to speak, opportunities to question, and often opportunities to receive and respond to audience feedback, the format ideally allows the advocates and the audience to focus on ideas rather than on procedure. When the specific norms that regulate speaking times and opportunities recede into the background because they are understood and accepted by all parties, then the debate can be an intelligent contest of ideas and not a desperate fight for time.

The lines quoted above come from a November 9, 1993 debate between then U.S. Vice President Albert Gore and businessman and former presidential candidate Ross Perot. The debate ostensibly focused on the question of whether the United States should adopt the North American Free Trade Agreement (NAFTA)—but it often seemed to be about something else altogether. The moderator for the debate, talk show personality Larry King, favored an open and freewheeling exchange. By avoiding an explicit format, the debate may have gained a bit of energy, but it lost a great deal of clarity as content was frequently submerged in conflicts over procedure. In the press, the debate was variously described as "sour"[1] and "nasty."[2] As columnist Maureen Dowd summarized the debate, "for ninety minutes, Vice President Al Gore and Ross Perot mostly bickered about who was interrupting whom, who was avoiding answering whom and who was lying about whom."[3] The example of this famous, or infamous, debate demonstrates the thesis of this chapter: format matters. While advocates and public debate planners have a wide variety of established formats to choose from, and while they may certainly craft their own format, the question of format itself deserves careful thought and clear expression. In this chapter, we will address the question of format by first looking at the basic elements that any format should have and then considering several existing debate formats.

Basic Format Elements

While several standard and time-tested debate formats exist, as a public debate developer you have the opportunity to design a format that best fits your needs. You don't have to be a debate expert to do this, but you should do it with an eye toward meeting the basic functions of a debate format and including the different elements of argument construction, evaluation and defense.

Effective public debate formats should address the following concerns.

- *Your format should be adapted to the attention needs of the audience, the subject matter, and the advocates.* As we discussed in chapter 5, planning should always begin with a consideration of your situation. Is the subject fairly technical and in need of developed and time-consuming explanations or will the themes be simple and well known? Is the audience coming to see a spirited contest, or are they coming basically to be educated? Different answers will yield different format choices.

- *Your format should promote the orderly development of arguments.* Arguments in a debate develop though predictable phases. After the debater articulates the basic thesis of her argument and supports it with reasons (the "construction" phase), her argument is subject to the responses of her opponents (the "evaluation" phase); she then answers these responses and reaffirms her position (the "defense" phase). While public debates are not locked into any specific sequence, they should allow time for each of these phases. We feel that public debates should incorporate questioning periods and audience participation as part of the evaluation and defense phases.

  Position Construction   At the beginning of a debate, the position of each side needs to be laid out. Controversial terms need to be defined, major claims need to be explained, and positions need to be supported with clear logic or quoted evidence.

  Refutation   Once their opponent's arguments are heard, advocates have a responsibility to provide a reaction. Refutation—the act of evaluating the reasoning, the support, or the implications of an adversary's argument—should occur as early in the debate as possible.

  Rebuttal   The act of defending your argument after it has been refuted is called "rebuttal." Generally, this defense of your arguments against attacks belongs in the closing phases of the debate. Often, in order to encourage final speeches to focus just on rebuttal (and to avoid the continuing articulation of more and more arguments), advocates are forbidden to introduce new arguments in the closing speeches of a debate.

Questioning   There is no more direct way to clarify information, to uncover flaws and to lay the groundwork for your own argument than to ask a question directly of the other side. By either allowing a specific time for questioning (often referred to as "cross-examination") or by allowing questions that interrupt an opponent's speech time (often referred to as "points of information" or simply "points"), you can add the excitement of direct interaction to your debate. Another method of interaction is heckling: the shouting out of (hopefully) witty remarks by opponents or members of the audience.

Audience Participation   Audiences often have a stake in the debate and may have a point of view that is not fully represented by the debaters. An excellent way to build audience involvement and expand the scope and interaction of the debate is to allow a specific time for the audience to ask questions, make short speeches, or both.

Preparation Time   While the majority of preparation for a debate should occur before the debate begins, advocates may need time to collect their thoughts and find information prior to their own individual speeches. As we will discuss below, most tournament formats set aside a considerable amount of time just for preparation—during this time, teammates may speak to each other privately, but there is no public discourse. This kind of preparation time offers little of interest to an audience attending a public debate, however. For this reason, we think it best for preparation time to occur at the same time as other activities: for example, a speaker might prepare for his speech while his partner is questioning the other side.

- *Your format should include equal and alternating speaking time.* A core principle of debate is that each side should have an equal opportunity to make its case and this suggests that the speaking time should be strictly equal for each side. The ultimate defense against charges of unfairness is, "You each had an equal opportunity to make your case." In addition, the need to respond to what the other side has said suggests that speaking time should alternate from one side to the other so that attacks may be made and responded to in sequence.

- *Your format should provide the first opportunity to the side supporting the proposition.* Generally, the proposition being debated will place the greater burden of proof on the side supporting the proposition (see our discussion of the burden of proof in chapter 6). For this reason, audiences will need a reason to accept a proposition before they need to hear a reason to reject it. Frequently, but not always, this principle also extends to giving the side with the greater burden of proof the last word as well. The greater the burden on the proponent's side—that is, the more unpopular or difficult their position is—the greater the reason to follow this convention.

- *Your format should include variety.* In order to retain interest, your public debate should include a mix of types of activities—speeches, questions, and audience comments—without any one activity dominating for an extended period of time. Particularly for debates on television or radio, the need to keep speaking opportunities short and varied is critical to maintaining a lively debate.

The remainder of this chapter will consider a number of different debate formats that embody these principles in different ways. Some of the formats are designed for tournament competition but could be easily adapted for public debate. Other formats are more specific to an audience situation.

A Taxonomy of Debate Formats

The basic principles outlined above can be satisfied in many different formats—and we will offer descriptions of a number of possible formats in the pages that follow. Before going into particulars, however, we would like to outline some of the basic decisions that debate organizers must make before choosing or adapting an existing model.

- *Teams or individuals?* In tournament settings, most debates are conducted by teams—that is, there are two or three individuals working together on each side of the debate. (In some formats, there are actually four teams in all, two teams on each side of the debate, working more or less independently.) But there are also tournament categories—most notably, Lincoln-Douglas debate—in which individuals compete (that is, there is only one debater on each side). Electoral debates, too, are almost always conducted by individuals.

  Either the team model or the individual model can work well in a public debate. One advantage of the team model is that it allows more people to get involved in a debate—and that can be a major consideration if the debate is being presented by a debating club or society. A team debate also offers more variety to the audience—they see different styles, personalities, and argumentative strategies, and so may find a team debate more interesting or entertaining. The individual model, however, may offer greater clarity: one debater, arguing a position from start to finish, is likely to be more consistent in language and style than two or three debaters who switch roles as they go along. But these tendencies are not absolute: it's certainly possible for a solo debater to be entertaining, and a well-coordinated team can be consistent and clear. The organizer's decision for one model over the other will usually be based on human resources—that is, who is available and who is involved.

- *Two sides, three sides, or more?* We recognize that our habitual perspective in this book has assumed that there are two sides to a debate. When a debate is centered on a simple, straightforward proposition, it invites two responses: agreement or disagreement. This binary opposition is central to virtually every kind of tournament debate.

  In the world of politics and policy, however, there are often more than two choices. Voters, certainly, usually have more than two candidates to consider. We began this chapter with an excerpt from a 1993 debate featuring Ross Perot; a year earlier, his Reform Party had garnered enough support for him to deserve a place on stage in the presidential debates, along with Democratic candidate Bill Clinton, and Republican President George H.W. Bush. Their three-way debates were messy but memorable. Citizens also face more than two options when deciding policy issues. In New York State, for example, many industrial factories along the banks of the Hudson River have closed in recent years. What should be done with the abandoned facilities? Some advocates argue that their towns should find new industrial tenants who will keep manufacturing jobs in the areas; others argue for rezoning the properties for residential development; still others want to convert the land on the riverbanks to public parkland. In a public debate about this issue, all three perspectives should be represented.

  Debate organizers have a choice, then, about the number of sides that will be part of their debate—and their choice will be shaped both by the issue being debated, and the nature of the audience for whom the debate is intended.

- *Audience participation or debaters only?* We have argued throughout this text that the audience comes first in a public debate—and it is only natural for the audience to become involved with the debate in a tangible way. We recommend that your public debate should include some component that allows audience participation—although we recognize that sometimes there are logistical or strategic concerns that make debate organizers choose to limit participation in the debate to the debaters themselves. At this point, we simply want to emphasize that this is one of the most fundamental choices that organizers must make before opting for a particular format. We would also note that almost all of the formats discussed below—many of which were developed for tournament settings—must be altered to include audience participation.

In developing a format for your public debate, you should approach these formats as illustrative and should not feel the need to adopt a format exactly as laid out: questioning styles and opportunities can be changed, the number and length of component sections can always be changed and adapted, and audience participation can always be added. We will refer generally to the side supporting the proposition as the "affirmative" and the side opposing the resolution as the "negative" side. All of these formats can also be followed by an audience decision or discussion period or both (see chapters 17 and 18).

The Policy Format (team debate with two sides)

Currently associated in the United States with high school and collegiate policy debate, this format has the advantage of strict equality: every speaker gets exactly the same amount of speaking and questioning time as any other. On the other hand, at least if used with the tournament time limits listed below, this format can make for a fairly long debate—as much as two hours if the standard allotment of preparation time is used.

9 min.	First Affirmative Constructive
3 min.	Questioning of first affirmative speaker (by second negative speaker)
9 min.	First Negative Constructive
3 min.	Questioning of first negative speaker (by first affirmative speaker)
9 min.	Second Affirmative Constructive
3 min.	Questioning of second affirmative speaker (by first negative speaker)
9 min.	Second Negative Constructive
3 min.	Questioning of second negative speaker (by second affirmative speaker)
6 min.	First Negative Rebuttal
6 min.	First Affirmative Rebuttal
6 min.	Second Negative Rebuttal
6 min.	Second Affirmative Rebuttal

Each speaker delivers a constructive as well as a rebuttal speech, e.g., the first speaker from the affirmative side delivers both the first affirmative constructive as well as the first affirmative rebuttal. The basic case for the proposition is laid out in the first affirmative constructive, and a case against the proposition, combined with a refutation of the affirmative's case, is provided in the first negative constructive. The following two speeches develop and extend those arguments and continue the refutation of the other side. Questions follow each constructive speech and you'll notice that the person doing the questioning is never the person who has to speak next; thus, the questioning time can also be used as last-minute preparation time for the upcoming speaker.

The Karl Popper Format (team debate with two sides)

Designed for members of the International Debate Education Association, this format is predominantly used in secondary school programs in Eastern and Central Europe and Central Asia. A simple design, this format accommodates three speakers per side and provides just one speaking opportunity for each speaker (although four of the six speakers also conduct questioning). As such, its strengths are that it includes a greater number of speakers and provides a gentle introduction to debate for less-experienced speakers. (You'll notice that the responsibilities are somewhat uneven: the first speakers on each team have a total of 12 minutes on stage; the second and third speakers on each team have 8 minutes apiece.)

6 min.	First Affirmative (Constructive)
3 min.	Questioning of first affirmative (by third negative)
6 min.	First Negative (Constructive)
3 min.	Questioning of first negative (by third affirmative)
5 min.	Second Affirmative (Rebuttal)
3 min.	Questioning of second affirmative (by the first negative)
5 min.	Second Negative (Rebuttal)
3 min.	Questioning of second negative (by the first affirmative)
5 min.	Third Affirmative (Rebuttal)
5 min.	Third Negative (Rebuttal)

One challenge of this format is to maintain continuity between the speeches. The third speaker needs to defend the same arguments that were extended by the second speaker and introduced by the first speaker. This need for continuity is present in other formats as well, but when speakers make only one speech each, there is a correspondingly greater need to communicate among the partners. The first speech from the affirmative side has the goal of laying out the team's main arguments. The first negative speaker follows, developing not only that team's case but also their refutation of the affirmative's arguments. The two speeches that follow are designed for extending the arguments and the refutation of each side, but not for introducing new arguments. A final speech from each side provides an opportunity to compare and summarize.

The Parliamentary Format (team debate with two sides, audience included)

The parliamentary format is probably one of the most recognized formats the world over. The format has the advantage of a relatively short duration (compared to other 2-on-2 competitive formats) and nearly constant interaction. The format includes the honorific titles of a European-style parliament: the team usually referred to as "Affirmative" is called "Government" and includes a Prime Minister and a Member of Government; and the team usually referred to as "Negative" is called "Opposition" and includes a Leader of Opposition and a Member of Opposition. These terms may or may not be used. Although the use of these terms might convey a special sense of importance or history, they are likely to create more confusion than they are worth in a public debate context—if only because the position taken by the "Government" team may not be the same as the position taken by the actual government in the country where the debate is taking place. (Say, for example, that the proposition states that "the United States government should ratify the Rome Treaty and become a party to the International Criminal Court." In a parliamentary format, the "Government" team would be called to affirm that proposition, which the federal government in Washington would oppose.)

7 min.	Government: Prime Minister's Constructive *"Points" allowed after first minute and before last minute.*
8 min.	Opposition: Leader's Constructive *"Points" allowed after first minute and before last minute.*
8 min.	Government: Member's Constructive *"Points" allowed after first minute and before last minute.*
8 min.	Opposition: Member's Constructive *"Points" allowed after first minute and before last minute.*
15 min.	Floor Speeches (2 minutes each)
4 min.	Opposition: Leader's Rebuttal
5 min.	Government: Prime Minister's Rebuttal

This format lacks specifically set-aside times for questioning, but includes the possibility for questions offered throughout the first phase of the debate. Once a constructive speech has completed its first minute but before it has entered its last minute, an opposing speaker may rise at any point and request a "point of information"—that is, the speaker requests permission to ask a question. At that point, the speaker holding the floor can either accept the question and answer it, before moving back into his speech, or he can say, "No, thank you," and continue on with his speech. The strength of this feature is that it offers a chance to address a point just after it has been made. A weakness is that, if overused, it can be distracting to the speaker and the audience. This method of questioning is considered at greater length in chapter 16. Another advantage of this format is that it allows for audience participation in the form of "floor speeches"—audience members may make challenges or ask questions of the debaters. (This format requires a firm-handed moderator to keep the floor speeches and responses within appropriate limits.)

A variation on the parliamentary format that is used at the World Debating Championships involves four teams at a time, two government teams and two opposition teams. While such a format permits the involvement of a much larger number of debaters, it also takes substantially more skill in order to maintain clear argument development and refutation.

The Lincoln-Douglas Format (individual debate with two sides)

Most of the formats considered thus far have focused on teams of debaters—two or more individuals working together on each side of the question. While team formats have the advantages of promoting a little more variety and in fostering the creativity that comes from teamwork, a one-on-one format has the advantage of promoting a simpler, shorter, and more personal contest. Getting its name, but not much else, from the famous debates between Abraham Lincoln and Stephen Douglas for the U.S. Senate seat from Illinois, the Lincoln-Douglas format offers a one-on-one debate including constructive speeches, rebuttals and questioning time in less than 35 minutes.

6 min.	Affirmative Constructive
3 min.	Questioning by negative
7 min.	Negative Constructive
3 min.	Questioning by affirmative
4 min.	First Affirmative Rebuttal
6 min.	Negative Rebuttal
3 min.	Second Affirmative Rebuttal

Though the total speaking times are equal, the affirmative speaks three times (beginning and ending the debate) while the negative speaks twice. Each begins with a constructive speech to lay out his principal argument, with the negative debater's speech being a bit longer so as to include both case development and refutation. The affirmative debater has two short rebuttals in which to refute the negative's case, defend his own, and conclude the debate. The negative debater has one relatively longer rebuttal in which to extend and defend his arguments and summarize the debate in his favor.

The "Town Hall" Format (team debate with two sides, audience included)

This is a format for two teams that includes a focused period for audience interaction. Based on a form of debate used at the National Communication Association's "Town Hall Debates" held at the association's annual conventions, this 50–60 minute format has proven to be useful and popular for public on-campus debates as well.

5 min.	First Affirmative Constructive
2 min.	Questioning of first affirmative (by second negative)
5 min.	First Negative Constructive
2 min.	Questioning of first negative (by first affirmative)
4 min.	Second Affirmative Constructive
2 min.	Questioning of second affirmative (by first negative)
4 min.	Second Negative Constructive
2 min.	Questioning of second negative (by second affirmative)
15 min.	Audience Speech/Question Period
3 min.	Final Negative Summary
3 min.	Final Affirmative Summary

Through the first four speeches, the first half hour of the debate roughly, the audience hears from each of the speakers, and hears each speaker ask questions and answer questions. The goal of the four constructive speeches is to lay out all of the arguments for one's side and to introduce all of the planned refutations against the other side. Up to this point, the debate follows the pattern of the policy debate format described above. After all four debaters have been heard, there is a 15-minute questioning period, during which audience members can make their own arguments or can directly question the speakers. A moderator can handle this audience participation period by providing individual speaking times to audience members who would like to give speeches from the floor (2 minutes, for example) or by simply letting audience members speak for a reasonable amount of time. The moderator should attempt to balance the questions and statements for the two sides as much as possible—for example, by allowing the other side time to answer or react to a question that was asked of their opponents. Finally, the debate ends with two summaries presented by each side. This summary, presented by one member of each team (it doesn't matter which one) reviews the main issues of the debate and provides reasons why the speaker's side should be chosen the winner.

A "Quick Debate" Format (individual or team debate with two sides)

Particularly in settings involving the broadcast media, debates sometimes must be accomplished in very short amounts of time. Debaters with experience in tournament debate, as well as public policy advocates, may feel that any issue worth debating needs at least an hour of debating time—but it is possible to offer the kernel of a debate, the fundamental give and take on the central controversy, in far less time. The following format requires only 10 minutes, and provides two speaking opportunities and a questioning opportunity to two sides.

2 min.	Affirmative Constructive
1 min.	Questioning of affirmative
2 min.	Negative Constructive
1 min.	Questioning of negative
2 min.	Affirmative Summary
2 min.	Negative Summary

This format requires speakers to have both discipline (selecting only one or two arguments) and a great deal of word economy. While the abbreviated format may not permit very complete argument development or extension, it does allow the basic points of view to be communicated and contrasted. As such, it might be ideal for a program that includes debate along with other activities—for example, a talk show or a radio call-in show. Starting such a program with a quick debate may be an excellent way to gain attention and briefly communicate the gist of the controversy.

A Three-Way Debate (team debate with three sides)

The formats that have been considered so far, and debate more generally, could be accused of presuming that all conflicts have only two sides. While it is certainly most common to conceive of disputes in a way that permits a single "pro" and a single "con" on a question, it is at least conceivable that a debate might involve more than two delineated sides. The more parties that are added, of course, the more we move from a debate to a discussion. Still, it is possible that three parties at least could engage in meaningful debate. For example, consider the proposition, "Resolved: That military action is a superior policy toward rogue nations than either economic sanctions or diplomatic engagement."[4] Debate on such a proposition would involve one affirmative (defending military action) and two distinct negatives (one defending economic sanctions, and one defending diplomatic engagement). Each side would have a responsibility to show that its solution was better than the other two. A debate accommodating three positions might be structured as follows.

6 min.	Affirmative, first Constructive
2 min.	Questioning by negative B
5 min.	Negative A, first Constructive
2 min.	Questioning by affirmative
6 min.	Negative B, first Constructive
2 min.	Questioning by negative A
5 min.	Negative A, second Constructive
2 min.	Questioning by negative B
5 min.	Negative B, second Constructive
2 min.	Questioning by affirmative
5 min.	Affirmative, second Constructive
2 min.	Questioning by negative A
3 min.	Negative B, Summary
3 min.	Affirmative, Summary
3 min.	Negative A, Summary

This format equalizes time with a varied speaking order; ensures that each debater speaks three times, questions both of his opponents, and is in turn questioned by both of his opponents. It is a little confusing, to be sure, but it remains possible to envision a setting in which it would not only be appropriate but would allow for a more comprehensive understanding of the issues.

A "Running" Format
The chief value of any format is that it lays out a clear understanding of who speaks when, as well as a clear understanding of who can ask questions, and when question can be asked. In some settings, however, it may be appropriate

to employ a less formal and less rigid system. A "running" format, as the name suggests, is a format that is worked out "live" by the moderator during the actual course of the debate. In other words, just as in a normal conversation, speaking turns and times are worked out in a reasonable fashion without applying strict rules and limits. A person speaks, within reason, until it seems fair to allow the opponent to respond. The response continues in turn until it seems like it is time to move on to another issue. If a question comes up it can be asked, and the debate as a whole becomes as self-regulating as a friendly discussion.

In the abstract, at least, this sounds very natural. In practice, on the other hand, it is quite difficult to achieve. Particularly in a debate in which the two sides have strongly conflicting interests and perspectives, self-regulation can quickly turn to bickering. The debate with which we began this chapter was intended to be a freewheeling exchange. It involved two public figures and probably one of the most experienced moderators in the United States. The fact that it still devolved into rancorous bickering should give caution to anyone contemplating this format. With a set format, debaters no longer wonder, "When do I get to speak? How long can I speak? When can I ask questions? When do I have to answer questions?" A set format removes much of the potential for conflict over procedure and keeps the conflict where it should be: on the content.

Still, there may be settings in which organizers might prefer to work with a natural and unstructured "running" format. For those settings, we suggest the following:

- The moderator has to be highly engaged in the debate. Rather than just letting people speak, the moderator must constantly ask herself questions like, "Is it time to move on?," "Did both sides get a chance to address this issue?," etc.

- The moderator has to be trusted by both sides, so much so that her decisions go unquestioned during the debate. If the moderator has decided that one side has gotten its argument out and that the other side should now be heard, that decision should be accepted without complaint by the participants.

- The moderator should ensure equality in all things—speaking times, questioning opportunity, and speaking turns (i.e., the same side shouldn't always be given the last word). One essential element is that the moderator, or an associate, should keep a running clock on both speakers to ensure that at all points during the debate, their respective speaking times remain roughly equal.

Conclusion

The format, of course, is not the content of the debate. Audiences attend debates to learn about their government's policies, to evaluate international relationships, to consider fundamental issues of civil rights, and a thousand other issues. They generally do not attend debates in order to learn about a format. While debate arrangements preoccupy organizers and experts, they rarely receive much notice from the audiences themselves. As a background consideration, though, the format is essential. If audiences leave the debate feeling that they have seen an exchange that was full and fair and allowed all sides to express their own views, to react critically to the ideas on the other side, and to summarize their positions, then it is probably the format that has allowed that.

In developing a format for your own debate, the best advice is to keep it simple, clear, and fair. A good format should fit your purpose and should encourage effective debate without calling attention to itself.

Notes

1. D. E. Rosenbaum, "Gore and Perot Duel on TV Over the Trade Pact," *New York Times*, November 10, 1993.

2. M. Dowd, "Personalities and Pictures: A Made-for-TV Debate," *New York Times*, November 10, 1993.

3. Ibid.

4. This proposition purposely violates one of the principles of phrasing propositions—focusing on one central idea—in order to accommodate three sides in this debate. Having a third entity in the debate would obviously change many elements including the burden of proof, the focus of refutation, etc. It is not our purpose to explain this format for argument fully but, instead, to suggest its possibility.

Chapter Eight

Attracting Attention

Introduction

The organizers of any activity involving an audience have one task first and foremost: to attract audience attention. A public debate is public only if it actually *has* a public. What good is it to prepare and deliver a great debate if nobody is there to hear it? Finding an audience and publicizing the event are therefore crucial for assuring the debate's success.

The first step, which we discussed in chapter 5, is to analyze the audience: who are they, and what are their concerns? This analysis helps to shape the topic of the debate, and plays a role in crafting the proposition. When it comes time to publicize the debate, organizers should be sure to phrase the proposition in a way that will appeal most directly to the target audience; this may mean choosing a negative statement over a positive one—or vice versa. If you hold a debate with the proposition "Universities Should Not Charge Their Students Tuition" at a university that already offers free tuition, chances are that nobody will come because the natural audience in this setting—the University's students—will not see it as an issue. Their tuition is already free, so why would they care to hear someone argue in favor of the status quo? However, if the same issue were to be worded differently—"Universities **Should** Charge Their Students Tuition"—the debate might attract the attention of those same students since it proposes a change that would affect their pockets, if adopted. In this case, the positive statement ("should") is clearly preferable to the negative statement ("should not").

Why Me to You?

The first question that needs to be answered in planning and promoting any debate is this: why ME to YOU? In other words, why do I feel compelled to bring this issue to the table and debate it in front of an audience, and, perhaps more important, why would YOU want to hear it? The audience needs a good reason to come and spend two hours of their time listening to a debate.

Why ME?

The importance of answering this question in any public address has been known for centuries, ever since Aristotle's *Rhetoric*, in which he defines the three types of proof that belong to the art of rhetoric: *logos, pathos* and *ethos*. *Logos* is the appeal to reason; *pathos* is the appeal to emotion; and *ethos* is the persuasive appeal of the speaker's character, or credibility. (For further discussion, see chapter 5, "Preliminary Steps" and chapter 11, "Making Your Arguments Compelling.") The audience always wants to know whether a speaker is qualified (professionally and personally) to address the issue being debated, especially if that issue is highly controversial or requires some level of expertise. It is therefore a good idea, for promotion purposes, to include some information about the debaters themselves and why they are participating in the event. This should be an important consideration even in the planning stage, when debaters are being chosen; inviting experts on both sides of an issue to debate, either as individuals, or as members of a team, may be a good promotional move.

Why to YOU?

This is the ultimate question. Why should the audience care? What is in it for them? In a public debate, the audience comes first. Their needs, their interests, their expectations and their attitudes should determine the choice of topic, venue, medium, debaters, format, proposition wording, timing and—promotion. In your publicity, you must tell them what you are going to tell them during the debate, and why. In other words, you must tell them what they will gain by attending or participating in your debate. Will they learn more about an issue, simply to satisfy their intellectual curiosity? Or do they have interests at stake—such as their money, their health, or the well-being of their families? Should they expect to be entertained? Moved? Inspired? Relieved? Whatever the case may be, any publicity campaign should make one thing clear: the audience should know what they will take with them when they walk out after the debate. The benefit may be as intangible as an enlightened mind, or an exalted heart, or an energized will—but the benefit must be promised.

All the aspects of thorough audience analysis required for preliminary steps and debate preparation (see chapter 5, "Preliminary Steps")—geographic, demographic, psychographic and behavioral characteristics[1]—should be used for promotional purposes as well.

Finding Your Natural Audience

The audience is what makes a debate an event; it is what makes debate relevant, worthwhile, and potentially an important force for effecting societal or political change. The audience is what makes or breaks the debate. This is why the audience has to be the primary concern every step of the way in preparing and publicizing a debate. Publicity is not about attracting any audience—it is about attracting the right audience. The right audience is the audience you want; it is the audience that needs to hear the debate you are offering. If you organize a debate at a nearby pub and provide free beer, you may attract a lot of people, but what for? It is important to get people to come for the right reasons and to participate as willing and concerned agents of change.

Directly Affected Audience

People who are personally affected by the issue being debated have the greatest incentive to attend and are the most important components of any audience. There is a reason why the public tunes into politicians when they talk about taxes: taxes affect their pocketbooks. A debate on whether universities should charge more tuition would be likely to attract students if they thought the outcome of the debate would affect what they pay. A debate about whether there should be a nationwide military draft would probably be most interesting to those who would be drafted if such a requirement were instituted. (It would appeal as well to their parents,

spouses and anyone else who would, in turn, be affected by such a requirement.) The relevance of the topic has to be made very clear in advance
and there should be a conscious effort to reach out to those who would be
directly affected, because it very often happens that those people aren't fully
aware of a controversial issue. In a suburban setting, for example, citizens
do not usually pay much attention to the rulings of the town zoning board,
even though the board's decisions may allow for the construction of new
housing developments that would have a significant impact on local traffic and local schools. Even national issues are sometimes not grasped fully
by the affected public: citizens may not recognize the long-term impact of
a change in tax policy, or the effect that a trade agreement will have on
manufacturing jobs. Again, publicity is vitally important and must be used
to reach even those people who are most directly affected and have the most
to gain from watching the debate.

Friends and Families

Even debaters have friends and families (contrary to popular belief)—and
friends and families are a natural part of the debate audience. They go to
the debate event just to see the debaters in action, the same way they would
go to see friends or relatives perform at concerts, recitals, plays or sporting
events. They find it exciting to watch a daughter (or son or brother or sister
or friend or classmate) debating in front of an audience; because they have
a personal connection with the debater, they have a greater investment in
the outcome of the debate. Friends and family are naturally supportive, and
can create good energy in the room. But even this audience can expand with
a little outreach—family members can be encouraged to bring their own
friends, and friends can be encouraged to bring their families. The inner
circle of friends and family can help with promotion as well, by forwarding
e-mails, making phone calls, and talking about the event in casual conver-
sations. Friends and family are both a guaranteed audience and a great
resource for attracting other audiences—so use them!

The Intellectually Curious

In every community, big or small, there are plenty of people who care about
issues that do not affect them directly or immediately, and they should be
recruited as part of the debate audience. You can call them "intellectually

curious" or "socially committed" (or both). The size of this subset of the audience will depend on the topic, and on how "hot" the topic is among the general public. Debates on cloning or a pending war are likely to attract larger audiences because these topics are part of the buzz of everyday life, both in the media and around the office water cooler. The only difficulty in attracting an audience for such hot topics is that they may be "overexposed" in the media. In today's world of 24-hour cable networks, saturation is more the rule than the exception. As a result, your potential audience of the curious and committed may feel bored or frustrated by an issue; they will tune out, literally and figuratively, if the debate seems like it will be "yet another bunch of talking heads rehashing the same topic." In situations like this, it is important to find a special niche, a twist, or a unique quality in your approach to the issue that will set your debate apart—and should be a major theme in your publicity. People who care about issues are often eager to speak about them and to ask questions—so it is a good idea to include audience participation in your debate as a way of attracting this group. Of course, the chance to participate should be highlighted in all of your promotional materials—if you want to use something as an attraction, you can't keep it a secret until after the people come in the door!

How to Publicize a Public Debate
The 4 Ps
Publicizing a debate is no different than trying to sell a product. Marketing an event like public debate and marketing a commercial product have a lot in common, and the same principles of basic marketing, or the four Ps—product, price, place and promotion[2]—apply. The **product** is the debate event itself, of course. The **price** can be interpreted on two levels: the first is the perceived value of the event to the audience (which they pay for with their attention and time spent attending the debate); the second is the cost of organizing the debate (the time and effort invested in the preparation and publicity, as well as any real monetary costs—for the venue, refreshments, flyers, posters, travel expenses and fees for experts, etc.). The **place** is the venue of the public debate; the location affects not only the size of the audience, but the character and mood of the event as well. A university setting will be likely to attract the university community and have a more academic

character, whereas a public debate at a town hall meeting will have a much more real-life, pragmatic flavor. (There is no need to discuss what kind of debate results when the venue is a local pub!) Finally, **promotion** is a necessary ingredient of any endeavor involving an audience, listeners, followers or customers, whether you are selling a product, an idea or an event.

Who Will Do It?

If the scope of the debate is grand and there is money available, responsibility for promotion can be given to people specially hired for that purpose; more frequently and realistically, the debate organizers themselves are in charge of the task. In university settings in particular, outside funding is usually limited, and it is common for debate groups or clubs to organize debate events from start to finish, doing everything from planning and promotion to the actual debating. The task of event promotion, therefore, often falls on moderators, questioners, respondents, coaches—and, as we mentioned before, on the friends and families of debaters who are willing and able to become involved.

In many circumstances, it is possible to arrange for debate sponsors—companies and organizations that are interested in supporting the event with money or with company products (refreshments, paper, computers, etc.). In return, the sponsor gains publicity or even increased sales (in a case where the sponsor's product becomes the "official" refreshment of an event, and only that product is sold at refreshment stands). When a sponsorship is established, debate organizers must feature it in their promotional materials—but sponsors are often happy to underwrite promotional costs. After all, the promotional material is a form of advertising, and it is in the sponsor's interest to see that the advertising is well done and travels far and wide. What is more, the sponsors have an interest in seeing the event itself well attended; they do not want to have their names associated with something that looks second-rate or unsuccessful.

Promotional Tools

There are many different vehicles suitable for publicizing a public debate: newspapers, television, direct mail, radio, magazines, the Internet, e-mail, newsletters of various organizations, bulletin boards, posters—you name it.

But the best method of promotion—because it reaches the greatest number of people at the lowest cost—is free coverage in the media.

Press Release

The first step in attracting any media attention is to write an interesting press release. The press release should answer the five Ws—**who, what, where, why** and **when**. This should be covered at the very beginning—the lead of the press release. The rest of the release—the body—should elaborate further on the lead and include quotes, background information, and any additional details.

For your press release to be effective, you must follow the standard format that news organizations expect. The release should be written on an organizational letterhead (if you are associated with an organization), or a news release form, with a name, address, phone number, fax number, and an e-mail address included. In the top left corner of the page there should be a date for release to the public, or the boldfaced phrase "FOR IMMEDIATE RELEASE." In the top right corner, there should be the name and phone number of the person who can be contacted for additional information. This should be followed by a short headline in bold capital letters, and the text itself should begin with the release date and location (city) of the release (see the example at the end of this chapter). The text should be typed, double-spaced and printed on only one side of the sheet. The ideal press release is only one page long; when there are additional pages, it is customary in the United States to write "MORE" at the bottom of the first page, and the end of the release is marked with "END" or "###". The standard conventions vary somewhat in different countries, so you should be sure to familiarize yourself with the expected format before sending your release.

Newspapers

Local newspapers are a great way to promote an event. They provide timeliness, broad coverage and high level of credibility. Newspapers can either publish a feature story about the debate (more common if the topic has some special relevance to the community) or list it in their calendar of events. The critical first step in trying to secure newspaper coverage is to send a press release. It is always a good idea to get the name of a contact person at the paper and to send the press release directly to that person. You should direct your release to the person who is most likely to be professionally interested in the debate topic or event. Depending on your topic, that person might be the science editor or a medical correspondent or the city editor; newspaper reporters and editors also have specific "beats" that may include your event or debate topic (some reporters, for example, always cover legal or judicial stories, and others handle any stories about schools and education). After the press release has been sent, you should follow up with a call after a week or so, to make sure that the contact person indeed received the release and to answer any questions about the event. If the debate event includes some expert debaters or guests, you can offer to arrange for an interview with some of the experts for the paper prior to the event. Interviews and interesting stories that provide context for a debate help to create a "buzz" in the media and can greatly increase the size of the audience.

Radio and Television

Radio and television are usually the best vehicles for promoting debates to wide audiences. Both vehicles—but television in particular—provide a very broad coverage and appeal to the audience's senses on more than one level. If you can afford it, advertisements are, of course, one very effective option. But if funds are restricted (or unavailable), it is worth spending some time and effort in trying to get some free exposure with Public Service Announcements (PSAs) or through talk shows. You should target local (as opposed to national) radio and television stations, since they are always looking for something of interest to the local community, and your event may suit their needs. The first step with the broadcast media is the same as it is with newspapers—you must create a good press release and make sure that it gets directly into the hands of the right person. And then—follow up, follow up, follow up.

Public Service Announcements.   Whether made for radio or television, Public Service Annoucements should be an exact length of time—usually 10, 20 or 30 seconds. They should answer the basic five Ws (who, what, when, where and why); they should use short sentences, catchy phrases and words that are easy to pronounce. Most radio stations will make a tape themselves from your written text without charging you; some will accept tapes that you have prepared yourself; others will simply have an anchor, newsreader or announcer read your copy live. (See the end of this chapter for a sample PSA designed for radio.) Television PSAs, because of the visual nature of the medium, require fairly sophisticated production values, and are best done by professionals. You may find that local cable companies allow the public to use their production facilities, with acceptable results; but a videotape made with a home camera, without high quality sound and lighting equipment, will inevitably look amateurish when broadcast—and that can do your event more harm than good.

Talk Shows.   Talk shows, whether on television or radio, are very appropriate vehicles for promoting a debate. If the show editor is convinced that your debate event is potentially relevant and interesting for their audience, you may be able to secure a talk show appearance for the debate organizers or for key expert speakers. Again, the press release should be mailed to the right person well in advance and should be followed with a call and a meeting with the director of the show.

Direct Mail

One common and cost effective marketing tool is mail directed at targeted audiences. Direct mail can be tailored to particular segments of the population and involves relatively small expenses (design, printing, copying, and mailing costs). The downside is that direct mail is frequently discarded without being opened (especially in more consumer-oriented countries like the U.S.), and even when it's opened, a direct mail piece may get less than a minute of the reader's attention. On the whole, though, direct mail is still considered quite effective; direct mailers just take it for granted that not every piece will hit its target.

Mailing Lists.   The first requirement for direct mailing is a mailing list—the names and addresses of your potential audience. Mailing lists can be developed "by hand" or acquired from other sources. Building a list by hand involves research, and good record keeping. Like charity, a good list begins at home: you should start by assembling information about the people in your organization, adding to that the names and addresses of friends and family that they provide. (Perhaps this seems redundant—why do you need mailing information for people you see regularly, or for people who will know about the debate via word of mouth? Think of it as planning for the future: if you are running a college debate club, sooner or later your debaters will graduate—but you want to keep them, and their friends and families, on your mailing list.) The next step is to gather information about local leaders: your mailing list should include the names of people who head civic groups, organizations, clubs and societies. You may be able to take a shortcut by consulting directories or membership rosters, which are sometimes available to the public. Organizations such as professional groups and associations, cultural and historical societies, sports clubs, community colleges and resource centers may provide these lists on special request. It is a good idea to send mail to key people with broad contacts in the field or in the community. Accompanied with personal notes, these mailings can be especially effective; if these leaders make announcements to their own membership, either at meetings or through their mailings, there is no cost to you as the debate organizer, and your event gains credibility. (Remember that direct mail does not always hit the intended target—but think of the return on your direct mail investment if your debate is about the legality of antiterrorism statutes, and the head of the local bar association decides to publicize the event to the association membership.) Finally, mailing lists can be built by hand at the debate event; it is a simple matter to ask attendees to provide their addresses if they want to hear about future events.

In commercial direct marketing, it is quite common for mailing lists to be sold or otherwise shared. Supporters of the local symphony orchestra, for example, will often find that they start to get mail from repertory theatres and dance companies—they have been identified as supporters of the arts, and artistic organizations are keen to reach them. It probably isn't practicable for debate organizers to start buying mailing lists, but it may be possible to borrow or share lists on an ad hoc basis. Say, for example, that your debate club is sponsoring a public debate about environmental legislation; you may find that a local environmental organization is willing to share its mailing list to publicize the event.

In any case, mailing lists must be maintained and updated when addresses or contact people change. (By the way, it is crucial for names on the list to be spelled accurately; nothing consigns a direct mail piece to the trash more quickly than a mangled name or title.) Mailing lists can be stored easily with commercial software, such as Microsoft Excel; mail merge programs allow for the production of personalized letters, labels, and envelopes. Personalized letters always work better than letters that begin "Dear Friend" or "Greetings, Fellow Debate Lover," and they will reward the extra time and effort required to produce them.

What to Include.   Direct mail can include postcards, letters, photographs, flyers, brochures, or anything that can be (legally) stuffed in an envelope. Design and the careful crafting of content are essential. The materials have to be visually appealing, easy to read and understand, and generally attention-grabbing. They also have to answer the basic who, what, when, where and why questions, with a particularly strong emphasis on why. Why should the audience come? What is in it for them? You should stress how the debate event will address their needs and interests and why the topic is relevant to their lives. Sell the benefit of the debate to the audience. Benefits command attention and induce action, so always mention them first. Another marketing mantra in promotion is: "Sales start on the cover." This holds true whether you are producing a one-page copy on an inexpensive paper or a dramatic multi-fold, multi-color brochure on glossy stock.[3] Leonard H. Hoyle, Jr., in his book *Event Marketing*, provides a few simple rules for flyer and brochure design:

1. use a contrast of dark text on light paper to make it easier to read;
2. avoid long paragraphs and verbose sentences—instead, use short, punchy sentences and simple lists with bullets and numbers;
3. have someone else do the final proofreading;
4. photographs and illustrations are welcome, but should be used with purpose, not just to fill space;
5. all photographs and artwork must be used with proper permission and credit;
6. type fonts should be used sparingly, and there should not be more than three fonts in any brochure;
7. bright, contrasting colors are more memorable and identifiable;
8. if there is some response expected of the reader (like a registration or RSVP form), it should be made easy to find and detach;
9. white (blank) space should not be overdone, but it does make reading easier on the eyes;
10. text boxes are good tools to emphasize special features;

11. be careful with special printing/folding/stock features, since they can dramatically increase production costs; and

12. create a mock-up prior to printing and get feedback from peers and focus groups about clarity, spelling, grammar, and overall effectiveness.[4]

Posters

Design.   Similar rules apply to designing posters—except that posters can handle less text and are meant to be teasers, designed to catch attention quickly and briefly. An effective poster catches the viewer's eye and gets straight to the point. Since a poster cannot contain many details, always provide a phone number and/or a Web site address for further information (if possible, on pieces of paper that can be detached from the bottom or the side of the poster, so that people can take them and use the information later). Posters are all about visual appeal, so they should be well designed and uncluttered, with any imagery complementing (not obscuring) important information. If your budget allows only for photocopying, not printing, you can still make your poster stand out by using colored paper. The poster should be as large as possible, yet not too large to be posted in certain venues. Either A3 (European) or 11x14 (U.S.) paper is a good size for most venues.[5]

Where to Post.   Posters should be placed in high-traffic areas, where they are likely to get the attention of the type of audience you would want at your debate event. Good venues include libraries, schools, community centers, outdoor kiosks, supermarkets, stores, shopping malls, launderettes, coffee shops, sports clubs, banks, hospitals, art centers, bulletin boards, churches, university campuses (in campus centers, dining halls and other central locations), subject-related departmental buildings, off-campus hangouts (pubs, cafes, bars, clubs), etc. You do need to make sure, however, that posting is allowed in your desired locations, and you should check from time to time to see that the posters have not been removed or covered with other posters.

Internet.   More and more people get their information on the Internet, and many people rely on the Internet exclusively, making it an increasingly important promotional tool. Debate organizers can create their own Web page or post information about the debate on existing Web sites. The basic rule of five Ws (who, what, when, where and why) still applies; you must also pay attention to structure, style, consistency and ease of navigation. There are certain technical requirements as well, and there are plenty of good designing software programs available (Microsoft FrontPage, 1st Page Web Editor, HotDog Professional and Macromedia Studio Program Suites like Dreamweaver MX and Macromedia Flash MX, to name just a few).

Final Notes

The above-mentioned tools and venues by no means exhaust the list of possible promotion vehicles. You can also publicize your event through direct e-mail, list serves, announcements in bulletins, newsletters, magazines, journals, and word-of-mouth. You are only limited by your imagination, the time and resources available to you—and the law. Make sure that, whatever you do, you get proper permission and authorization from all parties affected in the process of promotion. The last thing your event needs is legal difficulties which may jeopardize your credibility or endanger the event altogether.

Sample Press Release

Debate Association
SHYLI (South Hampton Youth Leadership Institute)
100 Europe Avenue
Claremont, NY 10021
211-212-2112   *fax* 211-212-2121
Debate@shyli.org

N E W S   R E L E A S E

FOR IMMEDIATE RELEASE   For More Information Call:
                                        Jennifer Lopez
                                        211-212-2111

Claremont Public Debate Festival
Scheduled on July 30, 2002

(Claremont, NY, May 1, 2002)—The first Claremont Public Debate Festival will close this year's SHYLI Camp on July 30, 2002, featuring SHYLI participants and Claremont public officials. Mayor Tom Cruise called the event a "culmination of the most exciting summer Claremont had in the last ten years."

SHYLI participants will showcase their debating and critical thinking skills, focusing on the hottest topics of the day. Education reform, U.S.-U.N. relations, minority rights, and the war in Iraq will be some of the issues debated. Claremont public officials have been invited as advocates and respondents.

The debates will take place in Cookie Hall at X University, 100 Europe Avenue, Claremont, starting at 9:00 AM and ending at 5:00 PM. Every debate will include audience participation and refreshments will be served.

"We are thrilled to be able to host this wonderful event," said Dr. Kitty Bird, President of X University "all these smart young people from all over the world will clash ideas and solutions with our most prominent experts and politicians. I hope all Claremont will come and participate."

# # #

Sample Public Service Announcement (PSA)

Debate Association
SHYLI (South Hampton Youth Leadership Institute)
100 Europe Avenue
Claremont, NY 10021
211-212-2112   *fax* 211-212-2121
Debate@shyli.org

PUBLIC SERVICE ANNOUNCMENT

TO: Public Service Director   Contact:
                                                        Jennifer Lopez
                                                        211-212-2111

:30 Seconds. Please run 7/15/02 through 7/30/03.

SHOULD THE U.S. GO TO WAR IN IRAQ? ARE OUR PUBLIC
SCHOOLS IN WORSE SHAPE THAN EVER? IS AFFIRMATIVE
ACTION EVER JUSTIFIED? SHOULD THE U.S. SIGN THE LAND
MINES TREATY? THESE ARE JUST SOME OF THE HOT TOPICS
SHYLI PARTICIPANTS AND CLAREMONT OFFICIALS WILL CLASH
ON THIS MONTH. COME TO X UNIVERSITY ON JULY 30 AND
HEAR CLAREMONT'S AND THE WORLD'S FINEST MINDS DEBATE
THESE ISSUES. ASK THE QUESTIONS YOU ALWAYS WANTED
TO ASK! VOICE YOUR OPINION IN FRONT OF YOUR FELLOW
CLAREMONTERS, AS WELL AS STUDENTS AND TEACHERS FROM
ALL OVER THE WORLD! DEBATES START AT 9 IN THE MORNING
AND END AT 5 IN THE AFTERNOON. THERE WILL BE PLENTY OF
REFRESHMENTS, SO PLAN TO MAKE A DAY OF IT. COME JOIN
US AT COOKIE HALL, X UNIVERSITY ON JULY 30—THIS IS YOUR
CHANCE TO BE HEARD, DON'T MISS IT!

Notes

1. P. Kotler, N. Roberto, and N. Lee, *Social Marketing: Improving the Quality of Life,* 2nd ed. (London: Sage Publications, 2002): 117–121.

2. L. H. Hoyle, Jr., *Event Marketing: How to Successfully Promote Events, Festivals, Conventions, and Expositions* (New York: John Wiley, 2002): 12–21.

3. Ibid., 109.

4. Ibid., 112–113.

5. S. Wilkinson, "Marketing Music Events," *Generator Information Marketing,* 1995, http://www.generator.org.uk/Infos_Frameset.asp?StyleNumber=1&Project= info_Marketing_Event.asp

Chapter Nine

Coaching and Preparation

[U.S. Senator and presidential candidate Robert] Dole's debate advisors sought to put him through a run of trial questions and answers, according to a participant, but the candidate cut him off: "What I want to hear is not questions and answers: I want to hear a strategy for winning this debate."[1]

Senator Dole was widely seen as turning in a less powerful showing during their debate than his opponent, U.S. President Bill Clinton, then running for reelection. One reason for this may be that the senator missed one thing: the winning "strategy" he was seeking was exactly what his advisors were already encouraging: practice, practice, practice. While some may feel that the secret to successful debates and public speeches resides in having a special strategy or an unexpected trick, in the long-run success comes from hard work and thorough preparation.

This chapter focuses on that process of preparing for public debates and it focuses on the role of those who help others prepare for public debates: namely, coaches. While most chapters in this book focus on one aspect of preparation or another, there are elements that relate to the preparation stages as a whole, and because there are individuals who will focus primarily or exclusively on the role of a coach, this chapter is provided in order to serve as a useful overview of the roles and processes involved in preparing for the presentation of public debates.

This chapter is intended for anyone who prepares and anyone who helps others prepare. In the context of a public debate, the "coach" may or may not bear that formal title. The coach may be a teacher, an event organizer, a consultant working for one side or the other, or even one of the debaters themselves. Coaching may be a role that is shared by several participants. Indeed, to the extent that the need to motivate and organize is common to just about any cooperative enterprise, coaching is a role that is often shared among several public debate participants. For that reason, this chapter is geared not just to teachers but to anyone who plays a constructive role in the planning and execution of a public debate.

After introducing some general elements of coaching motivation, and then considering one basic but important distinction between two modes or approaches to coaching, we will move on to consider the unique elements and responsibilities of preparation, at each of four phases in the debate: first, reaching important agreements; second, exploring the issues; third, preparing, practicing and developing individual speeches and questioning strategies; and fourth, moving into full-group practice.

Motivation and Leadership

Champions are made, not born.

Failure to prepare is preparing for failure.

It's what you learn after you know it all that counts.

Success is peace of mind that is the direct result of self-satisfaction in knowing you did your best to become the best you are capable of becoming.

These quotations are all attributed to John Wooden, the famed basketball coach of the Bruins at UCLA (University of California at Los Angeles), and though they may sound like clichés, they reflect truths not just about sports coaching, but about any instance in which we seek to motivate others to give their best in a challenging enterprise. Like a sports contest, a public debate can indeed be a setting in which individuals are called upon to find the best in themselves, conquer their fears, and improve their performance through practice.

Coaching is a highly individualized skill that varies based upon the personality of the coach, the personality of the individuals being coached, and the situation. If it were possible to amass a comprehensive description of the specific elements of coaching, such an accounting (by individuals more experienced than ourselves) would fill the remainder of this book. That, however, is not our purpose. Instead, we aim simply to provide a few general reminders on coaching prior to considering the unique attributes of coaching for a public debate, at each of four phases of preparation.

So, what does it mean to coach? Is it just the act of telling participants what they need to do, when they need to speak, what they need to say? Is it just the act of providing confidence and encouragement, cheering them up when they are feeling overwhelmed? Is it just serving as a support person for the true performers in the debate, providing an ear that they can speak to, another mind against which they can test their ideas? It is safe to say that coaching can be boiled down to none of these, but involves an aspect of each.

Because our first image of a "coach" may involve an individual in a gym, whistle in hand, perhaps we should first return to the field of sports. This time, we turn not to John Wooden, but to Craig Clifford and Randolph Feezell, two philosophy professors whose 1997 book, *Coaching for Character*,[2] was originally intended to aid sports team coaches in the process of promoting in their players a sense of respect for themselves, the game, and their opponents. The book developed a series of guidelines for coaches to follow in promoting this kind of sportsmanship. By substituting "public debate participants" for "players" and by shifting "sportsmanship" to the somewhat similar need to develop in debaters a concern for audience, opponents and the *entirety* of the event and not just their own performance, we found that many of the principles developed in this book apply quite well as advice for the public debate coach. Some elements of advice are:

1. *Be a good role model.* Demonstrate good preparation habits, good advocacy practices, and a good attitude toward the event.

2. *Emphasize the value of the entire event and the public's perceptions from the very beginning.* By speaking, first and foremost, of what the audience walks away with, and not just what each individual will say, you send the message that the debate's value is found in the understanding and appreciation that the audience gains.

3. *Remember to combine seriousness and play.* Debate is hard work, but the creative generation of ideas and arguments should also be enjoyable. That is a big part of why people debate. In this case, it is not a question of work vs. fun, because the work *is* fun.

4. *Talk about the relationship between the success of the event, and the debaters' personal success.* It is a cliché to say "when the audience wins, you win" but there is a truth contained in the idea that the more the audience understands, appreciates and enjoys, the greater the likelihood that a speaker's objectives will be attained.

5. *Regularly use language that focuses on the success of the whole event, not just on one's own performance.* Avoid an "us versus them" attitude toward the audience, and in many cases, toward your opponents as well.

6. *Expect a focus on the success of the whole event and the public's perception in both practice and in the debate itself.* Encourage participants to think about the audience from the very beginning, not just when the audience arrives.

7. *Establish norms, customs and traditions that reinforce a collective focus and esprit de corps.* A feeling of being part of something important is reinforced by social elements, such as group meals.

8. *Encourage participants to take the perspective of other participants in the debate and the audience.* Thinking of arguments and issues from another's perspective, or even role-playing, can improve a participant's perspective.

9. *Clearly deal with anything not suited to the goals of the event.* When something goes wrong, fix it right away.

10. *Reinforce good practice and good performance.* When something goes right, make sure that everyone knows it.

11. *Communicate the importance of a focus on the success of the whole event to supporters and sponsors.* Make sure that not only participants, but also those who attend or support the event also know that the most important "players" are the audience members and that equal respect is due to all.

12. *Promote reflexiveness by asking questions, not by giving answers.* From a coaching perspective, the question "Do you think that evidence is clear enough?" is always going to lead to more progress than the statement "that evidence doesn't make sense!"

13. *Expect participants to know the procedures and the plan for the event.* Commanding the time and attention of others is a privilege, even if it is one that requires a lot of hard work. No one "owes you" their attention; you have to earn it by being prepared.

14. *Show by your actions and your words that you care and that what you are teaching is important.* For participants to think that the event is important, the coach has to be sure that it is important and to convey that in words and deeds.

15. *Don't forget to have fun.* Debating is naturally fun, and an energetic approach to coaching can enhance that tendency.

Two General Approaches to Preparation

While some principles apply to all coaching situations, others will vary depending upon the approach that is taken. Let's imagine a spectrum that runs from a point of full and complete cooperation to the point of absolute and inflexible competition with many points in between; at the ends of the spectrum are the two general approaches or attitudes toward preparation described below.

The Cooperative Model

In some settings, our purposes will relate more to the success of the event as a whole than to the success of any of the individual participants. For example, an educational group that is hosting a public debate in order to generate interest in debating programs would have the most to gain by a debate that is successful for both sides, a debate that shows the give and take of positions, a debate that offers strong arguments on both sides, a debate that showcases the idea that dispute can occur peacefully and reasonably, a debate that demonstrates that there can be strong and credible aspects to both sides of a question. Given a purpose of that sort, if one side had all of the good arguments, or if one side were able to surprise the other with an argument that they had not planned, then the purpose of the event would be undermined. In this setting, both sides will be comfortable only if they know what to expect from the other side and are prepared to answer it. In this setting it makes sense for both sides to work together through all phases of debate preparation, to see themselves as a single unit with a common mission, and not as two separate teams with antagonistic interests. This sort of preparation would, perhaps, feature one coach who is coaching both sides rather than one coach for each side. While debaters using this model would certainly discuss many elements of their preparation as a team or as a side, much of the communication would occur at the level of the entire group preparing the debate. Several elements characterize this method of preparation:

- Meetings that feature both sides in attendance
- A coach or a facilitator who takes responsibility for the success of both sides
- Collective planning and analysis of issues, potentially prior to individuals choosing sides

- Relatively full exchange of information on the arguments planned by all participants
- Full debate practice, without the need for role playing or sparring partners

The Competitive Model

While cooperation has its advantages, there are clearly public debate settings in which it makes less sense. Imagine that a local environmental group opposes the development of a major shopping center in an environmentally sensitive area. They enter a public debate against individuals representing the development interests in the hope of championing their side of the question. Viewed from that group's perspective, an interest in creating the most powerful argument against development definitely exceeds their interest in making sure that the overall event is balanced. If both sides worked together and shared information, it would result in a more fair, comprehensive, and reasonable exchange—but it would also have the effect of helping the development interests, which is precisely what the environmental group does not wish to do. Thus, this group would be likely to do the bulk of their preparation on their own. They would be likely to receive coaching and facilitation from an individual who was working only for their side. Beyond establishing basic agreements on format, forum, and time, there would be little communication with the other side. Work within this model would then be characterized by the following elements:

- A coach or advisor for each side
- Few if any contacts beyond basic arrangements
- An effort to analyze and make predictions about what the other side will argue
- The use of role-playing in practice

Which Model Is Best?

Depending upon how you as an individual value "competition" or "cooperation," it is possible that you already see one or the other model as being natural and superior. Some individuals undoubtedly believe that a debate, by its nature, is always a competition and any sort of cooperative work decreases the value, the spirit and freshness of the exchange. (This vision is, of course, fairly prevalent in the world of tournament debating.) On the other hand, there are doubtlessly individuals who view any communicative enterprise as a cooperative one and would see any limit upon cooperation as a limit to the value and the reasonability of the exchange. However, the question of which model "fits" your debating situation can't be boiled down to a universal preference for one value or the other. There are times when cooperation makes sense and there are times when competition makes sense. And most important, there is a spectrum of possibilities between the two that could best fit the situation of your public debate. More specifically, the model that you use would depend absolutely on the goals of the event, specifically the extent to which educational values and advocacy values apply. (And these goals, of course, are shaped by the nature of your audience, and your own identity—if you are an advocacy group, you are likely to espouse advocacy values.)

Debaters who are most interested in education are seeking to equip the audience with the resources to make their own judgment about an issue, or to provide the audience with a greater understanding of the debate process. Debaters with a high interest in advocacy, on the other hand, are seeking to persuade the audience to agree with their preferred point of view. Some could argue, of course, that there is a false distinction between advocacy and education, but the difference depends upon the degree of autonomous judgment that you are expecting from your audience. Clearly, it is not an absolute distinction, but there are some settings in which interest tends more toward the goal of the audience receiving the information to permit them to make their own judgments, and there are other settings where the debate centers more heavily on the message itself and the goal is to have the audience make a greater commitment to a particular idea after attending the event.

The principle that we are proposing is that the higher the interest in advocacy, and correspondingly, the lower the interest in education, then the more we would prefer a competitive model of preparation. Conversely, the higher the interest in education, and the lower the interest in advocacy, the more we would prefer a cooperative model of preparation. This model acknowledges that there are gray areas, or instances in which our interests in education will be high, but our interests in advocacy will be high as well. In those settings it only makes sense to use a mix of cooperation and competition—for example, each side would disclose their main points without sharing complete information on what their responses and extensions were likely to be.

Keeping these two general tendencies (advocacy versus education) in mind, the figure below provides a visual representation of the situations in which a competitive or a cooperative focus would most appropriate.

Figure 1. Competitive and Cooperative Models of Preparation

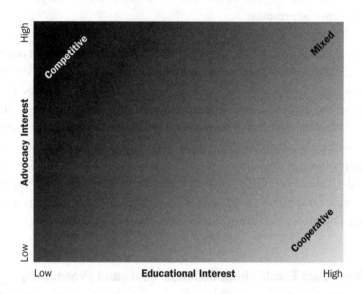

A high stakes debate with two sides of antagonistic interest, like the environmental debate discussed previously, may have the highest commitment to advocacy and the lowest commitment to a broad education on both sides (though of course, each side would seek to educate the audience on *their* side). In contrast, a debate in which a student group that has picked a current issue mostly because it would allow them to demonstrate a lively and interesting debate, not because of any particular personal commitment to the issues, would indicate a high interest in education and a lower interest in advocacy and would suggest a cooperative approach. One may question whether any debate that is both low in advocacy and low in education should occur, but such a debate could simply have the goal of entertainment. A much more common setting would be one in which advocacy interests and educational interests may both be high. For example, the event organizers could have a high interest in the educational aims of the event while the advocates themselves could have an interest in maintaining and defending their point of view against the opposition. In a case like this, a mixed model would be most appropriate and some elements of cooperation (sharing general argument content) and some elements of competition (avoiding joint practice and specific sharing of arguments prior to the event) may be present.

The degree of cooperation that characterizes the debate preparation process will depend to a large extent on the opinions of the event organizers and the advocates themselves. The greater the degree to which the most important aims relate to advocacy, the greater the impulse to compete. The greater the degree to which the most important aims relate to education, the greater the degree to which joint preparation will be important to the debate process. The choice that participants make for one method or the other will obviously influence the steps that follow, with those following a cooperative debate model pursuing collective work strategies and those following a competitive model developing arguments and practicing on their own. Overall, we can identify four phases of the preparation process.

Phase One: Establishing Common Goals and Procedures

Any cooperative enterprise risks losing a great deal of valuable time at the beginning if efforts are not undertaken to establish *a priori* understandings on common objectives and common ways of getting there. A public debate is an act of coordinated communication, and its planning requires a common focus. Everyone involved must ask: whom do we want to be talking to? For how long? About what? For what purpose? Even if a group believes that everybody is on the same page, so to speak, it is essential to make these understandings explicit. Where disagreements emerge, they need to be settled before the planning moves to the next phase. The first step is to have a meeting. Depending upon whether the planning for this debate is cooperative, competitive, or something in between, this meeting may take place among those planning one side of the debate, or among all of those who are involved in all sides of the debate. (Some elements [such as time, place, format and topic], of course, must be handled cooperatively and must be addressed or at least agreed to by all sides.)

The meeting could begin with a series of questions, that the coach or whomever is facilitating the debate can address to the group:

- Who is our target audience? Whom are we trying to reach?

- What is our goal for the event?

- How do we find the point of controversy or divide the issue? (see chapter 5)

- How do we express that controversy as a proposition that would be meaningful to our target audience and clear to the advocates? (see chapter 6)

- How much participation do we want from the audience? What do we want them to go away with?

- What do we as participants want to get out of the event? What goal do we have for ourselves as participants?

As we move through these and several other basic planning questions, it is predictable that some disagreements might arise. For example, imagine a group of university students jointly planning a debate on the possibility of a tuition increase: one participant mainly wants an educational experience for the audience; another participant is most interested in showcasing his own public speaking and argumentation skills. Still another debater is adamantly against tuition increases and wants, more than anything, for audience members to agree with her at the end of the debate. Clearly, some discussion and coordination of goals should occur before this group does very much planning for this debate.

That said, this scenario of conflict is not necessarily a disaster. The goals of participants do not have to be absolutely consistent in order for the debate to be a success. Debate is, after all, an activity of conflicts. For example, if opposing sides want the audience to walk away convinced of the superiority of their positions, and the moderator wants the audience to walk away exposed to the best of what each side has to offer, the goals are not identical, but they are surely complementary. It is important to go through this first phase of planning to ensure that the goals are consistent, not necessarily with each other, but with the overall purpose of the event. In simple and informal debate, this planning may occur in a basic face-to-face meeting, or (less ideally) in a series of contacts and letters. In more formal and more adversarial contexts and when these stakes are at their highest, these debate elements may be the subject of more than simple negotiating. In U.S. presidential campaign debates, for example, it has become common practice for the campaign staffs of the two contenders to meet and draft long and detailed "Memoranda of Understanding" which spell out every conceivable element (yes, right down to the size and shape of the lectern) and function like a contract for the event.[3]

Phase Two: Exploring the Issue, Refining the Focus

Once the parameters of the debate have been laid out, the next phase is to delve deeply into a discovery of the factual information as well as the disputes and controversies that characterize the topic under discussion. In this phase, participants will explore the audience's current knowledge and attitudes, will begin to engage in research on facts and arguments, and will begin to develop a list of the main issues that will evolve into the structure of the debate. If planners have adopted a cooperative model of preparation, then all of these actions would be taken by both sides of the debate, working in concert.

For example, if a group is working on a debate focusing on the International Criminal Court, then an initial search may focus on the factual background:

- What international agreement created the court? When?
- What nations have signed on? Which nations have not?
- What is the court's jurisdiction? Over what crimes and what citizens does the court have authority?
- Does the court have the power to arrest suspects and to enforce its decisions?

These and many other questions could be asked and together they would establish the factual foundation—viz., a grasp what the court is and what it does—that the advocates need before they can even think about building arguments. Once that factual foundation is laid, however, the investigation should turn to an identification of the ways in which the subject may be important:

- What does this audience already know about the court?
- Is there any way in which disputes about the court might affect them or might relate to their experience?

An investigation might reveal that most Americans in early 2004 knows that the court recently came into existence and know that the United States opted not to take part, but do not know much about why; the debate organizers might determine that the potential audience for their planned debate had a similar understanding. Advocates would thus be encouraged to explore these lines of argument: why should (or should not) the United States submit to the jurisdiction of the international court? At this time, advocates are ready to begin collecting arguments. Advocates for U.S. adherence to the court might find that:

- The court represents the next step in a long history of expanding protection for human rights.
- The court represents a unique opportunity to prosecute and deter human rights abuse.
- U.S. failure to participate deprives the court of needed legitimacy and effectiveness.

Those who oppose U.S. adherence to the court might in contrast find that:

- Previous efforts at international tribunals have been accused of political bias.
- An international court may put innocent soldiers and peacekeepers at risk.
- An international court would erode the sovereignty that serves as a cornerstone of stability and peace between states.

Having gained a broad understanding of the issues surrounding the court, advocates may find the debate focusing on the following questions in particular: does the court improve human rights? Can it escape a political bias? Can it function while at the same time respecting sovereignty? These questions, then, would serve as a common structure for the speeches, with each advocate turning to each of these issues in turn.

This process of constructing arguments for effective delivery is covered more comprehensively in chapters 10 and 11. But the coach's role in the process is to guide the participants through it. The most important element of this guidance is the coach's role in ensuring that participants don't rely just on their "top of the head" thinking and instead commit to investigate and research the issue fully. Especially when working with students who are very effective "brainstormers," as many students skilled in public debate tend to be, coaches need to get public debate advocates to look beyond the arguments that they can generate without much thought, and to explore issues more fully. The coach can accomplish this by making a list of questions that the debaters don't know the answers to, questions that might matter to the dispute, background that must be looked up. In this way, the coach focuses on material deficiencies that can only be resolved by a closer analysis and exploration of the issues. There is no upward limit to the amount of research that can be done. For more formal political debates, research can include community attitude surveys and focus groups as elements of audience and issue analysis, and it may involve commissioning investigation of specific questions.

Regardless of the level of the debate, the outcome of this phase should be a greater understanding of the issue and the available arguments. If the sides and the speaking positions have not already been established during phase one, then the information gained in phase two can be used to make a final determination of who is on what side and who is giving what speeches, according to the format that was developed (see chapter 7).

Analyzing the Opponent

As we will discuss in later chapters, one important part of developing an argument is "anticipation"—debaters must try to anticipate how their opponents will respond to the arguments that they make. To some degree, this is a matter of logic: debaters examine the structures of their own arguments, and identify vulnerable points. (For an extended discussion of this process, see chapter 14, "Refutation.") But anticipation also involves taking the measure of the people who will be debating on the other side; debaters must analyze their opponents in order predict what kinds of arguments they are likely to make. This tactic will no doubt seem familiar to anyone who follows competitive sports: in baseball, for example, professional teams produce reams of analytical studies, so that the pitcher on the mound knows what kind of pitch the opposing batter "likes to hit," and what kind he "can't hit"—and throws the ball accordingly.

Before going on, we should note the obvious: analyzing opponents is far more important in a debate emphasizing competition than it is in a debate emphasizing cooperation. But even in a cooperative debate, it is not a bad idea to develop a systematic understanding of what to expect during the debate, and knowing how an opponent is likely to argue is an integral part of that understanding.

In some instances, debaters will be familiar with their opponents' styles through past experience—this is the case when the debaters are part of the same club, or have faced each other in tournament competitions. But familiarity can also be gained through research, by looking up past speeches or writings by the opponent—especially when the subject of the pieces at hand is the debate topic or something similar. Research can allow debaters to get a sense of their opponents' political views or predilections: if the opponent has made a politically conservative speech about the death penalty, it is reasonable to predict a conservative perspective on civil liberties. At a deeper level, this conservative approach to the death penalty might suggest a habitual position about the role of government when in conflict with individuals—a position that might emerge in the context of a planned debate about reforming the tax code.

The analysis of opponents should also include a consideration of their style. Is the opposing debater serious, pompous or funny? What kind of rapport does he have with an audience? One-on-one encounters reveal a lot about a person's style, so engaging in a conversation with an opponent before the debate may help to predict his likely behavior during the debate.

After analyzing their opponents, debaters can prepare substantively. First of all, they can make educated guesses about what their opponents' arguments are likely to be, and they can prepare appropriate responses. When it comes to style, the rule is to play to your strengths and your opponents' weaknesses. Or, even better, you can use the philosophy of judo—use your opponent's strengths against her. What does this mean? If, for example, your opponent is known as tremendously charismatic and funny, and you're not exactly Jerry Seinfeld, then it probably would not be a good idea to try to win by developing a slick presentation. Instead, you should try to use your seriousness as an advantage, appealing to the audience by saying, "My opponent may make you laugh—she makes me laugh, too—but the bottom line is that we are dealing with a serious issue that requires a serious, logical analysis. And what's missing from my opponent's argument is logic. Here's why. . ."

Phase Three: Developing Speeches and Other Components

Once each person has a sense of what his or her role is, and what the main arguments are going to be on each side and on the whole, participants are ready to move toward more specific preparation of individual speeches and questioning periods. At this phase, the work will become more individual and the role of the coach will reflect more one-on-one, person-to-person, counseling. How the coach proceeds will depend a great deal on his own personal style—and more important, on each debater's working style. A part of the preparation of the coach will be to get a sense of that style. Is one of his debaters waiting for guidance or is she pressing ahead? Does her teammate need a lot of close work on content, or does he just need the coach to be a sounding board for his ideas? Obviously, the approach used by each person, and to each person, will vary.

Nonetheless, once attention begins to turn to individuals, several predictable challenges may result:

> **Problem: The script-driven debater.** This debater insists upon creating his speech word-for-word and he doesn't feel comfortable doing it any other way. In all likelihood, his delivery is wooden and he fails to react to developments and nuances in his opponent's arguments because he is "sticking to the script."

> **Solution: Extemporaneous delivery.** Emphasizing the need for fresh delivery and at least the appearance of spontaneity, the coach should ask the debater to practice using key word notes (see chapter 15) and reassure him by emphasizing that "it is only practice." Usually the speaker will become more natural and (gradually) more comfortable speaking from key words than he would be speaking from a script.

> Manuscript delivery is only called for when two conditions are met: 1) the exact wording is so critical that a single word out of place would be a disaster, and 2) the participant has sufficient delivery skills that he can pull off a scripted or memorized delivery and still make it sound conversational. In most cases, one or both of those conditions will not be present and the best bet will be to go with extemporaneous delivery.

Problem: The over-confident debater.   This debater is so sure of her knowledge and abilities that she does not see a need to practice or to plan in advance. She'll do fine, she believes, and too much practice may just decrease her natural spontaneity.

Solution: Demonstrate inadequacies, encourage teaching. Coaches should respond by *demonstrating* to this debater (and not simply telling her) that there are inadequacies that could be improved. This may involve handling some of the questioning and refutation personally, making the debater see that there are points in her own argument that she cannot defend. Second, the coach can emphasize for this debater the importance of being involved in practice as a benefit to the other (and presumably less experienced and talented) participants in the debate. In that way, the overconfident debater becomes a mentor for the others involved in the event. As many teachers can attest, there is no more effective way to get a student to recognize her own weak spots than to have her try to teach someone else.

Problem: The inflexible planner.   This debater needs to know everything the other side will be saying and can't embrace the flexibility called for in the situation. Not knowing exactly what the other side will say becomes a reason to not prepare.

Solution: Contingency planning.   Not being certain of the other side's approach becomes a reason to plan *more* not *less*. Assuming that it is impossible or inadvisable to give this debater as much information as he seeks, the coach should play the role of the opposition and generate a number of different argumentative strategies; the debater can then prepare "briefs" against each (see chapter 14, "Refutation").

Problem: The ghostwriter coach.   This coach, like the ghostwriter who writes books that famous people then put their name on, would much rather write the speech *for* a participant than help that participant develop her own content. To this coach, his own arguments are better, more original, and more strategic than any that could be developed by the advocates themselves.

Solution: Stick to coaching or become a debater yourself.   A track and field coach isn't able to run the race himself, and he wouldn't be helping the team much if he did. In a public debate, writing a speech for someone else to deliver can lead to a wooden performance, can leave the debater vulnerable to attacks and questions from the opposition and can lead to passivity—since debaters end up waiting for a coach to supply the content, rather than developing it themselves. If coaches feel that competitive spark and the need to create arguments and speeches of their own, they can always become debaters as well. Unlike track and field, and unlike tournament debating, there is no prohibition against participation by those who also advise and coach. However, coaches (whether they are also debaters or not) need to be clear on their role: as debaters, they should employ the skills and attitudes of an advocate, but as coaches, they should realize that their help is best offered by *facilitating* the development of an advocate's work, not by substituting for it. For participant-coaches, this creates the responsibility to prepare fully for their own role, while simultaneously encouraging and promoting preparation by others.

Phase Four: Practice

There is no such thing as a "practice debate" . . . All communication is influential. Still, any learning process involves a certain amount of trial and error, so provision for trying out ideas and techniques under conditions where "damage control" is possible has to be part of a systematic training program.[4]

Any debate performed before a live audience is by nature a spontaneous event. Directness in expression and flexibility in ideas are valued qualities for the public debater. The goal of the public debate, the desired outcome, is a moment of understanding, a transaction between a thinking speaker and a reacting audience; this outcome can never be achieved by a simple performance of something that has been prepared earlier, like a prerecorded tape. But the inherent liveliness of a public debate should not be seen as a reason for avoiding practice and preparation in advance. Avoiding a stale presentation does not require that we present our ideas off-the-cuff or off the top of our heads. There are several reasons why practice before a public debate is an essential element. First, practice allows you to identify your own flaws. Elements that may be incomplete or not fully developed may not be discovered until you practice. The argument that an opponent makes that you are not able to answer illustrates a critical weakness that can be corrected before the debate. Second, practice is a way of demonstrating to yourself your own capability for performing; in effect, practice is self-persuasion, a way of convincing yourself that it is something that you can do. Third, practice is an important way of smoothing out your performance. Anytime somebody is doing something new, from playing a sport to preparing a new recipe, the first couple of tries may be rough and unsteady, and the third or the fourth or the fifth are going to be better. Practice provides us with an opportunity to recognize flaws, smooth our performance, and convince ourselves that we are ready. Research, of course, indicates the advantages of practice, showing that even the quiet mental *imagining* of an event in our heads can substantially improve performance by conditioning our brain to respond effectively.[5]

In addition to smoothing our performance, practice also provides the ideal setting for constructive feedback. Perhaps the most obvious image of a "coach" is someone who plays the role of a critic, pointing out flaws, weaknesses, and inadequacies in one's performance. While criticism is undoubtedly a part of a coach's role, our view is more holistic; we see the coach as someone who not only identifies and finds weaknesses, but also identifies and builds upon strengths and contributes to the overall development of both content and attitude on the part of the debaters. There are several things that a coach should remember in giving feedback to public debaters:

- Don't forget constructive criticism. Often recognizing something done well is more important than realizing that something was done poorly. Letting the advocates know that they did something well will remind them to do it again when the pressure is on and will boost their confidence as well.

- Wrap your criticism in compliments. Some call this the "hamburger" approach: start with something soft and complimentary (the bun), then add an element of critical commentary (the meat), then end with something complimentary again (another bun): "Sasha, you are providing a lot of excellent evidence in this debate. However, you say that marijuana causes medical problems and I think that is really an unsupported point. But it should be easy for you, with the information you already have, to find this support and add it to your otherwise excellent argument."

- Always supply solutions to the problems that you identify. If you are going to tell someone that he doesn't look confident enough, there is a reasonable chance that you may be making him even less confident (now he has one more problem to worry about and that is his lack of confidence). Instead of identifying it as a failure, rephrase it as a solution: "You know, you would look much more confident if you made eye contact with the audience." "You would sound smoother if you used key-word notes only instead of that script."

- Be careful of modeling behaviors. The practice of giving "line readings" ("say it like this . . .") risks robbing the performance of its originality and risks substituting your judgment for the judgment of the speaker; you might end up depriving the speaker of a natural style. While there may occasionally be a cause to say "consider doing it like this," in general you can get farther by asking questions.

- Ask questions—criticize by asking questions rather than by making direct statements. Instead of saying, "I think that the support is insufficient on your second point," ask instead, "Do you think you have enough support for the second point?" "Do you think that the audience is going to understand that example?" "Do you think those statistics are recent enough?" In this way you are avoiding the defensive shield that pops up whenever we hear criticism and promoting the possibility that the speaker is actually going to reconsider his own views.

- Discourage participants' tendency to treat a speech or an argument as a finished piece of work. When practice is seen as a performance or as a dress rehearsal rather than as a laboratory for testing and refining ideas and approaches, then there is a chance that the participants are going to be resistant to changing anything or defensive toward even constructive criticism. That has to be set aside at the very start: "The reason we are here is to improve upon ideas, and while I don't want to shake your confidence or push you off track, I would like you to approach each of these speeches as pieces of work that *could* be improved. So during this practice I might ask you to experiment with a few things in order to test your preparation and the choices that you've made so far."

- Avoid arguing. Frequently, it will happen that your perception is simply different from that of the advocate. The advocate's investment in her own performance is going to cause her to disagree, and given the fact that she is operating within the mindset of debating, her brain will be ready to argue. The result is that a reaction from you will produce a denial or a rebuttal from her. The coach should resist the temptation to engage at that point. Since coaches are often former or present debaters themselves, it is often hard to resist. A better course of action, however, is to focus on the purpose of the criticism, and not the argument itself: e.g., "My role here as a coach is to share my perception, and whether we agree or not, there is a chance that *my* perception will be the *audience's* perception as well. So our question is not whether I am right or wrong, but the question is how do we deal with this possible reaction to your argument?"

- Emphasize "re-gives." Have the speaker do the speech again. Often, the real educational moment comes when the debater repeats and improves a speech or speech segment—and then *realizes* that he has done better. Just hearing that something is wrong or could be better is not enough. It is the process of fixing and rediscovering that leaves the greater impression. For this reason, coaches can't assume that just speaking about a problem constitutes improvement. It is essential whenever you identify something that can be fixed immediately, you ask the advocates to fix it immediately: "Why don't you try giving that speech, making that argument, asking that question, again?"

Conclusion

Coaching requires many of the same skills as those required of the advocate. Effective counselors and advisors have to size up the situation, and evaluate the advocate they are working with; they must select from a repertoire of strategies and apply the ones that seem to be the best fit. It is a responsibility that requires as much listening and learning as it does speaking and teaching. While all of the chapters of this text emphasize elements of preparation and public debate construction, it is the unique responsibility of the coach to bring them together in order to promote a debate that starts with a direction that is clear and agreeable to everyone involved, moves through a thorough analysis of issues and careful construction of individual speeches, then proceeds to comprehensive and constructive practice sessions and finally to a public debate that leaves audiences, participants, and organizers fully satisfied.

Notes

1. Adam Nagourney, and Elizabeth Kolbert, "After the Election: Anatomy of a Loss—A Special Report; How Bob Dole's Dream Was Dashed," *New York Times*, November 8, 1996. Quoted in S. Kraus, *Televised Presidential Debates and Public Policy*, 2nd ed. (Mahwah, NJ: Erlbaum, 2000): 130.

2. C. Clifford, and R. M. Feezell, *Coaching for Character: Reclaiming the Principles of Sportsmanship* (Champaign, IL: Human Kinetics, 1997): 100–104.

3. Kraus, *Televised Presidential Debates and Public Policy*.

4. R. O. Weiss, *Public Argument* (Lanham, MD: University Press of America, 1995): 177.

5. Associated Press, "Mental Sports Practice Helps by Training Brain, Study Says," *Hobart* (Australia) *Mercury*, January 23, 1995.

Chapter Ten

Reasoning With Your Audience

In our title for this chapter, the preposition "with" is important. There is a difference between reasoning *to* your audience and reasoning *with* your audience. While the former might suggest a demonstration of your own forethought and logical prowess, the latter suggests that you are inviting audience members to become partners in the process of developing, offering, and ultimately accepting or rejecting the reasons that underlie your claims in a public debate. This chapter will focus on this task of developing your arguments, which in many ways can be seen as the heart of your public debate. Through the use of argument, logic, and evidence, advocates in a public debate seek to convince the audience of the superiority of their side in the debate. While argument, logic, and evidence are doubtlessly complex topics that have been comprehensively addressed in other sources,[1] this chapter will address the elements of public reasoning and support that are most basic and most important to those who are debating before a large audience. We will begin with the step of uncovering and using the audience's existing beliefs and attitudes, then move through the stages of gathering information, and finally conclude with specific advice on developing and employing successful patterns of reasoning in the arguments that you develop for your speeches.

First, however, we should focus on exactly what we mean when we say "argument."

What Is an Argument?
Fans of the British comedy show *Monty Python's Flying Circus* might recall a sketch in which a man walks into an office and announces, "I'd like to buy

an argument." As it happens, however, he finds it hard to receive anything but contradictions in response to what he says:[2]

Man: Look, this isn't an argument!

Other Man: Yes it is.

Man: No it isn't! It's just contradiction!

Other Man: No it isn't!

Man: Yes, it is!

Other Man: It is NOT!

M: It IS! You just contradicted me!

O: No, I didn't!

M: Oh, you DID!

O: Oh, no, no, nonono!

M: You did just then!

O: No, no, nonsense!

M: (exasperated) Oh, this is futile!!

O: No, it isn't!

M: I came here for a good argument!

O: No, you didn't. You came here for an argument!

M: Well, an argument is not the same thing as contradiction.

O: (Pauses) It CAN be!

M: No, it can't!

M: An argument is a connecting series of statements to establish a proposition.

O: No, it isn't!

M: Yes it is! 'tisn't just contradiction.

O: Look, if I *argue* with you, I must take up a contrary position!

M: Yes but it isn't just saying "No it isn't."

O: Yes it is!

M: No it isn't! (Pauses and looks away, slightly confused)

M: (Continuing) Arguments are an intellectual process. Contradiction is just an automatic gainsaying of anything the other person says.

O: (pause) No it isn't.

M: Yes, it is!

O: Not at all!

M: Now look . . .

As this humorous sketch shows, the meaning of argument is not always clear and can itself become the subject of argument. We believe that the best way to look at argument is not just as a "connecting series of statements to establish a proposition" but more fully as *the use of reason-giving in an attempt to convince the audience of the truth or value of your perspective.* Specifically, we believe that there are four general principles that need to be kept in mind when applying this definition.

- *First, arguing is not "fighting with words."* When your friend says "I had an argument with my boyfriend" she may well be describing a conflict, but not necessarily a rational one. That is, one may have an "argument" without necessarily making any "arguments." Communication researcher Daniel O'Keefe explained this distinction between what he called "argument$_1$," which is something that one person can make, and "argument$_2$," which is something that two or more people can have.[3] In other words, an "argument" conceived as a claim with reasons isn't the same or even necessarily associated with "argument" conceived as a verbal conflict. Because public debate is a cooperative venture designed to explore options and enlighten an audience, it is far more likely to be characterized by arguments$_1$ rather than arguments$_2$. As Canadian logician Douglas Walton has noted, "the quarrel is no friend of logic and frequently represents argument at its worst."[4]

- *Second, argument is more than just assertion and contradiction.* The sketch indicates that for argument to get anywhere, it has to be more than simple disagreement. A statement, e.g., "The International Criminal Court is justified . . ." does not rise to the level of argument until it is accompanied by a reason, e.g., " . . . because past examples show that it can be an effective means of deterring human rights abuses." No matter how many times a statement is made, and no matter whether it is shouted or accompanied by fist-pounding certainty, it doesn't become an argument until it is accompanied by information that an audience sees as providing reasons.

- *Third, argument is more than just logic.* Reasons need to be present in order for argument to occur, but at the same time, argument should not be reduced to just the presence of logical reasoning. Instead, argument ought to be thought of as "motivated reasoning" where the motive is to convince an audience to adopt a new belief. Employing logical reasoning that fails to speak to a given audience (e.g., quoting your country's constitution to a group of anarchists), does not constitute argument as we see it. Instead, argument represents the use of logic in the service of developing audience conviction and this means that it is the subset of audience-relevant logic and reasoning that we are most interested in.

*   *Fourth, argument is more than just persuasion.* We don't make arguments just to demonstrate our ability or to hear ourselves speak—persuasion is the ultimate goal. But at the same time, it is only persuasion by means of good reasons that constitutes argument. Repetition may be effective as a persuasive strategy—say something over and over again and it starts to sound like common knowledge—but that doesn't make it an argument. You can "persuade" people with money or the threat of violence—but money and violence do not constitute reasons. Good delivery, eye contact, credibility, confidence, and dynamism are all essential aspects of good communication, but to the extent that they do not offer a reasonable basis for attaching greater truth-value to a claim, they can't be seen as aspects of argument. Persuasion that seeks not just action or recollection, but genuine *conviction* must involve an appeal to the audience's capacity to consider and accept good reasons.

In summary, argument can be seen as assertion and contradiction when accompanied by reasons, logic when motivated by a goal to persuade, and persuasion when accompanied by logical justification. A visual way to consider the relationship between argument, logic, and persuasion is contained in the following figure:

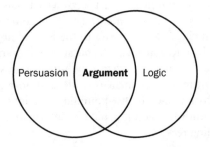

Argument always makes use of logic in the service of persuasion, but it can't be reduced to either logic or persuasion. By focusing on the use of logical reasoning in order to persuade, we are focusing on the most rational means of persuasion and we are focusing as well on applied logic—that is, logic used for a purpose. The next sections will provide a bit more detail about the complementary roles of logic and the audience prior to applying these perspectives to the practical tasks of developing strong and complete arguments for your own public debate.

Informal Logic: The Role of Reasoning

When we first hear the word "argumentation" or especially the word "logic," we may be tempted to envision a formal and mechanical application. Indeed *formal* logic aims toward a mathematical precision such that truth claims can be represented something like this:

$$\forall x, y, z, n \in \mathbf{N}. \ n>2 \wedge x^n + y^n = z^n \Longrightarrow x = 0 \vee y = 0$$

This construction represents formal logic, which carries a consistency and a certainty that permits us to talk in absolute terms about the truth or falsity of claims. Formal logic uses symbols, labels and forms that convert words into abstractions.

Formal logic does not, however, capture the more common elements found when humans give reasons for something. These elements are often captured in the phrase *informal logic*, or the search for the general rules of good reasoning that people use, or ought to use. By calling logic "informal," we don't mean to suggest in any way that it is casual or sloppy, but only to suggest that it eschews mathematical precision in order to include the subjectivities and probabilities that characterize human thinking and reason-giving in most situations. For example, if I make the argument that the death penalty is unjust, there is no way that I can represent my argument in a way that is *true* in any formal sense. Our willingness to see something as unjust is more than a mathematical calculation; it is of necessity a human judgment. But while I can't say that a claim like this is true in a formal sense, I can say that it is more or less assertable based upon the arguments that I have supplied in front of a specific audience. I could, for example, provide the testimony of a respected jurist: U.S. Supreme Court Justice Harry Blackmun concluded that America's experience showed that the death penalty could never be imposed fairly and consistently and said, as a result, "From this day forward, I no longer shall tinker with the machinery of death."[5] Alternatively, I could cite examples from the number of individuals who have been put to death only to subsequently be considered innocent based upon new evidence.[6] Or I could present a moral argument that killing is only philosophically justified in immediate self-defense, and as long as life in prison remains an option, the state need never kill a captured prisoner. Any of these arguments in the right situation and before the right audience could provide a reasonable basis for the audience to attach greater belief to the claim. The arguments do not make the claim "true," but by adding justification, they make the claim more likely to win adherence. Because effectiveness depends not upon an absolute truth standard but upon an audience-won sense of reasonableness, an emphasis on the public dimensions of logic is especially suited to a focus on debates before a large audience.

Enthymeme: The Role of the Audience

Effective argument in a public context involves more than "a connecting series of statements to establish a proposition"; to be effective it must also involve the integration of the advocate's reasoning with the preexisting knowledge, attitudes, and beliefs of an audience.

A substantial role for the audience in argumentation has long been recognized. The classic Greek teacher of rhetoric, Aristotle, captured the essential participation of listeners in the construction of good arguments through his concept of the *enthymeme*. Aristotle saw the foundation of formal reasoning in the syllogism—a series of statements, called premises, leading to a conclusion:

> **Major Premise:** All men are mortal.
> **Minor Premise:** Socrates is a man.
> **Conclusion:** Therefore Socrates is mortal.

The enthymeme is sometimes called a "truncated syllogism," because one of the terms is missing. If, for example, the speaker were to say only, "Socrates is a man, therefore Socrates is mortal," he would be depending upon his listeners to supply the missing premise (that all men are mortal). In other words, his enthymeme builds upon a belief or an attitude that is already held by an audience. This belief or attitude is part of the argument, but because it represents knowledge or belief that is already held by the audience, it need not be expressed explicitly. The utility of the enthymeme, however, is not in saving time. By identifying and adding to what the audience already thinks and knows, the enthymeme creates argument as a joint product of speaker and audience. As we will argue below, the enthymeme is especially fitting for certain types of argument.

For example, contrast the following arguments.

The Scientific Syllogism

Major Premise: All electronic products pose a risk of electrical shock.

Minor Premise: A television is an electronic product.

Conclusion: A television poses a risk of electrical shock.

The Rhetorical Enthymeme

(**Audience Premise:** Many television programs portray violence.)

Support: Studies show that an acceptance of simulated violence causes a tolerance for real violence.

Conclusion: Television is furthering the spread of violence in society.

The syllogism works because it is based upon an absolute and categorical statement: *all electronic products.* . . . In contrast, the sort of judgments and evaluations that more often characterize the most important human disagreements are less likely to take the form of such absolute statements. By dealing in probabilities and relationships, the enthymeme makes a conclusion that is more fitting to the way in which we usually deliberate about human affairs. Notice that in this case the enthymeme "works" only as long as the audience is willing to agree to and supply the identified premise. Average individuals who own a television might be expected to know and concede that television often portrays violence. A group of individuals who don't own televisions, or conversely a group of television executives who believe that television has increased its responsibility and reduced its level of violence in recent years, would be less likely to concede that belief. Thus, the effectiveness of the enthymeme depends to a great extent upon what the audience is bringing to the table. This, however, does not suggest that a good argument is simply that which the audience already agrees with. Instead, a good argument is an argument that builds off of the *reliable* prior beliefs and knowledge of an audience and supplies *additional justification or implication* for that audience. Furthermore, a good argument is one that survives criticism (or "refutation") from a reasonable opposition. In this case, the opposition could either question the extent of violence on television or they could question the relationship between portrayed violence and actual violence. In addition, they could question whether a mere tolerance for violence translates into actual violence. For the argument to be effective it would need to surmount these challenges.

Getting More Specific: The Components of an Argument

Earlier, we defined argument as *the use of reason-giving in an attempt to convince the audience of the truth or value of your perspective*, but at this point we need to get more specific about what counts as "reason-giving." What would lead one audience to consider the enthymeme above to be reasonable while another audience would not? The answer to this question requires an elaboration of the components of an argument. It is a good idea to consider these elements, not because we would refer to them explicitly when constructing arguments, but because we should consult them mentally when we are forming, appreciating, or criticizing arguments. Having a model in mind lets you know what to look for, what to strengthen, and what to attack.

The following model defines an argument as *a claim that is warranted by data*. Each of the central terms in this definition, however, requires a bit of explanation:

> **Claim:** That which you want your audience to ultimately accept. For the purpose of a given argument, this might mean the knowledge or the conclusion that you would like them to believe when the argument is concluded. For example, *adults should be able to choose whether to use marijuana or not* might be a claim advanced by a side that is urging liberalization of laws against the use of this drug.

> **Data:** Additional information given to the audience in order to support the claim. Words that would reasonably follow "because . . ." are offered to provide the audience with a justification for the claim. For example the information that *marijuana has been shown to have only moderate health risks* might be used as data to buttress the previous claim.

Warrant: An assumption or a logical relationship that connects the data to the claim. The additional supporting information (the data) needs to be logically related to the conclusion that you would like the audience to accept (the claim). For that reason, a connective statement that clarifies that relationship should be expressed or should be clearly implied in a complete argument. In the previous example, the warrant *adults should be free to accept moderate risks to their own health* could serve as a logical bridge between the data and the claim. We would emphasize that the warrant cannot be taken for granted as true—it, too, is arguable.

These three basic elements of argument can be represented graphically using a model developed by Professor Stephen Toulmin:[7]

A Basic Model of Argument

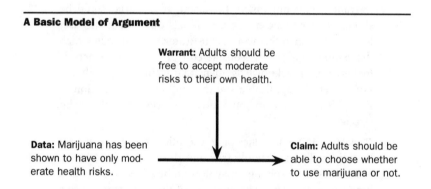

Warrant: Adults should be free to accept moderate risks to their own health.

Data: Marijuana has been shown to have only moderate health risks.

Claim: Adults should be able to choose whether to use marijuana or not.

Viewed in this way, it is possible to see an argument as an effort to get an audience to accept a claim by providing them with additional data that is connected to that claim by a clear warrant. Simply seeing this arrangement of statements in the form of an argument, however, does not mean that the argument is valid, or even necessarily strong. Both the data and the warrant could easily be open to question. Depending upon the situation, a given audience could accept them as self-evident or could look for further backing for these elements. For this reason, there are several other elements of the argument that may be present:

Backing: Additional information used to provide further support for the data or the warrant of an argument. For example, if the claim that marijuana bears only moderate health risks is seen as controversial by a particular audience, then it would make sense to supply research conclusions that document these risks. For example, a World Health Organization study found that most of the effects of marijuana use "are small to moderate in size" and that at current rates of use, marijuana is "unlikely to produce public health problems comparable in scale to those currently produced by alcohol and tobacco."[8] By the same token, if the audience is unlikely to automatically grant the notion that adults should be free to accept moderate risks to their own health, then it would make sense to provide further support for this notion by providing other situations (such as the use of tobacco or alcohol) in which adults are entrusted with similar choices.

Exception[9]: Special circumstances in which the data and warrant would not justify the claim. If the drug could be shown to harm society or individuals other than the user, for example, than this would constitute an instance in which the claim would not be considered true. This component is included as an acknowledgement that claims frequently are not universally applicable and that an honest recognition of a claim's limits can in some circumstances make the claim stronger.

Modality: In the presence of an exception, the claim will not be universally or certainly true and thus a qualifier like "in most cases" or "probably" may need to be added to serve as a limit upon the claim. The modality of the argument answers the question, "How certain are we that the claim is reliable?" The modality can highlight possibilities for qualifying or answering the argument.

We will add these elements to the basic model presented earlier to provide an expanded view of the elements of an argument:

An Expanded Model of Argument

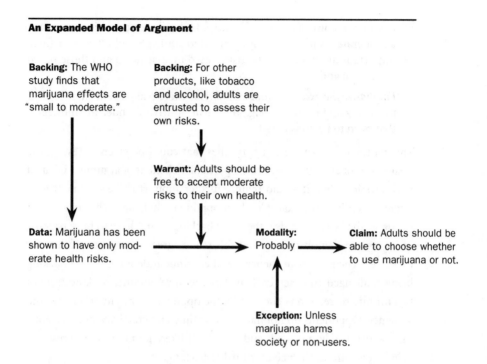

This model will be useful to advocates while they are understanding and evaluating arguments; in a public debate, it will not be as useful when they are expressing those arguments. That is, it wouldn't be wise in all likelihood for public debaters to say "I would now like to present my warrant...," simply because the term wouldn't mean much to an audience that is unfamiliar with Toulmin's model. It would be wise, however, for debaters to think about the warrant, or other elements, when they are thinking about how to defend or attack the argument. A debater who wished to advance the claim identified above could use the model as a mental checklist to answer the question, "How far do I need to go?" In other words a debater should ask, "Will this particular audience require an explicit warrant for my claim? Will my warrant require backing? Will my data be seen as sufficient, or will it, too, require further backing?" A debater wishing to attack this argument would have several options:

- *Question the data and its backing.* Was the World Health Organization study exhaustive? Are there other studies that contradict this result? What is their standard for what makes a health risk "moderate?"

- *Question the warrant and its backing.* Is the choice to subject oneself to a moderate health risk always granted to adults? Should it be? Are there important differences in the risks posed by marijuana and those posed by alcohol and tobacco?
- *Emphasize the exception and modality.* Is there real and substantial harm to society and nonusers (e.g., the harm of driving under the influence) that need to be considered?

This represents a sample of approaches that could be taken in testing the weaknesses of an argument. Once a particular element of argument is called into question, then it would require further support if the argument is to remain standing. For example, if an opponent challenged the backing for the data (the W.H.O. study), then that backing would have to have backing of its own (a demonstration that this study agrees with other studies, for example). The process in theory could continue indefinitely (each backing being challenged and each challenge met with yet another backing . . .) but this infinite regression is checked by the opponents, the situation, and the audience. Opponents do not have infinite time and creativity, not all claims can be *reasonably* disputed, audiences will likely grant some premises as being true without the need for further backing, etc.

In summary, a successful argument is a claim that is reasonably warranted by good data and capable of surviving all reasonable challenges. Because of the central role played by the notion of "reasonability" in this formula, our next subject is to consider the ways of locating and using the premises which underlie that sense of reasonability.

Locating and Using Audience and Opponent Premises

A premise is an element of your argument that the particular audience and opponent are likely to accept without explicit reasons. At first, this notion might seem counterintuitive: "Willing to accept? But if the other side is willing to accept it, then how are we having a debate?" But the fact is that opponents do not have to disagree about *everything* in order for a debate to take place. All debates, and all public argument generally, require some starting points. Two arguers may disagree on whether there should be an international criminal court, but still agree that the world needs *a way* to discourage crimes against humanity. They may agree that the government has a responsibility to regulate harmful products, but disagree over whether marijuana is a harmful product or not. These areas of agreement are likely to be found in all arguments. As Professor Robert O. Weiss noted, "If two individuals agree about everything, they don't need to debate; if they disagree about everything, they can't debate."[10] Clarifying where the agreements and disagreements lie, then, is essential to good debate.

The issue of locating and using premises is a practical matter of separating the claims you'll need to support from the claims that you will simply need to invoke or imply. One perspective on public advocacy might say that, "since this is a public *debate*, then nothing should be taken for granted—all arguments and claims should receive full support, whether we think that our audience or our opponents will grant them or not." That perspective may sound appropriate, but a bit of thought will quickly reveal that it is logically and practically impossible to support *all* potential elements of any argument. For example:

> The nations of the world should agree to reduce carbon emissions, because that will limit greenhouse gases.
>
> *So, why do we want to limit greenhouse gases?*
> Because that helps us limit global warming.
>
> *So, why do we want to limit global warming?*
> Because that helps us save the polar ice caps.
>
> *So, why do we want to save the polar ice caps?*
> Because that prevents the sea from rising.
>
> *So, why do we want to keep the sea from rising?*
> Because that will protect population centers and save countless lives.
>
> *So, why do we want to protect population centers and save countless lives?*
> Because human life is important and we have an obligation to defend it.
>
> *Why? . . .*

Of course, this exchange could continue indefinitely. But if your opponent is reasonable, the need for further justification will stop at some point. Why? Because the advocates will have reached a *premise*, a point that will be conceded by the advocates and their audience. Exactly where the premise lies will differ, naturally, based upon the situation. In some situations, the premise in the above exchange would be reached long before the opponent asked why it's important to defend human life: at a scientific conference on climate change, for example, it would probably be conceded by all that significant global warming would be a disaster and attention would focus instead on the means necessary to control it. In other words, the premise would be reached after the first question above.

The essential step in locating premises, then, is to figure out exactly what your audience and your opponent would be likely to concede without further argument. While nothing can substitute for a specific analysis of your own audience, opponent, and situation (see chapters 5 and 6), there are a few general considerations that apply here.

- *Use all available signs.* In most cases, you won't be able to read the minds of your audience and your opponents, and you also will not be able to poll them in advance on all of the specific elements of your argument. However, you can employ your best efforts to consider the motivation for the event ("Why are we holding it? Why did the audience come? What does that tell us about their opinions on this situation?"), the demographics of those who will be there (age, race, sex, etc.), the situation and any recent events that may influence their understanding and their commitments. It is also helpful to ask whether you are debating before an organized group or before an "accidental group" that is drawn together just by virtue of the debate itself. In the former case, it is possible for you to consider the history of decisions that the group has made and stances that it has taken in determining the premises that it will likely hold.

- *Check your assumptions.* Predict carefully and with a knowledge that you might be wrong. Neither demographics nor situation nor personal interest necessarily determine one's point of view. The rich man may support tax increases for the wealthy. The black woman may oppose affirmative action based on race. While we should be sensitive to the likely and predictable stances of our audience and opponents, we should never blithely assume that they hold for each person. The questioning period can be a good time to check and see what premises your opponent is likely to concede ("So, saving money is a good idea, right?"). Even in cases in which we have a good reason to believe that a given premise is reliable in a specific situation, it makes good sense to check that assumption verbally by referring to it in your speech: "... and I believe that we all agree that a rising sealevel covering Venice, Miami and

Amsterdam would be a bad thing." Explicitly stating that agreement can serve as a reminder as well. For example, if you were debating in front of members of America's National Academy of Sciences, you could note, "just last year, this body concluded that rapid climate change could have dramatic and far-reaching implications for both human society, and the ecosystem."[11] In this way, you signal that you don't find it necessary to spend time justifying a premise that has already been established.

- *When in doubt, justify.* If you are not sure whether a given premise will be conceded or not, then you are safer offering the argument anyway. Time will naturally prevent you from justifying everything, but if you have a good reason to suspect that some in the audience may find a premise controversial, then turning it into an argument can't hurt. In addition, if you think that your opponent might challenge you on a point, then it makes strategic sense to beat them to the punch by providing an argument for your stance before they get a chance to challenge it.

- *No premise is guaranteed to remain a premise.* One of the most positive, but also most unpredictable, aspects of a debate is that anything can be open to challenge. As long as the debate is being conducted in a setting that allows freedom of expression to its advocates, the debaters can at any time challenge a view that the other side has assumed to be an unassailable premise. They may even challenge a view that the audience would never have expected to need justification. Say, for example, that one team of debaters presumes that their audience and their opponents would support the legal concept of a right to privacy. They believe that the debate will center on the question of "how much privacy?" and not on the question of whether privacy itself is a good thing or not. The audience too, they assume, will think that privacy is a good thing. In the debate, however, they are surprised to learn that the crux of their opponent's case is that "privacy" is a negative concept overall: it breeds a philosophy of isolated individualism and harms the spirit of community. Once questioned, the team's premise that "privacy is good" now has to become an argument in answer to their opponent's challenge. Pressed, they have to think of reasons why the existence of a private sphere might be compatible with community, maybe even essential to community. So: even though premises serve as a foundation for our disagreements, that foundation is never 100 percent reliable. A premise represents our best effort to find a starting point or an ending point for our argumentation, but once challenged, all of the participants who are committed to a debate need to defend their assumptions.

Finding, Analyzing, and Using External Support (Evidence)

The reasoning process begins, then, with the articulation of claims (what you want your audience to believe), and the development of claims into arguments—that is, the identification of the warrants and data that support your claims. As we have just discussed, some parts of your argument can be identified as premises—that is, as points that do not need to be argued but that will be accepted by both your opponents and your audience. But that leaves the claims that do need to be argued and that require support. The next stage is to begin the process of developing that support. There are two distinct yet complementary sources that we can turn to in developing our arguments: ourselves and others. The use of our own resources of logic and reasoning is essential, but so too is the use of support from others. The use of external support (sometimes called "evidence" or "research") is an important complement to our own knowledge and reasoning in many situations. This section will focus on the question of when and how to use external support.

Step One: Know When to Use External Support

Few of us are experts on everything on which we speak. For that reason we frequently need to find material support for our own ideas by researching the ideas and knowledge of others. Citing outside sources that are neutral and authoritative can also build our own credibility. Some speakers feel that by using external support or evidence they are somehow silencing their own voices and just parroting the views of others. Certainly, this is an extreme to be avoided, but equally worth avoiding is the extreme of just relying on your own assertions when you don't have the knowledge or expertise to back them up. The effective use of external support can be represented in the following diagram:

External Support—Finding a Happy Medium

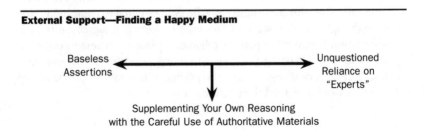

Baseless Assertions ←——————————→ Unquestioned Reliance on "Experts"

Supplementing Your Own Reasoning
with the Careful Use of Authoritative Materials

Some claims (matters of logic, perspective, or the application of common knowledge) may be supported through our own knowledge and reasoning. Other claims, however, require that we turn to outside resources. When we lack the knowledge, the experience, or the expertise to fully support a claim, *or* when we need to build our own credibility for an audience, then we would help our own case by turning to external support. One communication researcher reviewed the substantial body of research on the question and concluded that, as a general effect, the use of evidence enhances persuasiveness for all sources when the evidence is presented with named sources and with identified source qualifications.[12] And the more involved the audience is with a topic, the more the use of evidence matters, not only for its probative and informative effects, but also as an essential way of building credibility for the speaker. Thus, there are two reasons to use external support: 1) to support your arguments and 2) to signify outwardly that you have prepared, and are therefore worthy of belief.

Step Two: Brainstorm Prior to Research

Before beginning the search for useful sources, it helps to take a few moments to clarify what you are looking for:

- Analyze the proposition. Identify the main issues and terms contained in the topic for the debate.

- Identify your thesis. Make sure it can be expressed in a single, clear, and simple sentence.

- Generate a list of synonyms and related words for the key words in your thesis and your proposition.

- Make a list of the questions that you will need answered (information that you don't have at present).

- Make a list of the controversial claims that you expect to make that would most likely require external support in order to convince a skeptical audience.

- Identify the timeframe in which you are most interested in locating information. Matters of current events (politics, economics, international relations, etc.) will likely require very recent support, while matters that are philosophical, legal or moral will have less of a requirement for currency.

Step Three: Find Useful Material Sources

The next step in gathering external material is to locate sources (books, articles, Internet Websites, etc.) that will be relevant and appropriate to your topic. At this stage, it is important to use whatever is available to you at local libraries, newsstands, or universities. Using the widest variety of sources will also ensure that you are not just receiving information from one particular (and limited) perspective or area of expertise.

As you search for information, consider including the following sources:

- Books
- Encyclopedias
- Newspapers
- Magazines
- Specialized journals
- Computer databases
- CD-Roms
- Electronic publications on the Internet
- Organizations' Webpages on the internet
- Interest groups
- Government officials
- Independent experts (university professors, activists, etc.)

For a source to be useful, it should meet the following criteria:

1. *Authoritative*. It is from someone who is an expert on the subject or who has investigated various facts and opinions.
2. *Timely*. It is recent enough that the facts haven't substantially changed since it was written.
3. *Clear*. It makes understandable claims supported by identifiable reasons.
4. *Pertinent*. It supplies information relevant to the points that you would like to make.

Step Four: Locate Useful Information and Quotations Within Your Sources

The next step is to locate and record the information that you may use in the debate. If you have secured a photocopy, a computer printout, or a personal copy of a text you would like to use in your debate, then you can mark that text indicating the beginning and ending of useful quotations and sections.

The sections that you decide to keep for potential use should meet several criteria. The selected portion should:

1. *Support or inform a clear argument for your side.* Background information is important, but the relevance of any information should be tested to see if it leads you back to a relevant argument in the debate.

2. *Include claims as well as reasons, not just the author's assertion.* "Space-based missile defense will never work" is a powerful statement, but it remains just a statement and not an argument unless it is accompanied by a reason—no matter who said it.

3. *Be quoted "in context."* When you use the words or ideas of another, you need to ensure that you are not employing those words or ideas "out of context"—that is, in a manner inconsistent with the author's intent. The question is, "Would the author agree to the way in which you have used his or her words, including your selection, emphasis, and implication?" Fair representation demands that your best answer to that question be "yes."

The sort of arguments that you are likely to find in external material parallels the forms of reasoning that we may find in any argument. These forms of reasoning are covered in the next section. In selecting and evaluating the worth of the information that you've found, you may wish to keep in mind the following uses and considerations:

External Material May Be Used To . . .	But You Should Ensure That . . .
Provide a factual description: *"The process of cloning has several steps . . . "*	• Your source is qualified to describe the matter in question. • The description is clear enough to be understood by the audience. • The description is complete and representative.
Introduce statistical support: *"Unemployment has increased to more than 7% in the last month . . . "*	• The statistic uses clear units of measurement and an appropriate base-line. • The statistic is recent enough to be relevant. • The statistic uses a reasonable sampling method (e.g., random sampling). • The statistic includes an indication of reliability (e.g., level of significance, confidence interval, etc.)[13]

External Material May Be Used To . . .	But You Should Ensure That . . .
Describe the results of research: *"Viewing simulated violence in a laboratory setting causes people to tolerate violence . . . "*	• The research appears in a peer-reviewed publication. • The methodology of the research is identified and supported by the practices of the field. • The strength and the significance of the relationship is reported.
Report what happened: *"After three days of protests, the police entered the building and seized the painting . . . "*	• Your source was in a position to observe or to consult reliable records. • Your source is free from an obvious bias or conflict of interest.
Provide a qualified opinion: *"The President is far more effective in matters of foreign policy than any of his challengers . . . "*	• Your source has acknowledged expertise on the matter on which they are offering an opinion. • Your source has identified the support for their reasoning, i.e., the basis on which their opinion rests. • Your source is free from an obvious bias or conflict of interest.
Illustrate with an example or a narrative: *"Joe suffers from diabetes, but unfortunately, his employer does not provide any health insurance . . . "*	• Your example is real (not invented, or a composite). • Your example is reasonably typical of the phenomenon you are describing. • Your example is free from exaggerated appeals to emotion.

Step Five: Record Your Information in a Useful Format

Once you have found a clear, well-supported, useful, and in-context section that you would like to keep, the next step is to save it in some fashion so that you can find it easily when you are preparing your case and subsequent speeches. One of the easiest ways to retain information is to keep it on an index card with other information that will help you to use the material in an argument. Your note card should include the following information:

1. *A label.* One short sentence, phrased as an argument, that identifies your most likely use for the information during the debate. The shortest and clearest labels will often be formed in a subject-verb-object fashion: e.g., "The International Court upholds fairness."

2. *The source.* Include all information necessary for you to locate this source again (to check for errors or to find additional information), to reference the material during your speech, to provide information to others (e.g., if you are quoted in the media), or to build credibility

for the information if that credibility is challenged. This section should include the name of the author, his or her qualifications, and if published, the name of the article, the name of journal, newspaper or book, its publication date, and the page number of the specific material that you are using. Having this full information will prevent the practice of making empty references such as "I've read that ..." or "experts say ..." that do not carry much if any credibility.

3. *The quotation or information itself.* If you are quoting, then be careful to reproduce the text exactly as it appeared in print (it is easiest just to cut it out of the article, presuming you have a photocopy).

Once it is completed, your index card may look like this:

> **Your Label**   a clear sentence, phrased as an argument
>
> **The Source**   Author, his or her qualifications, the name of the article, the name of the journal, newspaper or book, its publication date, and the page number of the specific material that you are using.
>
> **The Quotation or Paraphrase**   ". . . . .
> . . . .
> . . . .
> . . . ."

Of course the index card represents fairly low-level technology in today's computer age. Many debaters have abandoned the practice of taking notes on paper and organize their information in computer spreadsheets or document files instead. These methods have their advantages, the biggest being the ability to search for a specific piece of text (e.g., "Where is the quote that includes 'long national nightmare?'"). But one advantage that the lowly index card still retains is its ability to be easily sorted and transported from the library to the stage. In the heat of the moment, when placing the final touches on their notes prior to stepping up to the lectern, most speakers find that it is still easier to handle a small index card than it is to fuss with a laptop. Thus, even if you do gather and keep your information electronically (which is increasingly easier to do thanks to electronic databases and the Internet), it is still a good idea to print out your notes and keep them in a sortable card-like format as you prepare your speeches and engage in your debate.

Step Six: Use Your External Material in Your Speech

The ultimate purpose for collecting evidence is, of course, to use it in a speech. When presenting the information, remember that it is not the existence of the material but how it is used that best promotes persuasion. A great deal of empirical research has focused on the extent to which evidence promotes persuasion. Researchers long felt that the results were mixed: sometimes the evidence seemed to help the speaker, and other times it did not. Argumentation researcher John Reinard, however, analyzed the major studies to date and found a consistent result: when advocates identified and qualified their sources, then the use of evidence enhanced persuasion, but when advocates instead simply named a source without qualifying it (e.g., "Daniel Denning said . . . "), or used no evidence, then persuasion was reduced.[14] Thus, it is important to remember that the "who says?" part of the evidence is the most important part in a public context. Using external support is simply a form of reasoning, viz., reasoning by authority. If the reasoning isn't strong (i.e., if we are given no reason to consider the cited source as a credible authority), then the argument isn't strong.

In addition to presenting enough information to encourage the audience to place trust in the source of the information, advocates should also ensure that they are providing content that aids their case in a clear and compelling way. Debaters should always ask themselves, "Why am I reading this instead of just making the argument on my own?" Answers like " . . . because this source uses an example" or "because she references data," or "because he provides particularly powerful language," or "because this organization will be seen as highly credible to my audience" are all good answers.

Finally, advocates should remember that their time is finite and frequently quite short in a public debate. Long quotations and intricately developed arguments from another source may be quite compelling, but if you are not able to boil them down and reduce them to a very concise expression, then perhaps those arguments should be left for another occasion. Remember that although the audience will want you to support your arguments, your audience will want to hear from *you* and not from a bunch of experts that you have brought in on index cards. The best support is

The Article

Legalization of narcotics: myths and reality.

BYLINE: Califano, Joseph A.

BODY:
When the high priests of America's political right and left as articulate as the National Review's William F. Buckley and The New York Times' Anthony Lewis peddle the same drug legalization line it is time to shout caveat emptor—buyer beware. The boomlet to legalize drugs like heroin, cocaine and marijuana that they, and magazines like New York, are trying to propagate is founded in myths, not realities, and it is the nation's children who could suffer long-lasting permanent damage.

Myth: Legalization works well in European countries.

Reality: The ventures of Switzerland, England, the Netherlands, and Italy into drug legalization have had disastrous consequences. Switzerland's "Needle Park," touted as a way to restrict a few hundred heroin addicts to a small area, turned into a grotesque tourist attraction of 20,000 heroin addicts and junkies that had to be closed down before it infected the city of Zurich. England's foray into allowing any doctor to prescribe heroin quickly was curbed as heroin use increased.

In the Netherlands, anyone over age 17 can drop into a marijuana "coffee shop" and pick types of marijuana like one might choose flavors of ice cream. Adolescent pot use there jumped nearly 200% while it was dropping by 66% in the U.S. As crime and availability of drugs rose and complaints from city residents about the decline in their quality of life multiplied, the Dutch parliament moved to trim back the number of marijuana distribution shops in Amsterdam. Dutch persistence in selling pot has angered European neighbors because its wide-open attitude toward marijuana is believed to be spreading pot and other drugs beyond the Netherlands' borders.

Italy infrequently is mentioned by advocates of legalization, despite its lenient drug laws. Personal possession of small amounts of drugs has not been a crime in Italy since 1975, other than a brief period of recriminalization between 1990 and 1993. (Even then, Italy permitted an individual to possess one dose of a drug.) Under decriminalization, possession of two to three doses of drugs such as heroin generally was exempt from criminal sanction. Today, Italy has 300,000 addicts, the highest rate of heroin addiction in Europe. Seventy percent of all AIDS cases in Italy are attributable to drug use.

The Index Card

Legalization Increases Use—Netherlands Proves

Joseph Calfinao, Frmr U.S. Sec. Health, Ed., Welfare, <u>Society</u> May 15, 1998.

In the Netherlands, <u>anyone</u> over age 17 can drop into a marijuana "coffee shop" and pick types of marijuana like one might choose flavors of ice cream. Adolescent pot use there <u>jumped nearly 200%</u> while it was dropping by 66% in the U.S. As crime and availability of drugs rose and <u>complaints</u> from city residents about the <u>decline in their quality of life</u> multiplied, the Dutch parliament moved to trim back the number of marijuana distribution shops in Amsterdam.

And, how it would sound in your speech

If we were to make policies against marijuana more liberal, we would see an increase in drug use and crime. This was the experience of the Dutch. Former U.S. Secretary of Health, Education, and Welfare, Joseph Califano, observed that "In the Netherlands, anyone over age 17 can drop into a marijuana 'coffee shop' and pick types of marijuana like one might choose flavors of ice cream. Adolescent pot use there jumped nearly 200% while it was dropping by 66% in the U.S." Thus greater freedom means greater abuse.

going to be clear, vivid, to-the-point, and *brief.* Those familiar with competitive debate may have noticed that in some formats debaters rely on very long quotations and spend much of their time *reading* rather than *speaking.* That style may be appropriate in a setting that places a primary focus on policy analysis rather than on communicating to a common audience, but in a public setting debaters should try to avoid any quotations that require them to read for more than a couple of sentences or so—unless the impact of a longer quote is likely to be very powerful. One useful technique is to alternate between paraphrasing and quoting (being careful, of course, to convey the author's intent accurately and not to represent as a quotation something that is actually a paraphrase).

The example on the previous page shows how we might move from finding material in an article, to placing it on an index card, to finally using it in a speech. This evidence would carry an appreciable weight in a public debate. Not only is it from a former government official at the Cabinet level (the equivalent of a European minister) with experience in drug policies, but it also contains a clear international comparison and concrete numbers ("a 200% increase") along with a discussion of the implications of those numbers (increases in crime and declining quality of life). Finally, notice that the quotation as expressed in the speech is "framed" by the advocate's own words. Instead of just saying, "Here is what the former official has to say . . . .," the debater begins with his own claim ("If we were to make policies against marijuana more liberal, we would see an increase in drug use and crime"), and then supports that conclusion with the data from the former official, before ending with a reiteration of his own claim ("Thus greater freedom means greater abuse"). In this way, we get the sense that the advocate has *remained* an advocate. Instead of letting Mr. Califano do all the talking on this point, the phrasing makes it clear that the advocate's argument is primarily and ultimately an argument that he is making himself, with the support of Mr. Califano's testimony.

The conclusion to be drawn is that while evidence plays a supporting role, and can never fully replace the reasoning of the debater, there are many instances in which the authority and the specificity of quoted evidence can add to our understanding of the issues and make for a better and more persuasive argument.

Developing Successful Patterns of Reasoning

Now that you have learned about your subject area by making use of external sources, the next step is to draw upon these resources and the resources of your own mind in order to construct powerful reasons. The use of expert testimony that we discussed above is one form of reasoning (argument by authority), but it is far from the only form. Audiences don't form beliefs simply based on what an expert has said; they also form beliefs based on sound reasoning appeals. Indeed the best expert testimony will be effective not just because of the credibility of the source, but also because of the reasoning that the source displays. Audiences are likely to judge that claims are well supported when they conform to one of several familiar patterns of reasoning. The main patterns that we will discuss here are reasoning by deduction, example, cause, analogy, and sign. Each of these forms will be discussed and illustrated below.

The audience, of course, is not expected to know the specifics of these reasoning forms. They are not likely to know the difference between deduction and sign reasoning, but they will have a sense of what sounds like a "good reason" to them and what does not. The value of knowing these forms of reasoning lies in analysis, not in presentation. That is, a debater wouldn't say: "And now, if you are ready, here comes an analogy!" Instead, she might simply use the analogy knowing that the audience will recognize it and make sense of it. Knowing in your own mind that it *is* an analogy, however, and not a sign or a deduction, will help you to know what makes the argument strong and what may make it weak. In short, thinking about argument forms helps you to construct them and to critique them. Being able to recognize them isn't just a matter of making an academic classification; it is a way of knowing what to look for and what to emphasize.

Reasoning by Deduction

Deductive reasoning consists of moving from general principles to specific conclusions. The most familiar syllogisms taught in school are usually examples of deduction: All cats are mammals; Fifi is a cat; therefore, Fifi is a mammal. The reasoning works by a process of transference: that which we know about the general category or principle is transferred to the specific instance.

Violent acts committed against innocent people are always immoral, and that is why terrorism is immoral.

Warrant: Violent acts
against innocent people
are always immoral.

(**Data:** Terrorism consists   **Claim:** Terrorism
of violent acts against   is immoral.
innocent people.)

In this case, we are offered an argument by definition. The advocate is relying on the audience's knowledge of what terrorism is and adding the general principle that such violence against innocent people is always immoral in order to support the claim that terrorism (the particular case) is also immoral. (You will note that this example is another enthymeme: the data part of the argument is left unspoken, to be supplied by the audience.)

The advantage of deduction is that it is *structurally certain*, that is, if the support is true, then the conclusion must be true as well. If it really is the case that *all* violence against innocent people is immoral, and it really is true that terrorism consists of such violence, then the conclusion follows inescapably. The problem with deduction is that it rests upon the absoluteness or uniformity of some sort of category. Indeed, one way to recognize deduction is to look for the presence or implied presence of a word like "all" (e.g., *all* men are mortal . . .). This patterns works well in the case of an argument by definition, which is what we have with our terrorism example. Such a pattern may also work well in fields that embrace absolutes: religion, mathematics, and some philosophy. But arguments that deal with the vagaries of human and social affairs are more likely to be characterized by tendencies and relationships, not by absolute categorical connections. For that reason, many arguments that we might find in the public sphere would really be better characterized as *sham deductions*. Consider the following:

Baltimore is an American city, thus we shouldn't really expect it to have a very effective mass transit system.

The argument breaks down as follows: "American cities lack effective mass transit, Baltimore is an American city, therefore Baltimore lacks effective mass transit." The problem for this argument is that for it to work as a deductive claim, the first statement would have to be that "*All* American cities lack effective mass transit"; any visitor to New York, San Francisco or the District of Columbia would know that this is not true. Even though it may be true that *most* American cities emphasize automobile transit rather than mass transit, the statement isn't a universal; thus, we can't treat it as absolute. The claim that Baltimore lacks effective mass transit may be true (and one of your authors can assure you that it is) but the reasoning that supports it in this case is not.

Thus, advocates relying on deduction need to ensure that they are reasoning from a principle that really is categorically true. Advocates replying to an instance of deduction need only come up with one exception in order to indicate that the principle doesn't always hold true.

Inductive Reasoning

Deductive reasoning, as we noted above, moves from general principles to specific conclusions. Inductive reasoning moves in the opposite direction—that is, inductive reasoning begins with known, particular truths, and then draws a general conclusion on the basis of those truths. It would be an example of inductive reasoning to say: "Baltimore has no effective mass transit; the same is true of Detroit, Cincinnati, Hartford, Los Angeles, and Kansas City. Therefore, we can conclude that American cities do not have effective mass transit." The patterns of reasoning that follow (by example, analogy, cause and sign) are all types of inductive reasoning.

Reasoning by Example

One of the easiest (though not necessarily one of the strongest) patterns of reasoning is reasoning by example, which involves the presentation of one or more instances of the claim being true. To reason by example is to move from the truth of a particular instance to a general conclusion. If deduction means knowing that the filling of the whole pie must also be the filling of the piece of the pie, then reasoning by example means reasoning that the filling of your piece of the pie is most likely the filling of the rest of the pie as well. This is also a process of transference but moving in the other direction: what we know about the specific instance is inferred to be also true about the more general category.

> Promoting national parks is an effective way to protect the environment. A network of more than twenty national parks and sanctuaries in Belize has preserved that country's rich bio-diversity.[15]

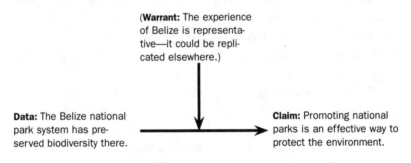

(**Warrant:** The experience of Belize is representative—it could be replicated elsewhere.)

Data: The Belize national park system has preserved biodiversity there.

Claim: Promoting national parks is an effective way to protect the environment.

The unstated warrant in this case, as in the case of all arguments by example, is that the example is representative. The assumption is that we can reason from the specific to the general because the specific in this case is a good example that doesn't differ in important ways from the larger case. Examples that are exceptional or unique are not good examples, at least from the perspective of reasoning. If Belize were the *only* nation in which national parks served as havens for bio-diversity, then the claim would hardly be reasonable.

This notion of representativeness can be difficult to assess. After all, if we knew what was true of the whole category, then we would hardly need the example. Often we use examples precisely because we cannot speak to the whole. The modern public opinion survey can be seen as an illustration in this regard. If we really want to know what British citizens think of Prime Minister Tony Blair, we would have to ask all of them. We can't do that, so instead we ask a very small minority, perhaps only a thousand or so. Such polls can be inaccurate, of course, if the people that you ask are not a representative sample. We could imagine a researcher interviewing people coming out of an unemployment office and concluding that nearly all Britons despise the prime minister. In reality, however, public opinion polls tend to be very accurate because researchers pay a great deal of attention to the representativeness of their samples. By ensuring that the small subset they consult contains the same diversity as the population as a whole (that is, the same mix of sex, age, income, religion, and dozens of other variables), survey researchers produce conclusions with a high level of reliability.

Those who do not conduct surveys but instead rely on more familiar examples are still subject to parallel considerations. They must also ensure that their example, at least in a rough sense, is typical of the category that they are talking about. If you wanted to give the audience a sense of the horrors of a particular disease, for instance, and you picked an example of an individual afflicted with the most extreme and horrific suffering you could find, then you might be building your emotional appeal but not your logical appeal. While examples may have other than logical uses (e.g., producing vivid images and creating identification), the use of the examples as a tool of reasoning always carries the implicit warrant "this is typical." Public debaters who are employing examples for that purpose should justify the representativeness of their example (e.g., "Joe is just one of thousands of individuals dealing daily with these symptoms . . .") and those who are in the role of responding to examples would be wise to question their representativeness (e.g., "So, how typical is it that the effects are this extreme?").

Reasoning by Cause

From the time we were small, we have all made sense of the world around us by understanding causal connections. We ask, "What happens when I do this?" and note the results of our action. This is how we explore and test our hypotheses. Forming and supporting causal connections remain a fundamental part of the act of advocating and evaluating. A *causal* relationship can be defined as a functional connection in which the presence or change in one thing results in the presence or change in another. Smoking causes lung cancer, sex causes pregnancy, and weight lifting causes the development of stronger bones. The simple existence of a causal relationship may be the focus of an argument, but more often the implication of a causal relationship is likely to be the most important part of the argument.

> People become infected with Guinea Worm Disease when they are forced to drink stagnant water infected with a para-

site. Thus, if we provide people with safe sources of drinking water, we can substantially decrease Guinea Worm Disease.

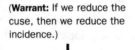

(**Warrant:** If we reduce the cuse, then we reduce the incidence.)

Data: People become infected with Guinea Worm Disease when they are forced to drink stagnant water infected with a parasite.

Claim: If we provide people with safe sources of drinking water, we can substatially decrease Guinea Worm Disease.

In this example, the advocate argues that because we know the cause, then we know the likely effects of a cause's removal. To say that "A" causes "B," means that in the presence of "A" we would expect to find "B," or that when we find more of "A" then we would find more of "B" or a greater risk of "B" as well. This simple one-to-one relationship, however, masks a number of distinctions between various types of cause. For example, something can be a *sole* cause (e.g., decapitation causes death) or a *contributory* cause (e.g., his lack of attention while driving on icy roads in a poorly maintained car caused the accident). In addition, a cause can be *necessary* or it can be *sufficient*. In the case of a necessary cause, the effect can't be present without the presence of the cause—the cause is necessary for the effect. In the case of a sufficient cause, the cause alone is all we need in order to produce the effect—the cause is sufficient for the effect. Let's take the example of fire. Oxygen is a necessary cause for fire (you can't have a fire without it), but it is not sufficient (simply having oxygen doesn't mean that there is a fire). Oxygen, a fuel source, and a spark, however, are sufficient for a fire. While these distinctions on what we mean by "cause" may seem technical, they do make a difference: rarely do causal statements on matters of social issues convey a direct and automatic one-to-one relationship. That is, the person is incorrect who thinks that she has denied the argument that smoking causes cancer by mentioning her uncle who smoked every day of his adult life and lived to be 100. A causal argument expresses a relationship that may have a fair amount of subtlety to it.

One specific danger to avoid is the attributed causal relationship that exists simply due to temporal or physical proximity. We can't assume that because two events occur together (in space or in time), then one is caused by another. For example, the months in which the highest number of frozen Popsicles are sold are also the months in which the greatest number of drownings occur: the higher the sales, the greater the number of drownings. That doesn't mean, however, that Popsicles cause drownings.[16] Popsicles and drownings may simply occur together coincidentally or, as is more likely in this case, both may be caused by a third factor (the onset of summer, a time when people swim more—and hence are more likely to drown—and have greater reasons to enjoy cooling snacks like Popsicles). Whether it's coincidence, or a third factor, that makes a statistical correlation between drowning and Posicles, the fact remains that they do not have a direct relationship with each other. (It would be different, of course, if you could show that people drowned when they were swimming far out to sea to eat Popsicles. . . .) When making or responding to causal arguments, it makes sense to ask a number of questions:

- Does the effect consistently follow from the cause?
- Is the cause alone capable of producing the effect?
- Are there other potential causes?
- What is the magnitude of the relationship (that is, what quantity of the cause is necessary to produce a specific amount of the effect)?
- Is there a *functional* relationship between the cause and the effort, or do they merely co-occur?

Reasoning by Analogy

When a famous and highly paid movie actor or actress needs to do something dangerous in the course of filming a movie, the director will generally use a "double"—that is, someone who looks like the actor or actress and has a greater willingness to risk bodily injury. So one person stands in for the other. An analogy is like that, in the sense that it uses one fact or phenomena to stand in for another: we talk about one thing in order to draw conclusions about another. Of course, you may have noticed that we just used an analogy in order to describe reasoning by analogy. More specifically, though, reasoning by analogy consists of comparing two cases or events and arguing that what is true of one case or event is also likely to be true of the other.

> Just as a nation would expect sovereignty within its own territory, tribes of indigenous people should have a right to control their own land.

(Warrant: Nations are comparable to tribes of indigenous people.)

Data: A nation would expect sovereignty within its own territory.   ⟶   **Claim:** Tribes of indigenous people should have a right to control their own land.

In this example, the advocate invites the audience to transfer what they know or feel about a familiar situation (the concept of national sovereignty) to what is perhaps a less familiar situation (the concept of sovereignty for indigenous tribes within nations). The warrant for all arguments by analogy will be that a sufficient level of comparability exists between the two compared cases or events. The weakness in the argument by analogy is therefore the possibility that important differences exist. Certainly, it could be charged that there are important differences between nations and indigenous tribes. Nations generally have international recognition and standing that tribes lack. However, it could be argued that important similarities exist that would support the argument. Indigenous tribes do have systems of law and government as well as customs that bind the population together. It is conceivable that an individual might think of himself as a Navajo first and an American second, for example. The issue is not whether there are differences, since there are *always* differences between the two cases. The issue is whether there are *differences that matter to the conclusion.* You could say that indigenous tribes are not like nations because they are not as large, but should their size affect the control over the land that they do have? Arguably not. (After all, if rights were commensurate with size, you would have to conclude that China has more rights than San Marino.)

In addition to assessing the comparability of the two cases, it is important to distinguish between two types of analogies, that are used in two different ways. Argument by analogy usually consists of a *literal* analogy in which we assert that there is actual and substantial similarity between the two cases. This is distinct from a figurative analogy. Figurative analogies also assert a comparison between two elements, but do so in a more stylistic or metaphorical way. When we began this section you may have objected, "But actors aren't like arguments!" And you would be right—fundamentally, one is a human being and the other is a concept. In this case, though, the difference isn't necessarily a problem because our analogy was merely figurative and was being used, as most figurative analogies are used, to explain something in a vivid and memorable way; in other words, we weren't trying to prove that something about actors was also true about analogies (for one thing, analogies are not willing to risk bodily injury!). That is an important distinction. When we use an analogy to prove something, then we are asserting that there is sufficient real comparability between the two cases to serve as a logical warrant. Argument by analogy can be a useful way of encouraging audiences to see similarities and transfer their knowledge and evaluation from the familiar to the less familiar, but care must be taking in creating and assessing analogies to ensure that the elements being compared truly ought to be compared.

Reasoning by Sign

If you want to know if it is warm outside, and you look out the window and see people walking around in shorts and T-shirts, then that is a good sign. If a boy wants to ask someone out on a date and she says she can't go because she really needs to wash her hair instead, then that is a bad sign. Signs are simply indications, messages for us to read in order to infer some other meaning. To an experienced tracker, a broken stick is a sign that some large animal has passed this way. Argument by sign means taking note of the existence of some phenomena and inferring the existence of other conditions that tend to accompany those phenomena. When the leaves turn color, it is fall.

Sign arguments can be confused with cause arguments, but a simple example should illustrate the difference: *The school bell just rang, so the buses should be along any time.* To interpret that as an argument by cause, one would have to believe that the ringing of the bell *caused* the buses to come. It didn't, however; the ringing of the bell signaling the end of a school day merely accompanies the arrival of the buses and for that reason the statement is an argument by sign. Cause arguments assert a *functional* relationship between the phenomena, while arguments by sign simply assert a correlation between the phenomena.

> Maryland's death penalty is racist in its application. A recent study indicates that that black offenders who kill white victims are four times as likely to receive a death sentence as black offenders who kill black victims.[17]

(**Warrant:** Harsher penalties for the killers of white victims is a sign of racism.)

Data: A recent study indicates that among black offenders, those who kill white victims are four times as likely to receive a death sentence as those who kill black victims. ⟶ **Claim:** Maryland's death penalty is racist in its application.

In this example, the advocate reasons from an observed disparity: the killers of one race are much more likely to receive a harsh penalty than the killers of another race. The warrant is that this disparity is a sign of an underlying condition or motivation, namely racism. The argument appears straightforward, but there are a couple of additional considerations in interpreting this and other sign arguments. The step of jumping from the observed sign to the condition it represents is an inference and that inference is only as strong as the connection between the sign and the condition. When using or evaluating sign arguments, you should always ask, "Is the sign a reliable indicator of what I want to prove? Or might it be an indication of an alternate condition?" In the example above, the disparity in sentencing is obviously a concern, whatever its source. But rather than being indications of simple racism, the differences in sentencing may be due to differences in demographics, where the crimes occur, or the habits of different prosecutors. The disparity might also reflect a difference in the nature of the crimes committed: typically, crimes of passion (where the victims are known to the killers) are not treated as harshly as crimes committed against unknown persons. Careful analysis may require that we look for other signs, or a consistent pattern of signs, before we confirm our judgment.

Conclusion

This chapter has sought to advance the argument that reasoning not only takes a central role in a public debate, but also takes on a unique form within that specific context. Argument means not just asserting or fighting, not just persuading or using logic, but reasoning *with* your audience: finding and using audience premises in a way that builds upon the audience's existing experience and knowledge. By using informal patterns of logic and forming enthymemes, public debaters forge a partnership with audience members. By locating and using external sources and combining that material with their own resources for analysis, public debaters build arguments that adhere to familiar patterns of reasoning and guard against possible weakness.

In making this argument, this chapter has quoted a number of different sources. We have referenced communication theorists, logicians, and experts who have studied a variety of the topics discussed. We have also discussed the indications, or signs, of good argument, developed and applied some general principles of reasoning, reported on some of the causes of effectiveness in persuading with argument, supplied a large number of examples, and even worked in a few analogies. The most important idea to be taken from this is that although we may have used some specialized terms in our discussion, reasoning is fundamentally about making sense, and knowing how to do that is important, no matter what your mission: winning a public debate, trying to talk a police officer out of giving you a parking ticket, or writing a chapter on reasoning. In a public debate context, though, the audience is likely to be diverse, the opponent is likely to be well-prepared, and the time is likely to be fairly short. In that context, we prize arguments that are clear, full and comprehensible upon initial presentation and are designed to withstand both a skeptical audience and an informed challenger. We succeed in that context by making our reasoning explicit and by remaining aware that offering proof is a continuing obligation to satisfy the audience and answer the challenges that might arise.

Notes

1. For example, see E. S. Inch, and B. Warnick, *Critical Thinking and Communication: The Use of Reason in Argument*, 4th ed.; R. E. Lee, and K. K. Lee, *Arguing Persuasively*; Richard D. Rieke, and M. O. Sillars, *Argumentation and Critical Decision Making*, 4th ed.; J. C. Reinard, *Foundations of Argument: Effective Communication for Critical Thinking*; K. C. Rybacki, and D. J. Rybacki, *Advocacy and Opposition: An Introduction to Argumentation*, 4th ed.; D. N. Walton, *Informal Logic: A Handbook for Critical Argumentation*.

2. A complete transcript of this dialogue can be located at http://wuzzle.org/python/argument.html.

3. D. O'Keefe, "Two Concepts of Argument," *Journal of the American Forensic Association* 13 (1977): 121–128.

4. D. N. Walton, *Informal Logic: A Handbook for Critical Argumentation* (Cambridge: Cambridge University Press, 1989): 4

5. *Callins v. Collins*. 510 U.S. 1141. See especially H. Blackmun's dissent, Legal Information Institute at Cornell Law School, http://supct.law.cornell.edu/supct/html/93-7054.ZA1.html.

6. M. L. Radelet, H. A. Bedau, and C. Putnam, *In Spite of Innocence: Erroneous Convictions in Capital Cases* (Boston: Northeastern University Press, 1992).

7. S. Toulmin, *The Uses of Argument* (Cambridge: Cambridge University Press, 1958).

8. W. Hall, R. Room, and S. Bondy, "A Comparative Appraisal of the Health and Psychological Consequences of Alcohol, Cannabis, Nicotine and Opiate Use," World Health Organization Project on the Health Implications of Cannabis Use (1995), Schaffer Library of Drug Policy, http://www.druglibrary.org/schaffer/hemp/general/who-index.htm.

9. Toulmin used the term "rebuttal" for this element. We've elected to use the word "exception" in order to capture a more accurate meaning for the role of this component and also to show a distinction between this element of an argument and "rebuttal" as it is used elsewhere in this book, namely as a label for the act of building up one's own argument after it has been attacked (see chapter 14).

10. R. O. Weiss, *Public Argument* (Lanham, NY: University Press of America, 1995): 87.

11. National Academy of Sciences, *Abrupt Climate Change: Inevitable Surprises* (Washington, DC National Academies Press, 2002).

12. J. C. Reinard, *Foundations of Argument: Effective Communication for Critical Thinking* (Dubuque, IA: William C. Brown, 1991): 107.

13. We lack the space to provide a full explanation of statistical concepts but individuals without a basic background in this area are urged to consult D. Huff, *How to Lie with Statistics*, reissue ed. (New York: W. W. Norton, 1993).

14. Reinard. 107.

15. Belize Audubon Society, National Parks Managed by the Belize Audubon Society, 2002, http://www.belizeaudubon.org/html/parks.html

16. This mistake, known as *post hoc ergo propter hoc* (after this therefore because of this), will be covered in chapter 14 with other fallacies of reasoning.

17. S. Levine, and L. Montgomery, "Large Racial Disparity Found by Study of Md. Death Penalty," *Washington Post*, January 8, 2003.

Chapter Eleven

Making Your Arguments Compelling

After hearing from several retirees about having to choose which medications to buy, Gore suggested the pharmaceutical industry should lower prices. As an example, he offered the plight of his mother-in-law, who spends $108 a month for a drug called Lodine, which helps relieve the pain of arthritis. Gore said his 14-year old black Labrador retriever Shiloh also suffers from arthritis and he has a veterinarian's prescription for Lodine. The difference? It costs less than $39 a month to fill the dog's prescription for what is the exact same drug.

"Don't you think that ought to be changed?" he asked as the crowd applauded. "Don't you think they ought to lower the price?"

—Account of Al Gore's presidential campaign in 2000[1]

In recent years, one of the hottest controversies in America has been the cost of prescription drugs. Millions of Americans take medication on a daily basis for a wide range of "ordinary" health problems: high blood pressure, high cholesterol, arthritis, allergies and asthma are common conditions treatable by drugs. But the cost of these drugs can easily run into thousands of dollars per year for only one patient; that cost is a significant burden for people who do not receive medications free or at reduced costs through health insurance plans. Elderly patients—who often have greater medical needs and smaller incomes—are particularly affected. Many critics have contended that the prices set by the pharmaceutical companies are unfair: that is, the prices charged do not accurately reflect the cost of producing the drugs. They recognize that drug companies are entitled to make a profit, but say that they should not be allowed to charge four dollars for a pill that costs less than a dollar to make. Moreover, critics say, drug companies have shown that they are willing to charge less for medications when their market is different: many drugs cost less when sold outside the United States, and there are cheaper versions of basic drugs that are produced for animal consumption. The pharmaceutical companies insist that the cost of their products must include their substantial expenses for research and development; they spend millions of dollars trying to develop drugs that never make it to the market, and the drugs that do make it to the market have to recoup that cost. As for varying prices in different markets, drug companies point to the high cost of meeting U.S. government regulations that control the production of drugs for human consumption.

When he ran for president in 2000, Vice President Al Gore made the cost of prescription drugs one of the themes of his campaign. While campaigning in Florida, Gore visited a pharmacy in Tallahassee, where customers told him that drug prices were so high that they could not afford to fill all of their prescriptions and stopped taking necessary medicines. The pharmacy owner told Gore that some residents went to a veterinarian so that they could buy prescribed drugs at lower prices. Gore remarked, "That's pretty bad, when you've got to pretend to be a dog or a cat to get a price break." [2] Soon afterward, the contrast between the price of drugs for humans and the price of drugs for animals became part of a Gore campaign speech. Addressing a crowd of senior citizens, Gore told the story quoted at the head of this chapter: his mother-in-law and his dog both took the same medication for arthritis, and the price for his mother-in-law's medicine was more than double the price of his dog's medicine.

In telling this story, Gore was trying to find a way to make his argument more compelling. As we noted in a previous chapter, "argument is more than just logic." If you are trying to demonstrate a geometric proof, logic will suffice; no mathematician needs to be persuaded by anything besides the numbers on the page. But the problems and controversies of political and social life are not as neat as mathematical theorems, and their truths are only rarely self-evident. What that means is that if you are debating in public, and want to persuade the audience to agree with your position, you will not be able to depend only on syllogisms and the other logical strategies that we discussed earlier; you will also need to use rhetorical techniques. (Rhetoric is defined in some sources as "the art of persuasion.") By using rhetorical techniques, you can connect your argument with your audience; these techniques make difficult arguments easier to understand; they change abstract concepts into concrete facts; they turn impersonal problems into personal issues; they make arguments memorable and forceful, often by engaging the heart as well as the mind. In short, an argument that is both logically sound and rhetorically effective can change minds. It can inspire the sympathetic, disarm the hostile, and sway the undecided.

Let's take another look at Al Gore's story. It is easy enough to infer his main position: prescription drug prices are too high. But how can he persuade the audience that his position is valid? He could construct a statistical argument by referring to the financial statements of drug companies, and showing how the profit margin of pharmaceutical companies compares with other service industries. Or he could mount a moral argument about the nature of profit in the health care industry; it's one thing to be maximizing profit when selling, say, designer handbags (for which consumers have no need), and another thing to be maximizing profits when selling drugs (which may keep consumers alive). But both of those arguments—even though they might be logically strong—would be abstract and fairly complex. Moreover, they would involve "taking on" the industry as a whole—an industry that is so large and varied that it might be hard for a listener to conceptualize it.

Instead, Al Gore chose to go with the particular, rather than the abstract: his story focuses on one particular drug, rather than on the profits of the industry as a whole. He also specified costs in a way that was easy for his audience to understand; he was addressing a group of senior citizens, who were more familiar with monthly prescription costs than with corporate balance sheets. It is even more significant that many audience members were probably taking the medication in question—for his example, Gore did not choose a drug used to treat a rare, obscure or foreign illness. His audience was able to connect with a drug used to treat arthritis more easily than they could with ivermectin, used to combat river blindness in sub-Saharan Africa. Gore also found a way to connect the drug pricing problem with his own personal experience: it wasn't just some nameless "senior citizens" he was talking about, it was his own mother-in-law. It wasn't just some animal, it was his own Labrador, Shiloh. Finally, Gore's story aims to make a point about a complex social problem by focusing on a fact that seems inescapably absurd and morally objectionable. The average listener will be bound to agree: it's just "wrong" that humans should be charged more than animals for the same thing.[3] (Even passionate animal lovers tend to value humans more highly than dogs.)

In sum, Al Gore's story about his mother-in-law and his dog is a good example of a rhetorical technique used to persuade an audience about the validity of the advocate's position. In the pages that follow, we will describe a number of other rhetorical techniques that can be used—and we will also discuss the weaknesses and drawbacks of using them.

Rhetorical Theory and Practice

As we have mentioned earlier, the teaching of rhetoric dates back to the classical period of Greece, when the Sophists trained young Athenian men to speak in public. Soon enough, rhetorical techniques were labeled and codified; this teaching was inherited and expanded by Roman orators and rhetoricians and formed the basis of rhetorical training during the Middle Ages and Renaissance. There are literally hundreds of different terms and techniques—curious readers should consult the *Silva Rhetoricae*, an online glossary written by Dr. Gideon Burton of Brigham Young University, for an exhaustive account.[4] Over time, rhetoric became a kind of art form—and like many other art forms, offered particular pleasures to the cognoscenti. In the same way that a balletomane can rhapsodize about the perfect execution of a balloté or an entrechat (while the uninitiated see nothing more than someone jumping), trained rhetoricians could appreciate the perfect insertion of an anacoulothon or epiphonema. This chapter, however, is not intended to explore or explain all of the possible rhetorical strategies available. We will confine ourselves to the simplest and most useful—those that can have an impact on an audience that would not even know what the words "rhetorical strategy" mean. We will draw examples from a few of the more celebrated speeches of the last century.

Syllogisms, Enthymemes, and Analogies

We do not intend to repeat our discussion of argumentation in the last chapter, but we would like to reiterate that an argument is never effective without good reasons—and it is important to remember to use the various logical strategies that we identified earlier, as well as the rhetorical strategies we will identify below. To launch this chapter's discussion of rhetorical strategies, we would like to revisit the analogy: yes, it is a form of logic, but it is also effective as rhetoric—partly because it engages the imagination.

An analogy, you will recall, is a form of comparison. The advocate wants to make a point about "A," but she begins by likening "A" to "B"; she then makes a point, or establishes a truth about B, and concludes by saying that the same thing is true of "A." To use a simple example: an advocate wants to argue that marijuana (item A) should be legalized. She contends that marijuana is like alcohol (item B). She points out that alcohol (B) is legal (throughout most of the West, anyway) and that attempts to make it illegal—e.g., Prohibition in America during the 1920s—have been disastrous. Therefore, she concludes, marijuana (A) should also be legal. (Like any other analogy, this argument is vulnerable at the point of comparison: if marijuana isn't really like alcohol, then the conclusion does not hold.)

The foregoing analogy is a fairly straightforward logical gambit: the advocate relies on the fact that her audience will accept her points about alcohol (that it is legal and should be legal), and will follow her to the more controversial conclusion that marijuana should be legalized. The advocate has used something acceptable for "leverage" to establish the controversial. Analogies are also used to simplify complex issues: if A is hard to understand, a speaker may make a comparison to a B term that is easier to grasp (e.g., North Korea's decision to convert fissionable material is the equivalent of an insane man loading a gun).

Sometimes, however, analogies are more fully developed—even to the point where they can engage the emotions as well as the imagination. Julius Nyerere, the president of Tanzania, used an extended analogy when addressing the Food and Agriculture Organization of the United Nations in 1963:

> Each underdeveloped country is like a man who desires to build a fleet of ships. First he builds a rowing boat. With this he sweats, carrying people across rivers until he gets enough profit to build a coaster. With the proceeds of coastal trade he builds first one, and later many ocean going ships. If, however, he tries to send his rowing boat into the ocean it will sink, and he will be back where he started. If, when he gets his coaster it does not flee from storms, that will sink and he will be back at the rowing boat stage. It is only when he has built up his fleet that he sends ships into hurricane areas.
>
> The economies of the underdeveloped countries cannot safely venture into the stormy ocean of unplanned international market-

ing until they are like oceangoing craft. They will get to that position more quickly if there is outside aid appropriate to the need of the time. But until then—regardless of whether aid is obtained or not—if the sea cannot be made calmer by international planning, then we must retreat from it while we build economies strong enough to withstand the unpredictable mischances of a "free market".[5]

Following the practice of many good analogies, Nyerere compares the known with the unknown, and uses a homely image (a man in a rowboat) to explain his position about a complex problem in international economics. This analogy is *figurative*, rather than *literal*. In other words, Nyerere is not trying to argue that underdeveloped countries are really like boats and that any statement about boatbuilding will also be valid about economics; rather, he uses his analogy to clarify a problem and highlight his response to it. (For an additional discussion of figurative vs. literal analogies, see chapter 14, "Refutation." A figurative analogy like the one used by Nyerere is hard to refute effectively.)

Anecdotes

An anecdote is a brief story; in the context of public debate, it is a story used to make a point. Take, for example, this story, told by the civil rights activist Malcolm X. Talking to an audience of black Americans in 1964, he said:

"... you'd get farther calling yourself African instead of Negro. Africans don't catch hell. You're the only one catching hell. They don't have to pass civil-rights bills for Africans. An African can go anywhere he wants right now. All you've got to do is tie your head up. That's right, go anywhere you want. Just stop being a Negro. Change your name to Hoogagagooba. That'll show you how silly the white man is. You're dealing with a silly man. A friend of mine who's very dark put a turban on his head and went into a restaurant in Atlanta before they called themselves desegregated. He went into a white restaurant, he sat down, they served him, and he said, "What would happen if a Negro came in here?" And there he's sitting, black as night, but because he had his head wrapped up the waitress looked back at him and says, "Why, there wouldn't no nigger dare come in here."[6]

There is, of course, a good deal of hyperbole in this passage: Malcolm X is deliberately exaggerating in order to make his point. (He doesn't actually want his listeners to change their names and start wearing turbans.) His real argument, however, is clear: white Americans, especially in the South, display an automatic, instinctive prejudice against black Americans. Black skin, he claims, is not the object of this prejudice; it is, rather, the cultural identity of black Americans that Southerners find objectionable. The anecdote is brief—a mere three sentences—but illustrates his point in a compelling way.

There are all kinds of anecdotes: some are humorous; some are pathetic; some are sketchy; some are told with an attention to detail worthy of a short story. No matter what shape they take, good anecdotes are about people—and that makes them one of the most powerful tools in a public debater's arsenal. Like analogies, good anecdotes succeed in turning the abstract into the particular; but more than that, they turn the abstract into something human—and they help an audience to relate to the issue at hand. Malcolm X was speaking to an audience of black Americans for whom racial prejudice was a real experience, even if they lived outside the segregated South (his speech was given in the northern city of Cleveland, Ohio); when they heard his story, they could wonder themselves if they would be treated differently if they were seen as black Africans, rather than "American Negroes." (It hardly needs to be said that Malcolm X's story would be heard differently by an audience of whites.) In public debates, the audience is of paramount importance, and the anecdote is a powerful way for an advocate to connect his audience with his argument.

Building Credibility

As we mentioned in an earlier chapter, Aristotle argues that an essential part of rhetoric is *ethos*—that is, an assertion of the speaker's personal authority and credibility. It is important, of course, for the speaker to have a good argument (*logos*), and it is important for the speaker to appeal to the emotions of the audience (*pathos*), but all of that can come to naught, says Aristotle, if the audience doesn't believe that the speaker knows what he is talking about. The speaker has to come across as knowledgeable and believable.

It is certainly true that some assertions of authority can backfire: audiences do not like to be told, either explicitly or implicitly, "You have to believe what I'm saying because I'm smarter [or better educated or more experienced] than you are." (One of your authors recalls with horror a high school teacher who told her class, "I'm not listening to your complaints because I have an advanced degree in education, and I've been trained in the best way to teach students your age.") A public debater cannot afford to sound arrogant or superior—and that is often what happens when the speaker touts his credentials.

But the effect can be completely different if the speaker refers to personal experience, rather than credentials. In 1984, Mario Cuomo—at that time, the governor of New York State—addressed the delegates at the Democratic National Convention (and, via TV, a nationwide audience). His speech, generally regarded as one of the most powerful keynote speeches in memory, included this passage about his own experience:

> That struggle to live with dignity is the real story of the shining city. And it's a story, ladies and gentlemen, that I didn't read in a book, or learn in a classroom. I saw it, and lived it. Like many of you. I watched a small man with thick calluses on both hands work 15 and 16 hours a day. I saw him once literally bleed from the bottoms of his feet, a man who came here uneducated, alone, unable to speak the language, who taught me all I needed to know about faith and hard work by the simple eloquence of his example. I learned about our kind of democracy from my father. And, I learned about our obligation to each other from him and from my mother. They asked only for a chance to work and to make the world better for their children and they asked to be protected in those moments when they would not be able to protect themselves. This nation and this nation's government did that for them.
>
> And that they were able to build a family and live in dignity and see one of their children go from behind their little grocery store in South Jamaica on the other side of the tracks where he was born, to occupy the highest seat in the greatest state of the greatest nation in the only world we know, is an ineffably beautiful tribute to the democratic process.[7]

There are elements of pathos in this speech—for example, Cuomo's evocation of his father's bleeding feet—but the primary thrust of the passage is to establish the speaker's authority and credibility: he emphasizes that he is talking about something he has "lived," rather than something he has "read in a book." He is trying to make a point about life in America: it is a country, he argues, where poor, hardworking immigrants are able to lead lives of dignity with the support of "this nation's government." He knows this is true because it has been the experience of his family. More than that, he recognizes that his family's experience has not been unique. Indeed, Cuomo explicitly draws his audience into the picture when he says, "I saw it, and lived it. *Like many of you.*" (Emphasis added.)

This passage, then, does more than simply establish the speaker's authority; it also connects the speaker with the audience. Again, any rhetorical strategy that builds a connection between speaker and audience is vitally important in public debate. Particularly when the debate is about social problems that affect the audience, it is important for advocates to let the audience know that they themselves understand such problems or are also affected by them. Here, we can refer back to Al Gore's speech about prescription drugs. No, he was not a senior citizen, like the people in the audience—but his elderly mother-in-law took arthritis medication, just like many of them. Moreover, his dog also took arthritis medication. The bottom line: he knew what he was talking about, and he was able to share the concerns of his audience.

Identification

At various points throughout this text, we have stressed the importance of establishing a connection between the speaker and the audience in a public debate. Here, we will revisit this topic in terms of the rhetorical concept of identification.

The concept of identification was central to the thinking of the influential theorist Kenneth Burke (1903–1997). Burke argued that persuasion is impossible without identification: "You persuade a man only insofar as you can talk his language by speech, gesture, tonality, order, image, attitude, idea, *identifying* your ways with his."[8] His point is that listeners are not persuaded unless they believe at some level that the speaker is like them and worthy of their trust. In practical terms, this means that the debater who wishes to persuade an audience must find common ground, something that he shares with his audience. The common ground may be as simple as a shared background or membership in a group; it may be as profound as shared ideas and values.

An almost perfect example of a speaker trying to identify with his audience can be found in a work of fiction, *Invisible Man.* The unnamed narrator of Ralph Ellison's 1947 novel is making his mark in the black community as a public speaker; in one scene, he addresses a crowd at a political rally, and talks about his experience of "dispossession." It is an experience, he says, that he shares with every black person in his audience; more than that, he sees that he and his listeners should both be united against those who dispossess them: "Look down the avenue, there's only one enemy." (Rhetorical theorists have noted that identification can be reinforced by antithesis—that is, by reminding the audience of the "other" that is opposed to both the speaker and the audience.)

In the conclusion of his speech, the narrator identifies powerfully with his listeners, embracing them with claims of kinship and community. Strictly speaking, he is an outsider, because he is a Southern black who has come north to New York City—but that is not how he feels:

> I feel that here, after a long and desperate and uncommonly blind journey, I have come home . . . Home! With your eyes upon me I feel that I've found my true family! My true people! My true country! I am a new citizen of the country of your vision, a native of your fraternal land. I feel that here tonight, in this old arena, the new is being born and the vital old revived. In each of you, in me, in us all.
>
> SISTERS! BROTHERS!
>
> WE ARE THE TRUE PATRIOTS! THE CITIZENS OF TOMORROW'S WORLD!
>
> WE'LL BE DISPOSSESSED NO MORE![9]

The example offered by *Invisible Man* is dramatic, and enlivened by metaphor and hyperbole—and so it may seem beyond the reach of the ordinary public debater. But there are more mundane ways to make a connection with the audience. Identity can be established through simple things like dress, manner of speaking and accent. It is a common sight to see political campaigners dressing to match their listeners. A candidate talking to workers outside a factory usually wears casual clothes; a three-piece business suit would mark the speaker as an outsider—and as someone who appears to be more in tune with management than with labor. Similarly, someone who talks in a way that seems overly formal or "stuffy" frequently puts off listeners; they prefer someone who speaks to them the same way that they would speak to him. (American voters seem to be particularly fond of politicians who use slang; Bill Clinton gained some fans when he told Democratic voters in New Hampshire, "I'll be there for you until the last dog dies."[10]) Regional accents, too, are often adapted (or adopted) to suit the audience; in 2003, some journalists noted that Democratic presidential candidate John F.

Kerry sounded distinctly different when his campaign entered the American Midwest.[11] All of these techniques can be used by the public debater.

Identification can also be established through various means of address. One simple rhetorical gesture is to address the audience as "friends" or as "fellows"—as in John F. Kennedy's exhortation to "my fellow Americans" and "my fellow citizens of the world"[12] or President Eisenhower's appeal to "my fellow citizens."[13] Whenever circumstances allow it, politicians are eager to establish more specific bonds of fellowship: Burke cites "the politician who, addressing an audience of farmers, says, 'I was a farm boy myself.'" [14] More creatively, John F. Kennedy claimed fellow citizenship with his audience at the Berlin Wall in June 1963: as a free man, he said, he was proud to say, "Ich bin ein Berliner"—"I am a citizen of Berlin." [15] The public debater can usually find similar connections, either literal or metaphorical.

One modern master of identification is former President Bill Clinton. He showed himself to be adept at identifying with the feelings of his audience—perhaps never more effectively than in his address in Oklahoma City on April 23, 1995. A few days earlier, a terrorist had exploded a powerful bomb in front of a federal office building, killing 168 people, many of them children in a day care center. Arriving in Oklahoma to speak to survivors, and to the friends and relatives of the deceased, Clinton began his speech by reminding his listeners of the private roles he shared with them. He was not just their president; as a spouse and a parent, he was a family man talking to families.

> I am honored to be here today to represent the American people. But I have to tell you that Hillary and I also come as parents, as husband and wife, as people who were your neighbors for some of the best years of our lives. [Clinton served for many years as governor of the state of Arkansas, which borders Oklahoma to the east.][16]

Clinton continued by stressing the feelings that he shared with his listeners—although he acknowledged that his suffering could not be as great as theirs.

> Today our nation joins with you in grief. We mourn with you. We share your hope against hope that some may still survive . . .
>
> But for so many of you they were also neighbors and friends. You saw them at church or the PTA meetings, at the civic clubs, at the ballpark. You know them in ways that all the rest of America could not. And to all the members of the families here present who have

suffered loss, though we share your grief, your pain is unimaginable, and we know that. We cannot undo it. That is God's work.

This was Clinton's first mention of God in his speech—and the inclusion was appropriate, given that he was speaking at a prayer service. After quoting a letter written by a woman whose husband had been killed in another terrorist attack (another instance of sharing), he offered his thoughts that the attack should provoke a passion for justice rather than hate. Again, he invoked God, and the shared values of the Judeo-Christian tradition, by saying that children should be taught that "the God of comfort is also the God of righteousness." The Judeo-Christian tradition was also invoked with a paraphrase from the Psalms, but Clinton's frame of reference was specifically Christian when he cited the words of a Christian saint: "As St. Paul admonished us, let us not be overcome by evil, but overcome evil with good." With all of these religious statements, Clinton identified himself as someone who shared the religious values of his audience. (According to recent surveys, the population of Oklahoma is almost entirely Christian.[17])

Clinton also connected to his audience by praising them, and their values. Consciously or unconsciously, he echoed the phraseology of Kennedy's speech in Berlin, during which the president had repeatedly said, "Let them come to Berlin."

> If anybody thinks that Americans are mostly mean and selfish, they ought to come to Oklahoma. If anybody thinks Americans have lost the capacity for love and caring and courage, they ought to come to Oklahoma.

This identification was further reinforced by antithesis, when Clinton stressed the common experience of his listeners (both in the room and across the country), while distinguishing them from the terrorists who had attacked them:

> To all my fellow Americans beyond this hall, I say, one thing we owe those who have sacrificed is the duty to purge ourselves of the dark forces which gave rise to this evil. They are forces that threaten our common peace, our freedom, our way of life.

In the peroration of his speech, Clinton returned again to his own personal experience, reminding the audience yet again of his roles of husband and father. More important, he connected his audience to his own experience by linking the children of Oklahoma to children he had met elsewhere and by giving a concrete example of the connection between Oklahoma and his own home, in the form of a memorial tree.

> Yesterday Hillary and I had the privilege of speaking with some children of other federal employees—children like those who were lost here. And one little girl said something we will never forget. She said, we should all plant a tree in memory of the children. So this morning before we got on the plane to come here, at the White House, we planted tree in honor of the children of Oklahoma.

In sum, Clinton's speech was effective because he recognized what his listeners were thinking, feeling and believing, and he made deliberate attempts to show that he shared the same thoughts, emotions, and beliefs. At the deepest levels, he identified with his audience.

Using Powerful Language
Figurative Language

In May 1940, three days after becoming Britain's wartime prime minister, Winston Churchill addressed the House of Commons. If he had said, "I want you to know that I am going to work hard and give this job everything I've got," he would not be remembered today as one of history's greatest orators. Fortunately for history, Churchill said this: "I would say to the House, as I said to those who have joined this government: I have nothing to offer but blood, toil, tears and sweat."[18] The power of his statement comes from his use of figurative language: the concrete imagery of blood, tears and sweat make his promise emotionally compelling. (Churchill also gets good mileage from the quick succession of blunt monosyllables: "hemoglobin, labor, teardrops and perspiration" would not have ended up in a dictionary of quotations.)

Figurative language is a broad category—it includes similes, metaphors, symbols, synecdoche, and a whole host of rhetorical devices. You will find that the most powerful speeches on record abound with this language. Lincoln, in his first inaugural address, spoke of the "mystic chords of memory" being touched "by the better angels of our nature;" John F. Kennedy, in his inaugural address, announced that "the torch has been passed to a new generation of Americans"; Martin Luther King told the crowd at the Lincoln Memorial, "I have a dream"; Ronald Reagan, quoting a poem by John Magee, said that the astronauts who died in the *Challenger* disaster had "slipped the surly bonds of earth to touch the face of God"; Bill Clinton promised voters that he would "build a bridge to the 21st century." In every case, these speeches were made powerful and memorable by figurative language.

Vivid Language

Public debaters make a more powerful impression on an audience when the language that they use is vivid and forceful. Take this example from Mario Cuomo's speech to the Democratic National Convention in 1984:

> We speak for senior citizens who are terrorized by the idea that their only security—their Social Security—is being threatened. We speak for millions of reasoning people fighting to preserve our environment from greed and from stupidity. And we speak for reasonable people who are fighting to preserve our very existence from a macho intransigence that refuses to make intelligent attempts to discuss the possibility of nuclear holocaust with our enemy.[19]

Cuomo uses a string of highly charged words—"terrorized," "greed," "stupidity," "macho intransigence"—to dramatize policy issues that might otherwise seem emotionally neutral. Suppose he had said merely, "Our party will act to preserve Social Security and safeguard the environment; we will also discuss arms reductions with the Soviet Union." Such words might have conveyed the policy positions of his party but little else. Cuomo's vivid language does a better job of injecting passion into the discourse.

Repetition

In his famous speech at the March on Washington in 1963, Martin Luther King used the phrase "I have a dream" no fewer than nine times. That may be a few too many times for anyone who is not as passionate and inspired as Dr. King—but the repetition of phrases can be a very effective tool. King repeated a substantive, meaningful phrase, almost as if it were a slogan. (A proper slogan is a political war cry that is used over a long term, like Bill Clinton's invocation of the "Third Way," or George W. Bush's claim to "Compassionate Conservatism.") It can also be effective rhetorically for a speaker to repeat a grammatical pattern, rather than a meaningful phrase. President George W. Bush did so when speaking about the war on terrorism: "We will not waver; we will not tire; we will not falter; and we will not fail."[20] So did Winston Churchill after the loss of Dunkirk: "We shall fight on the beaches. We shall fight on the landing grounds. We shall fight in the fields, and in the streets, we shall fight in the hills. We shall never surrender!"[21]

Contrast, Comparison and Choices

It is a classic rhetorical strategy to say what something *is* by saying what it *is not*. Good speakers often use contrast to emphasize their own ideas. When Martin Luther King was assassinated, presidential candidate Robert F. Kennedy offered this as part of his impromptu eulogy in Indianapolis: "What we need in the United States is not division; what we need in the United States is not hatred; what we need in the United States is not violence or lawlessness; but love and wisdom, and compassion toward one another, and a feeling of justice toward those who still suffer within our country, whether they be white or they be black."[22] (Note, too, the use of repetition.) Kennedy's rhetoric echoed the famous contrast made by his brother John when he was inaugurated as president in 1961: "And so, my fellow Americans, ask not what your country can do for you; ask what you can do for your country. My fellow citizens of the world, ask not what America will do for you, but what together we can do for the freedom of man."[23]

In a debate, of course, speakers are able to use the technique of contrast to distinguish themselves from their opponents. In essence, the speaker says, "This is what my opponent is saying [and it is wrong], and this is what I am saying [and it is right]." (This is part of the process of refutation, discussed in chapter 14.) But the contrast does not have to involve major issues or ideas; even a small rhetorical contrast can be effective. When he accepted the Republican nomination for President in 1996, Senator Bob Dole—age 73 at the time—said this: "Age has its advantages. Let me be the bridge to an America that only the unknowing call myth. Let me be the bridge to a time of tranquility, faith, and confidence in action."[24] When President Clinton accepted the Democratic nomination a few days later, he found a damaging way to paraphrase Dole's remark and offered himself in contrast: "But with all respect, we do not need to build a bridge to the past. We need to build a bridge to the future, and that is what I commit to you to do."[25] Subsequently, the bridge to the future became the Bridge to the 21st Century.

Another effective rhetorical strategy is to present the audience with a *dichotomy*, a choice between two mutually exclusive alternatives. Malcolm X did so in his address in Cleveland in 1964. He began: "The question tonight, as I understand it, is 'The Negro Revolt, and Where Do We Go From Here?' or 'What Next?' In my little humble way of understanding it, it points toward either the ballot or the bullet."[26] Throughout his speech, Malcolm X returned again and again to the dichotomy facing black Americans: if they did not exercise their voting rights effectively, he said, the alternative was violence. He also quoted the dichotomy offered by Patrick Henry in 1775, in the early days of the American Revolution: "Give me liberty or give me death."

Particularizing the Abstract

We opened this chapter with a discussion of Al Gore's attempt to particularize the abstract problem of health care costs by talking about the personal experience of his family. This strategy is especially important when the debate is about numbers so large that the audience has difficulty conceptualizing them. President Ronald Reagan acknowledged that difficulty when making a speech about the national debt, which was approaching a trillion dollars in 1981:

> I've been trying . . . to think of a way to illustrate how big a trillion really is. And the best I could come up with is that if you had a stack of thousand-dollar bills in your hand only four inches high, you'd be a millionaire. A trillion dollars would be a stack of thousand-dollar bills 67 miles high.

This image was so memorable that President Bill Clinton used it himself when addressing Congress: "I well remember twelve years ago President Reagan stood at this very podium and told you and the American people that if our national debt were stacked in thousand-dollar bills the stack would reach 67 miles into space. Well, today that stack would reach 267 miles."

Rhetorical Questions

A rhetorical question is a question that is asked for the effect, with no direct answer expected from the listener. It is a strategy that involves the audience and can be more effective than direct statement. Mario Cuomo used this technique effectively in his address to the Democratic National Convention in 1984:

> If July brings back Ann Gorsuch Burford [the controversial administrator of the Environmental Protection Agency]—what can we expect of December? Where would another four years take us? Where would four years more take us? How much larger will the

deficit be? How much deeper the cuts in programs for the struggling middle class and the poor to limit that deficit? How high will the interest rates be? How much more acid rain killing our forests and fouling our lakes? And, ladies and gentlemen, the nation must think of this: What kind of Supreme Court will we have? We must ask ourselves what kind of court and country will be fashioned by the man who believes in having government mandate people's religion and morality?

. . . How high will we pile the missiles? How much deeper will the gulf be between us and our enemies? And, ladies and gentlemen, will four years more make meaner the spirit of the American people?

It is also rhetorically effective for the speaker to ask questions, and answer them himself. Speaking of the peace talks called to end the Vietnam War, President Richard Nixon said,

No progress whatever has been made except agreement on the shape of the bargaining table. Well now, who is at fault?

It has become clear that the obstacle in negotiating an end to the war is not the president of the United States. It is not the South Vietnamese government. The obstacle is the other side's absolute refusal to show the least willingness to join us in seeking a just peace.

Humor

Jokes and funny stories are the stock-in-trade of promotional speakers and after-dinner raconteurs who have been given the task of entertaining audiences—but they are also useful tools for public debaters trying to persuade audiences. Even when an advocate has a serious purpose, and the problem at hand is dire, humor can be appropriate and effective.

The primary function of humor, in the context of a public debater, is to establish a relationship between the debater and an audience. If someone in the audience has been given the chance to laugh—or even to smile, or nod appreciatively—he or she is more likely to feel well disposed toward the person who provided that experience. We tend to pay more attention to people who have made us laugh, because we hope that more laughs will be in store. More important, we tend to like people who make us laugh—and we tend to believe the people that we like. In short, humor can contribute to the speaker's *ethos*, or credibility.

Humor can be used as an offensive weapon in a debate; that is, a debater can use humor to belittle an idea or a plan offered by an opponent. Take, for example, Winston Churchill's attack on protectionist economic theories: "It is the theory of the protectionist that imports are evil . . . we free-traders say it is not true. To think that you can make a man richer by putting on a tax is like a man thinking that he can stand in a bucket and lift himself up by the handle." This quip is tactically strong because it is hard for the protectionist speaker to respond: he probably doesn't want to get into specific reasons why he is not like a man standing in a bucket.

Humor can also be used effectively as a defensive weapon; audiences respond positively to speakers who are self-deprecating and can show that they "do not take themselves too seriously." One master of such humor was President Franklin Roosevelt, who began one re-election campaign speech by saying, "Well, here we are together again—after four years—and what years they have been! You know, I am actually four years older, which is a fact that seems to annoy some people." In the course of the speech, Roosevelt noted that he had come under attack for his military leadership during World War II. He responded by talking about his dog, a terrier named Fala:

> These Republican leaders have not been content with attacks on me, or my wife, or on my sons. No, not content with that, they now include my little dog, Fala. Well, of course, I don't resent attacks, and my family doesn't resent attacks, but Fala does resent them. You know, Fala is Scotch, and being a Scottie, as soon as he learned that the Republican fiction writers in Congress and out had concocted a story that I had left him behind on the Aleutian Islands and had sent a destroyer back to find him—at a cost to the taxpayers of two or three, or eight or twenty million dollars—his Scotch soul was furious. He has not been the same dog since. I am accustomed to hearing malicious falsehoods about myself—such as that old, worm-eaten chestnut that I have represented myself as indispensable. But I think I have a right to resent, to object to libelous statements about my dog.

Roosevelt's touch here is masterful: he knew that people in the audience had heard the accusations and attacks, and he defended himself by minimizing their importance in a humorous way.

A similarly deft defense was mounted by one of Roosevelt's successors, President Ronald Reagan. When Reagan ran for re-election in 1984, his age was raised as an issue. At 73 years old, he was already the oldest man ever to serve as president; his opponent, Walter Mondale, was only 56. During one presidential debate, a questioner asked Reagan if he thought he had the physical vigor to lead the country in a time of crisis. Reagan replied that he had no doubts about his ability, and added:

> I want you to know that also I will not make age an issue of this campaign. I am not going to exploit for political purposes my opponent's youth and inexperience. If I still have time, I might add, Mr. Trewhitt, I might add that it was Seneca or it was Cicero, I don't know which, that said if it was not for the elders correcting the mistakes of the young, there would be no state.

Reagan's questioner remarked that the president's response was like a home run hit over the outfield fence. Age ceased to be a serious campaign issue.

In closing, we should note that there are also some risks to using humor in a public debate. Jokes, in particular, are risky: if an audience finds a joke funny, it can be a major coup for a speaker, but if the joke goes flat, it does more harm than good. One consultant, Charles Francis of IdeaBank, Inc., recommends avoiding jokes altogether, and adding humor by means of amusing quotations from other sources. Even if the wit belongs to Mark Twain or Will Rogers, an audience will give a speaker credit for giving them a laugh by quoting it. Proverbs, too, can have the same effect: audiences know that the speaker did not invent the saying, "A fool in a hurry eats tea with a fork," but appreciates its inclusion.

It is also counterproductive to use humor that seems mean-spirited or personal. Sarcasm, invective and acidulous language may sometimes succeed in rousing the passions of a partisan audience, but they can come across as petty and unfair to people who are trying to make an impartial judgment. It is one of the premises of public debate that both sides should be treated with respect; if humor becomes mockery, it violates the spirit of the occasion.

Appeal to Emotions

In his book on rhetoric, Aristotle classified three kinds of persuasive appeal to an audience. *Logos* is the appeal to logic and reason; *ethos* is the persuasive appeal of the speaker's character; and *pathos* is the appeal to the emotions.

Many of the rhetorical strategies we have discussed in this chapter could be classified under the heading of *pathos*: humor, vivid language, and rhetorical questions, for example, are all ways to engage the emotions of the audience. Here, we would like to discuss a few techniques that have not been covered elsewhere.

The first technique is called *descriptio* in classical rhetoric; it is a vivid description of the consequences of an act. In debate, it is often used to characterize an opposing position—e.g., "If you support their proposal to legalize marijuana, you will see more crime; you will see more addicts strung out on the stoops of our inner cities; you will see more children abandoned by teenage mothers who are unable to take care of them; you will see longer lines at the unemployment office and more work for doctors and undertakers."

The second technique is an appeal made directly to the listeners by emphasizing the impact of a proposal on them personally—e.g., "If this legislation is passed, you will get a tax refund from the federal government—but you will also see, as a result, higher state taxes, and a weaker national economy that will affect the value of your savings and your ability to borrow money."

We would be less than thorough if we did not include children and the family dog under this heading, in the spirit of the quotation often ascribed to American publisher William Randolph Hearst: "Show me a magazine with a woman, a dog, or a baby on the cover, and I'll show you a magazine that sells." We began this chapter with Al Gore's evocation of his dog Shiloh, but he was by no means the first politician to bring his pet into the dialogue. Roosevelt talked about his terrier Fala; Barbara Bush, wife of President George H.W. Bush and mother of President George W. Bush, wrote an "autobiography" of her dog Millie; and perhaps most famously, Richard Nixon told the nation about a dog named Checkers. At the time, Nixon was a U.S. senator campaigning for the vice presidency, and he had been accused of taking inappropriate (and illegal) gifts. His defense—mentioning both a dog and his daughters—is a classic appeal to the emotions:

> One other thing I probably should tell you, because if I don't they'll probably be saying this about me, too. We did get something, a gift, after the election. A man down in Texas heard Pat [Nixon's wife] on the radio mention the fact that our two youngsters would like to have a dog. And believe it or not, the day before we left on this campaign trip we got a message from Union Station in Baltimore, saying they had a package for us. We went down to get it. You know what it was? It was a little cocker spaniel dog, in a crate that he had sent all the way from Texas, black and white, spotted, and our little girl Tricia, the six-year-old, named it Checkers. And you know, the

kids, like all kids, love the dog, and I just want to say this, right now, that regardless of what they say about it, we're gonna keep it.[27]

Using Audiovisual Aids

According to the Microsoft Corporation, there are more than 300 million users of PowerPoint software worldwide—and they make 30 million PowerPoint presentations every day. So there is no doubt that audiovisual aids are a customary and ubiquitous part of public presentations, from corporate board meetings to primary school classrooms. This fact raises a question: Are audiovisual aids an appropriate part of public debate?

Let's begin by examining what audiovisual aids do well. In the words of the well-worn proverb, "A picture is worth a thousand words"—and sometimes it is true that a picture can convey an impression of reality in a way that words cannot. If you want your audience to understand the ecological disaster of the Aral Sea, which has lost 75 percent of its volume in recent years, aerial maps will speak more eloquently than statistics. Graphs and charts can also make statistical material easier to understand and absorb.

Proponents of PowerPoint (and of its predecessors, the easel and the overhead projector) are also keen on using audiovisual tools to convey words. Famously, PowerPoint prompts users to create "bullet points," short and punchy tags of text. A typical PowerPoint screen will have three to five bullet points, with a total of about forty words of text. The logic of PowerPoint is that the bullet points help to emphasize themes and important points in the presentation; the audience is more likely to remember things that they have seen as well as heard.

But PowerPoint has its opponents, too. Critics of PowerPoint charge that it encourages oversimplification; complex ideas cannot be handled well by bullet points. Another charge is that PowerPoint steals the focus of the audience from the speaker's words: the audience focuses on the screen, waiting for the next slide, and does not listen carefully to the substance that the bullet point is meant to highlight. The relationship between the speaker and the audience is weakened—especially if the speaker, too, is focused on the screen and not on the audience. The effect of PowerPoint is particularly negative when physical conditions make it necessary to turn down the lights in order for the screen to be seen. When the speaker becomes a disembodied voice in the dark, a vital visual connection with listeners is lost.

On the one hand, PowerPoint seems to fit naturally with some aspects of public debate. Elsewhere, we have emphasized the importance of creating a clear structure of points and subpoints, and they would seem to fit easily onto a computer screen. But we have also talked about how important it is for speakers in a public debate to connect with the audience, and we think that elaborate visual presentations like PowerPoint undermine that objective. In our judgment, the minuses outweigh the plusses. Audiovisual aids in a public debate are best limited to pictures and graphics that are necessary to convey some part of the argument effectively.

Pitfalls to Avoid

If you do choose to use PowerPoint in presenting your side in the debate, make sure to avoid these common problems. You should not put huge amounts of text on the screen and then read the entire text out loud. This is not a good way to treat an audience of presumably literate people; it is also frustrating because the average person will be able to read the text much faster than you can speak it. (The "striptease" solution, where part of the text is invisible and is revealed only gradually, is worse than the problem itself.)

It is not a good idea to present images that are too small or complicated to be understood—for example, a chart with a lot of labels, or with labels that cannot be seen at a distance. Indeed, as a general principle, it is a mistake to use any visual material that cannot be seen by the entire room. (A nightmarish example we witnessed: "I know you people in the back probably can't see the cartoon that I have on the screen here, so let me explain it you. Charlie Brown and Lucy are playing baseball, and Lucy comes up the mound and says . . . ")

Conclusion

Audiovisual aids come with pitfalls—but so do most of the rhetorical strategies we have discussed throughout this chapter. Humor can fall flat; an appeal to the emotions can seem cheap and manipulative; even figurative language can seem artificial. A rhetorical strategy that backfires can actually derail a debate.

With that in mind, we return once again to our opening story, about Al Gore and the cost of prescription drugs. Although the immediate effect of Gore's story was positive (the newspaper accounts describe the applause of the crowd), the story did not stand up under intense scrutiny from the media and Gore's Republican opponents. Gore had quoted precise figures about the cost of Lodine ("While it costs $108 a month for a person, it costs $37.80 for a dog"), but was forced to admit that those prices had not come from personal experience—they were taken instead from a generic study of wholesale drug prices commissioned by the Democrats. What is more, Gore's campaign staff couldn't say with certainty that his mother-in-law and his dog took exactly the same brand-name drug, and they were unable to specify the dosages each took (which would affect the cost of the drug).

The result was that the issue changed from being the cost of prescription drugs to the personal credibility of Al Gore. Gore's opponent, George W. Bush, commented: "America better beware of a candidate who is willing to stretch reality in order to win points . . . I have always been concerned about Vice President Gore's willingness to exaggerate in order to become elected. . . . Now he's exaggerating about family members of his, in order to make a point on a very highly charged, very emotional issue."[28]

Three years later, Gore returned the compliment:

> Robust debate in a democracy will almost always involve occasional rhetorical excesses and leaps of faith, and we're all used to that. I've even been guilty of it myself on occasion. But there is a big difference between that and a systematic effort to manipulate facts in service to a totalistic ideology that is felt to be more important than the mandates of basic honesty. Unfortunately, I think it is no longer possible to avoid the conclusion that what the country is dealing with in the Bush Presidency is the latter.[29]

As they say in the language of the blues, "What goes around, comes around."

Notes

1. D. Wasson, "Gore Touts His Drug Plan in Florida," *Tampa Tribune*, August 29, 2000.

2. L. Kleindienst, "Gore Uses Florida As Setting to Start Weeklong Health-Care Focus," *Sun-Sentinel*, August 29, 2000.

3. Ibid.

4. Gideon Burton, *Silva Rhetorica: The Forest of Rhetoric* (Provo, UT: Brigham Young University, 2003), http://humanities.byu.edu/rhetoric/

5. J. Nyerere, "McDougall Memorial Lecture of the Food and Agriculture Organization" (speech, 12th Session of the Conference of the Food and Agriculture Organization of the United Nations, Rome, November 18, 1963), http://www.southcentre.org/mwalimu/speeches/written/mcdougall.htm

6. Malcolm X, "The Ballot or the Bullet" (speech, Cleveland, OH, April 3, 1964) in *Malcolm X Speaks*, ed. George Breitman (New York: Grove Weidenfeld, 1965): 22–44. Also available online at http://www.americanrhetoric.com/speeches/malcolmxballot.htm

7. Mario Cuomo, "A Tale of Two Cities" (address, Democratic National Convention, San Francisco, July 16, 1984), http://www.americanrhetoric.com/speeches/cuomo1984dnc.htm

8. K. Burke, *A Rhetoric of Motives* (Berkeley and Los Angeles: University of California Press, 1969): 55.

9. Ralph Ellison, *Invisible Man* (New York: Vintage, 1995): 300.

10. J. King, "Clinton Returns to New Hampshire," *Cable News Network*, February 18, 1999, http://www.cnn.com/ALLPOLITICS/stories/1999/02/18/clinton.nh/

11. "It wasn't a Boston accent, no, but presidential candidate John F. Kerry suddenly began dropping his g's yesterday as he sought to project a common touch during his 'Fighting for Working Americans' tour across Iowa." Patrick Healy, "Whirlwind Iowa Tour, Kerry Aims for Everyman's Vote," *Boston Globe*, December 23, 2003. See also Mark Leibovich, "Not Just Whistling Dixie: In South Carolina, Howard Dean Warms to His Universal Voter Message," *Washington Post*, January 2, 2004. "By 9:30 a.m., Dean is talking with a trace of a Southern accent. It's a subtle but discernible evolution, divined by a few members of the traveling news media . . . "

12. John F. Kennedy, "Inaugural Address" (speech, Washington, DC, January 20, 1961), http://www.jfklibrary.org/j012061.htm

13. Dwight D. Eisenhower, "Response to Little Rock," (speech, Washington, DC, September 24, 1957), http://www.nps.gov/malu/documents/eisenhower_little_rock.htm

14. Burke, xiv.

15. John F. Kennedy, "Remarks in the Rudolph Wilde Platz" (speech, West Berlin, June 26, 1963), http://www.jfklibrary.org/j062663.htm

16. William J. Clinton, "Oklahoma Bombing Memorial Prayer Service Address" (address, Oklahoma City, OK, April 23, 1995), http://www.americanrhetoric.com/speeches/wjcoklahomabombingspeech.htm

17. American Religion Data Archive, http://www.thearda.com/FR_Index.html?/RCMS/2000/State/40.htm

18. Winston Churchill, "Speech to the House of Commons," (address, London, May 13, 1940), http://www.winstonchurchill.org/i4a/pages/index.cfm?pageid=388#sweat

19. Cuomo, "A Tale of Two Cities."

20. George W. Bush, "Presidential Address to the Nation," (address, Washington, DC, October 7, 2001) http://www.whitehouse.gov/news/releases/2001/10/20011007-8.html

21. Winston Churchill, "Speech to the House of Commons," (address, London, June 4, 1940), http://www.winstonchurchill.org/i4a/pages/index.cfm?pageid=388#beaches

22. Robert F. Kennedy, "Statement on the Assassination of Martin Luther King, Jr." (address, Indianapolis, IN, April 4, 1968), http://www.jfklibrary.org/r040468.htm

23. John F. Kennedy, "Inaugural Address."

24. Robert Dole, "Acceptance Speech" (address, Republican National Convention, San Diego, CA, August 15, 1996), http://cgi.usatoday.com/elect/ec/ecr/ecr126.htm

25. William Clinton, "Acceptance Speech" (address, Democratic National Convention, Chicago, August 29, 1996), http://www.pbs.org/newshour/convention96/floor_speeches/clinton_8-29.html

26. Malcolm X, "The Ballot or the Bullet."

27. Richard Nixon, "Checkers" (address, September 23, 1952), http://www.americanrhetoric.com/speeches/richardnixoncheckers.html

28. Jake Tapper, "A Campaign's Dog Days," *Salon*, September 21, 2000, http://dir.salon.com/politics/feature/2000/09/21/bush/index.html

29. Albert Gore, "Remarks to moveon.org," (address, New York University, New York, August 7, 2003), http://www.moveon.org/gore-speech.html

Chapter Twelve

Listening and Note Taking in Public Debates

Imagine yourself observing a public debate. Most immediately, your attention is drawn to the individual speaking: the person who is standing at the lectern and making a speech. But what are the other debaters doing? When they are not nodding firmly in agreement (when listening to their teammates) or sporting pained expressions of incredulity (when listening to the opposition), they are likely to be engaged in the activities that serve as the focus of this chapter: they will likely be listening and taking notes. These are such essential academic skills that they are often taken for granted and given little emphasis in works on public advocacy and debate. More specifically, the subject of note taking in debate (or "flowing" as it is sometimes called) is often given only a small amount of attention or relegated to an appendix. This treatment, however, fails to recognize the importance of the nonspeaking roles in the debate. After all, as a debater, it you will in all likelihood spend far more time listening and writing than you will spend speaking. When you are listening—constructing, recording, and shaping your thoughts—you will most likely be doing that with a pen and paper. You will probably be creating your own view of the debate by listening strategically for the most important elements of the speech in progress, and writing them down in a useful and meaningful format.

One may argue that in the lively and decidedly oral setting of the public debate, it is simply unnecessary to spend a great amount of time writing. We agree that public debate advocates do not need to be stenographers. But listening carefully in order to take notes has shown itself to be an essential component in determining how we perceive and understand content as we hear it. In educational contexts, note taking has been extensively studied. Students who take notes have been shown to process information better than students who do not take notes.[1] And processing information well is one of the public debate advocate's most essential tasks.

As important as they are, the acts of listening and taking notes should never be likened to the activities of a tape recorder. That is, listening is not simply the act of retaining what is heard and note taking is not simply the act of writing what was said. Neither of these activities is 'neutral.' The listener and the note taker are engaged in purpose-driven activities. As we will see later in this chapter, the purpose that one has for listening and the way in which notes will be used subsequently in the debate have a large impact on what will be emphasized, what will be selected, and what will be retained. It goes without saying that unless you are one of the world's fastest writers (or listening to one of the world's slowest speakers) you are bound to write much less than what is being said, perhaps one word for every twenty or more words that are spoken. For that reason, your selection of what you notice, prioritize, organize and write down has a large influence on how the event is going to be captured.

In addition, it goes without saying that note taking is a personal act. Your notes are just that—*your* notes. What you would select and what you would find useful to record for your own or for an opponent's speech is not likely to be the same or necessarily similar to what another person would record and select. While there are certainly better and worse ways of taking notes, more and less useful techniques of recording, there is no unambiguously right way to take notes from a given speech. For this reason, debaters generally rely on their own notes rather than the notes of their partners. For one thing, it is often difficult to read someone else's handwriting—especially handwriting produced under the stressful conditions of a debate. More important, when you rely on your own notes, you are recognizing the fact that by taking notes you are mentally organizing what you are hearing. Many who have had the experience of being a student know that you take notes in class not simply because you want to re-read the notes again at a later time, but because the acts of recording and structuring are ways of processing the information; they aid your understanding during that moment even if you never look at the notes again.[2] Sometimes, instructors are very good at letting students know exactly when they have moved on to a new main point; more commonly, however, someone listening casually to an instructor will not realize that during the last twenty minutes the instructor has made three distinct points, supporting each one with two illustrations. The note taker is much more apt to have grasped the structure of the presentation. For this reason, debaters who want to have their full attention upon the content of the debate, in order to have the most informed perspective when giving their own speeches should be listening carefully and taking notes. The informed debater wants to be engaged in the mental acts of noticing and structuring while listening.

Strategic Listening

If our heading sounds odd, then it is only because we have conventionally (and, we believe, inaccurately) thought of listening as a passive process—we open our ears, we relax, we receive the information. Decades of research on the listening process and its successes and failures, however, have demonstrated that this model is anything but accurate.[3] Hearing (the physiological process of converting sound waves into auditory stimuli) differs from listening (the mental process of selecting, attending to, meaningfully organizing and retaining heard information) in essential respects. While we can't listen without hearing, we can hear without listening. Imagine debaters whispering to their teammates with questions like these: "*What was their second argument? Did they ever respond to our example? How does this fact support their side of the debate?*" Uncertainties like these may be symptoms of poor listening behaviors. If you aim to be an effective listener in the context of a public debate, you should maximize the experience by following a few important steps:

- *Focus your attention.* A public debate situation is replete with potential distractions: worrying about your own speech, communicating with your partners, thinking about the audience. All of these elements deserve your attention as well, but when another advocate is speaking, your ability to contribute meaningfully to the debate depends on your ability to prioritize your attention on that advocate's speech.
- *Construct as you listen.* Don't just pay attention to the words as they go by. Instead, actively try to identify the speaker's main ideas, support and strategy. "What is the most important element here?" is a good question to ask while you are mentally processing the information that you hear.

- *React as you listen.* Think about your own assessment. Can you critique the information? Supplement it? Extend it? Think of alternate or additional examples or support?

In addition, the strategic public debate listener should know her purpose. The act of listening can be just as purposeful as the act of speaking, and different situations will prioritize different elements of the speaking process. Writers on the subject of human communication commonly identify several types of listening that relate to different roles.[4] The following list represents those that may be the most appropriate to the public debate setting.

- *Appreciative Listening.* Appreciative listeners are attending to the information for the purpose of pleasure or enjoyment. They pay attention to both sides in the debate in order to gain equally from whatever each has to offer: new information and arguments, and the thrill of the contest. The appreciative listener is likely to be as open-minded as possible toward all points of view, but not necessarily neutral. Being appreciative doesn't mean that one is paying attention only to superficial aspects. You can appreciate the soundness of an argument, or the utility of a new perspective just as surely as you can appreciate a well-turned phrase or a powerful inflection.

- *Facilitative Listening.* The facilitative listener has the purpose of supporting clear and complete expression, not to support or oppose any of the claims in the debate. This type of listening is most suited to the role of respondent or moderator; the goal of the facilitative listener is not to attack anything that is being said, but to ensure that all views have received an opportunity to be heard and to be clarified. During a question and answer session, for example, the moderator would engage in facilitative listening to ensure that an unclear questioner has a chance to revise or extend his remarks if those remarks are not clear upon presentation. One technique of facilitative listening is to "mirror" statements—for example, "what I hear you saying is that . . . " or "if I understand you correctly, what you are asking the debaters is . . . "

- *Supportive Listening.* The supportive listener is an ally of the speaker, either a teammate or a supporter in the audience. Focusing on the strongest points in the message, the supportive listener would be actively thinking of ways to make them even stronger, to extend them, to add illustrations, or to add support. Weaknesses are noted, but only insofar as that attention helps the listener to generate responses to possible attacks. Supportive listeners are looking for material that they can use in order to support the same point or the same line of argument as the speaker.

- *Critical Listening.* The critical listener is paying particular attention to elements of proof in order to offer some sort of response or evaluation subsequent to the speech. Critical listeners are most likely individuals who are going to be refuting the arguments to which they are listening. Listening critically means distinguishing fact from opinion, distinguishing claims from reasons, and distinguishing good reasons from bad reasons. The critical listener does not automatically discount or reject everything that is said. Indeed the key to criticism is being able to separate strong from weak arguments, with the aim of offering a response that advances one's own position while still taking account of what is effective or strong in the other side's argument.

- *Aggressive Listening.* Aggressive listening shares, to some extent, the goals of critical listening, but takes them to an extreme. The aggressive listener is no longer critical—that is, the aggressive listener is no longer involved in the process of making distinctions and discriminations. Aggressive listeners are simply looking to attack everything that they are hearing. Rather than "listening," they are actually searching for ammunition. This fixation and the apparent need to deny or reject what the other side is saying can sometimes infect beginning debaters. Rather than trying to understand what the other side is saying, the aggressive listener is so busy thinking of an answer to everything that he is hearing that he may miss out on the larger understanding that permits the best response.

Viewed from an individual's perspective, listening is an internal process (something that takes place between your ears and your brain) but at the same time it has accompanying behaviors. These behaviors are important in the context of a public debate because they are witnessed by the audience. Typical debate arrangements permit the speaker to see the audience, but not necessarily the other debaters. The audience, however, can generally see the speaker as well as the other participants who are not speaking at the moment. For this reason, listeners need to be conscious of the behaviors that they are engaged in. Frowning, emphatically shaking your head (either yes or no), rolling your eyes, or laughing at inappropriate moments—any of these behaviors could be seen as rudeness or could be misinterpreted by the audience. For that reason, it is best to pay positive attention and to be aware of how your nonverbal behaviors might be received by your audience. (Viewers of the televised 2000 presidential debates will remember that at various points when George W. Bush was speaking, the microphones picked up audible sighs and groans from his opponent, Vice President Al Gore—and the audience reaction to this behavior was largely unfavorable.)[5]

Basic Methods of Note taking

Individuals who have learned debate within the context of tournament debating have likely focused on debate note taking (also called "flowing" or "flow sheeting") as the essential debate activity during nonspeaking moments. The ability to create a clear, legible, and organized flow sheet is seen as the hallmark of the experienced debater. There is a fair amount of agreement on the basic means of keeping track of arguments and ideas during a debate through note taking. The traditional flow-sheet has helped generations of debaters to keep track of what the other side is saying and prepare what they plan to say as well. While particular flowing habits and styles vary from format to format, there are a few common elements. Specifically, maintaining a flow sheet involves noting the key ideas and support quickly in abbreviated form and lining up the remarks of different sides and different speakers on a horizontal plane so that responses are placed next to the argument at which they are directed.

In this section, we will discuss the traditional debate flow sheet as well as a simplified version which may in some situations be more suited to a public debate setting.

The Traditional Debate Flow Sheet

In the traditional flow sheet, the paper is divided into columns and each speech is given its own column. A debate featuring three speeches from each side, then, could be represented on a sheet of paper with six columns. In the three-person Karl Popper debate format (cf. our description in chapter 7), for example, these columns would be represented as First Affirmative, First Negative, Second Affirmative, Second Negative, Third Affirmative, and Third Negative, progressing across the page from left to right in the order in which the speeches are presented. Sometimes note takers will use pens of different colors to indicate different speakers. Because each speech is represented and each argument is placed directly to the right of the argument that it is responding to, the note taker is able to see the issue develop as it alternates between the two sides and as it "flows" across the page from left to right. Hence the name of this note taking style. An example of a complete flow sheet on the subject the legalization of marijuana appears on the following page. Note that when using this method, it is possible to focus either on the elements of one speech (by reading down a single column) or on the progress of a specific issue (by reading across a specific row).

There are several advantages to this comprehensive style of note taking. First, it serves as a complete record of the points made in each speech. The third affirmative speaker, for example, was in a position to focus on her team's second argument (the pragmatic benefits of legalization) and point out that while the negative team initially advanced responses to this argument, the second negative speaker had dropped this point in his speech. Indeed, observers could note that after the first negative speech, the negative side never returned to a consideration of the pragmatic benefits of legalization. Second, the method allows the note taker to track the progress and evolution of a position. Focusing on the first issue in the debate, for example, observers could note that what began as a debate about free choice becomes a debate about the harms of drug use (since both sides agree that the state, to at least some extent, has a right to restrict harmful products).

The disadvantage of such a comprehensive approach is not only that it takes a considerable amount of attention to develop this record, but also that it might trick the note taker into assuming that the audience has the same understanding that he or she does. This "bird's eye" view of the positions and the extensions and refutations taken by all speakers in the debate is a powerful tool for the advocate who wants to begin his speech with a full and organized understanding of what has been said so far. But such a tool can be a liability if it creates in the mind of the advocate a privileged or "correct" understanding of the relationships between the arguments which the audience does not share.[6] Thus, the traditional flow sheet can be useful as long as it is used to aid and improve the clarity of an advocate's presentation to an audience that is not taking notes in a similar fashion. But that same flow sheet can be a liability if it serves as a barrier by creating a privileged or overly specific understanding of the debate on the part of the advocates. For debaters experienced in tournament settings, the flow sheet can also reinforce the temptation to introduce technical language and jargon into the debate (e.g., "they dropped their second point in N2R," shorthand for "second negative rebuttal"). As we have noted elsewhere, this kind of language is generally confusing to the audience of a public debate. In order to

First Affirmative	First Negative	Second Affirmative
Marijuana has few harms and should be legalized.	—Marijuana is not harmless, and should remain illegal.	
I. Free Choice —Choice is the basis of democratic society. —The state has a limited right to interfere—not justified for marijuana because: 1. Smoking marijuana doesn't hurt others' rights. 2. Marijuana isn't harmful enough.	The state has the right to limit choice. —Article 16 of Croatia's constitution: —health, public morality, and well-being justify limits. —Freedom requires responsibility. —State power to limit choice doesn't create risk—U.S. drug policy hasn't hurt democracy.	—Free choice is the most basic principle of a democracy. —You should have the right to decide as long as you don't hurt others.
II. Pragmatic Benefits A. Individual benefits —quality controls. —price controls. —avoidance of "forbidden fruit" appeal.	—drugs aren't of high quality. —lower prices on harmful things is bad. —If theft was legal, then more people would steal.	—Quality controls work in Netherlands. Humanist: marijuana effects equal to cigarettes & alcohol. —Price control means a fair price and no "middleman." —Theft can't be compared to soft drugs, theft endangers people.
B. Community Benefits —Taxes. —Reallocation of resources toward hard drugs, education.	—The state shouldn't receive money for harming health.	—State money can be beneficially used & reallocated. —One third of prisoners in W. Europe are in for drug crimes.

Second Negative	Third Affirmative	Third Negative
—Drugs are harmful enough to stop people from having a right to choose.	—Negative promotes paternalism (treating citizens as children) Oxford Dictionary —paternalism = controlling & denying responsibility and freedom of choice.	—Democracy doesn't mean anarchy. —Government still has a right to control in a democracy. People should not be permitted to risk themselves. —Example: seatbelts. —Legalization isn't necessary for democracy (all democratic countries but Holland ban drugs). —Laws set a standard for what is good and what is normal.
	They did not refute the pragmatic benefits.	
—The state shouldn't get money from harms to its citizens. Slavery was profitable but not moral.		

avoid this tendency and a more general disconnection between the debaters and the audience, some advocates have opted for simplified methods of taking notes for a public debate.

The Simplified Flow Sheet (two-column method)

For many advocates in a public debate setting, the traditional flow sheet will simply provide more information than is necessary. An alternative is to use a modified or simplified flow sheet in which only two columns are present. The left-hand column includes the arguments made by your opponents— the arguments that you will need to identify and respond to in your own speech. The right-hand column includes your own side's arguments as well as the points you will ultimately use yourself. During your speech you would refer to the left-hand column when identifying the arguments you are going to react to and make your own points from the right-hand column.

The two-column flow sheet is designed to serve as an aid to the advocate who is making just one speech and does not serve as a record of the entire debate. The material for both columns would be added over time while you are listening to the speeches which precede your own. For example, there may be a point in the first speech that seems to warrant a response, but then by the time you take the floor as the third speaker, it is no longer prominent or worthy of mention and so can simply be crossed out. On the other hand, a point that emerges late in the debate can simply be added to the column. An example of a simplified flow sheet using the same debate on the legalization of marijuana appears on the next page.

The simplified flow sheet has the advantage of helping you to focus on the crafting of your speech from the very beginning of the debate and may serve to prevent you from taking notes obsessively, including details that will not influence your own presentation. The note taker using this simplified system is making a moment-to-moment choice as to whether a given point that is being made deserves to be included or not. It is not a license to ignore previous speeches; it is more of a license to listen to them with an ear toward how they will impact your own upcoming speech. The disadvantage of this note taking style is, of course, that it does not serve as a full record of the debate and will not allow advocates to comment on the specific progression of an idea or on what each individual speaker has said in a debate.

The choice of whether to use one or the other of these note taking systems (or another alternative) is a personal one. Advocates who speak multiple times during a debate or advocates who are speaking to a specialized and debate-experienced audience may be well-advised to use the traditional flow sheet, while advocates who are giving just one speech to a nonspecialized audience might be more effective if they use the simple two-column method that places the priority on their own speeches.

Affirmative	Negative
Marijuana has few harms and should be legalized.	-Marijuana is not harmless, and should remain illegal.
I. Free Choice	The state has the right to limit choice.
—Choice is the basis of democratic society.	—Article 16 of Croatia's constitution: —health, public morality, and well-being justify limits.
—The state has a limited right to interfere—not justified for marijuana because:	—Freedom requires responsibility.
1. Smoking marijuana doesn't hurt others' rights.	—State power to limit choice doesn't create risk—U.S. drug policy hasn't hurt democracy.
2. Marijuana isn't harmful enough.	
—You should have the right to decide as long as you don't hurt others.	
—Negative promotes paternalism (treating citizens as children).	
II. Pragmatic Benefits.	
A. Individual benefits.	
—Quality controls.	—drugs aren't of high quality.
—Quality controls work in Netherlands.	—lower prices on harmful things is bad.
—Price controls.	—If theft were legal, then more people would steal.
—Price control means a fair price and no "middle man."	
—Avoidance of "forbidden fruit" appeal.	
B. Community benefits	—The state shouldn't receive money for harming health.
—Taxes.	—Slavery was profitable but not moral.
—Reallocation of resources toward hard drugs, education.	
—One third of prisoners in W. Europe are in for drug crimes.	

It is important to realize that either method of flowing serves only as a device to assist listening—an important device, but one that plays a supporting role nonetheless. "The flow" itself is unlikely to play the decisive role in public debate contexts that it sometimes plays in tournament debate contexts. At the tournament, the judge and both debate teams are frequently taking very detailed notes and the failure to give attention to even one small spot of ink can have devastating consequences when everyone is paying such close attention to a common written document. In public debate, chances are that only the most highly motivated audience members are taking notes, much less making a flow sheet. This is not a reason for public debaters to avoid flowing. Some debaters may feel that in order to experience the debate as the audience experiences it, it is better not to flow, and that is certainly an understandable perspective. Yet by giving up on note taking altogether, the advocate is giving up a very powerful tool for making the debate clear and comprehensive. A casual audience, for example, may not understand that the speaker that they just heard had essentially four reasons for opposing nuclear testing, yet when the next speaker tells them "my opponents offered you four reasons, and they are . . . ," the audience is likely to appreciate that explanation of the argument's structure even if they have not written it down themselves.

General Guidelines for Note Taking

No matter what style of written notes is used, there are some general guidelines that apply in all cases.

- *Keep It Simple.* Remembering that only a fraction of what is said will end up being recorded, it is important to record an advocate's *key ideas* and not the words that an advocate happens to be saying at any given moment. To discern the key idea, you must simplify and select. For example, the following might represent what is spoken and what is written:

   Spoken: "A hallmark of our nation's purpose and strength, free speech is not a mere luxury. Indeed, it is a necessity of a free people to use the power to speak without hindrance on any subject, to criticize as well as to compliment, that is one of the very building blocks of the form of government that we have come to call democracy."

   Written: "Free Speech promotes democracy."

An individual who is simply writing as the advocate speaks might be tempted to write the first thing that is heard: "hallmark of our nation . . ."—which is not the key point. Instead, the written version simplifies by pulling out just the main idea and writing it in a clear subject-predicate fashion. Asking "What is the subject?" (free speech) and "What is the action or evaluation?" (it promotes democracy) is a good way of arriving at brief argument labels. Remember that note taking is only an aid to memory and not a full recording of the event. It is a way of focusing response and prompting memory. In this case, the adage "less is more" often holds true. For example, studies have shown that students who try to take notes by writing down as much as possible of their instructor's words actually score lower in comprehensive tests.[7] In order to understand, we often need to reduce and to simplify.

- *Use Meaningful Abbreviations.* An alternate way of representing the argument above might be:

  Written: "F.S. $\longrightarrow$ Dem."

Removed from its context, that abbreviation may not mean anything, but for someone who has been studying and preparing a debate and dealing continuously with the ideas of free speech and democracy, and who recognizes the arrow symbol as "leads to," or "promotes," the phrase would have sufficient meaning and could be jotted down in less than a second.

There are some common abbreviations that are meaningful in a way which does not require much explanation. The = sign, for example can mean "is," "amounts to," "can be defined as," etc. The + sign obviously means "and," or "with" while the – sign can easily mean "without." An arrow can mean "increasing" or decreasing" or "promotes," "leads to," or "causes."

More specific word abbreviations would depend, of course, not only on the language that you are working in, but also upon the subject area and your familiarity with it. It is no savings in time to use an abbreviation that will tax your own recollection. If you have reached a point of familiarity on the free speech topic, for example, that "F.S." will have meaning to you, and it saves time to use it; otherwise, the use of "free speech" or "free sp." or "free spch" will suffice. It is a good idea to begin using some common abbreviations in your own note taking as you gather material and information for your debate and then to continue to use those abbreviations in your own speaking notes and in your own flow sheet.

- *Impose organization.* In many instances the act of taking notes will be an act of "creating order out of chaos." The structure of an argument may not be obvious to the individual who is casually listening; indeed, the structure may not even be obvious to the person making it. A trait often found in very inexperienced (or overly confident) speakers is to simply speak off the "top of the head," expressing thoughts as they enter the mind. Facing such a speaker, a note taker could say with exasperation, "It is impossible to take any notes because the speech has no structure." But that is not an acceptable excuse. Good note takers will find a structure even if they have to impose it themselves. Ideally, the note taker will be able to say, "Well, he spoke for four minutes without explicitly identifying any key ideas, but there were three essential claims that he kept coming back to and those are . . . " In a public debate, it is not really a concern whether those three points are the "right" three points or not. Audience members who are not taking notes will appreciate your suggestion of structure. Maybe if they had been taking notes themselves, they might have recognized three somewhat different points, or four points, or two. But the fact that you were the one carefully paying attention, and you are the one who will be speaking next gives you sufficient latitude to say, "*I heard* three essential points here, and that is what I'll be addressing in my speech."

All of these general note taking strategies are not skills that can be quickly learned, but at the same time they are skills that can apply, not only to taking notes in public debates, but to taking notes in any situation. Individuals who are used to recording minutes in meetings or in a classroom will find that the ability to simplify, the ability to abbreviate, and the ability to create organization are all essential skills for creating a useful record of an oral event.

Flowing the Other Side's Arguments

When you are taking notes from the perspective of an individual who is going to respond to the claims being made, then you are note taking with the specific purpose of getting enough information about the claim being made to permit you to identify and evaluate that claim appropriately. In this context, the general guidelines listed above apply, and some additional ones make sense as well.

- *Emphasize the Support.* Your primary attention should be placed on the reasoning and the evidence that your opponents offer. In addition to writing down the claim, you should also try to take note of the facts, examples, supporting analysis or quotations that they offer. Ultimately, you will be responding not to their claims or their implications but to their reasoning.

- *Record Your Own Reactions as You Write.* If you can think of a response as you are listening, then you may save time by writing the response rather than the argument that led to your response. For example, if the other side presents a quotation from 1963 on a matter of global economics, then instead of writing the source and its date, you might write in the space available for your own speech, "'63 is too old—too much has changed."

- *Group Similar Points Together.* Repetition in one form or another is a common feature in nearly all types of speaking. In a debate, your adversary will likely make several points that, while not identical, are similar enough that they can be grouped together and handled en masse. For example, "In their last speech, they made several arguments that basically all amount to one point, that free trade improves the global economy. However . . . "

- *Identify Areas Where You Have a Question.* When you hear a point that you think should be pursued in questioning, write a quick symbol: a question mark with a circle around it, for example. Generally there is not time to write out questions fully during the debate. But using the flow sheet method, it is a simple matter to employ a special symbol to indicate the points you would like to address through questioning. By making a quick mark and adding maybe one or two words, you will provide enough information to stimulate your recall of the line of questioning that you had in mind.

Flowing Your Own Arguments

Obviously you can't be writing as you speak, and you ought not speak from the top of your head. In a public debate, you should be both reacting to the events of the moment and speaking from some sort of a structured plan. This requires note taking before you speak and during the debate. These notes on the flow sheet will serve not just as a record of what was said but also as a plan for what you will say—and they are somewhat different in style and focus from the notes you will make about your opponent.

- *Write a Bit More for Yourself.* In flowing out your own speech, you want to capture the full power of the arguments as you intend them; you don't just want to capture the main ideas. In addition to recording the content, you want to include notes on the elements that will make your speech rhetorically effective—elements that may not be strictly part of the "proof" but that may be powerful and communicative nonetheless (see chapter 11, "Making Your Arguments Compelling"). Do not carry this advice to the extreme, however. Avoid the temptation to write a full-blown script for yourself; stick to key words (not sentences) that will allow you to speak extemporaneously.

- *Write Out Arguments in Advance When You Can.* If you know in advance that you are going to be making a specific claim in the debate, then it helps to have a likely version of your argument written in advance. Obviously, opening speeches are likely to be prepared in advance, but even after that there are certain predictable arguments that can be anticipated. For example, the defender of the International Monetary Fund (IMF) can expect that at some point in the debate, she will need to defend that organization against charges that its rigid economic plans contribute to poverty. She may not know exactly when that argument will be made, but she does know that it will be made. One technology for dealing with this situation is the familiar Post-it® note. This is a paper note with a weak adhesive that allows you to stick the note on another piece of paper, removing it and replacing it as you wish. If the IMF defender writes out her own brief response to the anticipated attack in advance, she can simply wait for the argument to occur and then add her note to her flow sheet, ready for her to use when she speaks.

- *Don't Forget About the Person Speaking.* It is important not to get so focused on preparing your own notes that you forget that you are supposed to be listening to and answering another arguer. This requires some getting used to and an ability to keep part of your mind on what is being said, while another part of your attention is on what you are about to say. This may require taking notes in two different places at the same time, keeping track of your opponent's arguments while at the same time filling in your own.

Flowing the Entire Debate

Members of the audience or respondents at a public debate may wish to have a comprehensive record of the debate at the end, either as a way of retaining important information, or as a way of focusing their own comments and questions. In this situation, the note taker is going to be writing not for the purpose of aligning himself with one side or the other necessarily, but for the purpose of accurately representing both sides of the argument. Many of the same skills considered above are needed by the nonadvocate note taker, but a few additional ones may also be necessary.

- *Use a Traditional Flow With an Extra Column.* Note takers who wish to have a comprehensive record will naturally want to know what each speaker said, and for that reason, they should use the traditional flow sheet. In addition, it will be a good idea to reserve an extra column on the right-hand edge of the flow sheet for their own assessments and reactions. Evaluators who expect to deliver a comprehensive critique of the debate may even want to create a section for comments on each speaker or each issue.

- *Don't Forget to Be an Audience Member.* Specifically, don't become so enamored of note taking that you forget to look up. As a nonparticipant, you should remember that you are part of the audience for the event; that is, you are experiencing it for the benefits that it holds. Taking notes is a way to sharpen your attention to specific details, but done to an extreme it can also serve to dull your attention to other features. For example, the more that you have your head down and your eyes fixed on your notepad, the less likely you are to notice eye contact, gesture, and even vocal tone and emphasis. While those elements may not be formal components of argument, they are important components of communication.

- *Be an Active Note Taker.* While you are not flowing for a specific reaction, like someone engaged in refutation might be, you should still remember that it is impossible to simply record. You should remember that you are selecting and reconstructing the elements of the exchange that are most important to you. This means that, even though you may not be giving any speeches, you are still in the situation of making continuous moment-to-moment decisions on the meaning, importance, structure, and priority of the arguments that you are hearing.

This chapter has sought to show that listening and taking notes, done well, reflect not the passive acts of an observer but the active engagement of a participant. What we write, how we organize it, what we pay attention to, and what we notice are all the result of constructive acts that help us shape the debate in a way that is meaningful to us. Like the skills involved in speaking, skills involved in listening and taking notes get better over time and they get better based upon the degree to which you pay attention and focus on improvement. If you engage in public debate or similar activities on a regular basis, then taking the time to notice how you are listening, and to work on how you are taking notes is time well spent.

Notes

1. S. McIntyre, "Lecture Note-taking, Information-processing and Academic Achievement," *Journal of College Reading and Learning* 24, no. 1 (1992): 7–17.

2. It has been found, for example, that note taking "enhances organizational processing" or aids the process of seeing relationships among the items of information that you are receiving. G. O. Einstein and others, "Note-taking, Individual Differences, and Memory for Lecture Information," *Journal of Educational Psychology* 77, no. 5 (October 1985): 522–532.

3. M. P. Nichols, *The Lost Art of Listening* (New York: Guilford, 1995).

4. E. Wolvin, and C. G. Coakley, *Listening*, 5th ed. (Dubuque, IA: Brown & Benchmark, 1996).

5. Martin Kettle, "Bush Retakes Lead As Voters Question Gore's Character: 'Sighs and Lies' Factor Starts to Hurt Vice-president," *The Guardian*, October 12, 2000, http://www.guardian.co.uk/US_election_race/Story/0,2763,381031,00.html

6. The flow has recently come under criticism from within the American policy debate community as creating a *reified* understanding of the debate; that is, creating a situation in which the representation becomes more important than that which it represents. The map is seen as more real than the territory. See W. E. Shanahan, "The Flow Is NOT the Debate: Ontology, Re(-)Presentation, and Violence" (paper presented at the annual convention of the National Communication Association, New Orleans, LA, 2002).

7. B. H. Bretzing, and R. W. Kulhary, "Note-Taking and Depth of Processing," *Contemporary Educational Psychology* 4, no. 2 (April 1979): 145–153.

Chapter Thirteen

Opening Speeches

It is axiomatic among speechmakers that the most important part of any speech is the opening. Some speakers say that the first thirty seconds determine the success or failure of a speech; in that brief time, the speaker must establish a connection with the audience and gain their willingness to listen to whatever is to follow.

In this chapter, we will discuss openings in the larger context of a public debate. As we have seen in our examination of debate formats (chapter 7), debates typically open with fairly extensive speeches, in which each side lays out its basic argument, either for or against the proposition. During the remaining parts of the debate, the basic arguments will be developed, extended, challenged, and defended—so the debate is by no means over when these "opening speeches" are done. And yet, these speeches are critically important: debaters must use them not only to explain their arguments, but also to connect with the audience. The opening speech can make or break a team's chances of success in the debate as a whole, the same way that the first thirty seconds can determine the success or failure of an individual speech.

In the pages that follow, we will look at the component parts of an opening speech: the introduction (including those crucial thirty seconds), the body and the conclusion. But before examining the parts, we should offer a few words about the function of the opening speech as a whole. Your primary purpose in making an opening speech is to articulate the main reasons that you have for supporting (or opposing, as the case may be) the proposition under consideration. It is also your purpose to distinguish your position from the position taken by the other side. True, if you are speaking first, you will not have heard the other side's position—but you can still anticipate what the other side is going to say, and you can explain, in a general way, what it means if the proposition is opposed. ("I will argue that the United States must become party to the International Criminal Court; if we do not, the result will be the death of more innocent people and continued impunity for war criminals.") Finally, your opening speech should put the debate itself in context; you should help the audience to see what the issue being debated is important and worthy of their consideration.

The Introduction

The heading of this chapter comprises two brief quotations. The first is a classic formula used by the comedian Bob Hope when he was entertaining troops in various locations throughout the world. The formulaic phrase, "Here we are in [location]," was always followed by a joke. True, the joke may not have been the equal of something by Oscar Wilde at his wittiest, but it performed an important function. In the first place, it was a strong start: Hope did not start with mumbled words about being happy to be there or some such rhetorical pabulum; the joke is confident—and it's worth listening to. (When a speaker begins by saying, "I'm happy to be here, and I'm really honored to have been invited and given this opportunity," you can be sure that the audience is not hanging on every word.) More important, Hope's joke connects him to the audience. It's not just that he knows where he is; his joke suggests that he knows how the soldiers feel about being in Yeongdeungpo: they don't think it's the equivalent of London or Paris, either. At the same time, he doesn't say anything to insult the place directly, and he doesn't insult his audience for being there. In short, with just a few words, Hope manages to establish a positive relationship with his audience. (Perhaps obviously, we have included the other quotation for contrast: many in the Peruvian audience were insulted that Alanis Morissette thought she was in Brazil.)

Bob Hope's opening line is a good illustration of some of the principles we want to outline in this discussion. The first major principle is that **the introduction—the opening of the opening speech—should be strong; it should demand the attention of the audience.** It isn't necessary to open with a joke, although that can be a successful tactic; jokes, when they work, are a great way to capture the sympathetic attention of an audience. (Jokes that don't work, on the other hand, can leave a speaker scrambling madly to get out of an oversized hole.) There are plenty of other successful tactics. Some speakers like to open with an anecdote; others like to open with a quotation, a question, a statistic, or a startling statement. (Consider this as an attention-getter: a headmaster at a demanding prep school was fond of saying to freshmen on opening day, "Gentlemen, I want each of you to look at the student sitting to his left and at the student sitting to his right. In all likelihood, one of them will not graduate with you four years from now—that is, if you graduate yourself.")

Our next two principles are concerned with the **psychological orientation** of the speaker and the audience. The second major principle is that **the introduction should establish a relationship between the speaker and the audience.** The debater needs to recognize where he is and who he's talking to. The average audience doesn't mind being flattered—although they are often quick to detect phoniness. (The good citizens of Wauwatosa, Wisconsin aren't going to believe that a senator from New Mexico has always wanted to visit because he's heard such great things about the Rivers and Bluffs Birding Festival.) Ideally, the debater will be able to find some kind of common ground with the audience: maybe she's been there before, or maybe her family has, or maybe she has spoken to a group similar to the one she's seeing now (e.g., "I have spoken to public interest research groups throughout the Northeast, and I have always been impressed by their knowledge, their commitment and their passion."). It can be a good tactic to recognize individuals in the audience and even introduce them to the audience at large (e.g., "I'd like to thank Ms. Brown for inviting me here today, and for telling me about all the work the people in your school have done for the environment."). It is true that in the context of a public debate—which by definition deals with controversial issues—there may well be hostile listeners in the audience, but the speaker cannot afford to let their presence affect the tone of her presentation; she must treat her listeners as potential friends, with whom she is exploring an issue in a rational and respectful way.

Our third major principle is that **the introduction should establish the character of the speaker**—what Aristotle called the speaker's *ethos*. The speech will not be persuasive unless the audience sees that the speaker is credible and authoritative. The speaker must be seen as trustworthy; more than that, the speaker must be seen as someone who is approaching the topic, and addressing the audience, with good will. The introduction is a good place for the speaker to establish her own relationship with the topic. If the members of the audience know *why* she is so interested in capital punishment, or animal rights, or bilingual education—whatever the topic is—then they will be more likely to become interested themselves.

Finally, we offer two principles concerning **logical orientation**. In the introduction of her opening speech, the speaker needs to offer the audience a kind of intellectual road map. This means, in the first place, that **the introduction should establish a context for the topic**. The speaker needs to show the audience why the topic is important and how she is going to approach it. Let's say, for example, that the debate is about the rights of illegal immigrants. There are different ways to think about the issue: some people see it primarily as an economic issue (i.e., illegal immigrants take jobs away from tax-paying citizens); some see it as a cultural issue, especially when illegal immigrants do not speak the primary language of the country (i.e., illegal immigrants "dilute" the strength of the indigenous culture); some see it as a legal issue (i.e., if the immigrants have broken the law, they should be treated like other lawbreakers). If the debater is in favor of amnesty for illegal immigrants, she might establish a historical context—viz., that people born in foreign countries came to America for over three centuries before the passage of the first immigration quotas in 1921. She might also note that immigration quotas, historically, have often been shaped by racist beliefs. Or she may put the topic in a conceptual framework: "The debate today is not about dollars and cents and costs and revenues; rather, the debate is about what kind of society we want to be. The debate is about whether this country intends to honor the invitation inscribed at the base of the Statue of Liberty: "Give me your tired, your poor, your huddled masses yearning to breathe free." Are we a society that welcomes people, no matter what color they are and what language they speak? Are we a society that cares about the poor? Are we a society that cares about others, not just about ourselves?" In any case, the context should make the topic more understandable; the debater should help the audience to connect the topic to things that they know and understand.

Our fifth and final principle is that **the introduction should offer an overview of the arguments that will follow**. There is much to be said for the element of surprise when you are trying to win a military engagement, and surprise is something you expect (paradoxically!) when you are watching a horror movie. But audiences at a debate generally don't want to be surprised; rather, they want to have clear understanding of what is going on. Of course, there will be twists and turns on the road as the debate develops, but they still want to have a sense of where the argument is heading. Accordingly, we think that debaters should sketch out, however briefly, the parts of their arguments (e.g., "My first point is that U.S. foreign policy should favor Israel in the Middle East because Israel is the only functioning democracy in that part of the world; second, I will argue that Israel, historically, has used military power for defensive, rather than aggressive purposes; and third, I will argue that the United States cannot and should not support Palestinian leadership that is dishonest and corrupt."). If listeners are given a framework during the introduction, then they will be able to fit what they hear later into that framework.

Summary of Principles

In sum, the introduction:

- should be strong and should demand the attention of the audience;
- should establish a relationship between the speaker and the audience;
- should establish the character of the speaker;
- should establish a context for the topic;
- should offer an overview of the arguments that will follow.

These objectives do not need to be addressed separately—it is quite possible to do two or more at the same time (as Bob Hope did in our opening example, with fewer than two dozen well-chosen words). It may also happen, given the time restraints of the debate format, that it is necessary to jettison some of these objectives. The introduction should not constitute more than 15 or 20 percent of the opening speech; if the opening speech is ten minutes long, it is certainly possible to accomplish all of these objectives in two minutes (after all, the entirety of Lincoln's Gettysburg Address takes only two minutes to read aloud); but if the opening speech is only four minutes long, there is not too much that can be achieved in forty seconds. We should also note that the significance of each individual objective will be determined by the particular context of the debate. If the debate audience is composed of students from the same college, and both debaters are also students there, then establishing a relationship with the audience will not be as important as it would be when the debaters are unknown outsiders. With some topics, it will be a matter of paramount importance to establish a context; with other topics, the context will be a secondary concern.

Pitfalls to Avoid

We noted that it is important to start out strong; the converse is that it is a mistake to begin with anything that is weak or apologetic. It is a common mistake to open with the words, "Before I start, I'd like to . . ."—because once you've opened your mouth, you've already started.

It is important to grab the attention of the audience—but it is a mistake to use an attention-getter that seems irrelevant to the topic at hand. This problem arises frequently when the speaker opens with a joke; the joke may help to relax the audience, but if it doesn't bear on the topic, it is a distraction that keeps the audience from focusing. Other opening tactics have their problems, too: quotations can work well, but not if they are too long and too complicated; a strong statement or question will fail if it sounds overly dramatic, or if the speaker seems to be wringing it for pathos. (If the topic is global warming, it is not a good idea to begin by asking, "How much longer are you going to watch the children of the world die?")

We have already noted that audiences are quick to sense phoniness when a speaker tries too hard to establish a relationship with them. It is also a mistake to drop names in an overly familiar way (e.g., "It's great to see that President Bob Hutchins is here tonight with his lovely wife Maud."). This kind of name dropping leaves the audience feeling like second-rate guests, sitting outside the charmed circle of familiarity.

Last, we'd note that is not a good idea to read the opening speech—even though it is essential for the speech to be prepared and outlined thoroughly beforehand. The problem is that reading a text imposes a barrier between speaker and audience: if the speaker's eyes are focused on the lectern, rather than on people in the room, the audience feels less important. Moreover, reading from a prepared text undermines the spontaneity of the moment; audiences respond more strongly to something that seems "live" and unrehearsed.

The Body

The body of the opening speech is the part where the debater offers his main arguments. These arguments—or points—must be organized and arranged in a clear and logical way, and they must be connected with strong transitions.

Organizing Points

In chapter 10, we discussed argumentation—types of logic, the component parts of an argument, patterns of reasoning, etc. At this point, we are going to discuss the presentation of arguments in the context of the opening speech.

In any debate, the argument begins with the resolution. The resolution articulates a statement about a controversial topic—a statement that takes a position. The debater's job is either to agree with that position or to disagree with it. To put it another way, the resolution gives each of the debaters a thesis, something that must be proved. The debater needs reasons and evidence to prove the thesis. (To employ Toulmin's terms, the debater must have a warrant and data to support the claim.)

In the course of preparing for a public debate, the advocates typically do some brainstorming: they try to think up as many reasons as possible to prove the thesis. But a public debate is definitely a place where less is more: the audience is more likely to be persuaded by a small number of strong reasons than by a barrage of reasons that are of indifferent quality. Debate preparation, then, involves winnowing; debaters may start with a dozen reasons in support of the thesis, but they need to test them and pick only the best—perhaps three or four out of the original number.

The winnowing process involves organization. As they make their selections, debaters should try to fit reasons into some kind of organizational structure. There are a variety of ways of doing this. One of the simplest ways is a topic outline—a framework of letters and numbers that clarifies the importance of points and their relationship to each other. The framework will be familiar with most readers:

1. Main Reason #1
   a. Subpoint
   b. Subpoint
2. Main Reason #2
   a. Subpoint
   b. Subpoint
3. Main Reason #3
   a. Subpoint
   b. Subpoint

Another method is to create a concept map that clusters ideas; with this method, a debater begins by writing ideas down in random positions on a page and then draws lines (or circles, or arrows) between and around them to show how various ideas should be grouped together. For example, one corner of the page might have a note that says that marijuana should be legalized because the war on drugs is prohibitively expensive; in another corner, there might be a note that says that legalized marijuana could be taxed by the state, just like tobacco and alcohol. In order to create a concept map, the debater would mark the connection between the two or add another note to link them. In a final version, the relationship might be expressed as follows:

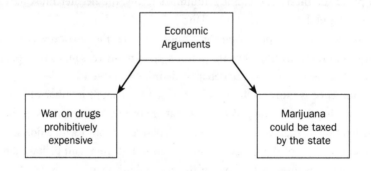

Whatever organizational tools are used, the debater should end up with a series of points. The points that clearly support the main thesis (that is, the resolution or the negation of the resolution) are the main points, and they should be logically independent of one another. You might argue, for example, that marijuana should be legalized because it poses no significant health risks; you could also argue that marijuana should be legalized because legalization would have economic benefits for the state. Both of those reasons directly support the thesis (that marijuana should be legalized), but they are independent: the first reason does not need to be valid in order for the second reason to be valid, and vice versa.

Usually, the debater will also create subpoints; as the name indicates, these are points that are logically subordinate to the main points. The chart above offers a useful illustration. The main point supporting the thesis is that the legalization of marijuana will have economic benefits for the state; the other points, about the expense of the antidrug effort and the possibility of tax revenues, are subpoints.

Arranging Points

There are many different ways to arrange points in a speech; there is no hard and fast rule about what should be first and what should be last. The best method is the one that is best suited to the type of argument being made. Here are a few patterns that are commonly used:

Chronological. A chronological pattern arranges points in a time sequence. Imagine that the debate is about the economic slowdown of 2001, and the debater's thesis is that the slowdown was caused by the actions of the Bush administration. In order to make her case, the debater could trace the government's actions, and their results, chronologically—e.g., "In January of 2001, the administration introduced a package of tax cuts, which led to x. Then in June of 2001, the administration raised the possibility of imposing tariffs on imported steel, and that caused y. . . . "

Spatial. A spatial pattern arranges points by location or geographically. If the debate topic was about the expansion of the European Union, the debater might arrange his argument to consider various areas in sequence: first, the effect of expansion on EU countries that border the proposed new members; second, the effect of expansion on EU countries distant from the new members; third, the effect of expansion on new members in Eastern Europe; fourth, the effect of expansion on new members in the Baltics.

Cause and Effect. We have discussed causal arguments in the context of patterns of reasoning (in chapter 10). Here, we are considering causal arguments as a broad strategy for supporting the thesis. Say, for example, that the resolution is that the debt of Third World countries should be forgiven. One way to approach the issue would be to outline the causes of Third World debt, with the intent of showing that the debt burden is unfair (e.g., the debt was incurred by corrupt dictators no longer in power; the debt was taken on with the encouragement of Western countries who wanted to build businesses in the Third World; the debt was backed by commodities such as oil, coffee and copper that lost value in international markets).

Problem and Solution. The first step in this pattern is to identify a problem that is implied or suggested by the resolution. The resolution might be this: "The U.S. federal government should provide health care coverage for all citizens." The debater would begin by identifying the problem with the current status quo—viz., millions of Americans do not have health insurance and are unable to afford medical care. The second step is to propose a solution; in this case, the solution is provided in a generic way by the resolution itself, but the debater needs to propose something more specific. The final step is to show why the proposed solution would work, why it is preferable to other solutions, and so on.

Topical. The foregoing patterns follow prescribed sequences; it is easy to determine what comes first and what comes last when you are using a chronological pattern. There is no prescribed sequence in the topical pattern, however; in this pattern, points can be arranged in different sequences—but they are always labeled to promote clarity. A debater arguing about immigration laws, for example, might say, "I have three arguments for enforcing the current immigration laws: the economic reasons; the legal reasons; and the cultural reasons."

Transitions

We noted earlier that it is important for debaters to provide an "intellectual road map" for the audience as part of the introduction to the opening speech. To continue the metaphor, it is important to include good transitions, which are like signposts along the way. Good transitions help the listeners to see where they are, and where they are going.

At a minimum, transitions can serve to remind audiences of the structure of the argument. If the speaker has said that she has three arguments for enforcing the current immigration laws—the economic reasons, the legal reasons, and the cultural reasons—she should introduce those reasons with an appropriate label (e.g., "Here are the economic reasons for enforcing immigration laws . . ."). Similarly, if she has said she has three reasons for changing the laws governing handgun possession, she will do well to number her reasons when she presents them (e.g., "and my third point is . . .). In this regard, we'd note that there are few things more frustrating to an audience than speakers who don't deliver on promises or who are inconsistent in their delivery. It is not a good idea to say "I have three points," before going on to identify only two points by number; it is even worse to switch from "point number one" to "point B."

Transitions should also be used to reinforce patterns of arrangement. A speaker using the "problem and solution" model (described above) could say: "Now that you understand the problem, and have heard my solution for it, I want to show you why my solution is the most practical and cost effective option available." Transitions can also be used to group two or three arguments together—e.g., "So far, everything I've said about this proposal has concerned its effect on children in bilingual classes; now I want to talk about its effect on you." This example performs two functions: it summarizes what has gone before and gives a suggestion of what is to come.

The simplest transitions are "additive"—that is, they indicate to the listener that something is being added to a sequence: "my next point is . . . ," "another reason is . . . " These are not, however, the strongest transitions—and can even be somewhat grating if they are repeated without any variance. The strongest transitions are ones that establish logical relationships between ideas. When a speaker says, "The government's actions have created higher levels of unemployment and, *as a result*, higher levels of crime," the transitional words ("as a result") indicate that the speaker sees a causal link between two points. Causality is not, of course, the only logical relationship possible; transitions can also indicate similarities and differences. (It is especially important to indicate differences when responding to an opposing idea—e.g., "you will hear from our opponents that the air strikes in Kosovo constituted an act of imperialism, but we feel that *they were something very different*; they were intended to save a people, not to conquer them.") Transitional words can also be used to emphasize a point: "This debate is, *in fact*, about class warfare."

Transitions are an important part of keeping the audience focused. It is easy for an audience to get lost when listening to arguments for the first time; they do not have the leisure of readers, who can go back and re-read a paragraph if they want. Transitions fix arguments within a logical framework and make them easier to grasp. Good transitions let the listener know what is most important in the opening speech.

The Conclusion

In many ways, the conclusion is a mirror image of the introduction. The introduction, we have noted, should provide a psychological and logical orientation to the listener; the conclusion should provide psychological and logical closure. And just as a good introduction begins with a strong opening, a good conclusion finishes with a strong ending. We should emphasize, however, that the introduction and conclusion *complement* each other; they are not the same thing, and it is a mistake to think of the conclusion as a simple repetition of the introduction.

The differences between the introduction and the conclusion will be apparent if we consider their psychological effects. The introduction offered the audience an orientation: it invited them into a relationship with the speaker; it encouraged them to become interested in the topic at hand. At that point, however, the audience constituted "virgin territory"; they had heard no substantive arguments. By the time of the conclusion, things have changed: they have heard arguments, and, ideally, they have been persuaded. They are not "in the same place" that they were when the speech began because of the experience of hearing the speech. It is the speaker's job, in the conclusion, to remind them of that. It may be helpful to think of the words of Buddha: "You, too, shall pass away. Knowing this, how can you quarrel?" Having made the appropriate adjustments, the question might be: "Now you know why the immigration laws are impractical, unjust and racist. Knowing this, how can you let them remain?" The conclusion is a good place for the debater to make her argument personal, by reminding her audience how they are affected by the topic. In some cases, it is appropriate to include a personal appeal to the audience to take action (by voting, for example), or to change their behavior. (This is only in some cases, however. If the audience is a high school class in West Virginia, and the resolution is about the Russian treatment of Chechnya, it will seem meretricious for the debater to encourage the audience to "go out and do something about it.")

Logical closure, like psychological closure, must take account of what has happened in the body of the speech. Naturally, the speaker's position in the conclusion will be the same as his position in the introduction, but his situation is different: when he made his introduction, his position was a proposition to be proved; now, he can regard that job as done. He is now able to remind his audience of what they have heard—e.g., "So here is what we have seen: the prohibition of marijuana is impractical and expensive; it is unjust, in that it denies the rights of ordinary citizens; and it is unnecessary, in that marijuana does no significant harm to users or to society at large. The conclusion is inescapable: marijuana must be legalized." If the speaker has dealt with complex ideas, it may be wise to repeat his points verbatim, instead of paraphrasing them; in any case, the main points of the argument should be repeated and the connections between them re-emphasized. Repetition will clarify the arguments and will help the audience members to remember what they have heard.

We have argued that the introduction should begin strongly, with no prefatory mumbles or rhetorical fillers; the conclusion should end on a strong note, too, with no apologies or diminuendos. This is not the time to say, "I guess that's about all I have to say. Um, thanks for listening." A simple restatement of the thesis, in a forceful way, can be an effective ending, but speakers can also use some of the tactics that we suggested for openers. A good conclusion can use a joke, a proverb, an aphorism, a quotation or even a snippet of poetry. If the speaker opened with a question, it can be especially effective to repeat it, with an answer: "I began by asking you how much longer this country can continue to sell arms to foreign nations and deny any responsibility for how they are used. The answer is 'No longer.' We must stop selling weapons now, before more innocent people die."

Pitfalls to Avoid

The potential pitfalls of the conclusion are kith and kin of the pitfalls that threaten the introduction. The conclusion should not be too long; it should not be weak or apologetic; it should not be read from a prepared text. It is also important that the conclusion remain consistent with the mood of the body of the speech: if you have closed your argument with a passionate denunciation of some policy as misguided, evil, and ruinous, the conclusion is not a good time to tell a joke. Finally, we'd note that the conclusion is not the place to add a new argument. Once you have indicated that you are wrapping up your argument—either explicitly (by saying "in conclusion") or implicitly—the audience will only be confused by some previously unheard point that does not fit into the framework that has been established. A new idea in the conclusion is merely an indication that the opening speech has not been carefully prepared.

Notes

1. Associated Press, "Readers Share Bob Hope Memories," *USAToday.com*, July 30, 2003, http://www.usatoday.com/life/2003-07-30-hope-memories_x.htm

2. "Alanis Closes Peruvian Gig with: 'Thank You Brazil!'" *Irish Examiner*, September 23, 2003, http://www.examiner.ie/breaking/2003/09/23/story114594.html

Chapter Fourteen

Refutation

"Anything you can do, I can do better.

I can do any thing better than you."

"No you can't."

"Yes I can."

"No you can't."

"Yes I can."

"No you can't."

"Yes I can, yes I can."

—*From* Annie Get Your Gun, *by Irving Berlin*

In the musical comedy *Annie Get Your Gun*, Annie Oakley and Frank Butler are stars—and rivals—in a Wild West Show. Annie begins her song by claiming that she is a bigger attraction than Frank, and then goes on to list her superior abilities: she can shoot better, sing louder, buy cheaper, dig deeper, and drink faster than he can. Every verse of the song ends the same way: when Frank refutes her ("No you can't), Annie reasserts her position ("Yes I can")—and she always gets the last word.

Theater audiences have always enjoyed the volleying contradictions in Irving Berlin's song, but audiences for a public debate expect something more when it comes to refutation. It isn't enough for advocates to contradict their opponents and repeat their original positions. A public debater needs to deal with the substance of an opponent's arguments and must reshape his original argument to respond to what his opponent has said. In this chapter, we will discuss the basics of refutation and rebuttal.

Definition of Terms

When you **refute** an argument, you are saying that the argument is either untrue or inaccurate. In debate, it's not enough just to say that an argument is untrue; rather, you have to *prove* that an argument is wrong, either with evidence or your own argument; you must show *why* the argument is false and erroneous. Refutation is, to borrow a term from competitive sports, an *offensive* maneuver; it is an attack on an opponent's argument. As a debater, you enter the public forum with your own set of arguments either for or against the designated resolution, and part of your job is to present those arguments; but it is also your job to show why your arguments are better than those offered by your opponent.

In a public debate, both sides will engage in the offensive maneuver of refutation; the corollary is that both sides will have to defend themselves. This defensive maneuver is called **rebuttal**—it is, in effect, a refutation of a refutation. When Debater A is attacked by Debater B, Debater A needs to respond; she needs to show why the refutation offered by Debater B is false or erroneous. In a broad way, she must reassert her original position, but she cannot simply repeat what she said in the first place; she must deal with the specific attacks that have been made upon her argument by her opponent.

Types of Refutation

There are four basic types of refutation: denial; reversal; minimization; and outweighing. The first two are sometimes grouped under the heading of direct refutation, meaning that both types flatly deny the truth of an opposing claim. The second two are sometimes grouped under the heading of indirect refutation, meaning that both types admit that an opposing claim is true, or partially true—but, nevertheless, should not be considered as significant or critically important.

Denial

A denial is a straightforward contradiction of a claim:

> **Claim:** The legalization of marijuana leads to an increase in crime.
>
> **Refutation:** The legalization of marijuana does not lead to an increase in crime.

We recognize that this example does not seem much more sophisticated than the contradictions we saw in Annie Oakley's song—but if we put the example in a fuller context, denial will be seen as a valid type of refutation. Let's say, for example, that the debater making the claim about the increase in crime has supported that claim with statistics about crime in the Netherlands, where marijuana has been decriminalized. The debater's opponent refutes this claim by denying it, and then offers his own evidence showing that the Dutch crime statistics are inaccurate, since they show no direct link between marijuana use and crime increase; the crime increase, in fact, can be attributed to other factors instead. Denial is effective if it is supported.

Reversal

In a reversal, or turnaround, the debater accepts part of her opponent's argument as true, but then shows how the part she has accepted supports her own position. In effect, the debater claims the point for her own side.

> **Claim:** If the government recognizes the validity of gay marriage, it will weaken society's respect for traditional marriage.

> **Refutation:** I agree that if the government recognizes the validity of gay marriage, it will weaken society's respect for traditional marriage—but that is exactly what I want to happen. It is unfair and discriminatory to judge that heterosexual unions are better than homosexual unions; traditional marriage does not deserve the respect that it has now.

Here, the refuting debater is accepting the causal chain offered by her opponent, but she is reversing the value of his conclusion. To use a fuller form, the first debater is saying this: "We should not recognize the validity of gay marriage because it will weaken society's respect for traditional marriage—and that would be a bad, undesirable result." The refuting debater accepts the first part of that sentence—yes, recognizing gay marriages *will* weaken traditional marriage —but claims that the result is good and desirable.

A reversal is similar to a denial, in that it contradicts part of what the opponent is arguing; but the reversal goes farther than a denial. A debater making a denial is, to put it metaphorically, kicking out one of the props supporting her opponent's argument; the debater making a reversal kicks out the prop, and then picks it up to use for support of her own argument.

Minimization

A minimization is a refutation of a claim that admits that the claim is true or partly true—but says that the claim is insignificant.

> **Claim:** The legalization of marijuana leads to an increase in crime.

> **Refutation:** The legalization of marijuana may lead to an increase in crime—but that increase would be so small that it should not shape policy.

Again, this example may seem unconvincing without a context—after all, how could any increase in crime be deemed insignificant? But suppose that the debater shows that crime rates, as a rule, are subject to fluctuation: crime rates go up and down all the time, sometimes apparently for reasons that are totally out of the control of policy makers. It has been shown, for example, that violent crime rises when there is an extended period of very hot weather and declines when the temperature changes. Some statistics may suggest that legalization will increase crime rates, but the potential increase shown is very small and would have no more impact on society as a whole than the usual seasonal fluctuations.

Outweighing

Like minimization, outweighing admits the truth of the claim—but it counters the claim by showing that the bad would outweigh the good if the argument as a whole were to be accepted.

> **Claim:** The legalization of marijuana leads to an increase in crime.

> **Refutation:** The legalization of marijuana leads to an increase in crime—but it is worse to deny the rights of the majority of marijuana users, who do not commit crimes.

In this type of refutation, the debater puts the claim in the context of the argument that it supports. The claim that "the legalization of marijuana leads to an increase in crime" is, obviously, meant to support the position that marijuana should be illegal. In refuting this claim, the debater puts it in a balance with his own claim, and shows that his own claim is more important. Statistics suggest that it is only a tiny percentage of marijuana users who commit crimes (excepting, of course, the crimes of buying, growing, or using marijuana). The vast majority of marijuana users, who are law-abiding, should be free—indeed, they have a right—to use a product that does no harm to others. So even if the legalization of marijuana leads to an increase in crime, that increase is a small price to pay for the greater good of giving ordinary citizens their rights. (As Shakespeare's Portia puts in *The Merchant of Venice*: "And I beseech you . . . To do a great right, do a little wrong.")

Strategic Considerations

Elsewhere in this book, we have emphasized the structure of arguments. Argumentative theory offers us many different models—from the syllogism of Aristotle to the claim-data-warrant model of Stephen Toulmin—but all of these models, whatever form they take, are analytical. That is, all of these models break arguments down into their component parts. What is more, the models delineate the relationships between the component parts.

For the sake of simplicity, let's look at the classic deductive syllogism as defined by Aristotle.

Major premise: All men are mortal.

Minor premise: Socrates is a man.

Conclusion: Therefore, Socrates is mortal.

Aristotle argued that the truth of the conclusion depends on the truth of the two premises. **IF** it is true that all men are mortal **AND IF** it is true that Socrates is a man, **THEN** the conclusion must be true. The corollary is that if either of the premises is shown to be untrue, then the conclusion is not proven to be true. For the sake of argument, let's say that Socrates is a dog, not a man. We can no longer conclude, on the basis of these premises, that Socrates is mortal. (To prove that, we'd need to construct a new syllogism with a new major premise: that all dogs are mortal.)

For the purposes of this discussion, the point is simply this: if one of the component parts of the argument fails, then the argument as a whole fails. Debaters should begin the process of refutation with an analysis of their opponents' arguments. What are the component parts of the argument? Which of those parts are significant? Which of those parts can be disproved? If the debater plans and executes his attacks strategically, then the opposing argument, like the walls of Jericho when Joshua fought his biblical battle, will come tumbling down.

We note in passing that in some forms of educational debate, arguments are often delivered with the parts clearly labeled. Lincoln-Douglas debaters, for example, typically offer an oratorical packing list that identifies definitions, criteria, value premises, and contentions. As a result, the business of refutation is somewhat simple: opposing debaters can run down the list, and decide where they want to aim their attacks. A public debate, however, since it is directed at an "untrained" audience, is not likely to include such a clear diagram of the component parts of an argument. Even so, the component parts are there, and it is the debater's job to listen carefully, to analyze, and to refute with precision.

A Model of Refutation

To illustrate possible targets for refutation, let's return to the logical model we used in chapter 10:

Warrant: Adults should be free to accept moderate risks to their own health.

Data: Marijuana has been shown to have only moderate health risks.

Claim: Adults should be able to choose whether to use marijuana or not.

The **claim**, you will remember, is what the debater is trying to prove. In a formal contest, it might be identical to the resolution, or it might be a subpoint in favor of the resolution. (The resolution might be, for example, that marijuana should be legalized; the claim above would support that position.) The warrant is an assumption or an underlying principle; it is something that connects the claim with the evidence that is used to support it. In the above model, that evidence is called **data**.

At the highest logical level, debaters can refute an opposing argument by attacking the claim itself. By attacking the claim, rather than the data or the warrant, the refuting debater isn't really addressing the truth of the claim; rather, he is attacking its relevance or its logical status in the argument as a whole. Let's say that the resolution is about the legalization of marijuana, but the debater has made a claim about the failure of needle-exchange programs set up for heroin users. His claim may be true—but it is irrelevant, given that the resolution is about marijuana. The refuting debater can attack this claim as "non-topical."

A claim can also be attacked if it is inconsistent with other claims that are part of the debater's argument. Suppose that the debater argues at one point that the legalization of marijuana will reduce marijuana use (this is the so-called forbidden fruit argument, which postulates that marijuana is attractive to many users only because it is illegal and would lose its appeal if legalized). It does not make sense for her to argue, at another point, that the government will be able to collect tax revenues from legal marijuana sales and that those revenues will increase as more and more people smoke marijuana. Both arguments cannot be true—so they can be refuted as inconsistent.

Most of the time, debaters will refute an argument by focusing on either the data or the warrant. To return to the model above: in order to refute the claim that adults should be free to choose whether to use marijuana, the first option for the refuting debater is to attack the data by offering evidence that shows that marijuana does not have "only moderate" health risks, but in fact causes long-term mental impairment. So even if the warrant is true, marijuana is ruled out because it cannot be classified as one of the moderate risks stipulated in the warrant. The second option is to attack the warrant itself. When the warrant says that adults "should be free," it is implicit that adults should be free to pursue this choice *without the intervention of the state*. In other words, the warrant is making an assumption about the proper role of the state itself. In order to refute the claim, a debater could argue that the state has a different role—viz., that the state has a responsibility to maximize the health of all of its citizens, and should eliminate health risks to the greatest extent possible. So even if we accept the validity of the data, the claim is disproved because even moderate health risks should be seen as unacceptable.

We should be clear that the debater mounting a refutation is by no means constrained to only one target: it is possible to attack both the warrant *and* the data, if both of them seem vulnerable. It is tactically wise to attack more than one target: if the audience remains unconvinced by the attack on the data—or if the debater who offered the data is able to rebut the attack successfully—they may be swayed by the attack on the warrant.

In chapter 10, we offered an expanded model of the above argument, and we reintroduce that model here in order to show how backing is vulnerable.

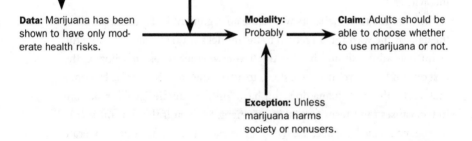

In the expanded model, **backing** denotes additional information offered in support of the data or the warrant. The **exception** is an admission, on the part of the debater, that the claim is not true in all possible cases. The inclusion of **modality** follows from the introduction of an exception; here, the word "probably" qualifies and limits the claim.

The backing of the data can be refuted if the opposing debater is able to challenge the validity of the backing (e.g., "the W.H.O. study was small, and did not include a valid control group") and/or is able to introduce contradictory evidence (e.g., "a study by the National Institutes of Health concluded that marijuana use has significant and serious effects on health").

The backing for the warrant above is similarly vulnerable. It could be argued, for example, that marijuana, as a psychoactive drug, is distinctly different from alcohol and tobacco, and those substances cannot be used as models to support the warrant. Alternatively, the refuting debater could argue that the state does not (and should not) offer citizens free choice about alcohol and tobacco; in fact, the state is publicly committed to reducing and eliminating smoking.

The exception in the above model opens the door for a refutation. The debater making the claim has admitted that adults should not be free to choose marijuana if that choice harms society or nonusers. If the refuting debater is able to establish that harm to society, and nonusers, is a general rule, rather than an exception to the rule, the claim will not stand up.

Refuting Patterns of Reasoning

So far, we have discussed refutation in terms of its targets—that is, we have looked at where a debater can direct an attack. Now, we would like to turn to methods of refutation. In chapter 10, we described different patterns of reasoning that can be used in constructing arguments and mentioned some of the weaknesses that should be avoided. Here, we will review those patterns in the context of refutation.

Deductive Arguments

A deductive argument is an argument that begins with known, general truths and draws a conclusion about a particular instance. Deductive arguments are inherently strong because they are self-contained: if the premises are true, then the conclusion has to be true—there is no need to consider any other evidence. In order to refute a deductive argument, you must disprove one of the general truths that lead to the conclusion. Typically, general truths include absolute words like "all" or "only": all men are mortal; all cows eat grass; only Red Sox fans know the true meaning of pain. A general truth can be disproved by pointing to significant exceptions, and establishing that "all" should be replaced by "most" or "some."

Say, for example, that a debater makes the following remark: "George W. Bush is a Republican, and that means that he cares only about the rich." There is actually an unspoken premise that leads to this conclusion:

> **Unspoken premise:** All Republicans care only about the rich.
>
> **Spoken premise:** George W. Bush is a Republican.
>
> **Conclusion:** Therefore, George W. Bush cares only about the rich.

There is no way to refute the spoken premise—Bush *is* a Republican born and bred—but the unspoken premise is vulnerable because it contains two absolute terms. The refuting debater needs simply to show that the statement is not true about all Republicans.

Inductive Arguments

An inductive argument is an argument that begins with known, specific truths and attempts to draw a general conclusion. Inductive arguments are weaker than deductive arguments because they are not self-contained. The specific truths with which an inductive argument begins are only part of a broader range of truths; you may base your conclusion on a dozen different examples, but there will always be examples you did not include or consider in your reasoning.

This is not to say, of course, that inductive arguments are bad and should be avoided. Indeed, most of the arguments you will hear in everyday life are inductive—a doctor considers specific symptoms, and makes a general conclusion with a diagnosis; a jury considers specific pieces of evidence in a courtroom, and concludes whether the defendant is guilty or innocent; even the weather reporter considers data received by various scientific instruments and concludes that rain will fall in the afternoon. The scientific method itself is inductive: researchers conduct the same experiment a finite number of times and always gets the same results; they conclude that if the experiment were repeated infinitely, the results would stay the same.

Nevertheless, inductive arguments are always vulnerable to refutation. The refuting debater needs simply to introduce matters—e.g., other examples, other signs, other causes—that were not considered by the debater when she drew her conclusions.

Reasoning by Example.   When a debater reasons by example, he draws a general conclusion from specific instances. Again, let's say that the debate is about the legalization of marijuana in the United States. In support of legalization, the debater cites the instances of countries that have legalized or decriminalized the drug, and shows that there has been no meaningful increase in crime or health problems, and that the countries have benefited by freeing up police and courts to do other work. The debater concludes that because legalization has had only positive effects in the countries he cited it will have a similar positive effect in the United States.

There are a few ways to refute this kind of argument. One is to adduce examples that do not support the conclusion; the refuting debater might argue that legalization has had disastrous effects in some countries. Another way is to challenge the quality of the evidence presented: the first debater has argued that there are no deleterious effects on public health, but his statistics come from a short-term study. The bad effects of using marijuana take years to appear, and it is wrong to conclude that there are no bad effects just because they haven't shown up yet in public health surveys; this is like arguing that smoking doesn't cause lung cancer because no one gets cancer the day after they smoke their first cigarette. A third way to refute this argument is to reject the applicability of the conclusion to the instance being debated. The evidence may suggest that the legalization of marijuana has no bad effects but that is true only in the sample countries—which have small populations, and where only a very small percentage of the population smokes marijuana. The United States, with a population approaching 300 million, is a completely different situation; according to some studies, more than one-third of adult Americans have smoked marijuana—which means that the population of American marijuana smokers is more than four times the size of the entire population of the Netherlands.

Reasoning by Cause.   A debater who is reasoning by cause is trying to establish causal links between events: something happened or is happening because of something else that happened first. In the physical world, causal chains are common and often seem irrefutable: the car stopped because you forgot to put gas in it; the roof collapsed because the tree fell on it; you broke your hand because you punched a concrete wall. But as any student of history knows, it is much harder to determine the causes of a particular event in the social world. Why did the communist system collapse in the Soviet Union? Because the government bankrupted itself trying to build weapons? Because the Russian people wanted democracy? Because the Russian people wanted money? Because the Soviet satellites wanted freedom? Because President Reagan approved development of the Strategic Defense Initiative?

Because glasnost destroyed the system of secrecy on which the communist system depended? All of the above? Some of the above?

The point is that, when it comes to causal chains, there are many roads that can lead to the same end—and the debater who wants to refute a causal chain can simply show one of the other roads. Say that the issue in the debate is unemployment. It is an incontrovertible fact that there are more unemployed people in the United States in 2003 than there were in 2000, and that many jobs have been lost in the manufacturing sector. A debater may well argue that the rise in unemployment is the result of policies by the Bush administration; the tax cuts have hurt the national economy, increased the national deficit, and made employers unwilling to hire new workers. The debater who wants to refute that argument needs to offer another cause: she might argue, for example, that the loss of manufacturing jobs is the result of globalization and the free trade agreements that were negotiated during the 1990s. It is much cheaper to hire labor in developing countries than in the United States, and American workers are no longer competitive on the world market.

Sometimes, the refutation of reasoning by cause may completely reject the cause proposed by the first debater ("The federal decision to deregulate the phone industry has nothing to do with the increased use of cell phones in this country . . . "). But it is also possible to accept the cause proposed, while minimizing or outweighing it ("The rise in child obesity may be partly attributable to the high fat content found in meals from fast food restaurants, but the biggest causes of weight gain are the poor quality of the lunches offered by the schools themselves, and the broad decline in children's physical activity").

Reasoning by Analogy.   An analogy is a comparison between two different items. Simply put, the logic of reasoning by analogy goes like this: "A and B are alike. Therefore, something that is true about A will also be true about B." Analogies are useful in order to explain difficult concepts; in debate, they are often used to make connections between controversial issues (e.g., the legalization of marijuana) and noncontroversial issues (e.g., the legalization of alcohol).

There are two basic types of analogies: literal and figurative. A classic literal analogy is the one just mentioned, which compares alcohol and marijuana. The two substances are alike, according to the analogy; the corollary is that if it is unwise or impossible or unethical to make one of them illegal, then it is also unwise or impossible or unethical to make the other illegal. Alcohol is legal, and that means that marijuana should be legal, too.

A figurative analogy does not focus on physical similarities between two items; instead, it proposes that two physically dissimilar things are similar in nature or function. In order to explain the restrictions on its software licenses, Microsoft compares them to airline tickets—some of the licenses are basic and restricted, like a low-cost economy class airline ticket. The analogy is meant to explain something that is not understood (a software license) by comparing it to something that is well-known (a plane ticket).

The simplest way to refute an analogy is to reject the validity of the comparison being made. Given the above analogy about alcohol and marijuana, a debater could say, "Yes, alcohol and marijuana are somewhat alike, but they are not identical—neither in the way that they affect the body chemically nor in their psychoactive effects. Therefore it is a mistake to construct public policy that presumes that they are identical; different substances demand different policies."

A figurative analogy is even easier to refute because the proposed similarities are more tenuous and are vulnerable to a literal approach: computers aren't planes, and software licenses are not something you buy so that you can travel for one day. Ticket pricing may be reasonable but that doesn't mean that software pricing is reasonable, too.

We note that most figurative analogies are more rhetorical than logical: when Canadian Prime Minister Pierre Trudeau remarked that having the United States for a neighbor is like sharing a bed with an elephant, he was looking for a colorful way to voice a complaint; his comparison did not really explain a difficult concept or make a controversial position more palatable. As a result, analogies like this are not susceptible to logical refutation—a debater would seem silly trying to argue that the United States is not an elephant, and North America isn't really a bed. (If, of course, Trudeau offered his comparison seriously and literally, it would be fairly easy to dismiss it.)

Reasoning by Sign.   Reasoning by sign is a method that uses independent indicators in order to support a claim. If you walk into a house and see a pair of size 14 sneakers in the hallway and an opened carton of milk on the kitchen counter, and you hear the sound of a stereo blasting metallic rock through the ceiling, you may conclude that there is a teenage boy somewhere in the vicinity. You do not have conclusive proof but experience suggests that the presence of these indicators correlates highly with the presence of adolescent males.

In debate, the signs that are correlated are often statistical: for example, a debater may argue that a rise in unemployment correlates with a rise in drug use. The debater may not have any hard causal evidence—that is, there may be no evidence that establishes that it is the newly unemployed who are taking drugs—but experience shows that one statistic is a good indicator of the other.

Arguments that depend on reasoning by sign may be refuted in much the same way as arguments that depend on reasoning by cause. Just as there are always potential causes other than the ones suggested by the debater, there are other ways to interpret signs. Teenage boys are not the only people who wear large sneakers (grown-ups wear them, too); they are certainly not the only people who drink milk; and heavy metal is also the favored choice of some girls, some preteens, and some middle-aged men. Unemployment may seem to correlate to drug use, but there may be a stronger correlation between drug use and the quality of the local police force.

Statistical correlations are also vulnerable in that they do not have predictive force. In the absence of causal links, it cannot be said with certainty that the future will be just like the past; proverbs to the contrary, there is always the chance that history will not repeat itself.

Common Problems and Logical Fallacies

So far, we have discussed refutation as it relates to different types of arguments and different patterns of reasoning. In the pages that follow, we will describe common problems and fallacies that can be refuted; these are logical flaws that appear in all types of arguments and all patterns of reasoning.

Flawed Evidence

Even experienced debaters sometimes make errors in fact—and those errors, of course, are the easiest to refute. If a debater should say that the top trading partner of the United States is Japan, it is a simple matter for the refuting debater to point out that the top trading partner is actually Canada, by a long margin.

Typically, however, evidence is flawed in subtler ways. Ideally, evidence is objective and impartial—but it often happens that it is faulty or biased instead. Statistical studies, for example, may be based on small or unrepresentative populations; advertisers are fond of saying that "recent studies show that our product is best"—but the wary consumer should realize that the study may have been conducted by surveying the friends and family of the company sales force. It also happens that studies are conducted by organizations that are not competent or credible—should you believe a survey published on the Internet when it was conducted by a middle school social studies class? The same caveat applies to individual opinions—is a pop singer an authoritative source for an economic policy analysis? Evidence can also become outdated. A 1975 study examining the attitude of Americans toward gay rights would not be very useful for examining that attitude today—too much has changed in the past few decades. When a debate centers on current social, economic and political conditions—as most public debates do—then the evidence must be recent in order to be valid.

Finally, we'd note that very often studies are produced or sponsored by organizations that have political motivations. Earlier in this chapter, we cited a statistic indicating that more than one-third of adult Americans have smoked marijuana, but it's worth noting that the statistic comes from a study by NORML (founded as the National Organization for Reform of Marijuana Laws), which takes a strong advocacy position in favor of decriminalizing marijuana. That does not mean that the statistics it produces are necessarily inaccurate; it does, however, suggest that the statistics should be corroborated from another, more disinterested source.

In sum, evidence must meet five standards: it must be accurate; it must be statistically valid (i.e., based on a large and representative sample); it must be produced by a source that is competent and credible; it must be recent enough to be pertinent to the issue being debated, when that issue is current and contemporary; and it must come from a source that is neutral and unbiased. A debater can refute evidence by showing that it fails to meet any one of these standards.

Flawed Reasoning

There are dozens of kinds of argumentative flaws; here, we include a description of the most common ones found in debate. A debater can refute them by identifying them for the audience.

The Hasty Generalization.   We noted above that one primary pattern of reasoning is reasoning by example. An argument based on this reasoning, however, is good only if it includes a sufficient number of examples. The hasty generalization is a fallacy because it is based on insufficient evidence—that is, on only one or two examples. It may be true that the Weimar Republic established after World War I was a weak and corrupt democracy; it does not follow, however, that all democracies after wars are weak and corrupt.

So: one example does not prove a general truth. The converse is that one example does not necessarily *disprove* a general truth—in other words, it is not logically strong to put too much weight on an exception to a rule.

Post Hoc, Ergo Propter Hoc.   This fallacy is sometimes found in arguments based on reasoning by cause. The Latin phrase means "after this, therefore because of this." In other words, this fallacy doesn't recognize the difference between "after" and "because." Just because one event comes after another event, it does not mean that the first event was the cause of the second event. It is true that Bill Clinton was elected president not long after the collapse of the Communist Party in the Soviet Union, but that does not mean that the two events were related causally.

Along the same lines, it is a fallacy to mistake coincidence for cause. In his discussion of historical causes in *War and Peace*, Tolstoy notes that he can hear church bells every time the hands on his watch indicate the hour—but that doesn't mean that his watch makes the bells ring.

Argumentum Ad Hominem.   The *argumentum ad hominem*—the Latin phrase means "argument directed at the man"—is an attempt to discredit an argument by focusing on the character or qualifications of someone who supports it. If, for example, the debate was about affirmative action, a debater would commit this fallacy by saying, "The government program in affirmative action began during the presidency of Richard Nixon, the only American president who was forced to resign from office." The logic is that if the idea was introduced by a "bad" president, it must then be a "bad" idea.

The *argumentum ad hominem* can also be launched directly at an opponent during a debate—e.g., "Why should we listen to a man who [choose
one] a) failed to vote in the last three elections; b) avoided the draft during Vietnam; c) divorced his wife to marry a woman younger than his
daughter; d) failed to file his federal income taxes; e) was a recruiter for
the Ku Klux Klan." (These accusations have actually been directed against
a) California Governor Arnold Schwarzenegger; b) President Bill Clinton;
c) Congressman Newt Gingrich; d) presidential candidate Rev. Al Sharpton;
e) Senator Robert Byrd.) Even if it is a common tactic, the *argumentum ad
hominem* is not a valid form of refutation because it does not address the
opposing argument directly.

The Non Sequitur.   The Latin phrase *non sequitur* means "it does not follow."
A non sequitur may look logical and sound logical, but it is a fallacy because
the conclusion does not follow from the premises that have been offered.
Take, for example, this syllogism:

> All successful movie stars are rich.
>
> Madonna is rich.
>
> Therefore, Madonna is a successful movie star.

Now, the first two statements are undoubtedly true—but the conclusion
does not necessarily follow, because there are other reasons why Madonna
could be rich. The problem here is not with the premises, but with the
conclusion drawn from them. In other words, one cannot refute this conclusion by disproving one of the two premises; the problem instead is with
the process of reasoning.

Debaters may not encounter too many arguments about Madonna—but
it is fairly common to hear people jump to conclusions when dealing with
policy issues. Take this sequence of ideas, for example:

> The cost of the Social Security program is going to increase
> in the coming decades.
>
> The amount of money being paid to Social Security will not
> rise at the same rate.
>
> Therefore, Social Security benefits should not be paid to afflu-
> ent people.

The problem is that the proposed conclusion is not logically necessary;
that is, it does not follow from the premises, even though the premises are

true. What *does* follow logically? With the addition of a condition, we could conclude the following: "If the budget of the Social Security program is to be balanced, we must either decrease its costs or increase the amount of money paid to it." Any plan—whether it is to cut benefits or to privatize investments—is something that does not follow from these premises. Other premises must be articulated, and other arguments must be made, in order to arrive at the above conclusion.

The Slippery Slope.   The slippery slope is a logical fallacy that presumes that a chain of events will result because of one single action—and that the results will get progressively worse. In a debate about the legalization of marijuana, a slippery slope argument would say that the legalization of marijuana would be followed by the legalization of other drugs, including cocaine and heroin, and that the spiraling crime rates that would follow would make it impossible to live in America's inner cities. The same slope often appears in arguments about civil liberties; it is said that any restriction of civil liberties will be followed by progressively greater invasions of privacy. The slippery slope is essentially a scare tactic, not a logical argument. Yes, it is possible to argue that one action is likely to be a precedent for other actions (e.g., if the school principal allows one student on academic probation to play in a school football game, it is reasonable to assume that other students on academic probation must be allowed to participate in other sports). It is not valid, however, simply to assume that one act will lead, via an asserted chain of events, to ever more harmful similar acts (e.g., if the school principal allows one student on academic probation to play in a school football game, then students caught bringing guns into school will be allowed to act as security guards at school dances).

Begging the Question.   Begging the question is a kind of circular reasoning: it is an argument that acts as if a question that must be asked has already been answered. Again, say that the debate is about the legalization of marijuana. One debater says that marijuana should be banned because it is harmful; when his opponent asks how he knows it is harmful, he replies, "Because it is banned now, and it wouldn't be banned if it were not harmful." Basically, the debater assumes that his position is right—and then uses that position to "prove" his claim.

A Format for Refutation

In a public debate, the clarity of the arguments is a matter of primary importance. Debaters need to present their ideas clearly so that the audience can grasp them readily; this is especially true when they are refuting arguments. If the debaters are not clear in refutation, it is easy for the audience to become confused about who said what; clear refutation helps the audience to grasp the most essential points in contention. In order to promote clarity, we suggest that debaters follow a simple format.

The first step in the format is to restate the argument that is being refuted: "My opponent says that the death penalty is a deterrent to violent crime, and that we will see more murders if the death penalty is abolished." It is important to restate the opposing argument clearly and fairly; generally, the audience will respond negatively if the restatement seems to be skewed or unfair. (So if the opposing team has said that they favor the decriminalization of marijuana, it is not fair to say, "They have argued that the government should promote marijuana and make it readily available to anyone who wants it.")

The second step is to state your own position in response: "But that claim is not true; the death penalty does not have a deterrent effect." The third step is to support your position with evidence: "First, we can see that the murder rate is much lower in Europe than in the United States—and the death penalty was abolished in Europe some time ago. Second, in many of the individual American states where the death penalty has been reintroduced, there has been no significant decline in the murder rate. Indeed, in some states the murder rate has gone up since the death penalty was reintroduced."

The fourth step in this format is to articulate the impact of the refutation on the opponent's argument: "So, we can conclude that the death penalty does not have a deterrent effect. In fact, it may have the opposite effect, because it creates a scenario where cold-blooded, premeditated killing is condoned by the state simply because it is the state doing the killing. The bottom line is that my opponent has not offered a valid reason for supporting capital punishment." (We'd note that in this sample, the refuting debater is offering a reversal or turnaround, one of the two types of direct refutation discussed earlier in this chapter.)

In summary, the four steps are:

1. Restatement of opposing argument ("They say that. . .)
2. Statement of response ("But we say that . . .")
3. Evidence and reasons in support of response ("Because . . .")
4. Impact of response ("Therefore their position is wrong . . .")

Rebuttal

As we noted earlier, rebuttal can be defined as a refutation of a refutation: that is, it is the debater's job to defend herself by showing why the attack on her argument has been invalid. Not surprisingly, most of what we have said about refutation is also valid about rebuttal: the rebutting debater can attack the warrant or the data in the refutation; she can offer alternatives to arguments that depend on signs or causes and reject analogies; she can expose logical fallacies.

The steps in a rebuttal are similar to the steps in a refutation. Again, the debater needs to begin by clearly identifying the point that is in controversy—and may begin by challenging the accuracy of the refuting debater's statements. ("They said that I am in favor of granting illegal immigrants all of the rights of citizenship, but in fact I said I am in favor of only two things: the children of illegal immigrants should have the right to public education; and illegal immigrants should be allowed to obtain valid driver's licenses. I do not believe that illegal immigrants should be allowed to vote, or hold public office, or do any of the other things that are open only to U.S. citizens.") If the refuting debater has been grossly inaccurate, the rebutting debater may simply dismiss the refutation ("There is no reason for me to defend a position that I never took in the first place").

If, however, the refutation has been fair and accurate, the rebutting debater must address the substance of the argument—that is, the statement and support (steps 2 and 3 in the refutation model). As an example, we'll reuse our debate about the legalization of marijuana. Suppose that in her original argument, the debater has included the evidence that one-third of all adult Americans have smoked marijuana. In the course of cross-examination, she has acknowledged that the statistic came from a study sponsored by NORML. In the course of his refutation, the opposing debater has challenged the validity of this evidence: "She told you that one-third of adult Americans have smoked marijuana, but that information came from an organization that is committed to the legalization of marijuana, and they have an incentive for making the number of marijuana users as high as possible."

How would the first debater rebut this attack? She might simply reject the charge of bias: "My opponent implies that this data is biased, but he has no hard evidence for this challenge; he has only his own presumption that it is biased. Besides, a position of advocacy does not necessarily mean that data is prejudiced: the American Cancer Society is devoted to wiping out the disease, but that doesn't mean we shouldn't trust their data about how many Americans have cancer." Another tactic would be to introduce new evidence in support of the point: "The study by NORML is not the only one that shows that marijuana use in America is widespread. In fact, studies done of high school age students show that their use of marijuana is even higher than that of the adult population. The Partnership for a Drug-Free America found that over 40 percent of teenagers had used marijuana—and their bias (if they have one) would be to deflate that figure." Still another tactic would be to minimize the importance of the refutation: "I have no reason to believe that the data is biased, but let's say that it is—let's say that only a quarter of Americans have used marijuana, instead of a third. That still means that there are millions of Americans—more than 70 million Americans, actually—who have used marijuana. And it is still only a tiny fraction of those people—a few hundred thousand at the most—who have committed crimes while smoking marijuana. My point remains true: most marijuana smokers are law-abiding citizens. Marijuana does not increase crime, and it should not be banned for that reason." As this example shows, the rebutting debater needs to reinforce her original point, but she cannot simply repeat what she said before; she must assert it in a new way, after refuting the attack that has been made on it. Finally, she must underline the impact of her rebuttal—that is, she must point out that because the refutation has been invalid, her original point still stands in favor of her position.

Part Three

Presenting a Public Debate

Chapter Fifteen

Delivering Your Arguments Effectively

Introduction

A badly delivered speech is like overcooked broccoli with no salt or pepper—it may be nutritious, but you wish you didn't have to eat it. How many great ideas and interesting thoughts have been wasted because they were presented with the enthusiasm of a dead fish? How much good information and persuasive argumentation have fallen on deaf ears because of poor speech delivery?

Samir, a neophyte debater, knows this all too well. He used to think that what you say is what really counts—if you have good arguments and support them well, why should it matter how you deliver them? After all, he had always gotten good responses to his articles in the school paper. He knew he had good ideas, did his research thoroughly and wrote well; that much was clear to everybody. Yet when he and his classmates decided to organize a public debate at his school about the hot issue of the day—school uniforms—the audience thought his carefully prepared speech was about as interesting as a lecture from the school nurse outlining the principles of personal hygiene. As he was explaining his case (and wishing it was all over already), he could hear people talking; he could see them shifting in their seats, eyeing the door, and generally looking bored by what he had to say. Needless to say, this discouraged him quite a bit. He didn't understand what went wrong; why wouldn't the audience listen to him? Didn't they care if their school introduced uniforms and tried to infringe upon the students' self-expression? Perhaps he should have just written about it in the paper . . .

The guys from his media class happened to record the whole debate on video; even though it pained him to re-live his failure again, he decided to watch the tape and see for himself what had happened. And there he was, slouching behind the lectern, head buried in his notes, reading off the paper as fast as he could (he remembered thinking: "If I read this fast enough, it will be over sooner"). He hardly looked up during the entire speech, and his intonation was as flat as a can of Coke that's been open a week. He was clutching his notes and speaking under his breath as if he was trying to keep the whole thing a secret. As he was watching, Samir had a hard time understanding what he was saying on the tape, even though he knew the speech almost by heart. If he couldn't understand himself, how could the audience? The moral of the story became clear to him: having good ideas, doing your homework and being a good writer certainly help, but these things are not enough unless you can deliver your thoughts with enthusiasm, clarity and poise.

A few weeks later, Samir and his friends decided to stage another debate, and Samir promised himself that he wouldn't act like that timorous bore he had seen on the tape. When he took the lectern, he tried a few things: he slowed down, made a conscious effort to look up at the audience, put down his notes so that he could gesture freely, projected his voice more, and actually thought about what he was saying and how it might sound to someone else. After the first few sentences, he noticed that everyone was looking at him and a few people were nodding in agreement. Nobody else was talking. It was just his voice and his ideas, making their way slowly but surely into the minds of his audience. Samir felt strangely excited, as if he were hearing his own arguments for the first time; he started liking this whole public speaking business. He'd have to do it again sometime soon.

Styles of Delivery

There are many different styles of speech delivery—and each is appropriate (or inappropriate) as determined by the occasion. As Aristotle noted centuries ago, the kind of oratory to be employed by the speaker is determined by consideration of the audience, and its expectations.[1]

Take, for example, the American president's State of the Union address. The speech and the occasion are highly formal; in fact, the speech is delivered in order to satisfy an obligation stipulated in the Constitution, which says that the president "shall from time to time give to the Congress Information of the State of the Union." The speech is broadcast all over the world and every word counts. Every utterance provides an opportunity for a hot debate among news anchors, pundits and politicians: What exactly did it mean? What new policies will be translated into action? Typically, the president speaks for about an hour from a prepared manuscript. (For many years, presidents have read their speeches from a teleprompter, which scrolls the projected manuscript on transparent screens visible to the speaker but invisible to the audience.) There is nothing casual or spontaneous in the speech; every word is scripted and rehearsed. The situation is ritualistic: the speech is studded with lines that are designed to elicit applause, and even standing ovations. (The leadership of the Congress is given the opportunity to preview the text before it is delivered, and they plan the responses of their parties—they determine when they will sit silent, when they will clap, and when they will stand and holler.) The speech and the response may seem somewhat stilted—but formality is what the audience expects; no one wants to hear a State of the Union address that sounds made up on the spot, or that is filled with off-the-cuff remarks.

The style used in the State of the Union address, however, would be entirely inappropriate and impractical for, say, a classroom debate on the advantages of Plato over Aristotle. In that case, a more extemporaneous, spontaneous style would be the right choice, because the students listening are sitting in a familiar setting and would expect their classmates to use "everyday" language.

In our view, the appropriate style for a public debate will almost always be somewhere in the middle of the spectrum of styles—not as formal as the State of the Union and not as casual as an interview on talk show. To provide a theoretical framework for this discussion, we will describe three basic styles on that spectrum:

Memorized or Read

In the most formal style of speaking, the text is memorized or read in its entirety. The speech is written in advance and presented exactly as written. Often the manuscript is distributed to the press and the audience in advance; delivering the speech serves only a ritualistic function. Some examples are the already mentioned State of the Union address, inauguration speeches, and the Queen's Address in the British Parliament.

Impromptu

At the other end of the style spectrum, we have impromptu delivery, also known as ad hoc or "off-the-cuff" speaking. (The word "impromptu" comes from the Latin phrase *in promptu*, meaning "in readiness." The expression "off-the-cuff" dates from the days when men wore stiff linen cuffs on their formal shirts; a gentleman who anticipated being asked to speak, say, after a dinner would pencil some notes on the end of his sleeve ahead of time and then surreptitiously read "off his cuff" as he spoke.) The impromptu speech is given with no advance notice. It is created completely on the spot, on the spur of the moment—improvised rather than prepared.

Some speech tournaments include the category of impromptu speaking—and most speakers would rather wrestle an orangutan on a high wire over a piranha tank than stand up before an audience and improvise a speech about a topic that seems to have dropped from the sky. It's worth noting, however, that impromptu speeches are fairly common in everyday life: whenever you are called on in class or at a meeting or during a meal with a group of friends and asked to speak; whenever you feel compelled to "say a few words" because it somehow seems appropriate or necessary, even though you did not plan on it beforehand; whenever someone sticks a microphone in your face and asks you what you think; then you are making an impromptu speech.

Extemporaneous

The extemporaneous style of speaking lies midway between reading a prepared text and impromptu delivery. Extemporaneous speaking is not plotted fully ahead of time, as with the first style; neither is it something that is composed fully on the spot, as with the latter. Extemporaneous speaking does require preparation; the speaker focuses on preparing ideas, doing research, and assembling evidence. But the speaker does not prepare every word that will be said—and in that respect, it is similar to impromptu speaking. The extemporaneous speaker works freely from an outline, rather than a fully written-out manuscript. As with impromptu speaking, the benefit is that the speech sounds lively and fresh—and avoids the occasional stiltedness that comes with reading a text.

The extemporaneous style is the best choice for most public debate occasions. While debaters should have their cases well thought out and researched in advance, they should let their words and sentences be created freely on the spot, especially when responding to their opponents' ideas. There is nothing worse than a static debate, composed solely of the exchange of previously prepared speeches—it's worse than watching a pop star lip-synch her way through a "live" concert. Good debates demand spontaneity, with advocates responding to what they have just heard, and changing their arguments as needed. An event that is scripted and unchanging does not properly deserve to be called a debate.

Vocal and Physical Delivery

Nonverbal communication is any kind of communication that does not use words. Researchers differ about the exact percentages, but most agree that the verbal part of any message on average conveys only 35 percent of the speaker's meaning, while nonverbal communication conveys the rest.[2] Some think that nonverbal behavior affects us five times more strongly than verbal messages, and, if they contradict each other (as they sometimes do), we are more likely to believe the nonverbal message rather than the verbal one.

Nonverbal communication can be divided into two major categories: vocal and physical. Vocal delivery includes anything that has to do with the use of voice: volume, speed, pitch, inflections, enunciation, pauses, stress. Physical (or kinesic) delivery refers to the body and its relationship to its surroundings: posture, head movements, body movements, gestures, facial expressions, eye contact, proximity, orientation, appearance.

Vocal Delivery

Pitch is the tone frequency of human voice. Pitch is determined by the speed at which vocal cords vibrate when air (breath) is forced through them by the abdominal muscles, thereby producing tone. If the vocal cords vibrate faster, the pitch will be higher; if they vibrate slower, the pitch will be lower. When we are nervous, we often breathe and speak faster—and, as a result, our vocal cords vibrate faster, and our voices sound higher in pitch than they normally do. A corollary is that most listeners equate a high-pitched voice with nervousness. Not surprisingly, speakers who want to sound calm and authoritative—for example, newsreaders and radio announcers—often train their voices to sound lower.

Volume is how loudly or softly one speaks. Though sometimes speaking in a softer, steady voice may make the speaker seem calm and collected, more often speaking too softly is associated with the lack of confidence and credibility. Aside from this perception, projecting one's voice is important in public speaking for purely practical reasons as well: a message that can't be heard is not going to persuade any listeners. Speakers have to reach everyone in the audience, even the man with the hearing aid sitting in the last row of the balcony. If the listeners have to strain to hear what is being said, they will soon get frustrated and give up trying, and the speaker's message will evaporate into thin air.

Enunciation has to do with the movement of speech organs. Good enunciation depends on the proper use of tongue, teeth and lips to produce sounds of vowels and consonants clearly. In the mouth of a speaker with unclear diction, "What is the matter?" becomes "Wassamadder?" Words are slurred together, and consonants are replaced with lazy substitutes, or disappear altogether. (Most English speakers find "t" harder to say than "d" or "s" because they must take the trouble to press their tongues against the back of their teeth to make the sound.)

In public speaking, good enunciation is important simply because clear diction is easier to understand than unclear diction, and listeners will never agree with someone that they can't understand. But good diction has other positive connotations as well. Listeners perceive that clear diction is a reflection of clear thinking; what is more, good enunciation connotes a higher level of education—and that connotation can add to the speaker's credibility.

Speed is the rate at which words are spoken and is another aspect of vocal communication that affects the audience's perception of the speaker. Speed is not interpreted independently; listeners perceive it in combination with all the other nonverbal signs and interpret it accordingly. So a fast speaker may be seen as nervous, if other factors contribute to that impression; alternatively, a fast speaker may be seen as passionate or excited. Similarly, slow speech may indicate confidence, if other factors point that way; but in some cases, it may indicate the opposite, that the speaker is uncertain.

So it is impossible to say in an absolute way how a debater's rate of speech will be perceived by the audience. Nevertheless, we would advise debaters to speak somewhat more slowly than they would in a regular conversation—if only because slower speakers are easier to understand. This is especially true when the content of a speech is complex, and the ideas offered are unfamiliar to the audience. In offering this advice, we are conscious that speaking slowly is not common practice in many tournament debates. Beginner debaters especially tend to speak too fast, partly because they are nervous, and partly because they try to cram as much information into the time allotted as possible. But even experienced policy debaters are prone to fact-cramming, and speaking very fast has become the norm in American Policy Debate style (even though unpracticed listeners will sometimes find such high-speed debates to be literally incomprehensible). In public debates, however, speakers should adapt to the needs of the audience and focus on good communication. Sometimes squeezing in more information—as opposed to communicating and explaining well the information already there—is not always the best idea.

Pauses are very important in public speaking. They can be full of meaning—thus the terms "pregnant pause" and "poignant silence." Beginning debaters are all too often afraid of silence and fill it instead with so-called vocal pauses, such as "like," "um," "okay," and other words and sounds that do not convey meaning. Minimally, these vocal irruptions are perceived as indications that the speaker is not as ease; sometimes, disfluencies like "er" and "um" are taken to mean that the speaker is being dishonest. (Think of police shows or courtroom dramas on television: a broken pattern of speech is usually meant to show that the witness is lying.)

It is far better, then, to create a moment of silence, rather than a moment of babble. A silence can be used to give the audience time to digest what has just been said, or to mark a moment of transition in the speech, before a new point is launched. Psychologically, a silence underlines the last words spoken and makes them resonate in the listeners' minds in a lasting way; similarly, a silence can create anticipation for the next point that is to come. Pauses are a powerful tool.

Inflections are changes in tone within an utterance. In a regular conversation, we naturally change our intonation to express our mood, define meaning, or indicate a question. In public speaking, we should do the same to make our messages sound natural and to convey their meaning effectively.

It is for this reason that we discourage debaters from reading their speeches. Speakers reading from a script very often fall into a monotone; when intonations are flat and inflections are absent, the audience finds it much harder to grasp the meaning of what is being said. Inflections help to tell the listener what is important in what is being said.

Stress is similar to voice inflection. A stressed word is spoken somewhat louder than the other words in a sentence; this change in volume draws attention to what is important. Stress can also change the meaning of a sentence completely. If you say, "I love *Peter,*" stressing the word "Peter," it means that you love Peter, as opposed to John. If you say the same sentence stressing the word "*I,*" your emphasis indicates that you may have a rival, and it is you who love him, not someone else. Let's try saying the same sentence stressing the word "*love*": this time you may have been challenged about your feelings for Peter, and you want to make the point that you do indeed love him and do not hate him. Stressing a certain word can have two purposes: either to indicate which word or phrase in the sentence is the most important or to distinguish a particular concept from its implied opposite (as in the examples above). Vocal stress is another very powerful tool to convey your meaning effectively.

Physical Delivery

Posture is the way one stands or sits: upright or slouching, relaxed or erect. The posture used by the speaker can weaken or strengthen the message being delivered. A slouching posture is perceived as weak and will make even the most forceful words seem less emphatic. An upright, firm and open posture, however, conveys strength: it visually reinforces a powerful verbal message. Perhaps more important, posture conveys an attitude toward the audience. By slouching, covering his body with his arms and shifting his body away from the audience, a speaker sends the message that he doesn't want to be there, compromising his credibility and his ability to communicate. A speaker who plants herself firmly and faces the audience, however, tells her listeners that she wants to be there and is eager to communicate with them.

The speaker can stand still, pace around the podium, or make a few steps here and there during the speech for emphasis. These are an important part of the speaker's nonverbal communication. Ideally, movements should be tied to meaning: the speaker can take a step, or change her position, when she is introducing a new point or making a transition in her speech. Movements that do not relate to the verbal message, however, can be distracting. If the speaker is continually pacing back and forth, the audience can end up paying attention to the pacing ("Will he turn now?" "Is she following a pattern?") instead of to the speech. Pacing also suggests nervousness and the inability to concentrate. It is equally distracting when speakers adopt a swinging or rocking movement during their speeches, often unaware that they are doing so; again, this kind of movement does nothing to reinforce meaning. And of course, standing stock-still does nothing to reinforce meaning either; no movement whatsoever can also look static and unnatural. Our recommendation, then, is that speakers should move a little, if only to seem natural—but their movements should always have the purpose of emphasizing the verbal message.

Gestures (arm and hand movements) are used to extend verbal message in many ways. Sometimes, gestures are used to illustrate people, objects, concepts or feelings—e.g., "Dennis is tiny—he comes up to about here"; "A typical land mine is about as big as this"; "Freud's theories explain only about this much of human behavior"; "I love you soooo much." Gestures can underline important words (when the speaker bangs his fist on the lectern and says, "This is outrageous!"), or they can serve instead of words (when the speaker gives the thumbs up sign). Gestures can reinforce the logical structure of an argument, or the internal structure of a paragraph ("on the one hand . . . on the other hand").

In everyday communication, most people use gestures extensively, albeit not consciously. In front of an audience, however, many speakers freeze, since they become acutely aware of every movement—and every gesture feels awkward. The problem is that using no gestures at all is even more awkward (and can leave the audience wondering, "Is she ever going to move her right hand? Is there something wrong with it?"). Just as we noted above with respect to movement, the other extreme—too much gesturing—is also bad, especially if it is repetitive ("How many times is he going to jab his forefinger in the air?"). The solution is to find a happy medium: speakers should use gestures to reinforce what they are saying, but the gestures must not be overdone or artificially choreographed. We know that this is easier said than done, but the secret is to stop thinking about gestures and to let them come naturally, just as they do in ordinary conversation. This will happen if the speaker concentrates on the speech as an important message he wants to communicate to the audience. If gestures remain problematic, a videotaped performance can provide a kind of shock therapy; the camera lets the speaker see how her gestures would be perceived by an audience, and she can identify bad habits that require correction.

Facial expressions are to the face what gestures are to the whole body. They can speak louder than words. Facial expressions can replace words (raising an eyebrow, blowing a kiss), support them (smiling, frowning), or frame them (indicating whether something is supposed to be funny, serious, important, etc.). They are largely used to communicate attitudes and emotions; many emotional facial expressions appear to be culturally universal and instinctive—no one needs to teach a baby how to smile or what a smile means.[2] A smile means the same thing in every culture. It is also a great way to handle new situations and begin interactions.

Head-nods usually act as reinforcers, which acknowledge and encourage the speaker. They also play a crucial role in floor apportionment; a head-nod gives the other debater permission to speak.[3] When a debater gets a question from the audience or his opponent, giving a head-nod means that the questioner can continue. Generally, a head-nod means, "I am listening, go on." Head-nods can also mean agreement—although not always. In the Bulgarian culture, for example, a nod up-and-down means "no," not "yes," as in the American culture.

Eye contact generally plays an important role in communicating interpersonal attitudes and establishing relationships. In public speaking, it is critically important because it establishes a connection between the speaker and the audience and enables communication. With no eye contact, there is no connection. Eye contact also serves to reinforce the message and lets the speaker check whether a point has been understood. Good speakers learn how to "read" an audience by observing their nonverbal behavior; the best speakers are able to adapt their styles and their messages when audiences seem unreceptive. There is no chance of adaptation without eye contact; a speaker who focuses on the lectern, or the projection screen, or the middle distance is not able to read the signals being broadcast by his listeners.

Proximity is the distance between speakers or between the speaker and the listeners. This distance depends largely on the occasion and our relationship with others. We all establish certain "zones" around ourselves—the space that we need between us and other people in order to feel safe and comfortable. There are public, social, personal and intimate zones each of us intuitively creates. The closer we feel to someone else, the less space we require to separate us. In most personal and social situations, the size of the required zone is determined largely by culture. Zones in personal situations can range from 40 cm to 1.2 m (for nonmetric readers, that's from about 16 inches to almost 4 feet); zones for social situations can range from 1.2 m to 3.5 m (almost 4 feet to 11.5 feet).[4] Northern cultures tend to have larger proximity zones—that is, Northern people require more space to feel comfortable than do people from Southern cultures. (This is not an absolute distinction, however: an American standing in line at a bank is likely to stand at least one and half feet behind the person in front of him; a Russian on a similar line will close to a distance of about 2 inches.[3]) In public situations like debates, a distance of more than 3.5 m is common between the speakers and the audience, depending on the size of the room, the audience and the level of formality (more distant is more formal). Debaters should also be aware that the audience is sensitive to the proximity zone surrounding the speakers on the podium; when senatorial candidate Rick Lazio walked across the stage and up to the lectern of opposing candidate Hillary Clinton during an electoral debate in 2000, it was widely perceived as rude and an invasion of his opponent's personal space.

Orientation is similar to proximity, but measures angles rather than distance—that is, a person's orientation is a description of the angle at which he sits or stands relative to another person or to the audience. Orientation varies with the situation. Those who are in a cooperative situation or who are close friends tend to adopt a side-by-side position; in a confrontation, negotiation or similar situation, people tend to sit or stand face to face; in other situations a 90° angle between individuals is most common.[5] (There are, of course, cross-cultural variations in these patterns as well.) In a debate, it is common for debaters to face the audience directly (especially when speaking). Typically, debaters sit side-by-side with their teammates, and at an angle to their opponents. Usually a sort of a triangle is formed with the audience as its base; the debaters sit at 90° to each other, and at 45° toward the audience.

Appearance speaks too. Debaters should not feel obligated to spend a month at a spa before any debate or to surgically alter the faces that they were born with. But much of our appearance—most notably, dress and hairstyle—is within our control, and it sends a message to the audience. It's true that Einstein was not a great dresser, and dress does not always spell success (to counter a phrase from the literature of self-help). Nonetheless, a pleasing appearance is one more factor that can help a debater to make a positive impression on an audience.

We would be foolish if we tried to prescribe a fashion standard for debaters—although we will go as far as to say that male debaters should probably not appear with a three-day beard (cf. Richard Nixon in 1960, discussed in chapter 11), and long-haired debaters of either sex would do well to secure their tresses away from their eyes. Beyond that, the way that we choose to present ourselves depends on the occasion and on our self-image. The only thing to keep in mind is that the debater's appearance should not distract from the message, and the way to avoid that is to dress appropriately—in other words, to meet the expectations of the audience. A good rule of thumb is to dress slightly more formally than the audience; it shows respect for the occasion and the listeners.

Adapting to the Setting and the Medium

A perfectly good speech can be easily ruined by the mishandling of visual aids, props or equipment that were meant to help it. Hiding behind the lectern, gesturing wildly with a microphone or fumbling with complicated visual aids do not exactly help communicate the message. There are some ways that the speaker can adapt to the setting and the medium and use them to her advantage.

Lectern

Lecterns and stands are useful if handled appropriately—they are, obviously, a good place to keep notes. Sometimes, however lecterns serve as a crutch; they become barriers behind which the speakers hide defensively, consciously or not. The speaker's desire for such a shield is only natural, since standing in front of an audience, completely visible from head to toe, is an emotionally vulnerable position. But there is an advantage to taking such a position: when the speaker is "exposed" (in full view, with no barriers), the flow of communication between speaker and audience is more open and unobstructed as well; as a result, the message exchange is that more effective.

A lectern is best used as a place for resting notes, so that speaker can leave both arms free for gesturing. When the lectern is big, or the speaker is small—or both—gestures need to be larger and higher so that they can be seen. It is up to the speaker whether to stand behind the lectern the whole time, or to step in front of it or next to it at times. It is even up to the speaker whether to use the lectern at all, and that choice should be based on his own personal preference and the occasion. Using the lectern indicates a higher level of formality, and sometimes that is more appropriate than not using it. The important thing to remember is to use the lectern not as a crutch, but as an aid.

Microphone

In some settings, the audience is just too large to be reached by a plain, unaided human voice. It is true that in distant times, the power of a speaker's voice was an essential ingredient of his effectiveness—historians tell us that Demosthenes, the famous Greek orator from the 4th century B.C., trained his powerful voice by shouting over the sound of waves with pebbles in his mouth. Only a hundred years ago, successful orators addressed crowds numbering in the thousands in outdoor settings.

These days, of course, we have microphones and tools to extend the human voice, and the ability to reach the top tier of a football stadium does not need to be part of the debater's vocal repertoire. Even though it is still important to be able to project well, sometimes it is not necessary to strain ourselves if we have microphones at our disposal.

Microphones come in all shapes and forms, but the biggest distinction can be drawn between the larger stick-shaped ones, and the little bug mikes that can be attached anywhere. Larger microphones are usually more effective, but they pose certain restrictions on the speaker. If the speaker holds the microphone in her hand, she is able to move freely around the podium, but she can gesture with only one hand, and has to be very careful to hold the mike close to her mouth whenever she is speaking. The usual pitfall is that the speaker starts gesturing naturally with the hand holding the mike—forgetting that it must remain close to her mouth—and her voice fades in and out as her hand moves (which drives the audience crazy). Putting the microphone on a stand (or attaching it to the lectern) improves matters somewhat because then the speaker is free to gesture with both hands; it creates other restrictions, however, because the speaker cannot move freely on the podium, and even head movements (turning to look at an opponent, for example) can cause her voice to fade out momentarily. (This is a particular problem with unidirectional microphones, which are designed to pick up sound only from the direction in which they are pointed. Omnidirectional microphones pick up sounds from a wider range; their disadvantage is that they can pick up unwanted noises.) The small "bug" microphones can be attached with a clip to a piece of clothing close to the speaker's mouth. They are far less conspicuous than stick microphones, and they allow speakers to move as freely as they wish; the problem with bug microphones is that they can pick up unwanted sounds (like the rustling of paper notes against clothing) and they must be properly placed to pick up voices without interruption.

Although sometimes necessary, microphones can add to the anxiety of inexperienced speakers who feel awkward about using them—but familiarity will overcome that awkward feeling. We know it sounds silly, but it helps to practice at home with any similarly shaped object (a phone, a water bottle, a stick), making sure that it is always close to your mouth whatever you do.

For public debates, technology is good—when it works. Sometimes it doesn't, and the prudent debater will take some precautions. Minimally, all technical equipment should be tested ahead of time; that will at least eliminate any surprises ("Hello? Is this thing on?") when the event begins. Debaters should test microphones to see if there is any feedback (a high-pitched wail that will send most listeners running for the exit). Feedback is a particular danger for debaters who like to move around the podium with the microphone; the mike may sound fine when used at the lectern, but a few steps in the direction of a loudspeaker can create a sonic loop that will deafen a dog. Another problem that will emerge in testing is echo; this sometimes happens if the equipment is not very good or if the space for the event is highly reverberant (churches and other stone buildings usually are). Echo is very distracting for listeners, and debaters need to compensate for it by speaking slowly, making more pauses, and enunciating even more clearly and deliberately than usual.

Visual Aids

Visual aids can enhance, explain or clarify an argument. They include everything from overhead transparencies, slides, videotapes, PowerPoint presentations and simple blackboards, to objects, models, photographs, drawings, or even the speakers themselves.[6] Many people think of themselves as being more "visual"; that is, they understand information better when they see it (through charts, pictures, photographs), than when they simply hear it. Even for nonvisual learners, pictures have an impact; if the speaker wants to evoke sympathy for starving children, one picture may be more effective than whatever description the speaker might offer. Numbers, too, are more easily grasped by most of us when they are presented in charts and pies, especially if the graphics are colorful.

There are a few general guidelines to follow. Prepare the visual aids in advance, keep them simple, and make them large enough for everyone in the audience to see. Display them so that they can be seen from any part of the room—but display them only when you are discussing them. (A visual aid that is on permanent display is an invitation to look at something besides the speaker.) When using visual aids, you must be careful to keep your attention on the audience, and to maintain eye contact with them. Finally, you must practice. There is nothing potentially more distracting and damaging to an otherwise perfectly good speech than a poorly handled visual aid. This is why visual aids should be well thought out and prepared in advance, along with the speech itself.

Camera

Sometimes public debates are videotaped for internal purposes, and sometimes they are even broadcast on television for a larger audience. The challenge for debaters is to balance the different media and audiences—they must decide how much attention they will pay to the immediate audience in the room and how much to the audience watching the debate on tape or on television. If a debate is being videotaped simply to allow for post-debate analysis, or to be filed in someone's archives, then it is clear that the focus of the debate should be on the people in the room, not on the camera. If, however, the debate is being recorded for broadcasting purposes, debaters need to have a much larger audience in mind and must play to the camera as well as the room. (Of course, all the guidelines we have articulated about audience analysis and argument adaptation apply to the broadcast audience as well as the immediate audience.)

In terms of delivery, speaking for the camera has some special challenges. One should be aware of framing issues: the closer the camera gets to the speaker, the more obvious every facial expression and gesture will be. Because the space around the speaker is limited by a screen frame, every movement seems larger than it would be in reality. Therefore, all facial, head, hand, and whole body movements should be reduced and made less abrupt, to avoid the "jagged" look. This is especially true if the debate is shot in a studio. Smaller spaces call for smaller movements. Another thing to consider is eye contact: it helps to treat the camera as just another member of the audience—it is a good idea to speak to it directly every now and then (but not all the time, because that will leave the immediate audience feeling excluded). If there is no other audience present, then the camera should be treated as the only listener.

Earlier in this chapter, we discussed proximity and zones in the context of nonverbal communication. When the camera is running, sometimes the lines between zones get blurred: public zones shrink to become the size of social zones, or even personal zones. Even though any broadcast utterance is of course public, viewers often feel that they are being addressed personally, because they are watching in the intimacy of their homes, often alone, and usually seeing a close-up of the speaker. So even if your broadcast audience numbers in the millions (if you are, say, running for president), you should not act as though you are addressing a vast crowd in a large arena; you should talk to the camera as if you are talking to one person, sitting in the living room at home.

Speaking Notes

"Preparation outlines" and "speaking notes" are different things, in reality as well as in name, and should not be confused. Preparation outlines serve the purpose described in their name—preparation. Once all the material for the case has been gathered, and all ideas brainstormed, the case is then out-lined in a sequence of arguments and constructed in the form of a speech. In this process, the relationships between ideas start to emerge, and the case starts to make sense (or not, in which case further revisions are in order). The preparation outline is for the speaker's eyes only; its purpose is to help formulate every thought and argument. Unfortunately, debaters often use their outlines during the event, only to discover that it is virtually impos-sible to navigate these notes and return to the right place again if they ever look up at the audience (and so they keep their eyes well glued to the page, eliminating all eye contact). The preparation outline needs to be adapted and completely rewritten for use in the actual debate; in other words, the preparation outline must be turned into speaking notes.

The first step is to read the preparation outline aloud several times, to see what it sounds like. The next step is to run through the text several times, adapting it to a speaking style (with short sentences, simple syntax, repetition as needed, and figures of speech), using the basic information of the outline but speaking extemporaneously every time. (Each time through, the speech should sound somewhat different.) After several such "runs," it is best to put the preparation outline aside completely, and to write a speaking outline from scratch, following the same basic structure (the introduction, the sequence of arguments, the conclusion), but including only key words and phrases, labels of arguments, crucial pieces of information, numbers and quotations. The rule is: no full sentences (except for quotes), no unnec-essary information, no clutter. Less is more: the less there is on the page, the easier it will be to use the outline effectively during the debate. You should leave a lot of blank spaces in between lines, use a large font, underline or circle more important words, and include cues for delivery (like "PAUSE!" and "BREATHE!").

Handling Anxiety

Shallow breathing, shaky knees, perspiration, heart palpitations—all are clear signs of fear. Whenever we are in danger, our body automatically starts releasing adrenalin, or the "fight or flight" hormone as it is some-times called. Adrenalin gives us a sudden boost of energy that allows us to flee from the source of danger or fight it, as the case may be. We share this characteristic with many other species: it is not uniquely human. However, in modern civilization, we rarely find ourselves in the life-threatening situations for which this hormone equips us. The closest some people ever get to real fear is—speaking in public.

One of the reasons why people generally feel such anxiety about public speaking may be that it exposes speakers to the judgment of others and makes them vulnerable to their scrutiny. This exposure grows exponentially with the size of the audience and the level of unfamiliarity with the situation. Expectations are high and the pressure is strong.

It is normal to feel some anxiety about public speaking. Even the most experienced speakers do. Some speakers say that if they don't feel any, it is a clear sign that they don't care and their performance usually suffers. The trick is to channel this anxiety into positive energy and excitement about the event—an excitement that usually transfers successfully to the audience as well.

The best way to manage anxiety is to be very well prepared. If you are confident about what you want to convey and know the information inside out, if you have a good grasp of the structure of your case and can visualize every argument without looking at your notes, if you have practiced your delivery and have a good idea what you will look like and sound like, then you should be in good shape. There is no reason to fall apart, even under a lot of pressure. Experience, of course, helps too: once you've gotten through a few debates without dying, you realize that the chances are good that you won't die in your next debate, either. There are also some relaxation exercises one could do to reduce the physical symptoms of stress, like slow and deep breathing, vigorous physical activity just before the speech, and vocal exercises.

Notes

1. R. McKeon, introduction to *Rhetoric*, in *Introduction to Aristotle* (New York Modern Library, 1947): 620.

2. A. Paese, *Body Language* (Ljubljana-Zagreb, Croatia: Zalozba Mladinska Knjiga, 1991): 10.

3. M. Argyle, "Non-Verbal Communication in Human Social Interaction," in *Non-Verbal Communication*, ed. R. Hinde (Cambridge: Cambridge University Press, 1972): 249.

4. Ibid., 248.

5. Paese, 24.

6. T. Maginnis, "How's Your Personal Distance—Watch This Space," *St. Petersburg (Russia) Times*, 1995, http://www.sptimesrussia.com/archive/lifestyl/122/how.html

7. Argyle, 247.

8. S. Lucas, *The Art of Public Speaking*, 7th ed. (New York: McGraw-Hill, 2001): 313.

Chapter Sixteen

Questioning

Speaker: For all of its imperfections, international law is the world's best hope for having a just and lasting world order. Just as individuals gain a better and longer life by forfeiting some of their freedoms to a government, nations would gain a safer and more secure existence by surrendering some of their sovereignty to a global system.

Question: Your argument by analogy seems to presume that nations are like individuals. Does that analogy hold? Aren't there important differences between nations and individuals?

Question: Your factual assumption seems to be that individuals gain a better life by forfeiting some freedom in exchange for government rule. Do you have support that indicates that life is indeed better with a government?

Question: Your argument seems to presume that the system of international law is fair and just and applied equally to all. But what if it isn't? What if international law is used as a tool by more powerful countries against less powerful countries? Is it still fair and just?

Question: There seems to be an infinite regress to your argument. You are saying that governments themselves need to be ruled—that the rulers themselves need to be ruled. Fine, but who rules the international rulers? What would we do if the international rulers were just as oppressive and resistant to popular control as some national governments are?

Question: Your argument sounds good in the abstract, but let's consider a concrete case like the International Criminal Court. Aren't there some powerful nations, like the United States for example, that have asked for and received special treatment? Is a system of law still just and fair in that kind of situation?

Question: I don't think I quite understand the implication of your argument. You are saying that the governments should give up some parts of their sovereignty. Specifically what parts?

Question: As you know some nations believe in democracy and others don't. How would an international world order function without interfering with one culture or the other?

Question: Can you think of an example in which international law has solved a conflict in a way that was fair for everyone?

All of these questions could no doubt be answered by the careful advocate of the original argument, and those answers would, no doubt, lead to more questions; in this way, the introduction of questioning into a public debate can grab attention and lead to the development of new ideas. Questions have a natural advantage over speeches in leading to a faster and more immediate development of responses and positions. By allowing a direct, side-by-side comparison of advocates and arguments, questioning periods also capture the spontaneity and quickthinking that public audiences prize. If the most negative image of a "public debate" is a boring speaker lumbering his way through an interminable speech, then one of the most positive images involves a spirited and direct exchange between two or more quick-thinking advocates who are challenging, refining, and developing their thinking and adding the element of wit through the process of asking and answering questions.

Viewed from another perspective, though, the questioning period does more than add interaction and spark to the debate. Questioning can actually be a means of seeking and revealing a sort of truth or knowledge. In his famous dialogues, for example, the philosopher Plato used questions as a means of encouraging all of the participants in a discussion to offer their points of view for critical analysis. More than just being a way to seek information, the question is a method of inquiry and testing in which both advocates participate in a search for a more reasonable argument. Certainly in public debates, this questioning between adversaries is not always likely to be cooperative, but still the element of participation persists. It is one thing to hear the statement made that "you can't support your point" and it is another to see that the advocate is unable to support her point after her opponent has posed the right question. Because it has been demonstrated openly, the weakness in this case is more forceful and more influential than a weakness that is merely mentioned. In this way the questioning period is particularly important to public debates. Rather than just helping another person, or a judge, to explore an issue or an argument flaw, your question in a public debate context showcases the problem, inviting your opponent and a room full of listeners to participate in the unfolding of a claim and the undermining of an idea, to follow along with you in the steps of tracing a line of argument to its conclusion.

Another advantage of the questioning period is that, by pulling speakers away from prepared speeches, it offers the chance to see the speakers thinking and advocating in the moment. As long-time debate coaches Maridell Fryar and David A. Thomas wrote, "On the one hand, a debater is probing another's mind for weaknesses and errors, and on the other hand, another debater is attempting to avoid making admissions which would weaken the arguments advanced in his speeches. The expression, 'thinking on your feet,' becomes a tangible reality."

The purpose of this chapter is to explore questioning as an important and lively component in public debates. Though it is possible to imagine public debates without questioning[1] it is hard to imagine why public debate planners would opt not to include an element that is likely to lead to the most dynamic engagement of the issues and the advocates. While differences in the way that questioning periods are included is one of the more obvious features that distinguish different debate formats, this chapter will focus first on the act of questioning itself, and not the specifics of individual formats for questioning. That is, prior to considering "cross-examination," "points of information," or "expert panels," we will address the practical, strategic and even philosophical considerations in the act of inquiring and interrogating through the asking and answering of questions. After exploring general goals for the questioner and general goals for the respondent, we will look at some of these specific ways of including questioning in the debate and some of the specific demands of each of these formats.

General Goals for the Questioner

> Never ask a question that you don't know the answer to.
>
> If you don't know, ask.

While these two statements seem to be in direct contradiction, they more accurately reflect two different goals of the questioning process. The first statement comes from the field of law; during the act of "cross-examination, " when a witness is questioned by the opposing attorney, it is strategically important for the questioning attorney to avoid being surprised or undermined by the witness answering the question. The second statement, perhaps the more intuitive of the two, simply reflects our interest in using questions to add to our own knowledge. These basic platitudes reflect merely some of the purposes that advocates have for asking questions. While debaters will not always know the answer to the question that they are asking, they should always know the reason why they are asking a question. There are at least five basic reasons for questioning.

1. To Clarify Your Opponent's Arguments

The first goal of questioning, at its most basic, is to clarify information. In order to react to and refute an opponent's arguments adequately, you need first of all to have a clear understanding of what that opponent is saying, and what that opponent isn't saying. In particular, you need to know the claim, and you need to know the support being offered for it. You need to know the implications of that claim, and you may need to know how that claim ties in to other claims.

> Do you have any evidence for your second point, that global trade hurts local business?
>
> Now, you make the argument that population is increasing dramatically, but how does that tie in to the rest of your argument? Is that a reason for more economic development, or less?
>
> I'm sorry, I missed the third reason you gave for your argument that capital punishment is ineffective. Could you tell me again what that reason is?

All of these elements may need to be clarified through questioning, both for our own sake—when we ask about elements of the argument that we may have forgotten or failed to notice on first presentation or that may have been unclearly presented—and for the sake of the audience. Particularly if our preparation stage has involved cooperation with the other side (see chapter 9), then we may have a sufficient understanding of our opponent's arguments. Still, we may seek to clarify for the benefit of the audience. We may know the backing for a point, for example, but in order to reinforce the audience's ability to appreciate the arguments that we will soon be offering, we want to clarify for them exactly what our opponents are saying and why.

Such clarifying questions not only allow the advocates to know clearly the claims that they are answering, but also, in the context of a public debate, they permit the audience to have a better understanding of the exchange as a whole. In public events, the advocates can sometimes forget that they are much more involved in the contest than the audience and for that reason they are understanding arguments, appreciating nuances and grasping distinctions at a level that is greater than that of most audience members. Because they are clearly participants, they are listening more carefully and they are drawing connections more easily. Audience members, on the other hand, because they spend large portions of their time as observers in the public debate, may not immediately see the connections and the implications of the arguments they are hearing. For this reason, questioners can pursue a strategy of clarification because they want the audience to understand the debate more fully; that understanding will be essential for audience members to appreciate upcoming arguments and refutations.

2. To Commit Your Opponents to a Position

Besides needing to understand clearly what our opponents are saying, we sometimes need to extract a promise from our opponents that they will indeed stick to supporting the position that we believe that they are supporting. Before investing precious time and attention in attacking a claim, we need to ensure that we understand, and be sure that the audience understands, that we are indeed attacking a position that our opponents are definitely, clearly, and unalterably supporting.

> So, your argument has been that international economic trading blocs always make things worse. I just want to be clear—in this debate you will defend the idea that we should roll back all such economic partnerships, like the European

> Common Market, and the North American Free Trade Agreement, correct?
>
> Now, you say that the death penalty is immoral. So what you are saying is that it is never ever justified, no matter how heinous the crime; it is never appropriate to take someone's life—is that right?

Questions of this sort can be viewed as a type of insurance. In addition to making sure that we are correct in our assumption about where an opponent stands, the question also acts as an open and public promise to the audience that the opposing side will not shift or modify their position once they are faced with an attack. The debate, after all, will never reach a point of clash if we are not able to predict and to count upon the stances that our opponents will be taking. The debater who answered "Yes" to the second question above would not be able to say, at some later point in the debate, "Well, we are not saying that the death penalty is *never* justified, we are just saying that our *current* reliance on the death penalty is unjustified because it is infected with racism. If we could remove the racism, then the death penalty could be justified." Obviously, an answer like that could instantly make irrelevant an argument from the opposition. For that reason, questioning designed to commit your opponent to a position makes good sense.

3. To Expose Flaws

Perhaps the most familiar reasons for questioning are to directly undermine the arguments of an opponent, to open up avenues of criticism, and to promote the realization on the part of the audience that a weakness exists. Eliciting the weakness through a question is more powerful and more dramatic than simply stating the weakness in a speech. The good advocate is able to do both: after eliciting the weakness through questioning, she reminds the audience of the weakness in a subsequent speech. Exposing flaws is most powerful when the individual being questioned is forced to acknowledge a weakness or reveals an inability to rebut an attack on the weakness effectively. The question then serves as a means of highlighting the weakness, so that when the point is made in later speeches, the audience is able to remember and attach significance to the problem.

> Now, you say that free speech can lead to violence, yet you give only one example.

> In support of your argument that the United Nations is effective you provide the testimony of Kofi Annan, but Mr. Annan really wouldn't have an interest in admitting that he is secretary-general of an irrelevant organization, now would he?

To use the question as a way to undermine the claims of an opponent is to engage in a form of refutation; that is, a form of weakening or denying your opponent's argument (see chapter 14). All of the methods of refutation have a counterpart in questioning. For example, those seeking to *minimize* a claim could ask, "So, how many people are affected, as a percentage of the entire population?" Those seeking to *outweigh* could ask, "Isn't our survival more important than our privacy?" In each of these cases, advocates would need to anticipate the refutations that they will make later; the questions are used to set up the refutation by drawing attention to the weakness that will be attacked.

4. To Respond to an Argument, Before it is Even Made

The fourth purpose for the questioner is to gain advance knowledge of what an opponent's argument or response is likely to be. This foreknowledge is useful because it can allow you to incorporate your opponent's response into the initial presentation of your argument. For example, if you are defending limitations on free speech and you anticipate that your opponent will say that the best cure for bad speech is more speech, you can use the questioning period to force that argument out into the open, even before you have delivered your own speech; when it's time for you to give that speech, you can note that " ... some limits are needed because the effects of hate speech cannot always be cured by more speech." The result is that when you are making the initial presentation of your argument, you are including a defense against an attack that you know is coming.

> **Question:** So, you believe that speech should be absolutely free?
>
> **Response:** Yes.
>
> **Question:** What about something like hate speech, directed against a specific racial group?
>
> **Response:** Well, the effects of damaging speech can be addressed by more speech ... speech that defends the group and responds to those attacks.

As discussed in chapter 14, incorporating the opponent's response in your own argument is a preemptive move and psychologically there are reasons to believe that a preemptive argument is going to be more powerful than simply waiting for the argument to occur and responding to it. There is some evidence to indicate that offering a response to an argument before an opponent has a chance to make the argument may have an "inoculating" effect. That is, because the audience has already heard reasons to oppose an argument, they have built-in defenses once they hear that argument.[2] In addition, it puts your opponents off balance by requiring them to defend their argument before they have even had an opportunity to make it.

5. To Elicit Concessions that Will Bolster Your Own Argument

The fifth and final purpose of questioning is similar to the fourth, in that it is anticipatory; that is, the questions are used to set up something that is to come. The fourth purpose was to anticipate your opponent's upcoming arguments; the fifth purpose anticipates your own. The goal of this kind of questioning is to get your opponent to agree to a point that will support the argument that you intend to make.

Say, for example, that the topic of the debate is the legalization of marijuana, and your position is that marijuana should remain illegal. One of your arguments is that the government has the right to keep citizens from hurting themselves (and you anticipate that your opponent will deny that the government has that right, and that government interference in personal choice constitutes an unwarranted intrusion on personal liberty). You know, of course, that your opponent is never going to agree to anything that is obviously a part of your argument—so it would be pointless to ask, "Do you think that the government has the right to keep citizens from hurting themselves?" You might gain a toehold, however, if you took an indirect approach, as follows:

> **Question:** I'd like to explore the question of governmental responsibility with you. We hear all the time about people committing suicide in public places—you know, someone jumps off a bridge, or from the top of a building, or dives in front of a train. You know what I'm talking about?
>
> **Answer:** Of course.

Question: And very often, in these situations, we hear about police officers or firefighters being involved—they're trying to get the guy to come down from the bridge, or surrender his gun, or whatever. My question is whether you think their involvement is justified. Should they be trying to stop someone from killing himself?

Answer: Yes, if it's a public situation. Law officers have to maintain public order, and the person committing suicide may pose a risk to other people, particularly if there's a weapon involved.

Question: So it's acceptable—it's even an obligation—for government officials to intervene to keep a citizen from doing something he wants to do.

Answer: In very particular and public circumstances.

Question: What if it's private? What if a cop drives by and sees some guy standing on his own front lawn with a rope around his neck, and he's tying the other end of the rope to a tree limb? Should he just keep driving, or should he stop it?

In this exchange, the questions are intended to elicit a concession from the opponent that can later be used—e.g., "My opponent admitted herself that the government has not only a right but an obligation to keep citizens from harming themselves—and that is what antidrug laws are intended to do." If the opponent is savvy, she won't admit much, and her admissions will be carefully qualified (as in "In very particular and public circumstances"). She can also make her own distinctions in response at a later time ("It's one thing for the government to stop someone committing suicide when the prospect of death is imminent; it is something completely different to stop citizens from taking drugs that are not lethal, or even particularly harmful"). Nevertheless, questioning aimed at defining points of agreement can be effective.

General Advice for Questioners

No matter which purpose an advocate has, there are several additional pieces of advice that should be kept in mind.

- Establish the context or the necessary explanation *before* asking the question. "Now, you say that gun crimes are highest among the lowest economic classes, right? But how are the poor able to afford their guns?" The first statement establishes the necessary context and may be more effective than just launching into "How do the poor afford their guns?"

- Think of the components of a good line of questions as a series. A good analogy here is volleyball: the ball is first "set" or positioned for attack, then there is the "spike" as the ball is sent swiftly over the net, and finally there is the prepared reaction to the return shot. Similarly, a good attack should be preceded by several possible set-up questions and followed by a reaction.

     Set-up 1: So one of the rights that international law tries to preserve is the right to self-determination, right? . . .

     Set-up 2: And what is self-determination? Is it the notion that if a distinct group of people does not wish to be governed within a system of law, then they have the freedom to form their own? . . .

     Set-up 3: In an international system of law, presumably there would be a single international system—a single global system of law, right? . . .

     Set-up 4: And it wouldn't be possible for a group to simply go off and find another world, would it? . . .

     Attack: So, wouldn't a system of truly international law prevent self-determination in the sense that it prevents people from being able to go voluntarily outside of that system and found their own?

     If the format permits it, then such a series could be executed through separate questions (for cross-examination); alternatively, or it could be built into a single question (for points of information or panel questions) through concise phrasing. In either case, the most strategic use of questioning is to build from conceded points to a point of challenge.

- Try to anticipate where your opponents are likely to go. Unless you are simply seeking clarification, you *should* have a sense of the likely answers that your opponents could reasonably supply. Having a sense of where you would like to end up allows you to react more effectively to your opponent's answers.

- Avoid treating the questioning period as a quiz show. A debate is a contest of ideas, not a test of knowledge and recollection. You don't "win" by simply coming up with a question that your opponent can't answer—e.g., "You said that NAFTA was a bad for Mexico. Could you tell me the median income in Mexico in 1990 and compare it with the median income in 2000?"

- Don't overrely on "trap" questions. Often the question that seems to trick an opponent and deprive them of any possibility of a reasonable answer is simply employing a logical weakness or taking advantage in an ambiguity of language: "So, are you still a heavy drinker? Please answer yes or no."

- Avoid aggression. Remember that it is a clash of ideas and not personalities. More strategically, the questioner should remember that adopting a more subdued and less confrontational style may cause the respondent to open up a bit more.

- Practice questioning just as you practice other parts of the debate. Given that speeches are seen as the more "controllable" parts of the debate, it is possible that a disproportionate amount of preparation time can go into speeches rather than questioning time. In order to keep the exchange fresh, a questioning period should not be planned out word-for-word and need not be executed the same way in the event as it was executed in practice. But practicing likely themes for questioning can ensure that once the speech is over, the speaker doesn't simply relax and "switch off."

- Work on developing concise questions, and avoid the appearance (or the reality) of speech-making while you are constructing or setting up a question.

- For the audience, begin with a question that captures their attention. Remember that the audience is likely to see the side-by-side comparison and the direct interpersonal exchange as one of the most exciting parts of the debate.

General Goals for the Respondent

It is less common to think of the question respondent as having a purpose. After all, they are "just answering the question," right? Actually, as long as respondents are maintaining their roles as advocates and not just passively submitting themselves to interrogation, then they are likely to have purposes that are just as vital as the purposes of their questioners. There are three main goals of the respondent.

1. To Provide Clarification.

Some respondents mistakenly believe that clarification is not their friend, and that making their arguments plain will only help their opponents. What these advocates don't realize, however, is that in keeping their opponents in the dark, they are keeping the audience in the dark as well; if an audience doesn't understand your argument, then they are unlikely to appreciate your side of the debate.

> **Question:** So, are you saying that all of development is bad?
>
> **Response:** No, certainly we are not, and I am glad you asked that. We are saying that we cannot stop developing, of course, but our position is simply that we have to develop in ways that are environmentally sustainable, in ways that add to and don't detract from the health of the ecosystem.

The opportunity to answer a question is an opportunity to provide your audience (and, yes, your opponent as well) with the understanding necessary to appreciate your side in the debate.

2. To Extend and Amplify Your Remarks.

Just because you are the one answering the questions, it does not mean that you cannot continue to build your case assertively. One way of looking at it is that by being asked a question, you are being handed a miniature speaking opportunity. In that mini-speech, you can add arguments and add support, both illustrating and extending your speech.

> **Question:** So you say that attempts at international justice are unlikely to work?
>
> **Response:** Yes, that is exactly what we said, and more than that, attempts at international justice *have not worked in practice*. In the former Yugoslavia, the UN Tribunal has left parties on all sides dissatisfied and has been perceived politically. And in Rwanda the vast majority of perpetrators have gone unpunished. International courts have simply failed to live up to the challenge.

While it is a good idea to add information and extend your case when you can, this should not be taken as a license to disrespect the time of the individual asking the question. Depending upon the format that has been chosen, there will be more or less time for you to answer, but in all cases you should resist the temptation to "filibuster," or to keep talking until a moderator or an opponent is able to shut you up. There is an art to handling this, of course. Your goal as a respondent is to fully use the time that you have been given, without appearing to intrude or trample upon the time of others.

3. To Counterattack

In order for the questioning period to have spark and life, the person answering the questions needs to respond not meekly, as if he is being interrogated, but firmly, reflecting his continuing role as an advocate.

> **Question:** So, in support of your claim that the United States shouldn't go to war in Iraq, you quote the opinion of a general, but he is *retired* isn't he?
>
> **Response:** Yes, that is right, the former commander of NATO forces in Europe with the entire weight of his career behind him. In response, it seems like you are quoting, let's see, a newspaper editor, a political adviser, and a president who has never served one day in the military overseas.

One advantage of the counterattack response is that it puts the questioner on the defensive. The questioner would like to move on to another question, but a good counterattack can create an implied need to respond to the attack that has just been made.

In all cases of responding to questions, the advocate should keep a number of additional pieces of advice in mind.

- Provide any necessary qualifying statements prior to providing an answer to the question. Sometimes questioners will seek a "yes" or "no" response, and may exert control over time and may cut you off before you've provided the full context. Thus, the audience may hear "Yes, the death penalty is moral . . . " and miss " . . . but only if we have a *certain* means of determining if someone is guilty." The better way to phrase the answer would be "*If* it could be shown that we have a *certain* means of establishing guilt, *then* I would say that the death penalty is moral."

- Try to anticipate where your opponent is going, but only answer the question being asked, not the question that *you think* will be asked in the future. It is important to think about your questioner's purpose in order to provide the best clarification and to avoid a misstep. However, you risk giving arguments to the other side if you answer a challenge that you think they are making before they actually make it.

- Take your time. As long as you are not stalling the process, you should feel free to think about your answer and to deliver it at a reasonable pace. You do have to respect the time of the audience and the questioner, but you don't have to rush into an instantaneous response.

- If you don't know the answer, say that you don't know, and then return to your argument. You are not in the debate just to display an encyclopedic factual knowledge of the issue. Some facts you won't know, and rather than drawing attention to this gap by trying to guess or to dance around the answer, the quickest way out is an honest admission.

- When in doubt, bridge back to your own argument. The strongest response is generally one that takes you back to one of the arguments that you are making. Even if you are not entirely sure where a questioner is going, you should keep in mind where *you* are going and seek opportunities to return to your main arguments.

  > You know, I'm not sure what the exact number of highway deaths each year is. But what I do know is that *every* death caused by drunk driving is an unnecessary death and until there is adequate enforcement of the laws against driving drunk, too many people are going to be lost on our highways.

  Some good bridging phrases are:

  What is important to remember . . .

  Let me put that into perspective . . .

  And, don't forget . . .

  This is essential to understanding the situation . . .

- Avoid defensiveness. The audience needs to see you as a confident advocate who is explaining, extending, and defending your case. You should not present the picture of a criminal suspect who is being questioned about where he was last night. Eye contact, a strong clear voice, and a willingness to talk and to explain all communicate that you appreciate the opportunity to take on these points.

- Practice potential lines of questioning in advance. Before the debate ask yourself, "If I was on the other side, what would I ask?" and think of likely responses to those questions. You are your own *best* critic in the sense that you are in the best position to see all of the avenues of possible weakness and attack.

- Answer concisely, and then expand upon that answer if the time or the format permits. Avoid the appearance (or the reality) of trying to steal time from the questioner.

Forms of Questioning

While many of the practical and strategic considerations in asking and answering questions apply independently of the process by which questioning is included in your debate format, some aspects of questioning depend upon how that feature is included in the debate. In this next section, we will consider several common ways by which questioning can be added to a public debate and the strategic considerations that apply in each of these settings.

Cross-Examination

Cross examination is an element of public discourse that finds its roots in the Anglo-American legal tradition. That legal tradition is based on an adversarial model in which one side is pitted against the other. One of the elements of this system is the right to confront witnesses. Thus, when a witness presents information for one side, the other side has the opportunity to question that witness. This questioning is called *cross*-examination because it is an examination by the other side (this is in contrast to *direct*-examination, which is questioning by the lawyer representing one's own side).[3] This element of legal communication has been incorporated into competitive debate for several decades; it is appreciated as a debate element because of its ability to allow a sustained face-to-face exchange during a specific period of the debate and to allow positions to be developed and explored through a series of questions and answers. There are a few essential elements of cross-examination:

- The questioner controls the time. The entire span of the cross-examination—not just the time in which they are actually speaking—"belongs" to the questioners. They are the ones who are charged with using this time to develop ideas for future speeches. Thus, the questioner has full authority to decide the subject and sequence of the questions and, importantly, to decide how long the answer to each question will be. In practical terms, this means that once a reasonable opportunity to answer a question has been provided, a polite "thank you" should signal the questioner's intent to move on to the next question, and the respondent should take the hint and cease speaking. Particularly when amplification equipment is being used, it is unlikely that the audience will be able to hear either party if they attempt to speak over one another.

- Civility is critical. Certainly this is true of all questioning situations (not to mention the debate as a whole), but because of the sustained back-

and-forth nature of cross-examination, the format permits anger an avenue to escalate more quickly than in other formats. For that reason, both the questioner and the respondent have a responsibility to keep the exchange calm, clear, and focused on the audience.

- More than in the case of other questioning formats, cross-examination should be used to develop support and positions for later speeches, not simply to gain a momentary advantage. For this reason, questioners during cross-examination will often avoid asking a question that draws the final and most important conclusion ("... so, you really don't have *any* support for this point do you?"). Rather than risking the possibility that the respondent will come up with a great answer when her back is to the wall ("Well ... we certainly do have that support, and you'll hear it in our next speech!"), a questioner will be wiser to wait and draw that conclusion during his own speech ("and remember when I asked her about her support for this point? She was able to come up with none").

- Cross-examination is done for the benefit of the audience. Because it involves just two people for a sustained period of time, cross-examination can have the appearance of a private conversation. It is crucial to keep in mind, though, that all questions and all answers are ultimately for the audience's benefit. That recognition leads to one feature of cross examination that some audiences may find odd—that is that during cross-examination the questioner and the respondent will often stand side-by-side, both facing the audience rather than each other. This is done to allow both speakers to keep their attention where it belongs.[4]

- A series of questions is preferable to a disconnected set of questions. The questions are typically asked in a series in which one question builds upon another. Because cross-examination formats typically allow several minutes (most often three) for the exchange, the investment of time into developing a line of questioning can be substantial.

   Question: So you say that guns ought to be allowed because a citizen's best protection is to have a gun, is that right?

   Answer: Yes, that is right.

   Q: But protection against what?

   A: Well, protection against criminals.

   Q: Any criminals, or violent criminals?

   A: Chiefly, I am talking about violent criminals.

Q: All right, so we wouldn't be shooting shoplifters. We would be shooting people who are committing violence against us, right?

A: Right.

Q: And what sort of violent criminals would be the most dangerous?

A: Well, I know you want me to say "criminals with guns . . ."

Q: . . . Exactly!

A: . . . and it is true, of course, that a gun in criminal hands is a dangerous thing.

Q: So it seems like guns are the root of the problem.

A: Well, yes and no. Someone willing to break the law is always going to be able to get a gun. The question is whether the law-abiding citizen is able to protect herself or himself.

Q: So, to you the answer to the gun problem is "more guns"?

A: That oversimplifies it, but yes. By allowing law-abiding people to defend themselves, we make ourselves safer.

At its best, cross-examination is a cooperative struggle in which both parties have the challenge of explicating and defending their own views and the opportunity to undermine each other's views. The element that makes cross-examination unique and engaging is the existence of a sustained series of questions. To fully exploit the advantage of cross-examination, both advocates need to be thinking about where the questioning is going, and need to be seeing each question as part of a larger sequence which is ultimately oriented toward making a point to the audience, and to the other side. Questioners within this format need to have an objective and a plan for stepping-stone questions that might lead to that objective, as in the previous example, but they also need to be flexible enough to engage in a real dialogue and to follow the thread where it leads. The ability to follow up on an unexpected answer that comes from an adversary is often more important than sticking to a planned series of questions. Given the nature of the event, it is generally impossible to write out all of the questions beforehand. Instead, the advocate should simply have his objectives and stepping-stones in mind.

Points of Information

One advantage of cross-examination is that it permits a sustained exchange within a dedicated time period. But one disadvantage is that the questioner needs to wait until her opponent's speech is finished, and does not have the freedom to ask a question when the moment is ripe. One format style that allows questioning *during* an opponent's speech is called "point of information" and it is most associated with the parliamentary format for debate (see chapter 7). This debate format is modeled on a British-style parliament and for that reason contains some of its elements. Most typically, members of the team that is not currently making a speech are allowed to ask questions at any time other than during the final summary speeches and during the first or last minute of any other speech. In order to ask a question, the speaker will generally stand (sometimes raising one hand and placing the other hand on top of his head[5]), and say something like "will the speaker yield?" or "on that point . . ." When this occurs, the individual giving the speech has three options: she can agree to the question, she can decline the question, or she can say that she will take the question later. It is not considered rude to refuse or delay a question, particularly if you are in the middle of explaining an argument or providing a reason. The speaker is in control of her time while she is speaking, so formally at least, she is the only one to say whether she will or will not entertain a question. On the other hand, it may be considered rude or (worse) defensive to turn down *all* requests for questions. In a typical six- to eight-minute speech, a speaker may wish to entertain two or three questions. If fewer, it could look like the speaker is afraid of whatever the other sides wants to ask. If more, there is a risk that the speech will turn into an interview.

> **Speaker:** . . . hopefully, by this point in the twenty-first century we have evolved, so that we no longer assume that one man's ability to kill another man confers any kind of moral authority. War in this case is nothing more than murder with another name. Anytime we take up arms against another . . .
>
> **Questioner:** Will the speaker yield?
>
> **Speaker:** Yes, go ahead.
>
> **Questioner:** So you are saying all war is bad, even wars that are designed to stop genocide and mass murder?

> **Speaker:** Yes, well, genocide and mass murder generally take place in conditions that are created or aggravated by a war, so they would be part of what this side of the debate would condemn. There are three moral harms to legitimated killing . . .
>
> **Questioner:** Will the speaker yield?
>
> **Speaker:** No, not now. Those three moral harms are . . .

As this example shows, the use of points of information creates a sort of "constructive intrusion" that at its best can provide an opportunity to make a point when it most needs to be made, and at its worst, could upset the equilibrium and flow of the speech. For this reason, points of information are best used when the speakers involved are experienced and confident, able to maintain their own flow of thought while addressing and accommodating the thoughts of others.

When using points, the following considerations are important.

- The respondent, which in this case is the person giving the speech, needs to maintain control of the question. This means not only choosing whether and when to respond to a request for points of information, but it also means deciding how long to answer, and how to direct that answer back into the flow of the speech. The effective speaker will attempt to direct the force of the question into the argument that he or she is making at the time.

> Yes, good question, I do believe that freedom of expression is important for journalists and that is precisely why they bear such a high responsibility for getting it right. They have the freedom, yes, but with that freedom comes an awesome responsibility and that leads directly to my next point: they have been failing in that responsibility.

- The question needs to be phrased in a self-sufficient manner. Unlike the case of cross-examination, points of information provide the opportunity to question only on a one-shot basis. After the answer is completed, the speaker moves back into his speech and the questioner must ask the speaker to yield again before she has the opportunity for another question. For this reason, questioners will most often not get the chance to set up a question or follow a line of questions. Concise and powerful phrasing is critical. Basically, the question needs to be phrased in such a way that *the principal effect is accomplished just in the asking,* and does not depend upon a particular follow-up or a conclusion. In this way, the point of information is less conventionally a "question" and more like an argument in question form.

Since you admitted earlier that the International Court could not enforce its judgments in a noncooperating nation, then the International Criminal Court couldn't have prosecuted Pol Pot, could it?

- Moderators bear a special responsibility to make sure that this format is clear to the audience. For an audience that has never seen a parliamentary debate before, it may not seem natural that people are periodically jumping up (possibly with their hands on their heads) and interrupting a speech in progress. At first blush, it might seem terribly rude to the audience. For this reason, the moderator should take care to explain that this questioning opportunity is an element of the debate, that it is designed to add some liveliness to the debate and to allow questions to be asked when they matter most, and that the speakers are prepared for it and ultimately bear the responsibility of deciding whether or not they are going to take a question.

- A certain amount of grace and cooperation is necessary from both sides. The responding party needs to be cooperative enough to allow a reasonable number of points to be made, but should not take so many that she is essentially giving away her speaking opportunity. The questioning party needs to exercise some restraint in picking the right times to request a point (and not be continually jumping up like a jack-in-the-box). In the case of a planned public debate, advocates have the opportunity to reach a rough agreement concerning the number of points that each speaker should allow.

- Don't ignore the opportunities for entertaining interplay in the requesting, granting, or refusal of points of information. As long as it fits the tone of the debate, consider employing some wit in how questions are requested and accepted. There is no rule about the phrases one must use to request, accept, or deny a point. For example in one public debate between Towson University and Cambridge University in 2001, a female debater who had been interrupted many times by a male speaker from the other side finally declined his request for a question by saying, "Seth, I know you must hear this from your girlfriend all the time, but 'not now.'" As long as they are in good taste, considering the speaker and the situation, witty retorts like this can project confidence and add to the fun of the event.

- Speakers, don't be afraid to take a reasonable number of points. It is wise to plan your speech with less than the full amount of material necessary to fill the time allowed. In this way, you'll be prepared to use the points from the other side to make up a minute or so of your speech. In addition, taking these points will make you look stronger and more confident and will also provide you with the opportunity to integrate them into your own speech.

- Questioners, don't be discouraged by the speaker's failure to take a question. No speaker would be well advised to take *every point*, and the questioner can still communicate a message even though the request for a point has been denied. A hearty "On that point . . ." just after a speaker has provided an illustration, for instance, may cause the audience to speculate about what might be wrong with what the speaker just said. (This is much like a trial lawyer shouting "Objection!" when he thinks his adversary has violated a rule. Even when the objection is overruled by the judge, it has an impact.)

Panel and Audience Questioning.

A final way to introduce questioning into a public debate is to allow the audience or an invited panel to question the advocates. At a specific point in the debate (during or after), the moderator will invite questions and direct them to one or more of the teams debating. This method of questioning is less familiar to individuals who are experienced in tournament formats of debate, but can be an excellent way of including an another perspective that is likely to be distinct from that of the advocates.

The format for panel or audience questioning is naturally going to be less technical than that of other means of questioning. Still, some advance planning and communication are essential. In the case of panelists, once they have been invited or otherwise designated, the next step will be to give them some practical advice on how to generate and prepare their questions. Panelists might be encouraged to do a little bit of general investigation if they don't already possess expertise in the subject and to think of a couple of potential question themes without locking themselves into specific questions. Then, when they are hearing the debate, they can refine and focus their questions to make them potentially reactive to something that was specifically said during the debate.

In the case of general audience questioning, there are two advance steps that could be taken. First, you may want to identify specific individuals who could be counted on, and who have agreed in advance, to ask a good question in order to get the ball rolling. These "icebreakers" may be necessary in the event that the moderator opens it up for questions only to discover that no one wants to go first. Particularly when the debaters are very good, members of the general audience may be less confident in their ability to speak up and they may need to be coaxed into it by a couple of "planted" audience-member questions. Second, the moderator should let the audience know at the very beginning of the debate (or even earlier, on the posters) that there will be a questioning period. In this way, audience members can be thinking about likely questions as the debate progresses and will not be surprised by the announcement of a questioning opportunity. Eliciting general audience questions may be the most challenging way to promote a successful interchange. The reason for this is that audience members, unless they feel comfortable really challenging the speaker, may simply ask informational questions or request additional detail. This does give the speakers additional chances to explain, but it doesn't really challenge their arguments in any way. For this reason, it will be essential for the moderator to explain, prior to the questioning period, what sort of questions can and should be asked (see chapter 17). The emphasis here is that the audience can both request information and challenge the advocates.

> At this point in the debate we have heard a great deal from the debaters, and now we want to hear from you. Specifically, we want to hear your questions. Was anything in the debate unclear? Did you find yourself wanting to challenge any of the facts or conclusions that you heard? Did you notice any weaknesses or inconsistencies? Do you wonder what the debaters would say to an argument that you have in mind? Do you think that the two sides have left anything out in their responses? Feel free to ask your question of either side, or both sides. Yes, go ahead . . .

There are a few key considerations for advocates and planners in the use of audience or panel questions.

- Panel and audience questions should be seen as discussion openers. Questions in this setting function not as instances of interrogation but as openings for discussion. The implication of this is that questions are valued not simply for their ability to undermine a specific claim or to refute an argument but for their ability to generate interesting follow-up and development. Panelists in particular should not see themselves as aligning specifically with one side of the debate or the other, but should instead see their questions as offering a perspective that expands the dialogue.

All of you offered some very interesting arguments on the responsibilities of the mass media. You seem to agree that the media has a social responsibility, you just disagree on whether they are meeting that responsibility. But I found it curious that none of you mentioned the responsibility to simply tell the truth. Certainly the media ought to operate in ways that avoid violence, encourage racial harmony, promote better government, etc. But isn't the first obligation of the news media in particular to just tell the truth, whatever the consequences?

- The moderator should play a direct role in regulating the questioning period. Particularly in the case of the general audience, we can't expect expert questioning from a nonexpert audience. Some questioners may begin to make speeches, never coming around to a clear question. Others may ask several questions before yielding the floor. The moderator in this case will need to step in and ask something like, "O.K., what is the most important question in what you've just said?" The moderator also plays a role in deciding which side of the debate answers first and in keeping a rough tally of the time that each side has spent answering in an effort to balance the speaking opportunities for each side. If questioning seems to lean more heavily on one side or the other, the moderator can ask something like, "Are there any questions for the affirmative side?"

- Audience and panel questions should be seen as providing the questioners with a speaking opportunity. Because the question is a "mini-speech" by an individual who is not otherwise receiving a recognized speaking opportunity, it is probably more acceptable than in other formats for the questioner to provide a bit of personal background before asking a question. After all, the questioners have not had other speeches in which they could have made their context or their perspective clear. Still, this idea cannot be taken to an extreme. Any clear question should be capable of being set up and asked in a minute or less. Because the question is likely to be a "one-shot" opportunity (much like points of information), questions should be phrased so that the work is done by the initial question and any prefatory remarks. That is, audience and panel questioners cannot ask set-up questions. In the event that one of the debaters has misunderstood or failed to answer a question, the questioner might be permitted a brief follow-up, at the moderator's discretion. If a longer sequence of questioning is desired, however, the cross-examination format is more suitable.

- The tone of the advocates in responding to audience and panel questions should be a bit different from the tone used with other debaters, since the audience shouldn't be thought of or treated as an adversary. Instead of attempting to "refute" or undermine the questioner, the effective speaker will attempt to include and build upon the questioner's information. For example, it should be fairly common to begin one's answer with some sort of affirmation, such as "that is a good question," or "that raises an important issue . . .", etc., and then to follow it up with a reaction to the question itself and a return to one's own side in the debate. (Many commentators theorized that U.S. presidential candidate Howard Dean lost support in the 2004 Iowa nominating caucuses after he told an elderly questioner at a town meeting, "You sit down. You've had your say and now I'm going to have my say."[6])

Conclusion

We have considered the role of questioning in a public debate, the purposes for the questioner and the respondent, and the specific demands of different formats for questioning. The specific way in which questioning is used in a given debate should be based upon the purposes and the situation for that debate. Certainly, combining various formats for questioning is possible (for example, allowing points of information during the debate, then panel questions after the debate). The many advantages of questioning in promoting and showcasing quick thinking, wit, and argument development have led to it being a nearly ubiquitous feature in public debates. In fact, several American presidential debates are constructed almost entirely out of candidate reactions to either panel or audience questions.[7] In most contexts, however, the balance of speaking time and interaction time is likely to be suited to the situation. With all of the advantages that questioning provides, perhaps the only time when a questioning period is *not* included in a public debate is when debate organizers feel that they need absolute control over a message and do not want to risk an unexpected question. In those situations, debate is itself probably not the best model. But the fundamental point is that for planners who are looking for lively opportunities to develop content and show interaction, the only question left is: "Why not ask questions?"

Notes

1. Indeed a once-dominant debate format, known as the Oxford style, didn't feature questioning and this lack was significant enough that when a new American debating organization was established in 1971 it came to call itself the "Cross Examination Debate Association" in order to emphasize that format distinction.

2. For an explanation of this persuasive theory, see W. J. McGuire, "Inducing Resistance to Persuasion: Some Contemporary Approaches," in *Advances in Social Psychology*, ed. L. Berkowitz (New York: Academic Press, 1964): vol. 1.

3. While direct examination could, in theory, be included as an element of debate, it wouldn't make much sense. In a legal context, direct examination is necessary because witnesses are just witnesses—they aren't advocates; for that reason they cannot directly address the court. Debate speakers, in contrast, *are* advocates, and for that reason, they are perfectly able to speak for themselves without needing one of their colleagues to elicit the information from them.

4. Some coaches have taken this idea to the extreme and instructed questioners and respondents to *not look at each other at all* during cross-examination. We find this advice, however, to be unnecessary and artificial. It is natural during questioning, for example, to look to your opponent when you are asking or being asked, and then to return attention to the audience once the question is being answered. One way to facilitate this is for both speakers to stand at roughly a 45 degree angle to the audience, or halfway between facing each other and facing the audience.

5. This is a curious affectation that, we are told, has something to do with early parliamentarians needing to keep their starched white wigs firmly on their heads as they jumped up to ask a question.

6. J. Wilgoren, "One Church, One Microphone, Two Hopefuls," *New York Times*, January 12, 2004.

7. S. Kraus, *Televised Presidential Debates and Public Policy*, 2nd ed. (Mahwah, NJ: Lawrence

Chapter Seventeen

Moderating the Debate

"Gentlemen, get this thing straight once and for all. The policeman isn't there to create disorder. The policeman is there to preserve disorder."

Richard Daley, mayor of Chicago, September 9, 1968[1]

When Mayor Daley made his famous Freudian slip in 1968, he was defending the behavior of the Chicago police force during violent confrontations with antiwar protesters at the Democratic national convention. Hundreds of protesters were arrested, most notably Abbie Hoffman and Jerry Rubin, the leaders of the Youth International Party—the Yippies. Hoffman and Rubin, along with five other leaders, were charged with crossing state lines "with the intent to incite, organize, promote, encourage, participate in, and carry on a riot" and put on trial. The case of "The Chicago Seven" captured the nation's attention and raised the question of how far America could go in its commitment to free expression and tolerance for political dissent. The trial was marked by mutual contempt and hostility. Hoffman, for example, called the judge a "tyrant" whose idea of justice was an "obscenity"; he appeared in court one day wearing his own set of judge's robes, which he took off and trampled on the ground. Rubin, at one point, raised his arm in a Nazi salute to the judge and shouted, "Heil Hitler!" In response to continued heckling, the judge ordered one defendant (later separated from the trial) to be bound, gagged and tied to a chair; the judge's actions were so harsh, in fact, that he was rebuked by an appeals court for "unseemly conduct in court" and for procedural errors that caused the convictions of Hoffman and Rubin to be overturned.[2]

Fourteen years later, Rubin and Hoffman had moved in different directions. Hoffman continued to be active in radical politics and committed to progressive ideals; Rubin, however, went to work briefly for a Wall Street investment bank before becoming a professional organizer of personal and business networks. Once partners, Hoffman and Rubin had become opponents; they decided to explore their disagreements in a series of public debates, staged at various college campuses in 1984. The two adversaries met at Western Washington University, a medium-sized public university on America's West Coast, and one of your authors was selected as the moderator of that debate.

The moderator's primary role is to serve as a genial host and facilitator for the debate; the moderator introduces the participants, sets the tone, and encourages an atmosphere of civil and productive dialogue. Moderating is generally a pleasant and uncomplicated experience. But this was not the case in the debate between Hoffman and Rubin: they had something else in mind. Just before the start of the debate, Abbie Hoffman pulled the moderator aside and said, in essence, "Look, what we are going to do is basically just go at each other, and we are going to ignore your attempts to set any sort of time limits or turn-taking behavior. That's part of the show—so don't worry about it." What ensued for the next hour was exactly what Hoffman had predicted: there was absolute bedlam as both advocates played to the crowd and pursued each other with zeal. They interrupted each other and spoke at the same time, while the moderator watched helplessly—but the audience loved it.

This example shows that roles can be altered to serve virtually any purpose in a public debate. Hoffman and Rubin turned the moderator into a foil in order to suit their purposes for the event. But this story also shows how important it is to have a moderator as a controlling influence in a public debate. Without an effective moderator, a debate can quickly degenerate into something other than a civil and reasonable dialogue. In this particular debate, Hoffman and Rubin ignored the moderator deliberately because they thought that the audience would find their heated confrontations entertaining—just "part of the show." But most public debates seek to create more light than heat; entertainment plays a secondary role to enlightenment. For that to happen, there must be a moderator who can promote the orderly exchange of ideas.

This chapter will focus on the role of the moderator (also known as the master of ceremonies or as "Madame Speaker" or "Mr. Speaker" in British debating). We will examine the responsibilities of the moderator before discussing the best way to choose an individual to fulfill this role. We will also review the moderator's tasks, both before and during the debate.

The Moderator's Role

As we noted in chapter 7, the primary purpose of any debate format is to ensure fairness: formats are designed so that all participants are given an equal chance to be heard. It might be said that the moderator of a public debate has a similar purpose: he or she is there to ensure fairness. In part, that means that the moderator is the guardian of the format who must see to it that rules are followed—but there is more to the job than that. The moderator must also ensure fairness when addressing the audience, introducing speakers, and explaining the structure of the debate.

1. Addressing the Audience: Setting a Tone and Establishing Purpose

The moderator serves as host for the event and generally will be the first person to speak to the audience. As a result, the moderator has a responsibility to set a tone for the event; in his opening comments, the moderator helps to establish audience expectations for the debate that will follow. The moderator should remind the audience of the importance of the question being debated and should characterize the conflict in an evenhanded way. Compare the following examples:

> A. Ladies and Gentlemen, we said we'd start at 8 o'clock, so let's get started. Let me introduce our first speaker . . .

> B. Of all the important issues facing this country right now, there is none more important than the question of our security. We need to protect ourselves, but the security of the country sometimes comes into conflict with individual freedom. Can we protect ourselves without losing freedoms? Or is that impossible? Because we want to address these questions, we have arranged this public debate . . .

> C. The most important conflict in this country is about the future of our environment. On the one side, there are the people who are committed to protecting the environment for future generations, and on the other side there are the

greedheads who would rape the Earth for the sake of their
profits. We have both sides here tonight . . .

It is obvious (we hope) that the second example is the best of the three. The
first example represents a missed opportunity; it does nothing to introduce
the topic or set a tone. The third example fails because it is biased; it shows
a clear prejudice toward one side in the debate. The second example, in
contrast, is balanced, and helps to orient the audience toward the topic of
the debate.

The moderator, of course, is not a participant in the debate itself and
does not take a position of advocacy. Nonetheless, some of the suggestions in our chapter on opening speeches (chapter 13) are apposite in this
situation: the moderator's opening remarks should be strong, and should
demand the attention of the audience; they should establish a relationship
with the audience; and they should create a context—albeit a neutral context—for the debate.

2. Introducing the Speakers

The moderator's second major responsibility is to introduce the participants in the debate. This is not simply a matter of reciting names and job
titles; rather, the moderator must introduce the speakers in a way that says
to the audience, "Here is someone you will find interesting." The moderator can do that by highlighting something in particular from the speaker's
resume of experience, or, if possible, by telling the audience something that
they don't know about the speaker. As for names and job titles, it is critical
for the moderator to have full and accurate information about each participant. It would not do to introduce Henry Kissinger as "someone who had
important jobs in the government back in the 1970s." (More precisely, *Dr.*
Kissinger (note the use of his preferred honorific) was National Security
Adviser and Secretary of State for both President Richard Nixon and
President Gerald Ford.) It is also important for the moderator to ascertain
the proper pronunciation of both personal names and organization names.
(*The Congressional Quarterly*, by the way, publishes a list of Frequently
Mispronounced Names of members of Congress.[3] Senator Michael Crapo
of Idaho pronounces his last name "CRAY-poe.")

Many speakers who are well-known or famous customarily provide
their own biographical information to debate organizers; in any case, the

moderator must assemble appropriate information for all of the participants involved—whether they are well-known or obscure. And in making the introductions, the moderator must be scrupulously evenhanded: if one speaker's introduction is festooned with mentions of awards and accomplishments, and the other speaker is introduced with only a name, the audience will in all likelihood become predisposed toward the speaker with the longer introduction. It is true that all debaters are not created equal, and some will arrive with more impressive resumes than their opponents; nonetheless, the moderator should try to minimize this imbalance, rather than maximize it.

3. Explaining the Structure of the Debate

As we noted in chapter 7, public debates can take many shapes and forms. The corollary is that the spectators at a public debate do not know quite what to expect; they are not like spectators at a baseball game, who enter the stadium knowing that there will be nine innings and that each side gets three outs. The public debate audience does not know how much time has been allotted to each side; it does not know the ground rules governing direct exchanges or questioning periods; it may not even know exactly what the resolution is. It is the moderator's job to inform the audience about these matters, so that they will know what to expect during the debate.

The moderator must begin by articulating the resolution or the question at stake precisely. In other words, it is not enough to say, "Tonight, these advocates will argue about the conflict between security and personal liberty." Rather, the moderator should say something like this: "Tonight's debate is focused on the following statement: 'Resolved: individual civil liberties should not be abolished for the sake of national security.' The team seated to my right agrees with that statement and will support it tonight; the team to my left disagrees, and will negate that statement."

After articulating the resolution, the moderator should explain the format briefly. Here is how it was done by television newscaster Jim Lehrer when he moderated the first of the presidential debates between Bill Clinton and Bob Dole in 1996:

> [The debate] will last 90 minutes following a format and rules worked out by the two campaigns. There will be two-minute opening and closing statements. In between, a series of questions, each

> having three parts. A 90-second answer, a 60-second rebuttal, and a
> 30-second response. I will assist the candidates in adhering to those
> time limits with the help of a series of lights visible to both.
>
> Under their rules, the candidates are not allowed to question each
> other directly. I will ask the questions. There are no limitations on
> the subjects. The order for everything tonight was determined by
> coin toss. Now, to the opening statements and to President Clinton.
> Mr. President.[4]

As this example shows, the explanation of the format does not need to be
exhaustive; at this point, all that is needed is a brief account of the guidelines.
The audience (and the debaters) can be reminded of the format as necessary
throughout the debate—e.g., when Lehrer introduced the opening statement
of President Clinton's opponent, he said, "Senator Dole, two minutes."

We should emphasize that the purpose of this introduction is simply to
give the audience some idea of the rules that are in place, so that they can
follow the sequence of events. That means it is *not* an attempt to give the
audience a set of judging criteria; when listening to the debate, they should
not be trying to determine who did the best job of following the rules.
Generally, public debates should be judged on the basis of substance, rather
than on the basis of form. (The rare exception would be a public debate that
was designed to showcase debating skills—in that case, performance and
adherence to form would be elevated in importance.)

4. Maintaining Order

We take it as a given that any public debate is governed by a set of rules
that create time limits, establish speaking order, and delimit the content of
speeches—and that these rules have been approved by both sides in the
debate. It is part of the moderator's job to make sure that those rules are
followed.

We do not mean that the moderator is supposed to act like an umpire or
a referee, ready to impose punishments for any infractions of the rules. The
moderator is, rather, more like a traffic controller—that is, someone who
manages the flow of the debate, makes sure that participants stop when they
are supposed to stop, and go when they are supposed to go.

A large part of the moderator's job, then, is keeping track of the time—
although that does not mean that the moderator needs to time the event
personally. Indeed, it is probably more efficient to have another person keep

time and display it in a way that is visible to both teams and to the moderator. (In the excerpt from the debate above, Lehrer mentions the use of lights; time cards are also effective.) Violations of time limits are not necessarily cavalier or malicious; even with knowledge of the rules and an awareness of how much time is passing, debaters can get so caught up in a thought that their words spill over the border. We don't think it does much damage to the principle of fairness if a debater's response takes 35 seconds instead of 30 seconds, and there is little to be gained for the moderator to interrupt if he or she judges that the debater is finishing a thought. But when the debater's violation is substantial, the moderator may interrupt, as in this exchange from the Gore-Bush presidential debates in 2000:

> **Gore:** . . . Last week he said that they were spending 3.7 billion dollars, or 4.7 billion dollars on this.
>
> **Moderator:** Mr. Vice President.
>
> **Gore:** Okay.
>
> **Moderator:** Time is up. Governor Bush, two minutes.
>
> **Bush:** I'm absolutely opposed to a national health care plan . . .[5]

The moderator may also interrupt when other rules are violated. Again, this can be done in a genial way—and again, we will use the example of Jim Lehrer moderating the Gore-Bush presidential debate.

> **Bush:** Yeah, I agree. I just—I think there has been—some of the scientists, I believe, Mr. Vice President, haven't they been changing their opinion a little bit on global warming? A profound scientist recently made a different—
>
> **Moderator:** Both of you have now violated—excuse me. Both of you have now violated your own rules. Hold that thought.
>
> **Gore:** I've been trying so hard not to.
>
> **Moderator:** I know, I know. But under your rules you are not allowed to ask each other a question. I let you [addressing Gore] do it a moment ago.
>
> **Bush:** Twice.[6]

Generally, the moderator should interrupt only when he judges that the violations—exceeding allotted time or breaking other rules—represent an imminent risk to civil and productive dialogue. Because an overly intrusive moderator can do as much harm to the debate as an unruly advocate, the moderator must exercise careful judgment before interrupting.

5. Facilitating Interaction and Engagement

The moderator's final responsibility—to facilitate interaction and engagement—will be shaped largely by the ground rules of the debate as determined by the participants. At one extreme, the ground rules may limit the moderator's job to introducing the event and enforcing the rules. But it is also possible for the moderator to be more significantly involved, both formally and substantively. Say, for example, that audience participation is incorporated into the design of the debate. In that case, the moderator might take an active role in determining which members of the audience are allowed to speak. The moderator might also determine which audience questions are posed to the debaters. In one of the Gore-Bush debates, for example, audience members wrote their questions on index cards that were given to the moderator; he had the responsibility of arranging the sequence of those questions.[7] Moreover, he was given the ability, as moderator, to ask follow-up questions—in other words, he was involved substantively in the debate, and could ask the participants to clarify their answers or to respond more directly to the question that had been asked.

It is also possible to design a debate in which the moderator poses his or her own questions. In this case, of course, the moderator must remain a neutral party. That means that the moderator cannot cross-examine a speaker the same way that an opponent would; it is certainly possible, however, for the moderator to raise issues with both of the debaters (or teams) involved. Imagine that the debate resolution is the one that we used above: "Resolved: Individual civil liberties should not be abolished for the sake of national security." It would be fair—and would promote direct "clash" or conflict—if the moderator asked this: "You have both spoken in broad terms about civil liberties and the Patriot Act, but I would like to hear what you think specifically of the provision that allows the government to access borrowing records at public libraries. Is this a significant invasion of privacy? Is it justifiable for the sake of national security?"

Choosing a Moderator

In describing the role of the moderator, we have emphasized the importance of neutrality: the debate cannot be fair if the moderator favors one side over the other. That does not mean that debate organizers need to find a moderator with no personal opinions or no involvement with controversial issues; even a person with passionate beliefs can adopt a neutral position for the course of a debate. Nonetheless, we recommend that the moderator be someone who is publicly neutral about the issue at hand; if the debate is about the conflict of security and civil liberties, it is not a good idea to invite a moderator from the American Civil Liberties Union (or, conversely, someone who has written newspaper op-ed pieces that criticize the ACLU). Minimally, the moderator should be someone who is unaffiliated with either of the two parties involved in the debate—in other words, if one side of the debate is represented by the campus Sierra Club, the president of the club should not be acting as moderator.

The moderator's job also requires public speaking skills. The moderator should be someone who is comfortable in front of an audience and who will be able to introduce the debate and the speakers with confidence. Moreover, the moderator should be a person with flexibility and good judgment: maintaining order requires the ability to respond to situations as they unfold, as well as sufficient assertiveness to control the situation when necessary. It is also important for the moderator to be genial and good-humored; a good moderator provides a calming center when exchanges become intense and keeps the debate on track with an easy hand. In this context, we offer a caveat about choosing a moderator on the basis of prestige or celebrity. It very often happens that highly respected officials—or professors, or writers—do not have good public speaking skills. So even if they have expert knowledge of the matter in question, they do not make good moderators because they cannot execute some of the job's main responsibilities.

The moderator should also be familiar with the topic and with the process of debate. Without understanding the topic, the moderator will not be able to provide an effective introduction; neither will he or she be able to take on a more substantive role in the progress of the debate, if that is allowed by the format. A moderator does not have to be an experienced debater in order to be familiar with the process but should at least have witnessed enough debates—either educational debates or public debates—to understand how debate formats actually work.

When searching for a moderator, debate organizers should consider people who are used to speaking for a living: teachers, litigators, and people who work in the media are all good candidates. People who have had experience as debaters or debate coaches can also do a good job as moderators.

Finally, debate organizers should look for someone who is happy to play a secondary role. In a public debate, the spotlight is on the debaters themselves—not on the moderator. The event requires an individual with the sensitivity and humility to step aside so that others may shine.

The Moderator's Preparation Before the Debate

Because the moderator must introduce the participants in the debate, it is important for her to gather necessary information beforehand from the participants. The introductions should also be prepared before the debate, so that their accuracy and appropriateness can be checked with the participants. (A participant might say, for example, "I don't think it's necessary for you to tell the audience where I went to college—but I would like you to mention that I have published articles about global economics in *Foreign Affairs*.")

The moderator should also prepare her opening remarks before the debate. Here, we would acknowledge one of the time-honored principles of oratory: the shorter the speech is, the longer it takes to prepare it. (As President Woodrow Wilson once remarked, when someone asked him how long it took him to prepare a speech: "It depends. If I am to speak ten minutes, I need a week for preparation; if fifteen minutes, three days; if half an hour, two days; if an hour, I am ready now."[8]) The opening remarks should be short—just long enough to set the tone and establish the purpose of the event. The moderator needs to remember that she is the host, not the main event; her job is to introduce other people, rather than herself.

This is also the right time for the moderator to review the debate schedule and format. Presumably, the parties involved have agreed on the format as one of the first steps in setting up the debate, but it is important for the moderator to review that agreement and make sure that everyone involved understands it the same way.

Finally, it is important for the moderator to check on the facilities where the debate is being held. Setting up the debate physically (e.g., supplying chairs, lecterns, microphones) is the primary responsibility of the debate organizers, but the moderator should ensure that the facilities are appropriately arranged, and that everything is in working order. (If, for example, lights are used to cue debaters to the passage of time, the moderator should make sure they are clearly visible.)

The Moderator's Participation During the Debate
The Opening

After ascertaining that the house is settled (i.e., there are no long lines of people milling about in the lobby of the auditorium), and the sound system is functional, the moderator begins the debate. We will recapitulate the responsibilities we outlined above.

Step	Sample
1. Welcome the audience.	"Good evening, ladies and gentlemen, and welcome to . . .
2. Identify the event.	. . . the first of a series of debates sponsored by the International Affairs Society of Northwestern Massachusetts State University.
3. Identify yourself and your role.	My name is John Wellington Wells. I am the secretary of the International Affairs Society, and tonight I will be serving as moderator of the debate.
4. Identify the topic and justify its importance.	Of all the important issues facing this country right now, there is none more important than the question of our security. We need to protect ourselves, but the security of the country sometimes comes into conflict with individual freedom. Can we protect ourselves without losing freedoms? Or is that impossible? Because we want to address these questions, we have arranged tonight's debate, which is focused on the following statement: "Resolved: individual civil liberties should not be abolished for the sake of national security."

5. Identify the participants and build credibility for them.	Seated to my right is Mr. James Sloane, who agrees with that statement and will support it tonight; on my left is Ms. Elizabeth Davidson, who disagrees, and will negate that statement. Mr. Sloane is Associate Director of the American Civil Liberties Union's Washington National Office. He was formerly . . . Ms. Davidson is a Deputy Director in the Office of Information and Privacy at the U.S. Justice Department. She has written. . .
6. Explain the format.	The first part of the debate will last sixty minutes following a format and rules worked out by the two debaters. There will be two-minute opening and closing statements. In between, a series of questions, each having three parts: a ninety-second answer, a sixty-second rebuttal, and a thirty-second response . . .
7. Highlight any particular audience involvement.	After the conclusion of the first hour, the floor will be opened to questions from the audience. Those of you who wish to address a question to Mr. Sloane should come forward to the microphone at the front of the left aisle; questions for Ms. Davidson will be made from the right aisle . . .
8. Introduce the first speaker.	On the basis of a coin toss, the first speaker tonight will be Mr. Sloane, defending the resolution that individual civil liberties should not be abolished for the sake of national security."

After the First Speech

After the debaters begin speaking, the moderator has a choice: his participation can be regular and automatic, or it can occur on an "as-needed" basis. Regular and automatic participation would involve managing every transition in the debate: after the first speaker finished, the moderator would introduce the next step (as in the example given above from the presidential debate, the moderator would say, "Ms. Davidson, you have two minutes for your opening statement."). Subsequently, the moderator would indicate the time allotted for questioning, for refutations, and so on. If, on the other hand, the moderator chose to participate on an as-needed basis, he might speak only when a time limit or rule had been violated or to introduce a major change in procedure (e.g., "At this point, we will open the floor for questions.").

The moderator should choose his model of participation to suit the occasion. If the audience consists of debate practitioners, or other people who are familiar with debate practice, the regular and automatic announcement of speeches would probably seem unnecessary. For an audience of neophytes, however, the signposts offered by regular introductions might be entirely appropriate.

It is also up to the moderator whether to use a gavel to maintain order. In some ways, the gavel presupposes the possibility of an unruly debate or an unruly audience—it is a simple machine designed to make a noise that will carry over the sound of people talking or shouting. It is not quite as loud as a starter's pistol, but it serves the same purpose. So the gavel can be an effective tool for crowd control. At the same time, it should be recognized that the gavel can have a provocative effect—if it is used too zealously, the audience may act up just for the fun of watching someone pound a desk with a piece of wood. The gavel must be used judiciously.

Dealing with Problems

We have already discussed the moderator's role in dealing with infractions committed by the debaters: the moderator must ensure that time limits and rules are respected or else the debate can quickly spin out of control. We have not, however, discussed the moderator's role in controlling the audience.

There is no universal law governing the behavior of audiences at public debates; rules and standards need to be determined as appropriate for each particular situation. At the presidential debates, for example, the audience members are enjoined to silence. They are allowed to laugh, of course, if something seems funny, but they are prohibited from applauding to show support for a particular statement by the candidate. For some public debates, that kind of restriction may be appropriate; in other situations, that kind of silence may seem deadening. (Just think of a sports event where the spectators seem to be "out of the game.")

In most cases, audience activity will follow the rhythms of the debate itself: audience members are likely to talk to each other at the conclusion of a speech, when one speaker is stepping down from the lectern, and another is stepping up—even if that change takes place in a matter of seconds. It is the moderator's responsibility to see that those sporadic eruptions of conversation remain sporadic, rather than constant. The debate will not succeed if there is an unbroken undertow of noise, and the moderator needs to admonish the audience as necessary.

Heckling

To put it simply, heckling means speaking out of turn: while the recognized speaker—that is, the speaker who "has the floor"—is talking, the heckler yells out a question or comment. This doesn't mean, however, that a heckler is necessarily a disruptive agitator who should be hustled out the door by the security force; indeed, heckling is an accepted practice in the British House of Commons. Members of Parliament often voice their approval or disapproval without being "recognized" by the House Speaker. (One corollary is that heckling is also encountered in the competitive debate format known as Parliamentary Debate.)

In a public debate, then, it is possible to allow heckling by the debaters—it is more likely to be seen when the debate is conducted by teams, rather than individuals. But the other possibility is to allow heckling from the audience; some debate organizers feels that it makes the event livelier if debaters are challenged directly by the people whom they are trying to persuade.

We do not think it is possible to prescribe a universal rule about heckling; we would neither ban it, nor proclaim it an essential component of a good public debate. The appropriateness of heckling depends largely on the context of the debate and its participants. We will note, however, that the moderator's responsibilities increase almost exponentially when heckling is permitted: the moderator must decide, in a disinterested way, when the heckling has become excessive. (Generally, this will be when the heckling is so loud or so insistent that the speaker cannot be heard.) In this case, the moderator must use his authority (and his gavel) to silence the hecklers—and that may be as easy as putting the genie back in the bottle or the toothpaste back in the tube.

Closing the Debate

We noted that the moderator generally opens the debate; not surprisingly, the moderator generally closes it as well. Minimally, this means that the moderator announces that the debate is over and thanks each of the participants individually. As in the opening, it is appropriate for the moderator to make brief general remarks about the debate—although such remarks must be neutral and impartial.

In our next chapter, we will discuss the incorporation of judgment into the model of the debate—that is, the incorporation of some mechanism that allows the audience, or a panel of judges, to say who "won" the debate. When such a mechanism is used, it is the moderator's job to manage the process, and to provide ultimate closure by announcing the winner, before bidding the audience a final farewell.

Conclusion

In sum, the moderator can be seen as one of the unsung heroes of public debate. The moderator isn't the star of the show; it isn't often that spectators will fill a hall just because they want to see someone moderating, and you will not hear many members of the audience murmur as they leave, "What a great debate! That was the best moderating I've seen in the past twenty years!" But it's clear that the moderator fills a vitally important role—by setting a tone for the event, by explaining ground rules and procedures to the audience, and by maintaining order and promoting interchange between the debaters and between the debaters and the audience. If the moderator is weak, the debate can devolve into a chaotic shouting match; if the moderator knows his business and does it, the debate can be an interesting, enlightening and rewarding experience.

Notes

1. Adam Cohen, and Elizabeth Taylor, *American Pharaoh: Mayor Richard J. Daley: His Battle for Chicago and the Nation* (Boston: Little, Brown, 2001): 482.

2. Doug Linder, "Famous Trials: The 'Chicago 7' Trial," in *Famous American Trials* (Kansas City: University of Missouri–Kansas City, 2004), http://www.law.umkc.edu/faculty/projects/ftrials/Chicago7/chicago7.html

3. "108th Congress: Guide to Frequently Mispronounced Names," *National Association of State University and Land Grant Colleges* (2003), http://www.nasulgc.org/cferr/BoHS/108thCongress_PronunciationGde.pdf

4. Debate transcript of First 1996 Clinton-Dole Presidential Debate: October 6, 1996, *Commission on Presidential Debates*, http://www.debates.org/pages/trans96a.html.

5. Debate transcript of Third 2000 Gore-Bush Presidential Debate: October 17, 2000, *Commission on Presidential Debates*, http://www.debates.org/pages/trans2000c.html

6. Debate transcript of Second 2000 Gore-Bush Presidential Debate: October 11, 2000, *Commission on Presidential Debates*, http://www.debates.org/pages/trans2000b.html

7. Debate transcript of Third 2000 Gore-Bush Presidential Debate.

8. Josephus Daniels, *The Wilson Era; Years of War and After, 1917–1923*. (Chapel Hill: University of North Carolina Press, 1946): 624.

Chapter Eighteen
Ending the Debate

In the political world, debate is usually part of the decision-making process; debate is followed by a vote. That is the procedure in the General Assembly of the United Nations as well as in the United States Congress; the same sequence was followed in the *ecclesia* of 5th century Athens, and in the tribal councils of the Ibo in precolonial Nigeria. Political leaders argue with each other because decisions must be made. "Winning the debate" and "winning the vote" are almost synonymous terms.

But public debates—as we have defined them in this book—are not set in legislative chambers, and it is only rarely that spectators have the power to cast votes that determine policy. In other words, the link between debating and decision-making is not as strong in public debate as it is in political debate. Does that mean it is meaningless to talk about "winning" a public debate? Hardly. Even when there is no vote to win, there are ways to gauge results—and this chapter will discuss various methods of incorporating such assessments into the fabric of a public debate.

Evaluating Persuasion

Before launching our discussion of evaluative systems, we would like to reiterate a few simple truths about public debate. The first thing to remember is that debate is a persuasive activity. The debater's job is to persuade the audience, by means of her arguments, that she is right about an issue. In practical terms, that means that she agrees (or disagrees) with a statement—the resolution—and she wants her listeners to share her position.

On one level, this makes the evaluation of debates seem like a simple business: did the debater persuade the audience? Or did her opponent?

But if we stop to ponder the meaning of the word "persuade," it will become clear that evaluating debates is not that simple after all. There are situations where persuasion has a binary clarity: in a court of law, for example, a juror will listen to the words of the prosecutor and the defense attorney and will be persuaded to vote guilty or not guilty. But the courtroom is meant to be an antiseptic, controlled environment: the jurors enter the jury box with no prior knowledge of the case before them; they decide on the basis of carefully delimited evidence. Contrast that with the situation found at a typical public debate. Say that the resolution is about the legalization of marijuana. Does the audience enter in a state of ignorance? Do they enter without their own ideas and opinions? No—the auditorium is part of the real world, not a clinical lab.

What, then, does it mean to persuade the audience? There may be some spectators, no doubt, who are changed immediately and completely by the debate; they are the ones who leave saying, "I used to think it was OK to legalize marijuana, but after what I've heard tonight, I think it would be the wrong thing to do." In our experience, converts like these are in a distinct minority. But we do not believe that they are the only people who have been "persuaded." It is much more common for the effects of persuasion to be delayed or subtle. Listeners may find that they have a new way of thinking about a problem or a different attitude toward it; they may find that they have to modify their own positions to take account of opposing arguments. And these shifts in thinking may not happen during the debate or immediately afterwards; very often, a debate provides a proverbial shock to the system, and the accommodation of new information or new ideas may take hours, or days, or weeks. What is more, the listener's thinking may change in ways that are significant, yet partial—rather than thoroughgoing. A supporter of abortion rights may decide that partial-birth abortion should be banned; an advocate of gun owners' rights may decide that mandatory trigger locks are a good idea; a civil libertarian may concede that government surveillance of bank transfers is a justifiable means of tracing the money that supports terrorist organizations. Such subtle changes are not surprising, given that debate often deals with complex issues that call for complex responses (even if the structure of debate creates a dichotomy between two starkly opposed sides).

It is our own belief that debates should be evaluated on the basis of substance—that is, on the quality of the arguments and counterarguments offered by the debaters. But even this is a complicated business, because the typical listener finds it easy to separate the dancer from the dance. That is, the listener is able to separate the debater's position from the debater's performance and say, in so many words, "I don't agree with the arguments that she made, but I think she did a better job of presenting her position than her opponent did." (Or, conversely, "I agreed with what he was trying to say, but he did a poor job of getting his points across.") The point is that the listener, in evaluating the debate, can make two distinct—and contrary—judgments. The listener may decide that she is not persuaded—by the person she thinks did a better job of debating.

Evaluating Performance

In raising the matter of performance, we have recognized that it complicates the process of evaluating debates because it utilizes a criterion other than persuasion. Furthermore, we recognize that evaluating performance is a complicated business in and of itself—performance can be understood as skill in argumentation, or fluency of delivery, or ease of manner.

Performance can be evaluated, first of all, on the basis of *debating skills*. Using this basis, the listener pays close attention to the following:

- the quality of the debater's main argument;
- her success in asking questions that weaken her opponent's arguments, or else set up an attack on those arguments;
- the thoroughness with which she refutes her opponent's arguments;
- her success in defending her argument against her opponent's attacks.

In short, the listener who evaluates on the basis of debating skills is judging the debater's success in the opening speech, in cross-examination, in refutation and in rebuttal.

More narrowly, performance can be evaluated on the basis of *speaking skills*. Here, the listener would judge:

- the volume and clarity of the speaker's voice;
- the fluency and articulation of the speaker's delivery;

- the speaker's use of vocal variety (contrasts in pitch, volume, rate, stress and tone);
- the speaker's success in making eye contact with the audience.

Finally, performance can be evaluated on the basis of less tangible criteria. Listeners judge debaters on the basis of whether they sound sincere; whether they seem relaxed and confident; whether they seem respectful and avoid mean-spiritedness. One of the most famous presidential debates—that between John F. Kennedy and Richard M. Nixon in 1960—was judged by many viewers on the basis of just such intangibles. Nixon—pale, sweating, his five o'clock shadow poorly covered by a product called "Lazy Shave," and wearing a gray suit that blended into the studio background—seemed weak and uncomfortable. With his tanned face and his navy blue suit, Kennedy exuded youth and vigor (even though he was actually in poor physical health and only four years younger than his opponent).

Again, we will register our own beliefs about this issue: we think that if debates are to be evaluated formally, the greatest weight should be given to argumentation. If "performance" is to be considered, it should be construed to mean debating skills, as outlined above.

Options for Evaluation

Given the complexity of evaluation—that is, given the coexistence of persuasion and performance, and the multifarious nature of performance—some debate organizers elect to dispense with formal evaluations altogether. This is not an act of cowardice or convenience; rather, it is a recognition that evaluative systems can create a false impression of accuracy. Telling an audience to vote for the "best debater" is a bit like taking a poll to determine who is the "entertainer of the year"—when the possible candidates include opera stars, rock guitarists, actors, comedians, pop princesses, country western singers, classical violinists and professional wrestlers. In the end, there may be one person who wins the title, but it's hard to say exactly why. In the same way, the "best debater" may be chosen by obscure and conflicting criteria, and so is best left uncrowned. But there is no reason to think that a debate without a declared winner is fundamentally incomplete; a good debate offers listeners its own rewards.

If, however, debate organizers decide to include evaluation as part of the process, there are more choices to be made. The first task is to choose the evaluators. In the foregoing discussion, we have talked about the audience doing the judging, and that is one possibility. But another possibility is to create a panel of judges to evaluate the debate.

The Panel of Judges

Debate organizers can have different reasons for creating a panel of judges. They may feel, for example, that it is either cumbersome or impossible to survey the reactions of the audience as a whole; surveying the reactions of a modest number of judges is undoubtedly more practicable. In this case, the panel would be composed of audience members, either a random sample or a representative sample. (A representative sample would be chosen with regard for the various constituencies of the audience.) Alternatively, a judging panel can be assembled for the sake of providing expertise that the average audience member does not have—and that can be expertise regarding the topic at hand or expertise regarding debate. A panel of politicians and social policy activists, for example, could be expected to know more about public housing issues than a randomly selected group of college students; debate practitioners certainly know more about refutation and rebuttal than the ordinary citizen.

Whatever the reason for assembling a panel of judges, there are choices to be made about their function. We realize that the use of the word "judge" may imply that the panel will make a decision designating a winner—but that is not necessarily the case. (After all, in many courtrooms, the decisions are made by juries, not judges!) Instead of designating a winner, the panel of judges may be asked simply to provide evaluative commentary on the debate: they may say what they think was good or bad, and successful or unsuccessful, without taking a formal vote to determine a "winner" and a "loser." (This is analogous to the model used by television networks after a presidential debate: typically, they seek the reactions of three or four commentators, but they do not tabulate their votes and announce a victor in the debate.) This model presupposes that the judges will be able to talk directly to the audience at the close of the debate; there is no point in keeping evaluative commentary private.

Alternatively, the panel of judges can be asked to declare a winner of the debate—and this process can be closed or open. A closed process will be familiar to anyone who has ever watched a Miss Universe pageant: the judges make their decisions, and the results are announced by the master of ceremonies; individual decisions, and the reasons supporting them, remain secret. A closed process has the advantage of being dramatic, as well as clear and decisive—but it offers no educational benefits for the audience or for the debaters. To put it another way, no one benefits directly from the judges' expertise; there is no opportunity to learn why a debater's performance was good or bad.

The benefits are greater if the judging process is open. An open process combines the definitive judgment of the closed process with the evaluative commentary approach described above. The judges cast their votes, but those votes are explained publicly to the audience, either by each of the judges individually or by someone chosen to speak for them. These explanations have a constructive value for the debaters and can help to clarify the debate for audience members.

Criteria for Judging With a Panel.   One of the advantages of creating a judging panel is that it allows for greater control over the criteria for judging. It is true that judging remains a complex and complicated business, even with a panel, but the small scale of the panel makes it easier to articulate and explain the criteria that should be used. These criteria should not be treated as privileged information for the judge, however—the audience should also be told how the judges are expected to make their decisions. With a judging panel, a public debate is able to mirror—for good or for ill—a competitive educational debate, in which judges are given formal instructions along with their formal ballots. Instructions and ballots vary from league to league and are differently configured for different types of debate. Some ballots require judges to "disaggregate" performance into separate categories, each individually rated; the American Forensic League, for example, asks judges to award points in analysis, reasoning, evidence, organization, refutation and delivery to each debater, and to add those points to determine a winner.[1] Other ballots are more holistic, and ask judges to say who had the best "overall" performance—it is up to the judges to determine how much weight should be given to the persuasiveness of the argument, and how much weight should be given to debating skills, speaking skills, and intangibles.

When a panel of experts on the topic is asked to judge, their evaluation will, of course, include their assessment of how well the debaters mastered the issues under consideration. Because they are experts, they will be able to say with some authority whether the debaters have been thorough, fair and accurate; experts will not be swayed by a skilled debater who has distorted or misrepresented facts.

A panel of judges is also able to adopt a formal position of neutrality. It is a common perspective in judging competitive educational debate that judges should disregard their own opinions about the topic being debated. That is, judges are asked to imagine themselves as blank slates, who can respond only to what they hear in the course of a debate. Practically, this means that a judge who has a membership card for the National Rifle Association in his pocket must vote for the debater who advocates the abolition of private handgun ownership—if, that is, the antigun debater has done a better job debating than his pro-gun opponent. More than that, competitive debate judges are constrained from engaging in a private shadow debate with the contestants. It may happen, for example, that the affirmative debater presents a case with an egregious logical flaw that the judge notices; although the judge may note this flaw in his comments, he cannot hold the debater accountable unless the debater's opponent has pointed out the flaw in the course of her refutation. To put in another way, the debate is supposed to take place between the two contestants (or the two contesting sides)—not between the contestants and the judge.

It is implicit in the foregoing that a panel of judges adopting a stance of neutrality will put more weight on debating skills; they will consider "persuasion" formally, rather than personally. They will not consider whether the debate persuaded them or changed their minds in a real way; rather, they will consider whether they would have been persuaded if they were someone else who had no personal opinions. In a sense, this makes the debate similar to one of those computer simulations that television broadcasters use when they can't get actual pictures of an event. The debate still has value, but it is more artificial than real.

Summary. The following table summarizes the formal possibilities discussed above. We note that there is further variety possible within each option—no matter what the composition, the function, or the mode of operation, a judging panel can be instructed to judge holistically or to consider specific aspects of the debate; the weight given to specific aspects (e.g., debating skills, speaking skills) can also vary.

Composition of Panel	Benefit	Function	Mode
Random or representative sampling	Manageable survey of audience reaction	Evaluative commentary	Open: commentary directed at audience
		Decision (designating winner and loser)	Open: decision and comentary
			Closed: decision only
Experts on topic of debate	Greater illumination of topic	Evaluative commentary	Open: commentary directed at audience
		Decision (designating winner and loser)	Open: decision and comentary
			Closed: decision only
Experts on debate practice	Stonger emphasis on debaters' performance	Evaluative commentary	Open: commentary directed at audience
		Decision (designating winner and loser)	Open: decision and comentary
			Closed: decision only

Evaluation by the Audience

As we have argued throughout this book, the audience is an integral part of any public debate. Public debates are not held for the edification and the amusement of the debaters themselves; the debaters take the floor because they want to change the minds of the people who are listening to them.

It is right and fitting, therefore, to give the audience the task of evaluating the debate, even if the audience members can claim no special expertise in debate or in the topic under consideration. Public debates are not designed for the ears of experts; any person with an open and attentive mind is qualified to be a judge.

In the discussion that follows, we are presuming that the audience is actually rendering a decision, and designating a winner of the debate. Before discussing the logistics of effecting and communicating this decision, we will consider some of the ethical dimensions of audience voting.

We noted above, in our discussion of persuasion, that the audience members at a public debate are very likely to have their own opinions about the controversial issue that is being addressed. Furthermore, we think it is unlikely that a public debate will radically change a substantial percentage of opinions that are firmly held. We may want to take these facts into consideration in designing our method of evaluation.

The difficulty facing us is best explained with an example. Let's say that the resolution is our now familiar example that marijuana should be legalized. And let's say that the audience for our debate is composed of college students; 50 percent of them firmly believe that marijuana should be legalized, 30 percent of them firmly believe that marijuana should remain illegal, and 20 percent are undecided. What results might we expect in a vote after the debate?

It is possible, of course, for the audience members to adopt the ideals of the expert judge and to vote strictly on the merits of what they have heard—meaning that the chapter president of NORML sitting in the audience would vote against legalization if the antilegalization debater did a better job. And the corollary is that either debater could win. But what if the audience members cannot or will not assume a neutral position? What if they vote for what they really believe? In that case, it is clear that the legalization side will win, even if there are a few defectors, and even if the antilegalization debater captures most of the undecided voters. Starting with a base of 50 percent in favor of his position, the legalization debater does not have to gain much ground to win a majority; for the antilegalization debater, however, the odds are all but insuperable.

There are two primary techniques for eliminating bias in choosing a winner. One technique is to exclude the partisans on both sides of the proposition and give voting rights only to the undecided. (This is the method used in some presidential debates: the audience in one of the Clinton-Dole debates was limited to voters who had not made up their minds about which candidate they preferred.) In this scenario, the winner of the debate is the advocate who captures the greatest number of undecided votes. There are, of course, practical difficulties with this method, beginning with the challenge of identifying who is truly undecided. It is also problematic to make partisans feel that they have been disenfranchised.

The second technique—and in our view, the most appropriate one—is to poll the audience twice, once before the debate and once after it. The winner of the debate is decided on the basis of the shift in audience opinion; the debater who gained the most votes would be declared winner—even if his supporters were in a statistical minority. Say that the antilegalization debater gained most of the undecided votes in the above example, and increased support for his position from 30 percent to 45 percent; he would win, even though the legalization debater had the support of the majority of the audience.

The shift in opinion does not need to be measured in binary ("yes" or "no") terms; in chapter 5, we included this sample of a questionnaire, which measures degrees of agreement:

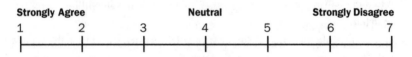

Granted, it would not be easy to tabulate the results of such a survey by hand, but if the appropriate computer technology is available, you should certainly consider using this model because it is capable of capturing more subtle shifts in opinion. It would show, for example, if support for a proposition had weakened, even if the number of supporters for the proposition remained unchanged. (Before the debate, there might be 50 audience members who placed themselves to the left of the neutral line, with an average rating of 1.8; after the debate, there might still be 50 people on that side of the neutral line, but their new average of 3.1 shows that they do not agree as strongly as they did before.

Logistical Considerations.   The method used to tally votes will be determined largely by the size of the audience. If the audience is small—fewer than 100 people—it is possible to determine a winner by a show of hands. (We are assuming that the voters have no reason to keep their votes secret.)

For larger audiences, some kind of paper ballot is more practicable. We would recommend against using a ballot where voters have to check off a debater's name; ballots like this take too long to sort and count. (We would also caution against any kind of ballot likely to produce hanging chads.) It is much faster and easier to use colored index cards. With this method, each spectator entering the auditorium is given two differently colored cards; at the end of the debate, he is told to submit the blue card if he wants to vote for the affirmative or the yellow card if he wants to vote for the negative. Even a large number of cards can be sorted and counted quickly—and speed is important, given that the debate is over, and the only business left is the announcement of the decision. The cards can be printed with "affirmative" and "negative" labels, if time and budget permit, but that isn't absolutely necessary. We'd note that this method can be used for the double polling procedure described above; it is necessary only to add a third color representing "undecided." Whether two or three cards are used, debate organizers need to provide card collectors, each with the responsibility of gathering votes from a finite segment of the audience (100 or so spectators).

We will mention two more methods, one utopian and the other less than ideal. The utopian method is to count votes electronically. If the audience members are able to register their votes by punching buttons at their seats, or by tapping computer screens, the results will be available almost instantaneously. Most debate venues do not come rigged with such equipment, however, and it is probably prohibitively expensive to install electronic devices for only one debate. Nevertheless, debate organizers are encouraged to consult information technology personnel; it may be feasible to set up a low cost system. (Given the almost universal prevalence of cell phones, it may be possible to set up a "vote by phone" system without breaking the bank.)

The less than ideal method is to let audience members vote with their feet. At the end of the debate, listeners can be instructed to move to one side of the room if they favor the affirmative and to the other side if they favor the negative. Then the respective groups are counted. The problem is that this process is messy and doesn't work well if the vote is lopsided. The other podiatric voting method makes the exits from the room critically significant: when they leave via one exit, audience members are counted as voting affirmative; when they leave by the other, they are counted as voting negative. The problem here is obvious: when the decision is announced, there's no one left to hear it (except the debaters).

Conclusion

We began this book by describing the public debate that took place on the campus of Western Washington University after students protested against the sale of *Penthouse* magazine in the campus bookstore. We will close the book by returning to that story.

As we noted in our earlier discussion, the *Penthouse* debate did not end with a vote—but it ended with the best of all possible outcomes: listeners remained in the hall after the debate ended and kept discussing the issue. In other words, the debate did not close the issue; rather, the debate inspired further dialogues. More than that, the debate helped to shape those dialogues: the sale of the magazine was understood in the context of the conflict between women's rights and the right to free speech, among other things. We believe that the *Penthouse* debate did what public debates do best: it promoted understanding, the respectful exchange of ideas, and the peaceful resolution of differences. In doing so, public debates strengthen the very foundations of democracy.

Notes

1. "American Forensic Association Debate Ballot," National Catholic Forensic League, http://www.ncfl.org//ballots/bltpol.htm

About the Authors

Ken Broda-Bahm spent eighteen years teaching debate and argumentation, the past eight at Towson University in Maryland. Since 1994, Dr. Broda-Bahm has been a consultant for the International Debate Education Association and has presented seminars in debate and advocacy in seventeen different countries. As a founding developer of the Southeast Europe Youth Leadership Institute, Dr. Broda-Bahm helped to design one of the first youth institute programs designed to teach public debate. Dr. Broda-Bahm is currently a Senior Litigation Consultant with the firm Persuasion Strategies, a service of Holland & Hart, LLP. In that capacity, Dr. Broda-Bahm conducts research and provides communication advice and coaching to attorneys preparing for trial. Dr. Broda-Bahm holds a doctorate in Speech Communication from Southern Illinois University, Carbondale.

Daniela Kempf has taught debate, advocacy and argumentation for ten years: abroad, for an international debate education program to students and teachers from over twenty countries from Albania to Mongolia, and in the United States, at Emerson College and Marymount Manhattan College, where she currently teaches advanced public speaking and debate. Ms. Kempf also served as public debate curriculum codesigner for an international youth leadership program and now promotes the worldwide land mine cause for a nonprofit organization dedicated to advocacy on international issues. Ms. Kempf lives in New York City with her husband, whom she met debating and teaching debate. Ms. Kempf holds a master's degree in Political Communication from Emerson College in Boston.

William Driscoll earned a master's degree in English Language and Literature at Oxford University before beginning a career in education. He has taught English, classics, theater, history and political philosophy at various high schools in the New York City area and served for many years as a debate judge at Regis High School. He also worked for ten years as a college counselor and college admission officer. He is the author of *Discovering the World Through Debate*, and has edited two collections of essays in the series of IDEA Sourcebooks on Contemporary Controversies.

Index